"*The History of Genocide in Cinema* is powerful, painful and poignant – the rest is commentary. In 18 thoughtful essays this book offers both a concise and clear general history of multiple genocides and the attempts to portray them in film. It grapples with major issues associated with these films, including the difficulty and necessity of representation and the tension between a fidelity to history and an appeal to a popular audience. It has added many – perhaps too many – films to my 'must see' list. The reader will come away with a sense of 'deja vu, all over again' as patterns of genocide and their presentation in film emerge and one recalls not only the violence and the indifference of the past but the anguish of our day as sadly genocide is not confined to the history and the cinematographer's task continues, perhaps these films will serve as a warning, more likely they will not but the mission to bear witness has only become more urgent in our time."

Michael Berenbaum, Professor of Jewish Studies and Director of the Sigi Ziering Institute at the American Jewish University in Los Angeles

THE HISTORY OF
GENOCIDE
IN CINEMA

Atrocities on Screen

Edited by

Jonathan C. Friedman and William L. Hewitt

I.B. TAURIS

LONDON · NEW YORK

Published in 2017 by
I.B.Tauris & Co. Ltd
London • New York
www.ibtauris.com

International Library of Twentieth Century History 92

ISBN: 978 1 78453 422 6
eISBN: 978 1 78672 047 4
ePDF: 978 1 78673 047 3

A full CIP record for this book is available from the British Library
A full CIP record is available from the Library of Congress

Library of Congress Catalog Card Number: available

Printed and bound by CPI Group (UK) Ltd, Croydon, CR0 4YY

Contents

Contributing Authors

Teresa A. Booker is a tenured assistant professor of Africana Studies at John Jay College of Criminal Justice and a member of the doctoral faculty of Criminal Justice at the Graduate Center of The City University of New York. She holds a doctorate in political science from the Graduate Center and graduated with an honors BA from the University of North Carolina at Charlotte. Her dual areas of expertise are found in the international relations and public policy subfields. Within the former, her research interests include peacekeeping, peacemaking and restorative justice. Within the latter, she focuses on the implementation and evaluation of policy. Dr. Booker is a co-author of *Walking with Indigenous Philosophy: Justice and Addition Recovery* (2014) and editor of two books: *Public Space, Public Policy and Public Understanding of Race and Ethnicity in America: An Interdisciplinary Approach* (forthcoming) and *Keeping it Holy: Southerners, the South, and Themes of Justice* (manuscript under review). She has published in the following peer-reviewed journals: *The National Journal of Urban Education and Practice*, *International Journal of Restorative Justice*, *The Journal of Pan African Studies*, and *The International Journal of Regional and Local Studies*.

Kristin C. Brunnemer, PhD, is Professor of English and Film at Pierce College, Washington. She is the co-author of *Term Paper Resource Guide to Latino History*, as well as several articles on film and television. Her areas of interest include film and visual culture, comparative minority discourses, television studies, and popular culture.

Glen M.E. Duerr is Assistant Professor of International Studies at Cedarville University in southwest Ohio, USA. He holds a PhD in Political Science from Kent State University, an MA in Political Science from the University of Windsor, and an (Honors) BA in History and Political Science from the University of Western Ontario. He has lived in three countries, the United Kingdom, Canada, and the United States, and has conducted intensive field research in two others. His research revolves around nationalism, secession, federalism, conflict, and genocide.

Eda Dedebas Dundar is Assistant Professor of English at Bogazici University, Turkey and a former postdoctoral fellow at the University of Nevada, Reno. She received her PhD in Comparative Literature from the University of Connecticut in 2013. She is currently working on her book, tentatively titled "Adapting Shahrazad's Odyssey: The Female Traveler and Storyteller in Victorian and Contemporary Middle Eastern Literature." Her research interests include women writers from the Middle East, human rights narratives, and contemporary Anglophone literature.

Mark V. DeStephano, a native of Palisades Park, New Jersey, and a Roman Catholic priest of the Jesuit order, was awarded his bachelor's degree in Philosophy and Spanish from Fordham University. He earned four degrees in theology from Regis College of the University of Toronto: Bachelor of Sacred Theology, Master of Divinity, Master of Theology, and a Licentiate in Sacred Theology. Following these studies, he continued his education at Harvard University, where he was awarded his master's and doctoral degrees in Romance languages and literatures, with specialization in medieval and golden-age Spanish literature. For the past 20 years, Dr. DeStephano has been Chair and Professor of the Department of Modern and Classical Languages and Literatures, and Director and Professor of the Asian Studies Program at Saint Peter's University in Jersey City, New Jersey. Named a "Scholar of the People's Republic of China" in 2005, Dr. DeStephano has spoken at many conferences and taught at various universities throughout Asia, including Peking University, the Central University for Nationalities (Beijing), Beijing Union University, the Catholic University of Macao, Guangxi Normal University, and Hong Kong Baptist University in China, Chung-Ang University in South Korea, the University of the Philippines, and Assumption University in Thailand. His research focuses on medieval European literatures and on issues of race, ethnicity, gender, sexuality, and identity in Asian and Latino cultures.

Lynne Fallwell holds a PhD in German History from the Pennsylvania State University and currently directs the Office of Competitive External Scholarships at Texas Tech University. In addition to publishing on various aspects of film theory and leisure studies, the Third Reich, and comparative genocide, her first book. *Modern German Midwifery, 1885–1960* was published by Pickering & Chatto in 2013. She is presently finishing a book-length manuscript on the implications of post-war Germany as a vacation destination for American tourists.

Clinton Fernandes is Associate Professor in the School of Humanities and Social Sciences at the University of New South Wales, Australia. Before becoming an academic, he spent 15 years in the Australian Army and served as the Australian Intelligence Corps Principal Analyst (East Timor) in the final years of East Timor's independence struggle. In 2008 and 2009, he assisted the Australian Federal Police's War Crimes team on the subject of the Indonesian military and the East Timorese resistance. From 2007 to 2009 he served as the Consulting Historian for *Balibo*, a feature film about the murder of six Australian-based journalists in East Timor in 1975.

Jonathan C. Friedman is Professor of History and Director of Holocaust and Genocide Studies at West Chester University in West Chester, Pennsylvania. He received his PhD in 1996 in Modern European, German, and Jewish History from the University of Maryland, College Park. After working as a historian at both the United States Holocaust Memorial Museum in Washington, D.C. and the Survivors of the Shoah Visual History Foundation in Los Angeles, California, Dr. Friedman began his tenure at West Chester in 2002. He is the author or editor of seven books, including *The Lion and the Star: Gentile–Jewish Relations in Three Hessian Communities, 1919–1945* (University Press of Kentucky, 1998), *Rainbow Jews: Gay and Jewish Identity in the Performing Arts* (Lexington Books, 2007), *The Routledge History of the Holocaust* (Routledge, 2011), and *The Routledge History of Social Protest in Popular Music* (Routledge, 2013).

Gloria Galindo has a PhD from the University of California, Santa Barbara. Her research specializations include contemporary Latin American studies (literature, film, and thought), film studies, and trauma and memory studies. She has written articles on Latin American/Spanish literature and film in international scholarly journals. She is currently writing a postdoc on post-traumatic culture in contemporary Latin American film at Roskilde University.

William L. Hewitt is Professor Emeritus of History at West Chester University. Professor Hewitt's areas of specialization include Native American history, genocide, film, and gay and lesbian studies. He has published an historical novel *Across the Wide River* (2003) and the book *Defining the Horrific: Readings on Genocide and the Holocaust in the Twentieth Century* (Prentice Hall, 2003).

Iuliia Kysla is a PhD candidate in the Department of History and Classics at the University of Alberta, Canada. A native of Kherson, Iuliia received her BA and MA in History from the Kyiv-Mohyla Academy National University, Ukraine in 2004 and 2006. She then continued her graduate studies at the Central European University in Budapest, Hungary where in 2010 she got her second master's degree in Central European History. In 2010–2011, she served as an executive editor of the Ukrainian peer review journal *Ukraina Moderna*. She is currently working on a doctoral dissertation entitled "Rethinking the Postwar Era: Soviet Ukrainian Writers under Late Stalin, 1944–1953."

Meriem Lahrizi is a PhD candidate in Technology and Education at Rabat Mohamed V University, in Agdal, Morocco. In addition to teaching high school English in Morocco, she also works as an in-country consultant for the International Research and Exchanges Board. Her research interests include the relationship between technology and society, genocide, American studies, and cultural studies, as well as skills for intercultural competence and living in a diverse, global society.

Sarah Maddison is Associate Professor in the School of Social and Political Sciences at the University of Melbourne. Her areas of research expertise include reconciliation and conflict transformation, indigenous political culture, and social movements. In 2015 Sarah published a major monograph, *Conflict Transformation and Reconciliation* (London: Routledge) based on research in South Africa, Northern Ireland, Australia, and Guatemala. Her other recent books include *Black Politics* (2009), *Beyond White Guilt* (2011), and *Unsettling the Settler State* (co-edited with Morgan Brigg, 2011).

Mark Malisa teaches at the College of Saint Rose in Albany, New York. His research interests include international education and anti-globalization as well as the preservation of African languages. He is also the author of

"Ubuntu is Utopia: The Individual and Community in African Philosophy" which was published in C. Ellis and C. Jones, eds., *The Individual and Utopia: A Multidisciplinary Study of Humanity and Perfection* (Surrey, England: Ashgate Publishing). He is currently working on "Apartheid and Anti-Semitism: European Intellectuals, Africans, and Jews in Apartheid South Africa" scheduled to be published in Frank Jacob, ed., *Intellectual Anti-Semitism from a Global Perspective*. With Adelina Nyabu, he is currently working on an article called "It Was Not Always Like This: The Rape of Women as a Colonial Legacy in African Literature and History," which will be published in P. Uwakeh, ed., *Under Fire: Critical Discourses on African Women in War and Conflict*.

Armen T. Marsoobian is Professor and Chair of Philosophy at Southern Connecticut State University and is Editor of the journal *Metaphilosophy*. He received his PhD from the State University of New York at Stony Brook. He has twice served as the Nikit and Eleanora Ordjanian Visiting Professor in the Department of Middle East, South Asian, and African Studies, at Columbia University. He has lectured and published extensively on topics in American philosophy, aesthetics, moral philosophy, and genocide studies. He has edited five books, including *The Blackwell Guide to American Philosophy* and *Genocide's Aftermath: Responsibility and Repair*. His most recent books, *Fragments of a Lost Homeland* and *Reimagining a Lost Armenian Home* (both I.B.Tauris), are based upon extensive research about his family, the Dildilians, who were accomplished photographers in the late Ottoman period. He has organized exhibitions based upon his family's Ottoman-era photography collection in Istanbul, Merzifon, Diyarbakir, Ankara, London and Yerevan. Further exhibitions are planned for Thessaloniki, Boston, New York and Los Angeles. He has received the Hrant Dink Foundation Prize for Historical Research for his work on the Armenian genocide.

Jane Mills is Associate Professor at the University of New South Wales where she teaches Film. With a radio, television, and documentary production background, she has written and broadcast widely on cinema, censorship, feminism, and human rights. Current research projects include screen literacy, cosmopolitanism, geocriticism, and sojourner cinema. Series Editor of *Australian Screen Classics*, Professor Mills' recent books include: *Loving and Hating Hollywood: Reframing Global and Local Cinema* (2009) and *Jedda* (2012).

Barbara A. Moss is Associate Professor of History at Georgia Highlands College in Georgia. Her area of specialization is southern Africa, and her research interests include nineteenth- and twentieth-century colonialism, gender, passive resistance, and religious beliefs. She earned a BA degree in African American Studies from Howard University, an MA from Northwestern University, and a PhD in African History from Indiana University.

David Pettigrew, PhD, has been Professor of Philosophy at Southern Connecticut State University since 1987, where he also teaches a course on Holocaust and Genocide Studies. He lectures and writes about the genocide in Bosnia. He created a documentary film with his son Jonah, titled *The Geography of Genocide in Bosnia: Redeeming the Earth* (2011), which was an official selection of the Srebrenica International Film Festival in 2011. In addition, Pettigrew has co-translated and co-edited eleven books on philosophy and psychoanalysis, including J. D. Nasio's *Oedipus: The Most Crucial Concept in Psychoanalysis* (SUNY Press), which was named by *CHOICE* as an "Outstanding Academic Title" for 2011. He has authored essays on the work of Jacques Derrida, Martin Heidegger, Jacques Lacan, Maurice Merleau-Ponty, and Jean-Luc Nancy, among others. His essays have been published in Arabic, Bosnian, English and French. He is Co-director of a book series, *Contemporary French Thought*, published by the SUNY Press. Pettigrew was a credentialed international observer for the municipal elections in Srebrenica in 2012, and is a member of the steering committee of the Yale University Genocide Studies Program.

Cathy J. Schlund-Vials is Professor of English and Asian/Asian American studies at the University of Connecticut; she is also the director of the UConn Asian and Asian American Studies Institute and president-elect for the Association for Asian American Studies. She is author of two monographs: *Modeling Citizenship: Jewish and Asian American Writing* (Temple University Press, 2011) and *War, Genocide, and Justice: Cambodian American Memory Work* (University of Minnesota Press, 2012). She has three co-edited collections that are published, in press, and forthcoming: *Disability, Human Rights, and the Limits of Humanitarianism* (Ashgate, 2014); *Keywords for Asian American Studies* (NYU Press, 2015), and *Asian America: A Primary Source Reader* (forthcoming, Yale University Press).

Zachary Vincent Smith is a former law enforcement officer who is currently a student in the master of arts program in Holocaust and Genocide Studies at West Chester University. His research focus is on film and representations of diverse subjects related to Jewish history and the history of genocide.

Introduction

William L. Hewitt and Jonathan C. Friedman

West Chester University

Would you want to watch depictions of horrific, even grotesque, events such as a genocide, depicted on film? People who slow their vehicles to see a traffic accident, psychologists explain, often feel a cathartic rush while observing the suffering of others at a safe distance. Similarly, by watching together the suffering of others on film, we insulate ourselves from the trauma of the victims and voyeuristically may derive similar feelings, something akin to the reaction which viewers of horror and slasher films experience. "By eliciting emotions, watching movies can open doors that otherwise might stay closed," claims Birgit Wolz, a psychologist specializing on movies as therapy and author of *E-motion Picture Magic*. "Because many films transmit ideas through emotion rather than intellect, they can neutralize the instinct to suppress feelings and trigger emotional release." Wolz observes further that moviegoers who seek out the horror genre tend to be the same people who enjoy skydiving, rock climbing, and extreme skiing. "Riding at the edge of death is, somehow, strangely enough, what makes them feel most alive," Wolz asserts. "For many moviegoers, the horror genre allows them the opportunity to experience events and people who otherwise wouldn't enter their lives."[1] Is this what draws people to films about genocide? Are the viewing experiences in fact analogous?

If people want to see vicariously what a genocide may have been like, the past century offers a wealth of examples. The organization Genocide Watch estimates that 100 million civilians around the globe have lost their lives because of genocide in the past seventy years. Political scientist Rudolph J. Rummel has argued for a number closer to 150 million over the period from 1900 to 1987, 85 percent of which one can attribute to totalitarian and authoritarian regimes, specifically the Soviet Union, China, Khmer Rouge in Cambodia, Vietnam, Yugoslavia, and Nazi Germany and its fascist allies. World War II, history's deadliest military conflict, accounted for 72 million of these deaths – 47 million civilians in total, 12 million of whom the Nazis murdered in the Holocaust, the genocidal wartime policy of the German state. To put it another way, it is estimated there were over 550 million people in Europe (including the Soviet Union) on the eve of World War II. By war's end, one out every eight European citizens who had been alive in 1939 was dead by 1945; two out of every three European Jews, 1.5 million Jewish children. In terms of real numbers, the 72 million killed well exceeded the entire population of Germany as of 1933.

The century of mass genocide evolved coterminously with the century of mass media, and the visual and performing arts have aided efforts to document and raise awareness of genocide, however uneven this may be. Film historian Leshu Torchin attests to this unevenness, pointing to both failures and successes in her recent publication, *Creating the Witness: Documenting Genocide on Film, Video, and the Internet* (2012). One need only consider the worldwide impact and criticism of the 1978 miniseries, *The Holocaust: The Story of the Family Weiss,* on the memorialization and academic discussion of Nazi Germany's extermination of 6 million Jews. By focusing on feature films on genocides, beginning with the genocides perpetrated in the era of the new imperialism (Congo and Namibia) and ending with the genocide in Darfur, this volume complements the monograph by professor Torchin and goes well beyond those that focus on specific films, such as Kristi Wilson's *Film and Genocide* (2012) and John Michalczyk's *Through a Lens Darkly* (2013).

To begin, we must present the etymology of the term genocide and advance our concept of it. As most who are familiar with the subject already know, Raphael Lemkin (1900–1959), a Polish-Jewish émigré who became a law professor and eventually a consultant for the US government, coined the term genocide. Growing up in a Jewish family in Wolkowysk, a town in eastern Poland, Lemkin mastered a dozen languages. The barbarity and vandalism that characterized the cultures he studied resulted, in his mind, in the premeditated destruction of national, racial, religious, and social groups. At the Madrid Conference of 1933, Lemkin presented his ideas about such predatory cultures. The delegates rebuffed him, but he continued his campaign through the 1930s, and he formulated his concept of genocide as the intentional destruction of national groups based on their collective identity. He coined his neologism in 1944 by combining both Greek and Latin roots: the Greek "genos," meaning race or tribe, and the Latin "cide," or killing. Lemkin emphasized ethnic and national groups, placed the crime in a global historical context, and demanded intervention and remedial action. He gave intellectual legitimacy to the new term in his book, *Axis Rule in Occupied Europe: Laws of Occupation – Analysis of Government – Proposals for Redress*. After the end of the war, Lemkin waged a successful campaign to persuade the new United Nations to draft a convention against genocide, to obtain the required number of signatures, and to secure the necessary national ratifications.[2]

On 9 December 1948, the United Nations Convention of the Prevention and Punishment of the Crimes of Genocide defined the crime as "any of the following acts committed with intent to destroy, in whole or in part, a national, ethnical, racial or religious group, as such:

(a) Killing members of the group;
(b) Causing serious bodily or mental harm to members of the group;
(c) Deliberately inflicting on the group conditions of life calculated to bring about its physical destruction in whole or in part;
(d) Imposing measures intended to prevent births within the group;
(e) Forcibly transferring children of the group to another group"[3]

Adding to the complexity of this definition are corollary terms such as democide,[4] crimes against humanity, and war crimes, the latter two of which emerged in the context of the Allied prosecution in Nuremberg of Nazi crimes committed during World War II. R. J. Rummel coined the term democide in 1994 to refer to the systematic and state-sanctioned murder of political opponents, a category unmentioned in the UN Convention, and while some may regard democide, war crimes, and crimes against human-ity as synonymous with genocide, there is a substantive widening of crimes committed under the former categories (including enslavement and mur-der for political reasons).[5] There are legal implications in the distinction as well. Crimes against humanity were framed as crimes committed against large numbers of individuals, while the initial rationale for a separate legal category of genocide was that it could be committed during peacetime (and hence needed decoupling from war) and more importantly, was framed as a group crime.[6] For this volume, it is clear that the authors have adopted a broader view of what constitutes genocide, especially with the inclusion of essays on imperialism, the Ukraine Famine and Cambodian genocide, all three of which had economic and political foundations.

Between the 1950s and the 1980s, the term genocide languished almost unused by scholars. A few scholarly commentaries appeared for a specialized audience. In 1975, Vahakn Dadrian's article "A Typology of Genocide" sparked renewed interest in a comparative context, as did Leo Kuper's *Genocide: Its Political Use in the Twentieth Century* (1981) and the subsequent volume on *The Prevention of Genocide* (1985). Edited and solo volumes by Helen Fein, R. J. Rummel, Frank Chalk and Kurt Jonassohn, and Robert Melson, among others, followed it.[7] The early literature drew on more than a decade of intensive research on the Holocaust. Holocaust studies became the foundation for the field and the locus for much of the work on genocide. A rich body of case study literature developed, as well, covering genocides such as those against the Armenians, Cambodians, and East Timorese – as well as indigenous peoples worldwide. The explo-sion of public interest in genocide in the 1990s, and the concomitant growth of genocide studies as an academic field, spawned a profusion of humanistic and social-scientific studies, joined by memoirs and oral his-tories. The wider culture also produced a steady stream of films on geno-cide and its reverberations, including *The Killing Fields, Schindler's List,* and *Hotel Rwanda*.

Films about genocide have often constructed their narratives around a single protagonist, usually a man (or, more rarely, a woman), who pursues some goal of achievement or endurance and then overcomes unimaginable hardship. According to *Time Magazine*'s movie critic Richard Corliss, the heroic structure of the "biopic" is not entirely or even primarily altruistic. It

4

more frequently than not translates into profits at the boxoffice. The recent release of *American Sniper* attests to this; the film ignited the four-day Martin Luther King weekend in January 2015, setting a record high grossing box office $90.2 million in three days, compared to James Cameron's *Avatar* which set the previous record at $68 million in 2010. Over the past two decades, biopics have also paid off in statuettes for Best Actor, e.g., Don Cheadle for *Hotel Rwanda* and Adrien Brody for *The Pianist*. Corliss snappishly observes that: "Making biopics, the movie elite feel like decent citizens; then they give themselves prizes. One hand shakes the other."[8]

Moviegoers may come to empathize deeply with the protagonist in a biopic, and Alison Landsberg, author of *Prosthetic Memory: The Transformation of American Remembrance in the Age of Mass Culture,* suggests, "cinematic identification might be crucial to challenging the spectator's fundamental assumptions."[9] Empathy is a vicarious, spontaneous sharing of affect provoked by witnessing and hearing another's emotional state. Author of *Empathy and the Novel*, Suzanne Keen, makes a distinction between *personal distress* and *emotional sympathy*: Personal distress, an aversive emotional response also characterized by apprehension of another's emotion, differs from empathy in that it focuses on the self and leads not to sympathy but to avoidance. The distinction between empathy and personal distress matters because empathy is associated with moral emotion (also called empathetic concern) and with *prosocial* or altruistic action. Empathy that leads to sympathy is by definition other-directed, whereas an over-aroused empathetic response that creates personal distress (self-oriented and aversive) causes a turning away from the provocative condition of the other.[10]

In addition to generating empathy, successful biopics and other films help to shape audience memory. Landsberg argues that movies create alternate realities, "a suspension of disbelief and identification with the protagonist: which might affect [audiences] so significantly that the images would actually become part of their own archive of experience." Landsberg is saying that audiences adopt prosthetic memories because of the alternate realities they see on screen, and convert them into their own authentic memories. For Landsberg, cinema has a kind of catalytic potential, "in which people experience a bodily, mimetic encounter with a past that was not actually theirs."[11] This possibility raises complex questions about reality and perception. Are these in an adversarial or complementary relationship to each other? Writer Isaac Butler has criticized what he dubs the "realism canard," or the assessment of fictional and non-fictional narratives against the backdrop of historicity:

> … in real life, people don't talk the way they do in movies or television or (especially) books. Real locations aren't styled, lit, or shot the way they are on screen … The problem, in other words, has *nothing to do* with whether it would *really* happen … It's about the world the show has created and its integrity.[12]

As journalist Noah Berlatsky pointed out in an October 2013 essay on the film *12 Years a Slave*, "whether something 'feels true' is often closely related to whether the work manages to create an illusion not just of truth, but also of accuracy."[13] Truth, and the empathy and potential change of consciousness which should spring from it, is thus in symbiosis with a commitment to precision. Historian Yosef Hayim Yerushalmi in his book, *Zakhor: Jewish History and Jewish Memory*, contends that when the structures of truth or collective memory prove inadequate and falter, historiography is a necessity.[14]

A longstanding believer in, and practitioner of, historical analysis of film narratives is Lawrence Baron, professor emeritus at San Diego State University, who first began teaching history students about the impact of motion pictures on Holocaust memory culture in 1989. His own initial source of Holocaust awareness had been film. He recalled seeing *The Diary of Anne Frank* (director George Stevens, 1959), and watching television footage of the liberation of the Nazi concentration camps with his father in the 1950s. The success of productions like the *Holocaust* miniseries from 1978, *Europa, Europa* (1990), and movies like *Schindler's List* (1993), and *Life is Beautiful* (1997) convinced Baron that movies and television probably did more to raise awareness of the Holocaust than college or high school courses. Baron's scholarship ensued from his teaching; *Projecting the Holocaust into the Present* (2005), resulted from his observation in the first years of the new century that there had not been a major survey on the topic published since the 1980s, when Annette Insdorf published *Indelible Shadows: Film and the Holocaust*, and Judith Doneson published *The Holocaust in American Film*. Baron, keenly aware of the oft-quoted argument that the Holocaust was a phenomenon that could not satisfactorily be represented (and, for some, should not), saw these arguments as out of touch with audience reactions to film in general, and Holocaust movies in particular.[15]

Films about genocides therefore can have wide impact, and yet their existence presents numerous challenges – of distorting history and historical memory and of inflicting trauma on and encouraging projection on the part of an audience. To answer the questions posed at the beginning, viewing a film about genocide is clearly not comparable to viewing a horror film. The impact of the viewing can be more traumatic, and hit audiences on a much deeper, visceral level of being. Viewing a film about genocide is more than just a rush; it has the potential to transform in both constructive and devastating ways.

Such viewing may also result in what Wayne Booth calls "coduction" in literary criticism. Booth's idea seems to embody something important about the way people process narratives. Booth says in his book on literary criticism, *The Company We Keep*, that when he encountered the story of a person, he would "see it against a backdrop of my long personal history of untraceable complex experiences of other stories and persons. Thus, my initial acquaintance is comparative even when I do not think of comparisons. If I then converse with others about their impressions – if, that is, I move toward a public 'criticism' – the primary intuition (with its implicit acknowledgement of value) can be altered in least three ways: it can become conscious and more consciously comparative…; it can become less dependent on my private experience…; and it can be related to principles and norms … Every appraisal of a narrative is implicitly a comparison between the always-complex experience we have had in its presence and what we have known before."[16] For Booth, the appraisal of narratives is a fundamentally ethical activity since narratives project human agency and therefore attitudes, values, allegiances, antipathies – in a word, moral positions. Working alongside deduction, a formal, structured, derivational style of reasoning, and induction, an empirical, data-driven, generalizing, style of reasoning, is coduction. In Booth's mind, coduction is what we do whenever we say to the world: "Of the works of this general kind that I have experienced, *comparing my experience with more or less qualified observers*, this one seems to me among the better (or weaker) ones, or the best (or worst). Here are the reasons."[17]

The question as to what makes an effective film about genocide begs perhaps *the* fundamental question, intimated by this introduction. It is the question raised long ago by the philosopher Theodor Adorno, and that is, can genocide be represented through a visual medium like film or any fictional medium at all? Is any attempt at staging, at best, an impossibility; at worst, a second violation of the victims? The concerns underlying these questions are legitimate, especially the fear of trivialization, but, as Baron and others have argued, film is such a powerful cultural access point, and it has the potential to reach millions of people. The question then becomes, can film be effective in changing consciousness, reducing prejudice, and helping even in small and indirect ways to prevent genocide? While much research on this question remains to be done, there are a handful of relevant studies that have been conducted over the past six decades, and the results have been promising, although admittedly mixed.

For instance, in the wake of 1947's Best Picture winner, *Gentleman's Agreement,* which starred Gregory Peck (the archetypical heroic male) in a film about anti-Semitism, psychologist Irwin Rosen queried target audiences to assess the extent to which the film lessened bias against Jews. He found that his experimental group showed a significantly more favorable attitude toward Jews one day after seeing the picture, although this change was slightly less dramatic two days later, suggesting a drop-off over time.[18] In 1960, sociologist Russell Middleton, writing for the *American Sociological Review,* conducted a similar study involving the film. His group also showed a reduction in antisemitic prejudice after exposure to the film that was greater than that of the control group (those who had not seen the film). Middleton, like Irwin, cautioned that the influence of *Gentleman's Agreement* may not have a lasting effect and that it might simply exert pressure at surface conformity.[19] But the two studies did record a change. In 2009, Princeton University psychology professor Elizabeth Levy Paluck published the results of a yearlong experiment in Rwanda that assessed the impact of a radio soap opera that contained messages about reducing intergroup prejudice. Although she concluded that the radio program did not necessarily change the personal *beliefs* of its listeners, their perception of *social norms* and their behaviors did change "with respect to intermarriage, open dissent … and empathy."[20] The authors in this volume begin from the perspective that not only is it preferable to have fictional representations of genocide and human rights abuses, but that it is crucial as part of an overall strategy to combat bigotry, dehumanization, and collective mass murder.

Our authors' understanding of what constitutes a film about genocide is similarly far-reaching, although narrower than the list compiled by genocide scholar Adam Jones, who includes such classics as *The Battle of Algiers* and *All Quiet on the Western Front*.[21] Most of the films under analyzes here address what most would agree were genocides of the past century. Some, like the film *Turtles Can Fly* and those on imperialism and others from Chile and Argentina, inspire discussion as to what distinguishes a film about genocide from a film about crimes against humanity or human rights abuses. Here is a summary of each chapter:

1. "Settler Colonialism and Genocide in Australia" by Sarah Maddison, Associate Professor of Politics, University of Melbourne, and Jane Mills, Associate Professor of Film Studies in the School of the Arts and Media at the University of New South Wales, Australia. This chapter discusses films made by Indigenous and non-Indigenous filmmakers that represent, misrepresent, or ignore the genocidal impact of settler colonial policies on Australia's first nation's peoples. These policies included appropriating land, destroying native languages and social structures, and attempting to remove Aboriginal people from the national landscape through massacre and by "breeding out the black." Films explored include those by indigenous directors Tracey Moffatt (*Night Cries – A Rural Tragedy*), Ivan Sen (*Dust* and *Toomelah*), and Warwick Thornton (*Samson & Delilah*), as well as those from non-indigenous directors Charles Chauvel (*Jedda*), Rolf de Heer (*The Tracker*), and Phillip Noyce (*Rabbit-Proof Fence*).

2. "No Good Samaritans: Explaining African Colonialism and Underdevelopment in Popular African Films" by Teresa A. Booker, Assistant Professor of African American Studies, John Jay College. This chapter sets the stage for a discussion of genocide in the twentieth century by beginning with a discussion of how European imperialism in the late 1800s has been depicted over time. Films to be discussed here include *Zulu, Heart of Darkness, Tsotsi, Blood Diamond,* and *The Last King of Scotland*.

3. "'White Saviors' Unable to *Save* the 'Other' in Hollywood's Genocidal West" by William Hewitt, Professor Emeritus, History Department, West Chester University. This chapter addresses the common threads of representation and interpretation of the Native American experience in many films including *Last of the Mohicans, A Man Called Horse, Little Big Man, Dances with Wolves,* and *Hidalgo.* Although showing different locales, time periods, and cultures, these films depict white characters who regret the genocide of Native Americans or indigenous peoples, and find redemption in embedding themselves in the cultures of the others.

4. "Genocide as European Empire Building: The Slaughter of the Herero of Namibia" by Mark Malisa, Assistant Professor of Education, College of St. Rose. This chapter examines the place of genocide in colonialism and European empire building as portrayed in the documentaries: *Racism: A History,* and *Namibia: Genocide and the Second Reich.* It focuses on Germany's genocide against the Herero in particular and the creation of the image of the non-European as inconsequential to European progress and material acquisition, as well as the resultant desensitization of the European mind to the genocides in Africa.

5. "The Armenian Genocide in Film: Overcoming Denial and Loss" by Armen Marsoobian, Professor of Philosophy, South Connecticut State University. This chapter gives an overview of the films *Ravished Armenia* (alternative title, *The Auction of Souls*), *Mayrig, Ararat,* and *La Masseria Delle Allodole* (English release, *Lark Farm*). It also focuses on two feature films from Soviet Armenia, *Nahapet* and *Karot (Yearning)*, and the never made major Hollywood studio film based on Franz Werfel's *The Forty Days of Musa Dagh,* a film project cancelled under political pressure by the Republic of Turkey. The chapter explores themes of silence, denial, and nostalgia.

6. "The Ukrainian Famine of 1932–1933 on Screen: Making Sense of Suffering" by Iuliia Kysla, University of Alberta. This chapter is an analysis of the one feature film on the Ukraine Famine, *Holod-33 (Famine-33)* directed by Oles' Yanchuk in 1991. It was shown in the year of the referendum on Ukrainian independence. The chapter provides the context for the film and investigates why there haven't been more features about the genocide in Ukraine.

7. "The Holocaust in Feature Films: Problematic Current Trends and Themes" by Jonathan Friedman, Professor of History and Director of Holocaust and Genocide Studies at West Chester University. This chapter traces the evolution of films on the Holocaust over the past 70 years, analyzing themes in recent films, including *The Grey Zone, Fateless, Everything is Illuminated, Esther's Diary, A Jewish Girl in Shanghai, Sarah's Key, In Darkness, Aftermath,* and *Ida.* The guiding questions for the article are: Have feature films about the Holocaust become less effective in recent years in their representations of the event? If so, can this be remedied?

8. "Slaughter in China on Film: Nanjing and 'Saving Asia' through Mutilation" by Mark DeStephano, Professor, Department of Modern and Classical Languages, and Director of Asian Studies Program, Saint Peter's University. This chapter examines three sets of genocidal events perpetrated by Japanese soldiers in China between 1933 and 1945, as portrayed by Chinese filmmakers: (1) the massacre at Nanking (*Black Sun: The Nanking Massacre*); (2) the chemical and biological experiments on Chinese by Japanese Army Unit 731 (*Men Behind the Sun*); and, (3) the mutilation of "comfort women" as part of the Nanking Massacre (*City of Life and Death*).

9. "Bangladesh: The Forgotten Genocide" by Lynne Fallwell, Professor of History, Texas Tech University. In 1971, during the nine-month Bangladesh War of Independence, Pakistani troops, with assistance of other militias, killed an estimated 3 million Bengalis. Yet, Bangladesh is sometimes referred to as a "forgotten genocide." Despite early media attention, including a 20-minute documentary by noted Bangladeshi filmmaker Zahir Raihan (*Stop Genocide!*) and a highly publicized concert, later released as a film, organized by George Harrison of the Beatles (1971), the extreme violence – including mass rape of Bengali women – quickly faded from international attention. Today, comparative studies of genocide often overlook Bangladesh as a case study. However, Bangladeshi filmmakers, starting with *The Clay Bird* in 2002, have begun to turn attention to the issue of genocidal violence within the nation's struggle for independence. In the last four years, three other feature films have been produced in country, with another due out in 2014: *Gohine Shobdo (Dark Resonance),*

Amar Bondhu Rashed (My Friend Rashed), Rubaiyat Hossain, and *Bastard Child*. This article traces the development of genocide themes within these productions, from initial passing references in the earlier works to a central narrative in Bangladesh's most recent filmic endeavor.

10. "Argentina's Dirty War on Film: The Absent Presence of The Disappeared" by Kristin Brunnemer, Professor of English, Pierce College. This chapter explores how films have addressed the period of kidnappings in Argentina in the early 1970s. These films are: *The Official Story (La Historia Oficial)* and *Captive (Cautiva)*.

11. "Featuring Acts of Genocide in Chilean Film" by Gloria Galindo, PhD, University of California, Santa Barbara. The films in this chapter, which chronicle the human rights abuses of the Pinochet regime in Chile, include the trilogy by Chilean instructor Pablo Larraín consisting of *Tony Manero*, *Post Mortem*, and *NO*.

12. "Screening the Killing Fields: The Cambodian Genocide on Film" by Cathy Schlund-Vials, Professor of English and Asian/Asian American Studies, University of Connecticut at Storrs. Focused on Socheata Poeuv's *New Year Baby*, Sambath Thet and Rob Lemkin's *Enemies of the People*, and Rithy Panh's *The Missing Picture*, this chapter considers the way film functions simultaneously in tandem and in conflict with the ongoing U.N/Khmer Rouge Tribunal. Officially known as the "Extraordinary Chambers in the Courts of Cambodia," the hybrid tribunal has struggled to prosecute former Khmer Rouge leaders and provide symbolic reparation for victims. This chapter considers the failures of the tribunal as a way to re-evaluate the ways these particular cinematic productions instantiate alternative sites of genocide justice.

13. "This Time We're Going to Hit Them Without Mercy" by Clinton Fernandes, Associate Professor of the Humanities, University New South Wales. Indonesian "operations" in East Timor Indonesia's 1975 invasion and occupation of East Timor till 1999 caused the largest loss of life relative to total population since the Holocaust. There have been a number of documentaries, some of critical importance in the campaign for independence, but very few feature films. The first feature film to be filmed and produced in East Timor, *A Guerra Da Beatriz (Beatrice's War)*, premiered in 2013. This paper explores how this and other films have dealt with the question of genocide in East Timor.

14. "The Guatemalan Genocide on Film: An Ongoing Crisis and Omission" by Zachary Smith, Master of Arts student in the Holocaust and Genocide Studies Program at West Chester University. In this chapter, documentaries of the genocide in Guatemala (such as *When Mountains Tremble, Granito,* and *Discovering Dominga)* will be analyzed against feature films such as *The Silence of Neto* (1994) and *Haunted Land: Le pays hanté, la Palabra Desenterrada* (2001), a film which tells the story of two survivors of the Guatemalan civil war.

15. "Cinematic Witnessing of the Genocide in Bosnia 1992–1995: Toward A Poetics of Responsibility" by David Pettigrew, Professor of Philosophy, Southern Connecticut State University. This chapter will explore the unique capacity of certain films to bear witness to the genocide in Bosnia. The films to be analyzed include *Welcome to Sarajevo, Shot Through the Heart, Baggage* [Prtljag], *Grbavica, In the Land of Blood and Honey, Srebrenica: A Cry from the Grave, and The Troubles We've Seen: The History of Journalism in Wartime.* The chapter will consider the extent to which such films enact a poetics of responsibility insofar as they enact a witnessing that provides for an authentic encounter with the singularity of the suffering of the other.

16. "'Truth' in Films About the Rwandan Genocide" by Barbara A. Moss, Georgia Highlands College and Mary Afolabi, Veritas University, Abuja, Nigeria. *Hotel Rwanda* in 2004, followed by *Sometimes in April* and *Shooting Dogs* in 2005, and *Shake Hands With the Devil* in 2007, have given audiences powerful representations of the 1994 genocide of over 800,000 Tutsi Rwandans at the hands of the Hutu militia. This chapter will analyze the filmmakers' representation of pre-genocide ethnic relations, depiction of the carnage, portrayal of the Hutu militia, role of the United Nations peacekeepers and the Rwandan Patriotic Front, and the complicity of the international community in the genocide.

17. "Stop a Genocide or Act in the National Interest? A Comparative Examination of *Hotel Rwanda* and *Attack on Darfur*" by Glen Duerr, Assistant Professor of International Studies, Cedarville University. This essay starts with an overview of the movies, and then presents a wider, in-depth investigation of key political issues alluded to in the films, revolving around the debate between acting to stop a genocide

versus acting in the national interest. These issues include: the reluctance of Western governments to intervene in Rwanda or Sudan, the role of prominent international organizations like the United Nations or the African Union, international media reporting, geopolitical restructuring in the post-Cold War era, and genocide since the Holocaust. This essay provides a comparative overview of the two cases using these lenses noting the similarities and differences in the cases of Rwanda and Darfur, as well as the depiction of genocide through film.

18. "Adults in Children's Bodies: *Disabling* Children in Bahman Ghobadi's Films" by Eda Dedebas Dundar, Assistant Professor, Bogazici University, Turkey. In this chapter, Professor Dedebas Dundar examines a number of the films of Iranian-Kurdish director Bahman Ghobadi, shedding light on the representation of both the Kurdish genocide of the 1980s as well as the US invasion of Iraq. Ghobadi's *Turtles Can Fly* (2004), a movie that portrays the lives of child refugees in a concentration camp on the Iraqi-Turkish border on the eve of the US invasion of Iraq, depicts characters who eagerly wait for their saviors but become disillusioned with the outcome. *Turtles Can Fly* and Ghobai's other films create "disabling" and disturbing narratives in the affirmative sense, which destabilize the trope of the Western savior.

From these articles, we gain a better understanding not only of how genocide has been represented in films over the past century, but also what constitutes an effective film about genocide. Many of the films under consideration here are regarded by film historians as classics in their own right, with strong acting, directing, writing, and cinematography. They suggest that at bottom, an effective film about genocide must begin with an attention to historical rigor, detail, and accuracy, as well as a sense of respect for the victims of genocide and a need to foreground their stories in the context of the trauma which they confront daily. There is an additional consensus among our authors that filmmakers should treat audiences as intelligent and capable of handling difficult imagery, multiple storylines, and even stories that do not necessarily have easy or happy endings. This latter strategy might not produce a commercially successful film, but it might actually get closer to the darkness above and below the surface which a representation of genocide seeks to reveal.

1

Settler Colonialism and Genocide in Australia

Sarah Maddison

University of Melbourne

Jane Mills

University of New South Wales, Australia

The arrival of British colonizers in 1788 saw the decimation of Aboriginal and Torres Strait Islander peoples in Australia. Within weeks of the First Fleet sailing into what is now known as Sydney Harbor, frontier warfare had erupted in the southeast of the continent, subsequently spreading north and west over the following 140 years. During this period, Australia's Indigenous peoples were engaged in ongoing violent conflict that belies the common characterization of Australian history as involving a relatively peaceful "settlement."[1] The invasion and colonization of *terra australis* saw Aboriginal and Torres Strait Islander peoples massacred, dispossessed of land, and contained through legislation that restricted their freedom of movement and association, later also subjecting them to assimilationist policies intent on destroying their languages and social structures, and that allowed for the widespread removal of Aboriginal children from their families. Over many years, Aboriginal and Torres Strait Islander people were pushed to the margins of Australian society both literally and figuratively, as the colonizing state sought to obliterate their existence in order to legitimize its declaration of the land as *terra nullius*, thereby justifying the refusal to negotiate treaties with Indigenous peoples or otherwise recognize their existing sovereignty.

The genocidal practices that underpinned this pattern of elimination and legitimation are typical of settler colonial societies. The emerging field of settler colonial studies emphasizes the distinct characteristics of nations with a permanent settler presence (notably Australia, Canada, New Zealand, and the United States), which avoided the "decolonizing gestures" experienced in the extractive colonies in much of the rest of the world.[2] Settler colonial societies perpetuate an eliminatory logic that seeks to permanently displace the Indigenous populations within their acquired territories, without any intention that the nation as a whole might one day undertake a process of structural decolonization.[3] This logic of elimination is inevitably genocidal, but in such a way that genocide cannot be understood as belonging to any particular period of history. Rather, genocide can be seen as intrinsic to the structure and institutions of settler colonial societies. As Patrick Wolfe has famously argued, "invasion is a structure not an event."[4]

It is in light of this complex engagement with the practice of genocide that this chapter discusses films made by Indigenous and non-Indigenous filmmakers that represent, misrepresent, or ignore the genocidal impact of settler colonialism on Indigenous peoples in Australia. Films explored include those by Indigenous directors Tracey Moffatt (*Night Cries – A Rural Tragedy*), Ivan Sen (*Dust, Toomelah*) and Warwick Thornton (*Samson and Delilah*), and non-Indigenous directors Charles Chauvel (*Jedda*), Rolf de Heer (*The Tracker*), Igor Auzin (*We of the Never-Never*) and Phillip Noyce (*Rabbit-Proof Fence*).

Denying the Australian Genocide

The complex logic of settler colonialism has meant that genocide remains a complicated and contested concept in Australian cultural and political discourse. Settler societies like Australia rest on a denial of genocidal practices that allow them to maintain a sense of moral and political legitimacy.[5] It therefore follows that representations of genocide in Australian feature films also reflect the nation's deep ambivalence about its relationship

17

with the original inhabitants of the continent. As a result, the filmic representation of genocide has not played a large role in the cultural history of Australia. Indeed, until relatively recently when a new generation of Indigenous filmmakers burst upon the cultural scene, films about any aspect of Australian Indigenous peoples were noticeable by their absence.[6] Since the inception of cinema at the end of the nineteenth century, the Australian film industry largely adhered to an unwritten rule that movies about Aboriginal and Torres Strait Islander peoples and issues were box office poison.[7] Writing little more than ten years ago, Peter Krausz observed that of over 1000 Australian feature films produced in Australia he could "only identify around 50 films that represent Aborigines in any way at all in the narrative."[8] In partial explanation, Chris Healy points to cycles of rememberings and forgettings in white social memory; arguing that "Aboriginal people and things appear and disappear from public culture in strange but definite ways. Aborigines are recognized and identified, then they are overlooked and disregarded."[9] Understanding settler colonial logic thus helps to explain the absence or refusal to represent filmically the genocidal impact of settler colonial policies on Aboriginal and Torres Strait Islander peoples, as to do so would be to acknowledge the illegitimacy of the nation's founding, and the "genocidal morality"[10] that has enabled the settler state to advance its eliminatory logic despite the evident cost to Indigenous peoples. No differently from the majority of Australians, filmmakers have largely found it easier to forget, evade or avoid the topic.

There is also a sense in which Australian filmmakers have lacked the audio and visual tools to represent the historical and contemporary reality of Indigenous genocide. For many, the vocabulary of genocidal discourse seems inflammatory in the Australian context, at odds with the national narrative of exploration and settlement. But the concept of genocide, defined by the legal scholar Raphael Lemkin as "the destruction of a nation or of an ethnic group"[11] is, of course, much wider than the popular understanding of the practice as one of mass extermination.[12] Leaving aside the question of intent, the concept of genocide tends to refer to the destruction of the foundations of life of the national group, including the destruction of language, culture, religion, and social institutions, with the intended aim of annihilating the group.[13] Indigenous peoples around the world have argued that colonial practices intended to absorb or assimilate a minority group into a dominant group are fundamentally genocidal in intent.

Yet despite this, until almost the end of the twentieth century there was little discussion in Australia of the conflict between European colonizers and the Indigenous peoples, and certainly not in terms of genocide. An exception was the historian Peter Read whose prescient 1981 pamphlet *The Stolen Generations: The Removal of Aboriginal Children in New South Wales 1883 to 1969* used for the first time the now widely accepted term "stolen generations" to refer to the state-sanctioned, forced removal of thousands of Aboriginal and Torres Strait Islander children during the twentieth century. Read argued that this policy constituted genocide, which:

> ... does not simply mean the extermination of people by violence but may include any means at all ... At the height of the policy of separating Aboriginal people from their parents the Aborigines Welfare Board meant to do just that.[14]

Yet these early claims held little legitimacy within the dominant settler society where, as Tony Barta argued, "most Australians have never seriously been confronted by the idea that the society in which they live is founded on genocide," despite the fact that "If ever a people has had to sustain an assault on its existence of the kind Lemkin described it would seem to have been over the last two hundred years in Australia."[15] The settler colonial mentality also explains the refusal to countenance a definition of genocide that includes cultural and assimilatory practices. Indeed, along with other settler colonial nations, Australia had specifically voted against the inclusion of cultural genocide in the UN definition. How could it do otherwise? The colonial project depended upon the destruction of Indigenous land ownership, societal structures and culture precisely in order to succeed.[16] Yet the criterion of "intention" and the actual wording of the crime in the UN Convention contributed to the absence of the word "genocide" from the Australian lexicon for many years. Colin Tatz suggests the very nature of the crime may also explain the reluctance to confront the historical reality:

> The degree to which the crime is widely considered abhorrent is indicated by the number of euphemisms used to not-name it – even while the crimes themselves are actually being carried out/put into operation. Almost all historians of the Aboriginal

> experience – black and white – avoid it. They write about paci-
> fying, killing, cleansing, excluding, exterminating, starving,
> poisoning, shooting, beheading, sterilizing, exiling, removing –
> but avoid genocide.[17]

Ultimately, however, the reality of this history could not be suppressed, and the political contest over the genocide in Australia made its way onto the nation's film screens.

Contesting Genocide on Film

The "not-naming" of genocide in Australia ended explosively in 1997 when the Australian Human Rights and Equal Opportunity Commission's report, *Bringing Them Home: The Report of the National Inquiry into the Separation of Aboriginal and Torres Strait Islander Children from their Families* (here-after *Bringing Them Home*) focused the nation's attention upon genocide as never before. The report concluded that twentieth-century government policies of removing between one in three and one in ten Aboriginal and Torres Strait Islander children, particularly lighter-skinned children, from their families amounted to crimes against humanity and were in breach of international laws prohibiting genocide. As the report argued:

> When a child was forcibly removed that child's entire commu-
> nity lost, often permanently, its chance to perpetuate itself in
> that child. The Inquiry has concluded that this was a primary
> objective of forcible removals and is the reason they amount to
> genocide.[18]

This first, overt mention of genocide in a government document unleashed a heated and ugly public debate. Indigenous and non-Indigenous politicians, public intellectuals, media commentators, filmmakers and many members of the general public took sides in what became known as the "history wars."

Five years after the publication of *Bringing Them Home*, Phillip Noyce's film, *Rabbit-Proof Fence* (2002), brought the Indigenous experience of child removal to the big screen. Set in the 1931, the film tells the real-life story of three young girls of the Mardudjara people living in the Pilbara region of north-western Australia: Molly, her sister Gracie, and their cousin

Daisy, aged 14, eight and ten respectively. Because they were considered "half-caste" in the racist language of the day, these children were among the many thousands of Aboriginal children who over a period of 70 or more years were removed from their families. In the film, we see the three girls transported 1,491 miles away from their home to a mission settlement from where, desperately homesick, they escape and follow the fence built to keep rabbits out of western Australia to walk all the way home. The story is extraordinary, extraordinarily moving – and true. It was first published in 1996 in a book written by Molly's daughter, Doris Pilkington Garimara, on which the filmmakers based their film.[19]

The film is remarkable in several ways, not least for its creation of a space in popular culture for the Indigenous experience to be seen and heard, although it does not ignore the benign intentions of some government perpetrators.[20] It also introduced Australia's stolen generations to international audiences. Referring to the end of the film in which the real Molly Craig and Daisy Craig Kadibil, now two very elderly women, are filmed on their land and speaking in their language, the esteemed US film critic Roger Ebert made the connection to the Nazi Holocaust:

> The final scene of the film contains an appearance and a revelation of astonishing emotional power; not since the last shots of *Schindler's List* have I been so overcome with the realization that real people, in recent historical times, had to undergo such inhumanity.[21]

While the word "genocide" is not actually mentioned in the film, it clearly depicts the forcible transference of children of the group to another group along with practices of eugenics and cultural genocide, as the Indigenous characters are forbidden to marry and have children with members of their own race, speak their own language, inhabit their own land, or learn their own cultural practices.

Like the reaction to the *Bringing Them Home* report, the film's critical response was loud, angry and frequently racist. Argument raged about whether white colonial settlement had indeed involved genocide and whether the child removal policy was done with or without good intentions. The argument also became mired in the issue of factual accuracy: had writer Christine Olsen and director Phillip Noyce exaggerated or twisted the facts? Opinion was further divided as to whether the film promoted an overly critical view of Australian history that unfairly judged the Australian state as perpetrators of genocide or provided "the approbation of the implementation of genocide [and] justifies the very act by obfuscating the crime as benevolence."[22]

Such debate about the veracity of historical experience is not uncommon to films that depict, discuss or allude to genocide. Take, for example, *Manganinnie* (John Honey, 1980) that offers a highly romanticized view of the frontier war period of settler history in Tasmania (then known as Van Diemen's Land) in the early part of the nineteenth century. It tells the story of a white settler family whose father participates in the notorious "Black Line." This was the human chain of every able-bodied male colonist, convict or free, that in 1831 swept across the settled districts in an attempt to corral all members of the Big River and Oyster Cove peoples and confine them in a small area in the south-east corner of the island. When young Joanna (Anna Ralph) becomes separated from her White family, the sole survivor of the massacre, Manganinnie (Mawuyul Yanthalawuy), "adopts" her and together they search for Manganinnie's people. Upon learning that none have survived, Manganinnie dies.

Based on the novel by Beth Roberts[23] whose stated aim was to "promote greater understanding about different nationalities and strengthen our bonds with the Aborigines,"[24] the film loosely references Trugernanner (Truganini), the Palawa woman who is popularly but incorrectly thought to have been the last surviving "full blood" member of her Oyster Cove language group. The film is variously criticized for aestheticizing violence by showing a massacre "in tasteful long shot or off screen," for depicting the Black Line as a massacre when all but five Aboriginal people escaped capture and of whom three were killed, and for perpetuating the myth that by the end of the century there were no surviving Aboriginal people in Tasmania.[25] As Karen Jennings writes: "If it is set against a backdrop of European massacre and Aboriginal dispossession, as its press notes proclaim, it is a very distant backdrop indeed."[26]

Another film that fails the veracity test so often demanded of filmic representations (or non-representations) of genocide is *We of the Never Never* (Igor Auzin, 1982). The film is based on the autobiographical account of Mrs. Aeneas Gunn who in 1902 was the first white woman to settle (with her husband) in an outback area some 300 miles south of Darwin in the Northern Territory. Jeannie Gunn's account reveals a tough-minded and racist, although not altogether unkind, woman. Both book and film, however, are accused of putting a rosy gloss on her account of white settler treatment of the traditional owners of the land of which they were dispossessed. Rob Gowland, for example, is critical of how publisher and filmmaker fictionalize the truth:

> Earlier editions of Mrs Gunn's once popular book recounted the 'nigger hunts' which her husband and 'the men' carried out … recent editions of the book have had the 'nigger hunts' deftly removed, so as not to offend. This tidying up of a true story may keep the shine on Mrs Gunn's image but [the film] portrays a false picture of both the author and her times … beautiful scenery, safe period atmosphere, bland relationships and – to satisfy modern attitudes – a heroine whose perception of Aboriginal culture was suddenly very ahead of her time.[27]

Other films accused of ignoring, sanitizing, or otherwise evading the truth of white settler genocidal crime are *Walkabout* (Nic Roeg, 1971) and *The Chant of Jimmie Blacksmith* (Fred Schepisi, 1978).[28] The first is the lyrical vision of a doomed encounter between two cultures personified by two teenagers, "Black Boy" (David Gulpilil) and "Girl" (Jenny Agutter), in the central Australian desert, as imagined by three English men: novelist James Vance Marshall (pseudonym of Donald Payne), screenplay writer Edward Bond, and director/cinematographer Nic Roeg. *The Chant of Jimmie Blacksmith* tells the story of an Indigenous "outlaw" who commits in graphic, violent filmic detail a series of murders of white people around the turn of the twentieth century. Schepisi's screenplay derives from the novel of the same name by Australian author Thomas Keneally who fictionalized the real-life story of Jimmy Governor from Governor's point of view.[29] What the two films have in common is the criticism that because the Indigenous protagonists both die – "Black Boy" commits suicide and Jimmie is hanged (as was Jimmy Governor) – the films perpetuate the common colonial understanding of Aboriginal and Torres Strait Islander peoples as a "dying race." The notion was, of course, comforting to the descendants of the settler colonial nation who wanted to ignore or forget their ancestors' participation and collusion in genocidal crime.

Cinematic Specificity

These and other filmmakers accused of using euphemism or dysphemism to hide or exaggerate genocidal truth are not necessarily or always guilty of falsifying historical fact. How films show and tell stories, their specifically filmic "language," needs to be considered when discussing truth and accuracy in feature films which are, after all, dramatized fictions.[30] Australian filmic representations of, or references to, genocide are no different from any other film; all depend upon the creative imagination of artist and viewer. Authors elsewhere in this volume may plead for absolute obedience to historical fact and for the filmic imagination to resist a specific trope or genre (comedy, for example) but cinema, as an art form, uses creative imagination to extend or compress what "actually happened" or reference it in ways that may hide, but can also illuminate actuality. Ultimately, meaning is not made only by the filmmaker(s) or the film text itself as audiences also participate in the meaning-making process and draw upon their own knowledge, experience, and understanding to make sense of what they see and hear. Sometimes viewers can "see" (that is, understand) what they don't actually see (or hear) on the screen. Equally, they don't always or necessarily see or understand what, to others, may be transparently obvious. As Larissa Behrendt writes in her monograph on *Rabbit-Proof Fence* in which she discusses the film's dramatic and poetic use of images and words to tell a story based on actual events:

> No film, not even a documentary (which *Rabbit-Proof Fence* doesn't pretend to be), can do anything other than *represent* reality – it can't *be* reality. Films use metaphors and symbolism as a means of telling a story and of making sense to their audiences. They may use close-ups, for example, to show a small part of a person, a thing or a place, in order to indicate the whole. They also use images and sounds to call up an attribute of that person, thing or place. We all read films differently and clearly some critics saw things that others didn't. Equally, some critics wanted the film to be something that others didn't.

Many Australian films help explain how a filmmaker might not actually use either word or image of genocide and yet an audience may "see" or understand that this is what the film or a scene is "about." One is *Jedda* (Charles Chauvel, 1955), an undoubted classic in the Australian film canon. This was the first film in the history of Australia's national cinema to have Indigenous characters at the center of the narrative and to cast Indigenous actors in the leading roles. It tells the story of Jedda, an Aboriginal baby whose mother dies and who is "adopted" and brought up by a white pastoralist couple, Sarah and Doug McMann, as a white child. Jedda (Rosalie 'Ngarla' Kunoth) is dispossessed of her family, nation, language, culture, and spiritual beliefs. In a poignant scene, she cries out that she cannot join her people at a *corroboree* (an Aboriginal ceremony involving song and dance) because she does not know their (her) language nor her people's cultural customs. Jedda is then abducted once again, this time by Marbuk (Robert Tudawali), an Aboriginal lawbreaker. The film ends with Marbuk and Jedda plunging to their deaths from a high cliff.

While there is no specific image of genocide as it may be commonly imagined, and the actual word is not mentioned, genocide nonetheless pervades the film and swirls in and out of each frame for those who look and listen closely. *Jedda* was made just four years after Australia ratified the UN convention and at a time when the issue of where Indigenous peoples fit into society was being widely debated throughout Australia. However, this is not necessarily what the filmmakers intended, nor what all audiences necessarily see or understand. Debate continues as to whether *Jedda* is racist or *about* racism, whether it is an Aboriginal text about survival as writer Mudrooroo maintains, or a "colonialist fantasy" that masks the truth of "frontier brutality," as Indigenous scholar and activist Marcia Langton argues.[31]

A film that represents genocide very differently is *The Tracker* (Rolf de Heer, 2002). In this film set in rough bush country in the 1920s, an Aboriginal tracker (David Gulpilil) leads three White men on the hunt for a Black fugitive accused of murdering a White woman. The senior policeman in charge (Gary Sweet) murders "bush blacks" on sight; a young constable (Damon Gameau) initially joins in but then takes a stand; a third man (Grant Page) disapproves but does nothing to stop the killing. Thus the film neatly represents perpetrator, victim, Aboriginal sympathizer, and colluding bystander. The tracker watches and waits for his chance to turn the tables, as the party rides further into the bush. When Gulpilil's character does eventually exact revenge, he gives the policeman a mock-trial in British court-style, and a British form of execution – hanging. White law is then superseded as the local Aboriginal people take the tracker and the young policeman prisoner. They already have the Black fugitive in custody, for the rape of a woman of their clan.[32] As film critic Paul Byrnes notes, "The story is fictional but we know that these things happened," and the strategy of non-Indigenous director de Heer, "is to make us feel them in a different way":

> … the movie is incredibly direct and confronting in showing cruelty and humiliation but it substitutes a series of paintings, created for the film by South Australian artist Peter Coad, for most of the explicit depictions of ultimate violence. These paintings disrupt the place that violent scenes usually occupy in violent cinema – there is no payoff for the viewer who wants the thrill of gore. Instead, each killing becomes a kind of instant history. The paintings could be from any time, representing a collective memory. Director Rolf de Heer is turning these despicable, unspeakable acts into a kind of cinematic cave painting.

Indigenous Filmmakers

In recent decades Indigenous filmmakers have also depicted genocide, often obliquely but also through a direct engagement with non-Indigenous cinematic representations. Tracey Moffat's experimental film, *Night Cries: A Rural Tragedy* (1990), for example, is an imaginative revisioning of what may have happened if Jedda had not plunged to her death at the end of Chauvel's 1955 film *Jedda*, as discussed above. In this film, a middle-aged woman (Marcia Langton) who is unnamed but unmistakably Jedda is looking after her aged, dying mother (Agnes Hardwick). Nothing is said or explained directly – indeed, for those who do not know *Jedda*, little would be explicable – but Moffat reverses the earlier film story: now the White mother (the adoptive mother character, Sarah McMann in the Chauvel film) has nothing and no-one other than her adopted Indigenous daughter to care for her. One scene in the film is particularly relevant here. In flashback, Moffat creatively imagines and represents genocide when the Jedda character remembers happy holiday times at the seaside as a child with her loving, White mother.

Disturbing this happy tableau, however, there is a wild wind that whips up long strands of seaweed that wrap themselves round the young Jedda, blinding and choking her. The little girl cries in fear and as the scene plays out, the strangling strips of seaweed look increasingly like strips of 35 mm celluloid. This scene can be understood as Moffat's critique of the Australian cinematic treatment of Aboriginal peoples and its collusion in refusing to remember acts of genocidal destruction of peoples, their nations, families, and culture or to give Indigenous people their filmic voice.

Night Cries is not a feature-length film and so falls outside the remit of this book. But to ignore it and other short films by Indigenous filmmakers is to ignore the fact that experimental and emerging filmmakers, including Indigenous filmmakers, cut their teeth on shorts (and, often, documentaries). Of these, one film stands out from all those that on close reading reveal or suggest ideas about genocide. This is *Dust* (2000) by Ivan Sen, a descendant of the Gamilaroi peoples of northwest New South Wales and southern Queensland, and also of Hungarian, German and Croatian descent.[33] Sen is one of Australia's most prolific filmmakers, Indigenous or otherwise. In addition to many shorts and documentaries, since 1992 he has made five features – four dramas and a one-hour documentary. "Director" is an inadequate description for Sen who is a "multihyphenate" as *Variety* dubbed him: on many of his films he is writer, director, cinematographer, editor, composer, sound recordist and sound designer.[34]

Dust is set on the cotton fields of far Northern New South Wales where cheap labor – mostly Indigenous workers – chip away at the weeds. In 23 minutes it shows and tells the story of a treacherous dust storm that brews alongside the relationships between the White and Aboriginal cotton chippers. Through the dust and dawn tones of the oncoming storm, a car makes its way to the cotton fields. In it are two young Aboriginal men, Leroy (Clayton Munro) and Vance (Wayne Munro) and their mother Ruby (Reta Binge) on their way to work. In another car are a young White couple whose relationship is not in good shape. On the cotton field the chippers encounter and provoke sexual and racial tensions and rivalries that threaten to explode violently. When the storm finally breaks we see that the historical violent tensions between the original owners of the land and the White colonial settlers were greater than anything that exists today. The film gives the audience the space to determine if the bones they see revealed as the storm blows the soil into dust are those of Indigenous ancestors who were peacefully buried here or if they mark the site of a genocidal massacre.

This is not to say, however, that there are no feature-length films by Indigenous directors that depict the outcome of over 150 years of physical, psychological and cultural onslaught of Australia's Indigenous peoples, their society and culture. We have space here to mention just two: Warwick Thornton's *Samson and Delilah* (2009), and Ivan Sen's third feature, *Toomelah* (2012).[35] The former, while ostensibly a love story of two Indigenous teenagers, Samson (Rowan McNamara) and Delilah (Marissa Gibson), growing up in a socio-economically disadvantaged community in Australia's red center, also imaginatively implicates the Christian Church in the historic disabling of Indigenous peoples and the relentless destruction of their culture and society in this part of Aboriginal Australia. As Therese Davis points out, the film's title is not just a biblical allusion:

> It is also an ironic residue of this particular colonial history: Old Testament names such as Samson and Delilah are commonplace in Aboriginal communities in Central Australia, especially those that began as Lutheran missions. Moreover, Delilah and Samson's return to Delilah's homelands speaks to long-standing political struggles between Aboriginal communities and the government of the Northern Territory over government funding for Aboriginal people opting to live in smaller family groups on their homelands, rather than in larger government settlements. By bringing these historical traces and others to the surface, the film reveals the complexities and contradictions of living in the aftermath of colonialism, making it a profoundly local, "insider" representation of Aboriginal experience.[36]

The film's representation of cultural genocide is treated with delicate filmic brushstrokes. Although not hesitant to depict cultural and societal destruction, writer/director/ cinematographer Thornton, a Kaytetye man, also represents survival for those who look closely.[37] In addition to the poverty, petrol-sniffing and cultural decay the film also shows "how Christian beliefs have been adapted by many Aboriginal people as part of a complex hybrid worldview."[38] The film reveals the complexities and contradictions of living in the aftermath of genocidal colonial and post-colonial policies in a community that no longer knows how to speak its own language or know its traditional customs and beliefs.

Toomelah is also seen by some audiences as a harsh and negative showing and telling of this aftermath while to others it both depicts reality and offers hope in a fictional filmic mode. Set in the actual community of Toomelah on the border of northern New South Wales and southern Queensland, Sen uses fictional story-telling techniques and local non-actors to depict a vivid picture of a small society in physical, emotional and cultural distress. The locality of Toomelah is, in fact, the third site to which the Gamilaroi people have been forcible settled. Sen's creative focus is on a ten year old boy, Daniel (Daniel Connors), who is unable to resist the allure of local small-time drug dealing. At first, the narrative seems to point Daniel towards a life in a cultural and societal wasteland comprising drugs, alcohol, child sexual abuse, domestic violence and jail – a borderland of cultural genocide that certainly exists in Australia today as a result of decades of government political policy and casual neglect. But Sen offers a shard of hope. When Daniel elects to return to school where he can start to learn his own language, the film says something important about borders: the borders that once protected the Indigenous nations' culture and language and that White settler Australians destroyed as part of the colonizing process need to be resurrected if the process of cultural genocide is to end.[39]

Conclusion

Like other settler colonial societies, Australia has a history of contesting the idea that genocide was committed on its soil. Politically this contest has played out in political debates over the making of treaties, the recognition of Indigenous land rights, constitutional reform, and the wars over (and eventual state apology for) the devastation caused by policies of child removal. The logic of settler colonialism drives a need for state legitimacy that rests on the denial, or at the very least the minimization, of all such genocidal practices. Indeed, it is a foundational settler fear that the acknowledgment of past (and present) wrongs against Indigenous peoples will reveal the fundamental moral wrong upon which the nation is built.

The response to claims of genocide, therefore, is one ranging from passive silence to outraged denial. These are not stories that can be comfortably accommodated within the settler nation's narrative.

Australian cinema has mirrored the ambivalence and hostility of settler colonialism. Unlike filmmaking in societies where genocide has become an uncontested historical fact, Australian filmmakers have approached the representation of genocide obliquely, often raising questions about whether their art is perpetuating the denial of genocide. Yet as a focus on Aboriginal and Torres Strait Islander peoples in Australian film has become more prevalent in recent years, these questions have become unavoidable for the Australian film industry. Increasingly, certain filmmakers have made bold statements about the continuing impact of the settler colonial genocide, and key among these have been Indigenous filmmakers. Often working outside of the mainstream feature film genre, Indigenous film simply cannot be ignored. Indeed, to do so would merely be to perpetuate the settler's desire to control the national narrative. Even as Aboriginal and Torres Strait Islander film becomes more mainstream, and Indigenous filmmakers begin to access the support and funding that has been available to their non-Indigenous counterparts for far longer, it will remain vitally important for the early and experimental work of Aboriginal and Torres Strait Islander filmmakers to be afforded recognition.

In a settler colonial context this work is important for reasons far beyond a need to support otherwise marginalized artists. In telling the stories of Australia's genocide from a uniquely Indigenous perspective, Indigenous film may offer an important counter-narrative to settler timidity about acknowledging the true horrors of the nation's colonial history. It is a rare opportunity for the victims of genocide to tell their own stories.

2

No Good Samaritans: Explaining African Colonialism and Underdevelopment in Popular African Films

Teresa A. Booker

John Jay College

It was Rudyard Kipling's 1899 poem, "The White Man's Burden," which provided the unofficial justification for nearly five hundred years of European colonialism in Africa, the Americas, and Asia. Less than one hundred years after the poem was written and the former colonies began claiming their own voices, developing world scholars like Walter Rodney contended that Europe was no Good Samaritan intent on doing right but a cunning foe that always meant to plunder and under-develop places like Africa for its own purposes. This viewpoint is clearly demonstrated by examining a series of African-themed films depicting life in the colonies once Europe's purported mission was cast away and the colonized were arguably left worse off than they were before their initial contact. The purpose of this chapter is to analyze the cinematic portrayals of imperialism in Africa. This analysis will proceed in four parts: (1) an overview of Europe's scramble for Africa; (2) a discussion of Kipling's "White Man's Burden" and Hollywood's contribution to Africa's stereotypes; (3) a summary of Rodney's argument regarding the nature of underdevelopment; and (4) an application of both Kipling's poem and Rodney's assertions to the following films: *Zulu* (1964), *Heart of Darkness* (1993), *The Last King of Scotland* (2008), *Blood Diamond* (2006), and *Tsotsi* (2005).

They Saw, They Formed Empires

For nearly 450 years, nearly all of Africa was controlled, for the most part, by six European countries. The initial exploration of the continent is attributed to Portugal's Prince Henry, "the Navigator" who commissioned his sailors to search for gold.[1] Hence, as early as 1450, (40 years before Columbus landed in the Caribbean on behalf of Spain), the Portuguese explored the West Coast of Africa and established as many as three forts along its shores to support the acquisition of gold and, ultimately, slaves.[2] By the mid-1600s, not only had the Dutch driven the Portuguese from their own forts, but they had also established an additional nine of their own, formed the Dutch East India Company, and were using the Cape of Good Hope "as a refreshment station for the scurvy-ridden crews of its fleets plying between Europe and Asia."[3] As late as the 1870s, though, less than 10 percent of the African continent was under European control. Greed, racism, and nationalist rivalries among the European powers propelled the so-called "Scramble for Africa" in the late 1870s and 80s, with Belgium's Leopold II leading the way in the Congo.[4] The Berlin Conference of 1884–1885 "formalized" the European takeover of Africa so that by the beginning of the twentieth century, well-over 90 percent of the continent was in European hands.[5] Although the Portuguese started the process of the Europeanization of Africa, ironically both Portugal and Germany came to possess only a minimal number of its countries. Spain and the Netherlands had even fewer possessions in Africa but, like Portugal, expanded their empire in the Americas and Asia Pacific, respectively. Belgium had only one colony, while France and Great Britain acquired the most. The French acquired eleven countries spread across North, East, West, and Central Africa, and the British about nine countries spread throughout the continent.

The White Man's Burden, Hollywood's Propagandists

The United States never acquired any of its own colonies in Africa. However, as a response to its colonization of the Philippines, Rudyard Kipling's poem, "The White Man's Burden," provided the unofficial rationale for the many centuries of European colonialism in Africa, the Americas, and Asia. According to Kipling, it was every colonizing White man's duty to serve God by working on behalf of "half-devil and half-child" savages. Those settlers and missionaries, Kipling warned, should expect to build ports that they might "not enter" and roads that they might "not tread," while slothful savages offered neither help nor praise.[6] Nevertheless, the motives of the colonizers were, in reality, far from altruistic.

Perhaps it was mere coincidence that that the notion of an altruistic do-gooder occurred to Kipling at the same time that three important contemporary phenomena were transpiring: (1) the advent of travel journals from eighteenth century missionaries and explorers (who were anxious to document what they considered to be the indolence, unbridled passions, and mental degradation of Africans),[7] (2) the creation of Edgar Rice Burroughs' *Tarzan of the Apes,* and (3) the birth of the motion picture industry. In fact, once "talkies" supplanted silent pictures, Hollywood became able to more easily capitalize upon the Western stereotypes of the African as a drumming, gyrating, cannibalistic practitioner of witchcraft. Predictably, body-painted actors holding spears and shields, and wearing feathers or bones were put forth as "bad." Undoubtedly, the African helpers, "wearing European shorts [to signify their] colonized savage status," were cast as "good" – even if duty called for them to also don "earrings, necklaces, and various rings and bones in their mouths and ears."[8] Unbeknownst to Hollywood, but just as Kipling warned, Tarzan and his mate Jane's "sloth life" not only led to their status as "noble" savages, but to the "heathen folly" of wearing hip-revealing loin cloths, half-naked skinny dipping, [and] animalistic yodeling as a form of communication, as well.[9]

Rodney's Underdeveloped Africa

Seventy years removed from Kipling, Guyanese scholar Walter Rodney enunciated a compelling rebuttal to the mistaken notion that Europe did Africa a favor with its uninvited and unwanted colonization. Underdevelopment is defined as the economic dependency of one country upon, often, a developed one. Since the underdeveloped country lacks "a capacity for self-sustaining growth" (due to it having been deprived of the opportunity of moving from one stage of growth development to another), it will be "held back" at that stage "forever," unable to go on to a further stage."[10] In *How Europe Underdeveloped Africa*, Rodney argued that, once a European country colonized a nation, its people ignored ethnic boundaries in favor of artificial ones designed for the colonizers' convenience. As they observed their new subjects, they made assumptions that led them to favor certain ethnic groups over others. Such favoritism, said Rodney, ultimately created a new "class of Africans indebted to Western Masters."[11] As a result, standards of living were raised for some Africans while lowered for others. Western culture was glorified and "linguistic hegemonies" for western languages established. When Europeans interacted with the locals, the locals were treated as "simpletons." Schisms between followers of traditional religions and Christianity or Islam were often a result. When exploiting Africa for its natural resources, Europe not only disrupted traditional economies and created jobs primarily benefitting Westerners, it furthermore created a separate class status for those Westerners living in Africa.[12]

The Films

Just how is Hollywood depicting Africa, 116 years after Kipling (and 43 years after Rodney)? Is it through the rose-colored lenses of the great White savior? Or, is it through a glass half-empty, compliments of European mistreatment? I propose that the answer is probably somewhere in between. To test this assumption, six notable films about Africa ranging from 1964 to 2008 will be discussed. The films were chosen based upon three presumed criteria selected by this author: their (1) depiction of colonialism, (2) general popularity, and (3) general rental availability. The films are discussed in the general chronology of the periods they represent.

The film *Zulu* (1964), directed by Cy Endfield, is set in South Africa during 1879, 9 years before Kipling penned his poem. The film recounts the attempts of British soldiers stationed in Zululand, South Africa to fight off 4000 Zulu warriors intent upon destroying them.[13] Not only must the soldiers fight for their lives, but they must also battle their own cowardice, an emotion induced by a pessimistic soldier who predicts that they will all die. The battle between the two groups of men goes to and fro until the British manage to gain the upper hand before, ultimately, being surrounded by the

Zulu. With their backs against the wall, the British decide to rally around a national song of unity before facing certain death. In the end, just when the British expect to be overrun and killed, the warriors unexpectedly stop and, instead, sing a song in honor of the bravery of those valiantly facing certain death. The warriors then leave the soldiers alone, rather than going for the final kill.[14]

The film's opening moments show a concerned missionary lamenting news that many lives were lost in a recent battle between British and Zulu soldiers.[15] His very presence underscores Kipling's suggestion that settlers' intents are to promote some greater, godly good. Historically, according to Gilmour, from the moment the British annexed the Cape of Good Hope from the Dutch in 1806, their missionaries spent the next hundred years spreading Christianity to as many natives as possible. In doing so, they "produced an array of linguistic texts – notably grammars, dictionaries and phrasebooks – [not to mention] songs, stories, and other kinds of narratives in African languages" just to spread the Gospel.[16] The additional theme of honorable settlers intending to do no harm occurs again in *Zulu* when both injured White and Zulu citizens are holed up in an integrated, fort infirmary. This scene suggests a brotherly relationship among equals. Nevertheless, it is undeniable that the 4000 shield-beating warriors outside screaming incomprehensible, guttural sounds are depicted as savages ready to pounce on the undeserving British. It is an indictment of the entire Zulu culture.

While acknowledging the non-harmful contributions of some missionaries, Rodney undoubtedly uses historical evidence to inform *Zulu* viewers that "civilizing missions were inextricably enmeshed with [an] economic motive" from their very inception with at least one minister bragging, "[T]he savage no sooner becomes ashamed of his nakedness, than the loom is ready to clothe him."[17] To underscore the infancy of South Africa's underdevelopment, Rodney calls attention to White settler arguments that Blacks who had lived on the land for thousands of years and Whites who had just appeared, had actually arrived in Zululand at the same time. Such arguments, in addition to others attempting to nullify ancient land rights on the grounds that property was not "competently developed," point to a disregard of ethnic boundaries in favor of artificial ones designed to suit the colonizers.[18] An additional signpost found in *Zulu* pointing to future underdevelopment of South Africa, according to Rodney, is the increased appreciation of Western culture and technology at the expense of indigenous culture. For instance, in *Zulu,* warriors stop to collect the rifles of the British dead rather than leave the rifles behind altogether. Similar sentiments can also be witnessed at the end of the film when the British are honored in song rather than being killed. This suggests that some kind of civilizing or contact elevation of the natives by just being in the presence of the valiant, self-sacrificing British. In light of the country's destiny, Rodney might well regard the film's serenade as worthy of the title "simpleton" for the soon-to-be underdeveloped group.

Heart of Darkness (1993), directed by Nicolas Roeg, is set in the Congo in the late nineteenth to early twentieth century, based on the 1899 novella by Joseph Conrad. The film recounts the travels of Marlow, a sailor who takes a job as a riverboat captain for a Belgium company that trades in Congolese goods. Marlow's job is to travel from his present location to Central and Inner Stations where he hopes to meet Kurtz, an upper level company man. Marlow's travels allow him to gain first-hand experience of how the Company regards the natives, the interest of company pilgrims, and the ill treatment of workers. His ship breaks down, stops to take on firewood, and is attacked by natives before reaching its destination. After learning that Kurtz has given up his job to be revered as a god and run with the natives to find ivory, Marlow eventually meets Kurtz who ultimately is transported from the native camps to civilization. Kurtz bequeaths to Marlow his personal effects – one of which is an "eloquent pamphlet on civilizing the savages" – before dying soon after in a lunatic haze.[19]

According to Viaene, the Congo's very foundation was built upon King Leopold's "commitment to the evangelization of Central Africa."[20] Consequently, Kipling would argue that one need not look any further than Kurtz's self-imposed civilizing mission – and the very documents he held dear – as proof of his desire to help others despite the risks. After all, even the noble savage cannibals who worked on Marlow's steamship were afraid of bad boogey natives who attacked them with arrows. Moreover, Kurtz was so zealous that he attempted to steal away to be closer to the natives.[21] Rodney, on the other hand, would counter that Leopold's evangelism created a "clerical elite" among those religious orders supplying missionaries to the Congo and those that did not.[22] As a contributor to the country's underdevelopment, the *de facto* creation of this social class of Westerners deprived locals of access to upper mobility.

At first, it is unclear when watching *Heart of Darkness* what goods could possibly be important enough for a company to risk transporting them by riverboat. After all, no trader would travel hundreds of miles simply for forest trinkets. It is only later that the "real" prize, ivory, is revealed once Kurtz resigns from his company job to become a god rather than heed the more altruistic calling of the ministry. Rodney would argue that no matter what traditional economy that might have existed locally, its attractiveness to the Europeans would have paled in comparison to the lure of elephant tusks. In fact, it is the distribution of the company's shipping stations – at the jungle's periphery, inner, and center – that reference the terms that would be used by the dependency theorists of the 1970s. Just as Leopold's Congo forced natives to harvest rubber, under penalty of amputation, Marlow's natives are similarly forced to work *Heart of Darkness* or else.[23]

The Last King of Scotland, (2008), directed by Kevin Macdonald, is "based on the book of the same title written by Giles Foden, [and set in] Uganda during Idi Amin's rule of the 1970s. The film admits from the beginning that it is based on true events."[24] Dr. Nicholas Garrigan voluntarily goes to Uganda to start his new medical practice. Soon, he crosses paths with the brutal dictator who quickly makes him his personal physician and, later, political advisor. Additionally, out of all of the women in Uganda, happenstance places Garrigan in the unfortunate position of being the paramour of Amin's third wife. The film allows the viewer, through the doctor's eyes, to experience the confusion and fear that he feels when hearing rumors, noticing political disappearances, and witnessing the bipolar behavior of the undeniably powerful Amin.

Dr. Garrigan represents the best of mankind, á la Kipling. He has randomly chosen Uganda with the mere tip of his finger because he does not care whom he serves. By helping "poor Africa," he is doing God's work in a country where people may not even believe in God. Half-devil and half-child savages are everywhere in Uganda. The people are superstitious, prone to believing in witchdoctors and omens. Enemies of the state are murdered, the unfaithful are dismembered, and even Garrigan is tortured (by impalement) for all his efforts. In the end, as Kipling might say (like the

British who eradicated sleeping-sickness in Uganda[25] and built its colonial railroad), Garrigan would never become a benefactor of his own deeds and sacrifice but would leave the country weary and without praise.

Despite witnessing it on screen, Rodney would probably doubt that Garrigan would have really served just "anywhere," pointing to colonial British motives to exploit Uganda for its ivory, rhino horns and slaves.[26] Furthermore, the Guyanese scholar would undoubtedly point out that the stage for Uganda's underdevelopment was set when colonial Uganda favored Asians (who arrived in the country to perform clerical and semi-skilled work) over natives. Asians were allowed to start businesses whereas "aspiring Ugandan entrepreneurs" were relegated to "gin and market cotton."[27] This action not only led to differing standards of living but, according to Asiimwe, three classes of citizens – Europeans, Asians, and Africans – where, of course, Western culture was glorified most of all. In *The Last King of Scotland*, Amin is seen praising Scottish culture, exchanging his shirt for a Western t-shirt, having Garrigan fitted for a tailored Western suit, and surrounding himself with "parties, and [other] eccentricities such as manicured lawns studded with peacocks."[28] Perhaps the pièce de résistance underscoring the aspersion of Amin's own culture is the actual title he gave himself: "Lord of All Beasts of the Earth and Fishes of the Sea and Conqueror of the British Empire in Africa in General and Uganda in Particular."[29]

The movie *Blood Diamond* (2006) takes place in Sierra Leone around the late 1990s, a time when diamonds were smuggled for money to purchase the arms needed to fuel the civil war.[30] Directed by Edward Zwick, the film depicts how members of the Revolutionary United Front are in conflict with the government. As a way to fund their missions and pay their troops, they raid villages and force those they do not maim or kill to either work in the diamond mines or serve as soldier conscripts. After being seized in a village raid, Solomon Vandy finds a large, rare pink diamond and uses it to entice white Rhodesian, Danny Archer to help him find his kidnapped son and scattered family.

Recognizing that British philanthropists repatriated ex-slaves to Sierra Leone for humanitarian reasons (i.e. in an attempt to stem the tide of new-found social problems like destitution and unemployment),[31] Kipling would encourage viewers to look no further for an example of the White man's burden more than a hundred years before. Despite the fact that Archer is a gun runner, opportunist, and occasional diamond smuggler, Kipling might have argued that Archer still gambled to help Vandy and his family search for the rare pink diamond, rather than simply dedicate himself to getting the smaller, more readily available conflict diamonds. Before dying, Archer was under no obligation to return the stone to Vandy or help photojournalist Maddy Bowen publish what he knew about the illegal diamond trade.

Rodney, by contrast, would argue that the fact that the diamond company Van De Kaap processes Sierra Leone's diamonds, and not the citizens of Sierra Leone, speaks to the exploitation of the country and its inability to produce finished products itself. The civil war had disrupted the local economy to such an extent that fishermen like Vandy could not make a living (although poor economic conditions might have been present before the war due to backwards, local management of the economy). The rare pink diamond is celebrated as the pinnacle of Western culture, but it only represents life improvement for Westerners like Archer who have the knowledge and ability to sell it on the black market. At the end of the film, Sierra Leone's state of underdevelopment is further underscored as the gem is safely stored in London among a million others while Africans continue forced mining.

Tsotsi (2005), directed by Gavin Hood, takes place in modern day South Africa and centers around David, a street thug and gang leader who calls himself Tsotsi. Tsotsi grew up among street vagabonds after he ran away from an abusive, alcoholic father and a dying mother. As an adult, he and his gang mug and murder subway riders, as well as each other in broad daylight. When Tsotsi hijacks a car that is driven by a Black, middle-class, South African woman, he finds that he has not only shot a mother but has nearly orphaned her child. Rather than abandon the child, Tsotsi takes care of it as best as he can until he eventually forces a nursing mother in his village to feed it for him. Tsotsi is ultimately caught – not by being apprehended for "doing bad", but upon returning the baby to its mother (who has survived) and father.

As in the case of *Zulu*, Kipling would argue that missionaries proselytizing across the Cape of Good Hope did their best to spread the Gospel to as many Africans as possible and in their native languages. Hence, the inability of Christianity to eradicate the gangster behavior that Tsotsi and others display simply underscores the savage nature of the people and the White man's continual burden. Rodney, of course, would offer an alternate interpretation, pointing out that Tsotsi's childhood flashbacks reveal a community already in semi-squalor – the one Tsotsi lives in as an adult. Tsotsi's neighborhood contrasts sharply with the middle-class Black baby's neighborhood which serves to glorify Western houses, cars, and gated communities. This suggests not only that the baby's parents may belong to a new class of Africans but also that Tstosi could belong to an entire ethnic group economically disadvantaged since the founding of the Cape, as well.

In conclusion, more than 500 years after Europe conquered Africa, Hollywood struggles with whether to tell Africa's story according to the White man's burden or Africa's struggle to survive despite the White man's visit to the continent. The truth most, likely, falls somewhere in between.

3

"White Saviors" Unable to *Save* the "Other" in Hollywood's Genocidal West

William L. Hewitt

West Chester University

When his twin brother is killed in a robbery, a paraplegic Marine, Jake Sully (Sam Worthington), takes his place in a mission on the distant moon, Pandora. The moon is inhabited by a race of ten foot tall, blue-colored humanoids called Na'vi, who sit on vast deposits of *unobtanium* "worth twenty million a kilo." As Sully later says, "When people are sitting on something you want, you make them your enemy so that you can drive them out." Sully enters the Avatar Program (because of his genetic match with his twin brother) where biologically engineered bodies that are a mix of human and Na'vi DNA produced a human in Na'vi bodily form to work for the colonizers. Jake learns of corporate head Parker Selfridge's (Giovanni Ribisi) intentions of eliminating the Na'vi. Selfridge remarks, "These savages are threatening the whole operation ... Killing them is bad. But there is one thing shareholders hate more than bad press, and that's a bad bottom line."[1] That the indigenous must go for the good of the colonizers is a "given," a trope that critics on the right of the political spectrum see as a critique of capitalism.[2] The film, James Cameron's 2009 blockbuster *Avatar*, sparked a sometimes fierce, sometimes confounded discussion:

41

Cameron's[3] long-awaited feature has been described as *Dances with Wolves*[4] meets outer space. That's not flattery. Critics have noted that *Avatar* promulgates more than its share of stereotypes, which, not coincidentally, are also myths of the West and key to environmental justice discussions. 'You know a movie has a narrative worth discussing when political analyst James Pinkerton admits on Fox News that '(its) meta-politics lean right, not left.'[5]

New York Times writer David Brooks explains that this is problematic because it "creates a sort of two-edged cultural imperialism. Natives can either have their history shaped by cruel imperialists or benevolent ones, but either way, they are going to be supporting actors in our journey to self-admiration".[6]

Jake begins to bond with the Na'vi and falls in love with Neytiri (Zoe Saldana), forcing him to take sides with the Na'vi. He becomes the "White savior," a classic Hollywood trope, "their Messiah, leading them into a righteous crusade against his own rotten civilization."[7] Classic "White savior" trope-themed-Westerns include: *A Man Called Horse* (1970); *Dances with Wolves* (1990); *Quigley Down Under* (1990); and *The Last Samurai* (2003). Although showing different locales, time periods, and cultures, these films depict White characters who regret the genocide of Native Americans or indigenous peoples, and find redemption in embedding themselves in the cultures of the others. They cleanse themselves of the corruption of European-American imperialism, thus exhibiting profound ambivalence about America's past as well as about modernity, and adopt the best of the other culture, resulting in their regeneration and redemption. In each of these movies, White society is in some way seriously flawed, and the White hero immerses himself in the exotic other society, emerging cleansed to what had tarnished his character in American society, realizing himself in another society in a way he never could in America. These films, moreover, comprise a genre that might be called "White messiah movies." In a two-way exchange, the White gives as good as he gets, not only giving advanced technology and tactics to the other, but usually saving the culture as well.[8] The larger story, of course, still is not the story of the "other," but of the White savior.

Last of the Mohicans

Michael Mann's[9] adaptation of James Fenimore Cooper's novel, *The Last of the Mohicans* and the 1936 screenplay based on the same is set in 1757 in the British American colonies. This was the time of the French and Indian War, when Britain and France battled over control of eastern North America. Under the guidance of Magua (Wes Studi), Major Duncan Heyward (Steven Waddington) leads a regiment to Fort William Henry. Also under Duncan's care are Cora (Madeleine Stowe) and Alice Munroe (Jodhi Mae), daughters of the colonel in command of the fort. On the way to the fort, however, Magua betrays the English by leading them into a Huron trap. The Huron kill the entire regiment, save for Duncan and the Monroe girls who escape unharmed due to the intervention of three Mohicans: Hawkeye (Daniel Day-Lewis), Uncas (Eric Schweig), and Chingachgook (Russell Means). The Mohicans escort the English trio to the safety of the fort, as Cora and Hawkeye grow closer in affections.

Hawkeye shares story lines with other White saviors, such as Jake Sully (Sam Worthington) in *Avatar*. Hawkeye lives in Mohican society, but he differs from these other examples of White savior in that he is not an outsider who first encounters the native culture in adult life, and becomes a "cultural traitor" so to speak. Rather, he is raised in that culture from infancy, and his consciousness is not in need of "conversion".

Two film versions of the novel were produced in the 1930s. The first, a serial directed by Reaves Eason in 1932,[10] is a classic 12 chapter nail-biter that includes almost as many textual distortions of the novel as it has cliffhanger endings. The famous character actor Harry Carey played Hawk-eye, with Chingachgook killed in the end. Uncas survives, and Hawk-eye tells the young Mohican that he is the last of his race. Michael Mann used the other 1936[11] version as the source for his 1992 blockbuster. Based on a screenplay by Philip Dunne and directed by George B. Seitz, the 1936 version stars Randolph Scott as Hawk-eye and Binnie Barnes as Alice Munro – the two star-crossed lovers unlike Mann's Hawk-eye and Cora. In spite of his misrepresentation of Cooper's novel, which has Uncas and Cora, the mixed race woman herself the product of miscegenation, in an interracial romance, Seitz's plot twist was surprising in 1936, given Hollywood under the Hay's Office's moral quagmire infused with racially-based fears of miscegenation.[12]

Michael Mann's 1992 film is about a love story of no consequence. *The Last of the Mohicans* is not finally about such peripheral action as two lovers (even if particularly White ones), but about the violent contest between the Native Americans and the intruders, White immigrants and settlers, and their military protectors, representing various powers, and its consequences; the most important – tragic – outcome being the destruction of the last vestiges of a race of Native-Americans.

A Man Called Horse

The hardened conventions and themes of the Western genre were examined, criticized, dismantled, and refined in the late 1960s and 1970s. The conventional Western's traditional thematic myth of Whites attacked by Indians, or seeking revenge against Indians became outmoded. New attitudes toward Native Americans included seeing them as proto-environmentalist victims of White progress and technology, not as opposition to White progress. *A Man Called Horse* (1970)[13] provides a good example of the revisionist Western of that era. Jack DeWitt wrote the screenplay for *A Man Called Horse* (1970), based on a short story by Dorothy M. Johnson, but he turned Crows into Sioux, their ancient enemies. Critics asked DeWitt why he had changed so much of the original story, showing the Sioux sun dance ceremony as being the Okipa ceremony of the Mandans (the Sioux did not practice elevation the way the Mandans did), and why he had Horse, played by Richard Harris, teaching the Sioux British military tactics. In response to this last question, he stated he had based the teaching episode on *Lawrence of Arabia* (1962) and as for the rest, at this date, who cares? When this conversation was repeated to Dorothy M. Johnson, she replied that if one thought *A Man Called Horse* was a bad film, one should see the sequel.

In Johnson's novel, the protagonist is a Bostonian, but a British substitute in the film provides more insulation for American viewers, thus reducing their discomfort by only indirectly addressing their genocidal past through the British surrogate. "Rather than a tale of INDIAN LIFE," Dave Georgakas wrote in an essay titled "They have not spoken: American

Indians in Film," *A Man Called Horse* is "really about a white nobleman proving his superiority in the wilds,"[14] offering what Philip DeLoria calls "a deep, authentic, aboriginal Americanness."[15] As Horse assimilates into Sioux culture, he saves a group of children from an enemy war party, gaining the respect of the Sioux. His epiphany occurs when he has his initiation into tribal manhood by having his flesh pierced and skewered by eagle claws, which are attached to thongs that hoist Horse in excruciating pain. The final battle scene – á la *Lawrence of Arabia*[16] – makes Morgan the primary warrior and the one most responsible for saving his adopted culture, using the White's own military tactics. Through a strange turn of events, he absolves the guilt of the audience by having the Indians massacre the invaders who are bent on annihilating them, thus giving White audiences the eye-for-an-eye justice that muddles issues of ethnicity, violence, and genocide.

Early in the story, John Morgan's (Richard Harris) guides are killed and he is captured by a band of Sioux warriors. He is beaten and mocked by the warriors who put a saddle on his back and call him Horse, before dragging him to their village where he is given to an elderly woman (Judith Anderson) as a servant. His attempts to escape end when he meets Batise, a captive feigning insanity to be spared by the superstitious Indians, who educates Horse in Sioux culture. This film framed Morgan's experience in anthropologically detailed daily Indian life of the Sioux in the Dakotas in the early 1900s, offering what Philip Deloria calls "rituals earnestly copied from a George Catlin painting."[17] It inverted the traditional captive narrative by focusing not on how someone will be rescued from their Indian captors, but rather how he is drawn to prefer their way of life to that of "civilization." Focusing on the White character makes Indians strange and exotic props, foils for his criterion of Westernized civility.

Little Big Man

Director Jake DeWitt ends *A Man Called Horse* with a massacre, and Arthur Penn's "progressive" Western *Little Big Man* begins with one. However, the film, and Thomas Berger's 1964 book upon which it is based, cannot exhaust the psychic energy and mythic trauma of the massacre with this single bloodletting. Therefore, throughout *Little Big Man*, Penn gives the audience another slaughter of Cheyenne at the Washita, and by inverting the conventions of the massacre, concludes with Custer's infamous "Last Stand;" this time the Indians do the massacring.[18] In this attempt to highlight American racism that supported genocidal "Manifest Destiny," Penn simplistically reverses the dichotomy of good Whites and bad Indians. Besides lacking analytical sophistication, it portrayed a maniacal Custer, thus diluting the association with the event by White audiences, and absolving them of the negative consequences of racism since the insane racist in the film in no way represented them or their government.

Penn's comic-ironic Western portrays another White character living among Indians. A 121 year-old curmudgeon named Jack Crabb (Dustin Hoffman), through a series of flashbacks, recalls that when he was a ten-year-old, after the massacre of his family, he was taken by a Cheyenne war party and given to a chief named Old Lodge Skins (Chief Dan George). Crabb is raised as a Cheyenne, a group who refer to themselves as "human beings." Old Lodge Skins articulates the dichotomy of White and Indian worlds when he says to Crabb, "The Human Beings, my son, they believe everything is alive. Not only man and animals. But also water, earth, stone. And also the things from them …. That is the way things are. But the white man, they believe EVERYTHING is dead. Stone, earth, animals. And People! Even their own people. That is the difference."

During an ill-fated battle with the cavalry, Crabb uses his whiteness to save himself and is returned to "civilization." But the dominant culture is lampooned during a series of misadventures with a religious family, the Pendrakes, revealing the hypocrisy of White civilization in stark contrast to the wholesome and honest Sioux way of life, thus asserting that the two cultures have been portrayed, in the past, inversely by the dominant culture's triumphal myth history. This inversion of the traditional interpretations of dominant and Indian cultures is termed a "gigantic distortion of the American Past," by traditional history defender and film critic Michael Medved.[19]

The Battle of the Little Big Horn, in *Little Big Man*, with a blustery egomaniacal Custer (Richard Mulligan), in effect stands for American treatment of Indians in explaining genocide by attributing it to the whims of a few unbalanced people, i.e., General Custer, and exonerates the settler-state system of responsibility for the very process on which its founding myth of expansion has been so resolutely based.[20]

Dances with Wolves

Almost 20 years after *Little Big Man*, the even more sympathetic *Dances With Wolves* (1990)[21] re-employs the storyline of Whites living among the exotic other and the massacre themes. The story had antecedents from the early twentieth century. In 1907, J. W. Shultz published *My Life As An Indian*, for example, telling a story that anticipates the one told by Kevin Costner in *Dances With Wolves* decades later, and marks a transition in the representation of Native peoples in American culture. Set in the mid-nineteenth century, just before the European-American invasions into the region reached their highest point, Shultz's book celebrates his years on the frontier living as a member of the Blackfoot tribe.[22] By identifying with the Blackfoot, who conveniently "vanish" at the end of the narrative, Schultz concealed his complicity in the conquest,[23] and by indicating that progress (rather than European-American acquisitiveness) conveniently deflected difficult ethical questions about centuries of slaughter of Native peoples and usurpation of their resources.[24]

Because of the shared colonialist themes in *Dances with Wolves* and *Lawrence of Arabia*, embattled writer Ward Churchill calls the movie "Lawrence of South Dakota."[25] *Dances with Wolves* reworks themes previously covered in *Broken Arrow, Run of the Arrow*, and as described in *Little Big Man*. In those earlier films, James Stewart, Rod Steiger, and Dustin Hoffman (respectively) had each married an Indian woman, an integral part of their assimilation within the larger Indian society. *Dances with Wolves* sidesteps a suggestion of miscegenation by conveniently having a White woman (Mary McDonnell) as a ready-made romantic interest living among the Sioux. Thus, at heart, *Dances with Wolves* was not so much a repudiation of WASP (White Anglo-Saxon Protestant) America as a paean to an alternative (and ecologically harmonious) culture in which a nice young WASP couple may find a home in an ode to a mythical bucolic suburbia.[26] The union of Dunbar and Stands-With-A-Fist implies that these two characters, cleansed of the corruption of European-American life by adopting Indian ways, hold the promise of a new and better white society that proves the ultimate goal of Dunbar's journey into the primitive.[27]

Theorist Claude Levi Strauss maintains that, "myths and narratives reconcile cultural contradictions and bring opposing forces and values together."[28] Dunbar goes to the Garden of Eden and has the opportunity to start over, to redress the wrong headedness of his people in the past. R. W. B. Lewis, in *The American Adam*, describes the historical development of the idea of a new American hero who would be "emancipated from history, happily bereft of ancestry, untouched and undefiled by the usual inheritances of family and race."[29] Film historian Richard Grenier asserts that this new characterization of the hero allows him to "violently reject 'evil America' and its diseased values without appearing patently disloyal" precisely because he chooses to join our own "Indigenous Aborigines."[30] By the end of the film, *Dances with Wolves* and Stands-With-A-Fist have donned buckskins, spoken the Sioux language, and adopted Sioux ways.[31]

Like Dunbar, Stands-With-A-Fist is redeemed after suffering a violent trauma which she recalls a massacre told as a flashback, described by psychologist Robert Baird as the most:

> distilled and powerful an embodiment of the massacre trauma as has ever been presented by Hollywood. Shot in soft focus at sunset, [dawn?] the scene begins slow-motion, as an idyllic view of a rustic farm and cabin; two frontier families are eating outdoors on a large table when ominous looking Pawnee warriors ride slowly in on horseback, their faces painted in bilious blues and bloody reds. At first it seems a peaceful meeting of two cultures, but then a tomahawk flies through the air, and the scene takes on added poignancy as the edit returns us to the horrified gaze of the young witness and, by a film dissolve, to the still-haunted Stands-With-A-Fist.[32]

The movie industry claimed with pride that *Dances with Wolves* was Hollywood's attempt to render justice to Indians through Kevin Costner's sympathetic telling of their proud history. Encountering the carcasses of bison skinned and left to rot on the prairie, for example, Costner's disillusioned cavalryman wonders, "Who would do such a thing? It must be people without values, without soul." He is, of course, talking about Whites. By contrast, among the Sioux, "Everyday ends with a miracle."

The attempt by Costner and other filmmakers to totally negate traditional Western themes, showing Euro-Americans almost without exception as sadists, thugs, or lost souls, did not sit well with Conservative film scholar Richard Grenier:

> In the 1860s, the period of *Dances with Wolves*, some of the greatest generals of the Union Army (Sherman, Sheridan, Custer) led American troops against the bloodthirsty Sioux, who erupted in the midst of the Civil War in one of the most savage Indian uprisings in history. All along the western frontier, the Sioux massacred. They pillaged. They raped. They burned. They carried women and children into captivity. They tortured for entertainment. By converting these Sioux Indians into gentle, vaguely pacifist environmentally responsible bucolics, Kevin Costner, in a state of holy empty-headedness, has falsified history as much as any time-serving Stalinist of the Red Decade.[33]

Grenier represents the side of an argument led by historian James Axtell who cautions that we use the word genocide sparingly and with extreme care, avoiding the fallacy of applying it wholesale to every Indian death in colonial American history, for example. Anthropologist James A. Clifton extends Axtell's disclaimer to the entirety of United States history, arguably claiming that, "In the over two hundred years it has existed as a nation, no US administration from George Washington to Ronald Reagan has ever approved, tolerated, or abetted a policy aimed at the deliberate systematic termination of Indians."[34] *Dances with Wolves'* hero presents the revisionist point of view making Dunbar the center of consciousness, and he is re-named, at first, without his knowledge and without dialogue so that viewers, knowing the title of the film, rename the character his Sioux brothers will name him. In this scene without dialogue, the audience also renames him, knowing the title of the movie, and thus participates in his reconstruction. A new name enables Dances with Wolves to shed the culpability associated with his official army duties as an "Indian fighter." Significantly, because his perspective provides the film's narrative center and thus the white audience's point of identification, it also symbolically purges white America of its responsibility for the terrible plights of Native Americans, past and present. It thus assures contemporary European Americans of the legitimacy of their power and possessions. Because real Indians were destined to disappear anyway, European Americans are the proper heirs of *Indianness,* as well as the land and resources of the conquered Natives.[35]

Although he has just recently attained the status of a Sioux warrior, Dunbar has the entire tribe depend upon him for their welfare as a skillful buffalo hunter and superior warrior." *Dances With Wolves*, in other words, actually reinforces the racial hierarchies it claims to destabilize, and it thus serves another primary function of going native, reinforcing a regeneration of racial Whiteness and European-American society.[36] In a scene depicting the first social interaction between the Sioux and Dunbar, he serves them coffee, shows them how he grinds beans, and sweetens their cups with sugar. They depart, after reflecting naiveté for innocence, displaying new tin cups obviously impressed by their introduction to Dunbar's products. Throughout the twentieth century, going native in movies has served as an essential means of defining and regenerating racial Whiteness and a radically inflected vision of Americanness. While those who go native frequently claim benevolence toward Native peoples, they reaffirm White dominance by making some (usually distorted) vision of Native life subservient to the needs of the colonizing culture.[37]

The third massacre in *Dances with Wolves* transforms the horror associated with that depiction into the Hollywood-sanctioned celebration of dispatching the US Cavalry. Dunbar has been captured by the cavalry as a renegade and is being taken by wagon in shackles to a frontier prison. When the Lakota attack and kill Dunbar's tormentors, one realizes that – even with 90 years of Hollywood history turned on its head – we have here the same cheer for the good guys; the skillful and precise application of violence in order to right the world; the promise of "regeneration through violence," which Richard Slotkin has so eloquently described.[38] Weapons go to those opposing genocide – we are willing to turn our technology over to the Sioux so that they can defend themselves from their enemies – the less civilized Pawnees,[39] just as the US needed to identify the good to help fend off the bad, an imperative in the wake of

American expansionism. Dances with Wolves implements vicariously America's post-Vietnam desire to not become directly involved in struggles elsewhere, but instead support friend against enemies. Dances with Wolves knows the implacable truth as the audience sees the truth as the murderous, cruel Pawnees emerge from the horizon bent on destroying "our" home (the Sioux village). With punkish haircuts and fierce facial paint jobs, they are not Native Americans but the treacherous Indians of movie lore, and Medved and Grenier's history. What had changed here – and it indicated the limits the Vietnam era still imposed – was that Whites, constrained from killing directly, gained that right vis-à-vis the people central to the spectacle.[40] *Dances with Wolves* appears to embrace what Annette Hamilton calls the "National Imaginary," that it seeks to contest, pitting the Pawnee (bad Indians) against the Lakota (good Indians) in ways that play-out the Western paradigms that the film strives to counteract.[41]

The film leaves the power of European-American society unchallenged at the end of the story. The Sioux disappear (as in virtually all other movies with Indians), thus eliminating any threat their presence poses to White privilege. In the film's closing scenes, the military redirects its efforts to the conquest of Indians. An epilogue instructs audiences about the fate of Dunbar's noble companions in the years following the end of the Civil War: "Their homes destroyed, their buffalo gone, the last band of free Sioux submitted to white authority at Fort Robinson, Nebraska. The great horse culture of the plains was gone, and the American frontier was soon to pass into history." The film's end then, is elegiac. Though regrettable, the Indian's fate, it seems, is inevitable in the face of White settlement.[42] Predictably, though, Dances with Wolves does not share the fate of "his" tribe. The final scene shows him leading his probably pregnant wife on horseback, ascending into the mountains. The scene carries heavily Biblical overtones. It recalls illustrations of Joseph leading the mule bearing a pregnant Mary, in search of a place for the birth of Christ, redeemer of a fallen world. Redemption for Whites, even a child of mixed parentage, plays a key role in *Dances With Wolves*, and the audience can breathe a sigh of relief at the good outcome.[43]

Hidalgo

Hidalgo[44] has much in common with Edward Zwick's *The Last Samurai*,[45] as both are set near the end of the nineteenth century and are about troubled Americans resentful of their government's treatment of Native American's who find personal redemption in cultures of the East. Tom Cruise's Nathan Algren goes to Japan with the intention of modernizing the Emperor's army, but instead embraces and learns the ways of the honorable Samurai. In *Hidalgo*, Viggo Mortenson's Frank T. Hopkins travels to the Middle East to compete in "The Ocean of Fire," a 3,000-mile horse race across the Saudi desert. Disney Studios purported *Hidalgo* to be "based on a true story," and the actual life of Frank T. Hopkins, who allegedly had been born at Fort Laramie, worked for Buffalo Bill, witnessed the massacre at Wounded Knee, and rode in the legendary long-distance horse race across Arabia called the "Ocean of Fire," none of which was true.

In the Middle East setting for the film, the Arab world is presented as desolate and primitive, similar to the Great Plains and the Outback. Hopkins enjoys the other's culture as a spectator, and is renamed by the other as Dances with Wolves was. But Hopkins, called the "Cowboy," "impure animal," and "infidel," remains an outsider reflecting recent American experiences at nation building. Screen writer John Fusco, who also wrote *Thunderheart*,[46] turns Hopkins' fictions into an allegory of race and redemption. In order to ameliorate the racist notion of white American superiority over darker skinned challengers, the movie foregrounds Hopkins' mixed race heritage. His mongrel of a horse, metaphorically representing a polyglot American society, inverts strength and nobility by competing against thoroughbreds and nobility.

The differences between East and West are highlighted in other ways. A wealthy Sheik Riyad (Omar Sharif)[47] admires Hopkins' firearm (technology), but he would have Hopkins castrated for cavorting with his daughter, Jazira (Zuleikha Robinson), a proto-feminist who detests her second class status. An attack by the Sheik's rivals delivers Hopkins from mutilation. Jazira's potential power is weakened, however, when she is kidnapped by one of the Sheik's evil, dark, Arab rivals, Prince Bin Al Reeh (Said Tagmaoui), but Hopkins' superiority is reaffirmed when he saves her.[48] The Prince wants to force her to "become his fifth wife. The youngest of his harem. No more than a slave in his house."[49] Film historians Matthew Bernstein and Gaykyn Studlar, in *Visions of the East: Orientalism in Film*, observe that, "In this sense the narrative of Western women in the Third World can be read as a projected didactic allegory insinuating the dangerous nature of the uncivilized man and by implication lauding the freedom presumably enjoyed by Western women.[50] The White hero by his actions denounces the sexism with which the film imbues traditional non-Western cultures; thus Hopkins civilizes the other in an enlightened masculinism.[51] Thus Princess Jazira stands in for submissive and mistreated Arab women wearing burkas, liberated by the American forces in Afghanistan, so that she and all Arab women, may decide their own destiny and realize their full potential. The vulnerable woman, threatened by a lustful male in an isolated desert locale – similar to the imagery of Rudolph Valentino in the *Sheik* (1921) – with a swooning woman lifted in his arms, gives voice to the masculinist fantasy of complete control over Western, or Westernized, women.

The rescue fantasy, when liberalized through the rescue of a woman from a lascivious Arab, has to be seen not only as an allegory of saving the Orient from its libidinal, instinctual destructiveness, but also as a perpetuation by contrast to the myth of the sexual egalitarianism of women in the United States.[52] Of course, the status of American women is in no way comparable to that of women living under fundamentalist male domination in the Middle East.[53] The exotic film context, nevertheless, gives voice to antifeminist backlash, responding to the threat that women will become totally independent. Puritanical Hollywood thus claims to censure the tyranny of the harem and female adventurousness.[54]

At the end of the film, Hopkins finds redemption by returning to his heritage and inner strength. At the point of total exhaustion near the end, and apparent defeat in the race, Hopkins is within seconds of giving Hidlago the *coup de grâce*; when a hazy vision of Indian Warriors miraculously instills vitality in Hopkins. Thus the shimmering influence of his synthesized heritage is what Hopkins needs to triumph. Hidalgo is a thinly disguised allegory about the Iraq invasion of 2003 – in which a surrogate for the American army – encounters good and bad Arabs in the desert where he respects Arab customs and womanhood, rescuing the woman from the bad Arabs and returning home having left the good Arab in power. The conclusion? All it takes is a smart American to make the difference. Hopkins returns to South Dakota, where he enlists a few Indians to help release penned-up wild horses, a metaphor for freeing Indians, and more importantly Whites, from their historically confining history.

Conclusion

On one level, the White savior trope undercuts the notion of White superiority. On a deeper level, however, the myth requires the depiction of bucolic communities of the other at peace, but threatened by genocidal adversaries who must be stopped by the intervention of a virtuous White man, and in the case of the above films, an American man. Even though Hollywood imbues the "White savior" with extraordinary characteristics, Larry McMurtry concludes in *Oh What a Slaughter*, "The impulse to turn whole groups of people into meat shops is not likely to be extinguished."[55] American warriors, scared and recovering after their culture sent them where they witnessed or participated in atrocities and genocide, seek redemption immersing themselves in the culture of the other, but ironically changing only that part of themselves that allows them to redeem themselves without losing their dominant cultural identity. These films show a progression from Vietnam syndrome antiwar films, to post 9/11 pro-war films with individual Americans triumphant at center stage. The quagmire of the Iraq war briefly resulted in a moment of cultural self-doubt and introspection (with anti-war films such as *Why We Fight* [2005], *In the Valley of Elah* [2007], *War, Inc.* [2008], and *Taking Chance* [2009]). Linda Williams suggests, in *Refiguring American Film Genres*, "The greater the historical burden of guilt, the more pathetically and more actively the melodrama works to recognize and regain a lost innocence."[56] But the tide has turned recently, and the success of a film like *American Sniper* (2014), about the life and tragic murder of Chris Kyle – the deadliest marksman in US military history, suggests that films which critique American foreign policy or war-making or suggest complicity in genocide might become even more scarce in the future.

4

Genocide as European Empire Building: The Slaughter of the Herero of Namibia

Mark Malisa

The College of Saint Rose

Meriem Lahrizi

The College of Saint Rose

Our chapter examines the place of genocide in colonialism and European empire building as portrayed in the documentary: *Namibia: Genocide and the Second Reich* (2005). We focus on Germany's genocide against the Herero in particular, and the creation of the image of the non-European as inconsequential to European progress and material acquisition, as well as the resultant desensitization of the European mind to the genocides in Africa. With the effective creation of anthropological/cultural racism, it became easier to portray European imperialism and empire-building in Africa as bringing 'civilization' to the uncivilized, and when the uncivilized resisted, genocide could be committed without any qualms. European myth, religion, commerce, science, fiction, and reality coalesced to legitimate what would later pass as one of the first European genocides in Africa. The documentary blends twenty-first century commentaries with twentieth century historical depictions of Africa, while tracing the Namibian genocide to the Berlin Conference of 1884, and its role in informing the Holocaust.

Narrated mostly by European scholars, the documentary contributes to a continued misleading Eurocentric view of Africa as a continent that can be rationally comprehended and controlled by Europeans, and African history as best told by European scholars. Although the documentary anesthetizes the ordinary viewer to the cultural, economic, and ecological violence brought by modernity, it also invites the reader to assess the role of movies and documentaries in the production and reproduction of historical events.

Not much is known about the Namibian genocide, and there are comparatively very few documentaries and monographs that deal with this topic. Historical documents from European scholars during the period of the genocide rarely portrayed events as atrocities.[1] British historians, including George Steer, often alluded to the "German colonial enterprise," while the resistance by the Herero was called the "rebellion," as if they were supposed to acquiesce to their murder.[2]

From Europe to Africa: Setting the Scene

Namibia: Genocide and the Second Reich traces the beginning of the Namibian genocide to events in Europe, particularly the Berlin Conference of 1884. As such, the reader has to understand genocide as part of European empire-building. Genocide, in other words, was not something that Africans practiced upon each other prior to the encounter with Europeans. The documentary begins by connecting the Namibian genocide to the Jewish Holocaust in Germany, and in so doing makes it clear that European disregard for African life contributed to the making of the Holocaust. The policy of exterminating Africans so as to build an empire, carried out in Namibia, was to later return to Europe and be used against the Jews.[3]

European empire building, to a great extent, can also be traced to its policies of colonialism in Africa. At the Berlin Conference of 1884, Germany gave itself a number of countries in Africa, among them Namibia (also known as German West Africa). Although there is a tendency to view Germany's colonial history as unique, it is not, and many European countries adopted policies that were parallel to that of Germany when it came to relationships with Africans. *Namibia: Genocide and the Second Reich* argues that all of Europe was involved in the rape and pillaging of Africa one way or another. Governments were complicit, and if governments rule on behalf of the people, then the people of Europe were responsible.[4] The genocides committed by Europeans have much in common: philosophy;

the intention of building empire, of stealing land; of using slave labor; of racism; of brutality; and rape.[5]

The Namibian genocide, according to Jeremy Sarkin-Hughes, was to a great extent, motivated by Germany's desire to have a new homeland in Africa. *Namibia: Genocide and the Second Reich* points out that in the nineteenth century, Germany, like most European countries, was faced with a problem of population growth and poverty, especially in its cities. While a significant number of Germans were migrating to the United States, Germany also desired to have an empire in Africa, and found Namibia one of the most suitable countries for settling its citizens. Although it was mostly desert, the country also had arable land as well as vast tracts of grazing areas, while its proximity to the ocean made international trade relatively easier than in land-locked countries.

Although the Berlin Conference gave (and is still, for the most part interpreted to give) the impression that the colonization and division of Africa was a peaceful process, European powers used their military might to seize the land from Africans in a brutal way. In Namibia, the German military general, General Von Trotha, with the blessing of the Kaiser, engaged in a systematic slaughter of the Herero. German military historiography glosses over the brutality of the genocide while making heroes of the German soldiers. In one official account the narrative goes:

> This bold operation shows in a brilliant light the reckless energy of the German leadership in pursuing the beaten enemy. No trouble, no deprivation was spared to rob the enemy of the last remnants of his capacity to resist. He was driven from water-hole to water-hole like a bear hounded half to death, until, having lost all will, he fell victim to natural forces in his own country. The waterless Omaheke would complete the task began by German force: the annihilation of the Herero people.[6]

What is left unsaid in this narrative is that the Herero, although formidable, did not pose a significant threat to the German settlers. Tensions escalated as the minority White sense of superiority justified rape and murder of the Herero, and theft of their lands. The tensions exploded in war with the Herero confronted by the might of the Kaiser's army led by *Oberbefehlshaber* (Supreme Commander) General Lothar von Trotha. The German forces decisively defeated the Herero at the battle of

Waterberg, then herded the population into the desert beyond the water-holes. Although the impression given is that the Herero were wandering in search of water, official German military history does not always acknowledge that German soldiers poisoned most of the water-holes that the Herero used.[7] In addition, many of the captured Herero were taken to concentration camps in Namibia, while some were sold to provide free labor to German colonial farmers and large companies. In the words of the narrator: "a new history of the colony was fabricated in which the events of 1904–1905 were transformed from a genocide to a glorious imperial war."[8]

Hannah Arendt observed that:

> African colonial possessions became the most fertile soil for the flowering of what later became the Nazi elite. Here they had seen with their own eyes how people could be converted into races, and how simply by taking an initiative in this process, one might push one's own people into the position of the master race.[9]

To a great extent, her observation was correct, but misses out on the genocide against Native Americans in the United States[10] and the Aborigines in Australia. Indeed, many scholars argue that the Namibian genocide and the Holocaust were modeled on the Native American genocide to acquire land and the use of African slavery to create wealth. The policy and practice of racism was not confined to Germany. Even the narrator acknowledges that the use of concentration camps, for example, was prevalent in other countries colonized by the British.

Racism

Racism played an important role in the making of the Namibian genocide. One can argue that the philosophy of European racial superiority had been central to Germany's self-understanding since the days of Hegel.[11] Africa and Africans, as it were, were not that significant when it came to the well-being of the Europeans. In addition, many Germans saw the colonies as something they could acquire as needed. The humanity of the Herero was of no consequence.

To a great extent, one has to understand racism as an economic system that helps Europeans acquire resources from non-Europeans. In the case of Namibia, the primary resource that the Germans needed was land, *lebensraum* (space for survival). In the documentary, General Von Troth ordered the extermination of the Herero civilians, women, children, and soldiers.[12] The Herero had to be dispossessed of their land. Europeans, as it were, had never envisioned living as equals or subordinates in the lands that belonged to other peoples. The documentary argues that between 1904 and 1905, between 60,000 and 10,000 Herero were killed. In the words of Major Von Francois, "The fact that the Africans possess the bulk of the land, to use and dispose of at their will, is not to be discussed but disputed with a rifle."[13] There was little room for negotiations or peaceful coexistence in the colonizer's mindset. Even those who swore and demonstrated their loyalty to the German settlers were killed by the Germans. Even those who took refuge in churches and missionary buildings were killed.

During the Namibia genocide, Germany and German soldiers did not consider the Herero to be human at all. Law professor Jeremy Sarkin-Hughes notes that Von Trotha viewed the Herero as existing below the level of the human.[14] As such, Herero could be slaughtered without any qualms, often with the blessing of the Second Reich. *Namibia: Genocide and the Second Reich* argues that the racial theories developed during the Namibia genocide helped fuel what was to later become the Holocaust.

What is astounding is the deliberate distortion of the life of the Herero by the German media, especially in Germany. This is especially so when it came to the depiction of the "sexual depravity of the Herero." The German media portrayed the Herero men as rapists (especially of European/German women), murderers of German civilians and children, and savages. *Namibia: Genocide and the Second Reich* points out that it was also true that the reputation of German soldiers as rapists, contrary to official German colonial historiography, was well known in Germany and a few newspapers pointed this out. What the media did was to fan a militaristic sentiment in Germany to annihilate the barbarians who were raping White women and killing White children. As pointed out elsewhere in this chapter, even during the war and genocide, the Herero did not kill women and children during the military confrontations with Europeans.

59

While the rape of Herero women by German soldiers is mentioned in *Namibia: Genocide and the Second Reich*, there were very few occasions when Herero women consented to marrying the German soldiers. More often than not, such women came from families that held power and property. Yet the official German colonial policy often forbade mixed marriages or interracial relationships of any kind. As such, the Herero realized that not only was their land stolen, but their women had been raped and rejected. For the German colonial government, the children of mixed marriages were viewed as polluting the purity of the Germanic race. Empire-building did not imply race-mixing between those viewed as superior and those consigned to an animal status. It was not unusual for the Germans to refer to the Herero and Africans as "baboons" or "vermin".[15] African/Herero lives did not matter at all.

As such, it would be a mistake to understand the Herero genocide as a product of renegade German soldiers or the racist philosophy of Hegel. Genocide was part of European nationalism in which only the lives and interests of Europeans were of consequence. To a great extent, genocide, as perpetrated by Europeans against non-Europeans, is tied to the ideology of capitalism. A close examination of what lies at the heart of racism as it is currently constituted reveals the horrors of modernity and capitalism that dehumanize both Whites and non-Whites. To give legitimacy to its apartheid policies, the South African Nationalist Party also used racist ideology, or a distortion of facts and history to justify the oppression of Blacks. Likewise, for close to 500 years, the United States also used racism against non-Europeans to build an unjust system that privileged Europeans.

Race has a way of finding its way into how human nature is portrayed in almost any historical context since the fifteenth century. Although there is an awareness of the problems caused by both Nazism and fascism when it comes to the Holocaust, there are many ways in which the depiction of Europeans and non-Europeans points to a belief in the superiority of German and European culture. In terms that sound Hegelian, the Herero are described as existing at a pre-civilization stage almost at the level of primates (baboons). Genocide perpetrated by Europeans is based on the belief that Europe and European values are at the core of a qualitatively better world belief. They adopted a Eurocentric belief that the salvation of the world comes from Europe, and through the world's adoption of a

European worldview. It is closely tied to the concept of capitalism which is not significantly different from racism. The implication here is that for non-Europeans, there is little hope when their world encounters that of Europe. As baboons and vermin, the Herero (Africans) appear as the least complicated, least evolved of all in the human species which Europe could destroy with no compunction, a sentiment that one finds in Hegel and most of European philosophy with regard to Africa.[16] The objective of genocide in empire-building is to pilfer resources, and when facing resistance, to exterminate.

But racism also depends on a deliberate distortion of what is known about non-European races, and changing the truth to make genocide possible. Prior to the genocide, the Herero were portrayed as a noble people with great customs worth preserving. They were admired for their pastoralism (and knowledge of cattle-breeding) and pacific relations. Yet, when it became necessary to destroy them, the propaganda machinery at home and abroad portrayed them as sub-human, criminals, murderers and rapists. In many ways, what the Germans were saying about the Herero – the negative portraits – were reflective of what the Germans were doing, what they were in terms of political conduct and relationships with the Herero. The Herero, who had not posed a threat to the German settlers, were depicted as warlike and a safety risk to be exterminated on sight.

Concentration Camps and Slave Labor

The Herero who survived the genocide and the poisoned water-holes were captured, sometimes through trickery, broken promises, and peace treaties. According to *Namibia: Genocide and the Second Reich,* those the Germans captured were 'shuttled around the country in cattle trucks.' To lull the Herero into surrendering, the German colonial army promised them forgiveness. Instead, the Germans herded them into concentration camps at Shark Island and Luderitz. Shark Island, moreover, turned into a death camp for those who were too feeble or too old to provide slave labor to the German colonizers. For the Germans, the Herero who were too feeble were not deserving of life. Many were exposed to the cold winter, and left to die. For Germans, the deaths of the Herero at Shark Island was a sport, a form of entertainment, hidden from the public, and yet open to those with power who could take pictures of the victims of genocide. Desensitized to the humanity of the Herero, German soldiers and prison guards took pictures, posing with the severed heads as trophies. The death of the Herero led to the continued depopulation of the country while confirming the "superiority" of the Germans.

The Herero who were captured also provided slave labor, similar to the Africans in the United States before the Civil War. The slave labor not only benefitted the German settlers, but also German companies. According to *Namibia: Genocide and the Second Reich,* many German companies profited from the slave labor, often renting prisoners and even holding them in their own small concentration camps. The building of cities, the development of new agriculture and forms of farming were made possible by such forms of labor. Even as they provided labor that brought about the economic wellbeing of the colonizers, many of the Herero were systematically overworked and starved, and then shipped to Shark Island for 'the final solution'.

While the use of slave labor was problematic, the Germans were also notorious for sexually abusing the women in concentration camps. However, the Germans often blamed the women, arguing that the Herero women were full of lust and taunted or seduced the German soldiers. Showing scant regard for the humanity of the Herero women, the German soldiers wantonly took advantage of the conditions in the concentration camps. Rape was a common practice, and very rarely, if ever, were German soldiers prosecuted for committing rape. While the documentary mentions the rape of women as well as some of the German generals involved, there is no testimony from the women who were raped.

Most of the monuments, the symbols of progress and development in Namibia, were built using slave labor. According to *Namibia: Genocide and the Second Reich,* even the present day parliamentary buildings were the product of slave labor. Most of the towns and ports were also constructed using the labor of those in the concentration camps. In addition to cities and industries, those confined to the concentration camps also provided the labor for building the railway system in Namibia. It is possible to argue that German soldiers and European empire-builders saw violence as one of the characteristics that set human beings apart from other forms of life and that Europeans had to assert their worldview through domination and conquest. Jeremy Sarkin-Hughes argues that the German soldiers who carried out the Namibian genocide knew of the Geneva Convention with regard to war and civilians, but chose to ignore it when it came to the Herero. Likewise, the British knew about the genocide against the Herero, but deliberately chose to ignore it, and sometimes collaborated by providing financial support to German explorers.[17]

The Herero who died at the concentration camps were often buried in mass graves, leaving little trace of their humanity or existence. Many of the mass graves were unmarked, rendering healing with the descendants of the Herero almost impossible. The few Herero voices that speak or appear in the documentary acknowledge that something terrible happened at the concentration camps, that their grandparents were murdered, and that they do not know where most of them are buried. A history, a tradition, and a people were destroyed by the colonizers.

History and Historicism

Namibia: Genocide and the Second Reich challenges the nature of history and the distinctions among fact, fiction and propaganda. In a way, it makes it clearer that how history is presented, whether from the present or the past, often serves an ideological purpose. This does not mean that the events did not happen: but the interpretation of events differs from one historical perspective to the other. This is also the case when it comes to the Namibian genocide. And yet history can be an instrument of either liberation or oppression.

But another way in which the German colonizers successfully presented the Herero genocide as inconsequential was refusal to acknowledge the European legacies of colonialism, xenophobia, racism, and class exploitation by whitewashing of language via euphemism. This was a process of not naming reality for what it is, to conceal the savagery from which Europeans reap benefits and privilege. Although modern Europe is largely viewed as a product of the 'discovery' and 'conquest' of the non-Western world, the documentary rarely refers to the colonial encounter and Europe's role in the creation of a sociology of knowledge systems built on prejudice and military violence. On the few occasions the natives rebelled, Germany, like other colonial powers, used its superior weapons to slaughter the rebels. As with many proponents of the superiority of Western civiliza-tion, Europeans do not always explicitly acknowledge that the process that created the modern world system did so at an enormous cost in ethno-cide, genocide, and ecocide suffered by the peoples and territories forcibly conscripted into service to *empire*. What makes Europe *better* is the way it oppresses the *other*. The Namibian genocide not only destroyed people, but ways of living that contested European thought and behavioral patterns.

For a while, Germany's portrayal of the genocide, could fall within use of history as ideology since it is not a view of the system of the real relations which govern the existence of individuals and nations, but the imaginary relation of those individuals and nations to the real relations in which they live. As an ideology, such history presents an atomized perception of real-ity and a system of ideas which expresses without reciprocity the more or less legitimate interests of a racial group, in this case, Europe. Among the characteristics of ideology is included a false consciousness, as well as a failure of genuine encounter, an almost willful destruction of the other in behalf of power. On the few occasions that the documentary speaks about the non-European other, the viewer rarely sees or hears the words that come from the Herero. Even when they speak, their worldview revolves around Europe. As such, there is no dialogue or encounter with the other that is based on mutual affirmation. Rather, the other is often ridiculed or excluded.

As a form of false consciousness, history as the ideology of Europe makes it possible for Germans to partially explore what the geno-cide meant, but perhaps selectively ignore problematic issues. While *Namibia: Genocide and the Second Reich* gives genealogy of Western racism and genocide leading to the Holocaust, it frequently negates or the troublesome nature of Europe's relationships with the rest of the world. One of the effects of an ideology is an uncritical appropriation by its followers so that it becomes universal and its worldviews and termin-ology are sheepishly regurgitated. As such, history can easily become a propaganda tool and a basis for constructing a false identity. When this happens, not only is there a distortion of history, but the pretensions of universalism go unquestioned. A diagnosis of the ills of modern society that deliberately revolves around the interests of Europe cannot lay any claim to universality since it hardly pretends that the humanity of the others really counts or matter. As such, European historiography might not offer much that might lead to the healing of countries which were victims of genocide.

Yet history or the past is a prerequisite for the continuous construction of the present identity, especially for the descendants of the colonizer and the colonized. However, remembering or re-creating the past through commemorating genocide is not simply the retrieval of stored information, but the putting together of a claim about past states of affairs by means of a framework of shared cultural understanding. Yet, in the twenty-first century political contexts in which talk of custom and ancestral ways goes on are of course very different from pre-colonial contexts or the years in which the genocides were carried out. In *Namibia: Genocide and the Second Reich* history as a discourse is a construct which cannot comprehend the whole of the past, especially as it is told from the perspective of those who benefitted directly or indirectly from genocide. However, it does not matter whether the recreated past is real or mythical in the sense of representing closely the actual events since political symbols radically condense and simplify reality, and are to some extent devoid of content: that is how and why they work. Perhaps it matters only whether such political ideologies are used for just causes, whether they are instruments of liberation or of oppression. Indeed, the documentary points out that the Germans have built statues to celebrate their victory over the Herero on the very sites of the concentration camps.

A Need for African Historiography and Histories of Genocide

Germany and Hegel's curse on Africa and the way Africa is perceived still has an impact on the Western episteme and Western ways of viewing Africa. Even many Africans and non-Africans have adopted the Hegelian view regarding Africa. In his *Philosophy of History*, Hegel (1831, 1995) presented an image of Africa and the African as a continent and a people not worth engaging.[18] In this one-sided conversation and one-dimensional gaze, Hegel consigns Africa to anonymity and invisibility while simultaneously establishing the superiority of Europe and/or White supremacy. In one sweeping paragraph, written through the eyes of a cultural and philo-sophical voyeur, the African world is depicted as destined to live in a per-petually primordial condition. The false projection, which also forms the basis for an irrational prejudice (is there any rational prejudice?) makes it possible for the European to ravish and annihilate the African and Africa without any compunction. Over time, different falsehoods, having given themselves the status of truths, take on a function with unforeseen conse-quences and often propagate myths under the guise of philosophical, sci-entific, or anthropological history. But Hegel also has established himself as one of the most insightful philosophers in the Western tradition. Yet, if Hegelianism lays the foundation for Western thought then Western civi-lization is constructed on an uncomfortable philosophy of race. As such, the destruction of the other, whether it is the Jew, the African, the Latina, the Arab, or the Aboriginal, has its roots in a distorted philosophy of race. However it is also true that not many scholars distance themselves from Hegel, and like Hegel, they leave Africa out of any discussions on issues related to life.

While the Hegelian worldview reveals that Europe's self-understanding depends on the negation of the *other*, African languages and philosophies offer a contrasting view of both gnosis and human nature and the relationship between thought and truth. In the docu-mentary, the language of communication is primarily English, the lan-guage of the colonizers. For the non-European, (and sometimes for Europeans) Africa is often different from the one depicted by Hegel and is frequently a source of nostalgia, of the remembrance of a bet-ter period in human history and the way life ought to be lived. Having been exiled from the human community in the Hegelian worldview, most Africans realized that Africa could not reconstruct itself through European languages, philosophies, and models of development. In the documentary, there is an acknowledgement of the ways such language makes the Herero foreigners in their own culture and country. The adoption of European languages, cultures, and modes of being is largely based on imitation, rather than originality. However, with imitation there is no genuine dialogue or reciprocity. It is beyond doubt that the reason for Africa's predicament is due to both racism and imperialism. In a similar way, race, cultural, and human consciousness are likely to be the source for its renaissance. That is, the rebirth of Africa will come through its self-discovery and affirmation of the values and languages that had been marginalized in the quest for *civilization*.

Hegel's portrait of the African personality in many respects legitimated the cultural and social racism prevalent in most of the Western countries even in the twenty-first century. After having stated that Negroes had no consciousness of religion or God, no understanding of what constitutes human nature, and no sense of development or culture, Hegel declared that "the only essential connection between the Negroes and the Europeans is that of slavery."[19] In many ways Hegel provided a blueprint for Western scholarship on Africa. Of course, anyone familiar with postcolonial Africa will be aware of the many individuals rooted in the African worldview who have changed the world for the better, for all people, not just Africans. Mandela and Nyerere as well as a host of other Africans created worldviews and cultures based on the best of what they remembered from traditions that had been debased by Hegel. They strove to create and provide new models of a harmonious world. The African languages at their disposal proved sufficient for fashioning alternative worldviews. The richness and complexity of the languages reinforced the cultural and linguistic diversity of those viewed as subhuman. One could argue that the superiority of any one language or philosophy over and against others is based on a false logic that assumes there can be no interdependence based on a mutual affirmation of the *other*. Of course, the emergence and 'rediscovery' of African languages and philosophy through European languages poses a different set of theoretical questions with practical implications. In *Namibia: Genocide and the Second Reich* there are hardly any references to African languages or philosophies of reconciliation.

The lasting impact and effect of the Hegelian worldview is the scientific and cultural racism that dominates the academic field in most parts of the Western world. Hegel's invitation for Europe to leave Africa leads to a superficial integration of the world against Africa, a pseudo-scientific rationalization of prejudice, and the formation of a false European utopianism based on a sharing of pirated and pirate treasures at a fictionalized brethren's cove. His proclamation of the superiority of Europe reads like nothing more than Narcissus' gaze at his reflection, and the consequent self-proclamation as the most handsome of all. However, there is counter-finality to, and in every self-proclaimed infallibility and perfection in almost every tradition and philosophy. If language in one capacity or another is part of the materiality of being, then the nonexistence of African and other nonwestern languages in philosophical discourses reflects in enterprises that present themselves as "detotalizations" reflects communities as based on the perpetual exiling of the other.

As a documentary, *Namibia: Genocide and the Second Reich* invites genocide scholars to explore changes and continuities in the practice of historical research especially in the early part of the twentieth century when written sources of information were mainly with the Europeans. What is apparent is that documentary and historical research, as well as the making of historical facts in everyday research, paying particular attention to the study of files and records kept in archives and libraries is a field that African historians need to develop. Traditionally, the history of knowledge production dwelled chiefly on the study of narratives and textual representations of the past from a European perspective. African historiography and historical research has the potential to critically examine the circumstances under which historians generated knowledge about genocide in colonial contexts.

The nineteenth century is generally acknowledged as the foundational period of history as a scientific discipline, the consolidation of the Enlightenment and Modernity. However, for countries in the global South, both the Enlightenment and Modernity were synonymous with genocide as European empires and nationalism grew. Africa and Africans can contribute to knowledge production about the genocides in African countries. More often than not, European languages often distort when it comes to history, for history generally serves an ideological purpose. This is especially the case when even medical and 'scientific' research with regard to the victims of genocide is ideologically designed to bolster white supremacy.

Medicine and Experiments

In addition to slave labor and rape, the Herero were also subject to medical experimentation by their German conquerors. Herr Doctor Eugene Fischer made the rounds to the concentration camps; it was there that he conducted his first "medical "experiments on race, genetics, and eugenics.

For "guinea pigs" he used both Herero full-bloods and the mulatto off-spring of Herero women and German men. Under his supervision, the preserved bodies and severed heads of Hereros were sent to Germany for dissection and study. Fischer later became head of the Kaiser Wilhelm Institute of Anthropology, funded by the Rockefeller Foundation for the study of heredity and eugenics. He co-authored the book *The Principles of Human Heredity and Race Hygiene*, which became the standard text-book in Germany on the subject. Hitler cited it in his *Main Kampf* (My Struggle), which became the Bible for the destruction of millions of peo-ple in his own goal of "racial purity". Hitler appointed Fischer as rector of the University of Berlin in 1933, where he taught medicine. Sometimes referred to as the "Father of German Genetics", one of his promising stu-dents was Josef Mengele, the so-called "Angel of Death", who went on to replicate his teacher's cruel experiments on Jewish children, and directed the operation of the gas chambers at Auschwitz.

Like all aspects of Herero suffering, the Germans turned it to profit. German universities and medical researchers requested body parts from Namibia and paid handsome sums of money for Herero human remains. German anthropology and philosophy had contributed to racism by pointing out the cultural differences between the races, and the access to body parts gave researchers an opportunity to engage in racial science and medicine. The practice of selling the skulls from murdered Herero was so widespread that German soldiers and prison guard, made a fortune from selling the skulls to scientists, museums, universities and hospitals in Germany. The medical experimentation, which often included measuring the sizes of the skulls and the eye color of the dead (in comparison with the Europeans) was used to prove the racial superiority of the German and Aryan races, and the inferiority of the Africans (Herero).

Namibia: Genocide and the Second Reich makes it clear that the roots of the Nazi genocide were informed by the practices during the Herero genocide. As such, the Herero genocide was a dress-rehearsal for the Nazi genocide. The only difference is that with the Herero, European countries and governments did not seem to care, and even collaborated in one way or another. In some cases, they were engaged in similar practices across Africa. Leopold of Belgium and Cecil John Rhodes of England had carried out similar practices in Congo, Zimbabwe, and South Africa. And, even as the genocides were going on in Africa, European settlers were systematically exterminating the indigenous peoples or placing them in "reservations" in North America where there was little hope for cultural regeneration and economic growth. Genocide was one of the ways European empires and colonies were created.

From Namibia to Germany: The Colonial Roots of the Nazi Holocaust

That there was a connection between the Nazi Holocaust and the Namibian genocide was made evident in the documentary. When the German economy collapsed after the First World War, the conditions that had made the genocide against the Herero possible were there. In Namibia, the Germans had portrayed the Herero as a threat to their safety and economic development. In addition, the Germans were quick to point out the racial inferiority of the Herero who were exterminated and had their property confiscated, while their women were subject to sexual abuse. The concentration camps that had worked so effectively to exterminate and dehumanize the Herero could be constructed to exterminate those who were seen as a threat to Germany's economic recovery and growth. The railway system that made for the efficient transportation of the Herero to the concentration camps was now used as the artery to transport the Jews to their extermination centers.

Almost all the methods used in the Nazi concentration camps in Germany had their origins in Namibia and other European colonial genocides. Just as the Germans had used "science" to prove the racial inferiority of the Herero, for the Third Reich, it became essential to portray Jews as vermin to be exterminated. The "Final Solution" had been tried in the colonies, the difference being that the lives of Africans were inconsequential to European empire-building. Effective control of the media had also made the dissemination of propaganda a lot easier.

Namibia: Genocide and the Second Reich shows the extent to which the Namibia Genocide had an impact on the making of the Holocaust. The German generals who formed the Storm Troopers had gained significant experience in Namibia. Among those who shaped the policies of the Third Reich included Von Epp (who had fought in Namibia) and Hermann

Goering, whose father had been governor of Namibia before the Herero genocide. The policies of the Second Reich were reborn in the Third Reich. Eugen Fischer, whose ideas on racism were developed in Namibia, played a huge role in the racism that was to shape the events in Germany. What the German doctor Mengele was doing to the Jewish prisoners at the concentration camps, the Germans had been doing to the Herero in Namibia with no protest from any European powers. It is not just fear per se, but the ideology behind it that drives one race to oppress another, or to view others as less than human. The notion of white superiority and purity also necessitated an ideology that portrayed blacks and other non-whites as inherently and irredeemably inferior. In many ways the lack of human dignity experienced by Africans is the direct result of the policy of white supremacy, especially in the colonies. White supremacy implies non-white inferiority. The creation of whiteness is also a product of colonialism and capitalism with regards to Europeans and empire-building

It is possible to argue that in this documentary, Africa and Namibia play a background role to the Nazi Holocaust, and highlight the discrepancies with regard to the treatment of Africans in European ethics. While there have been punitive consequences for Germany with regard to the Nazi Holocaust, it was not until 2005 that Germany offered Namibia a few million dollars to aid healing and reconciliation. In addition, German had qualms about acknowledging that genocide took place.

Twenty-First Century: Prospects of Reconciliation

Namibia: Genocide and the Second Reich is pessimistic with regard to the prospects of reconciliation between the descendants of the Herero and those of the German colonizers. Part of the reason is the reconstruction or re-writing of history by the colonizers and the silencing of the colonized. What Germany did was to glorify those who had committed the Namibian genocide as heroes and founders of a new homeland who had made the survival and prosperity of Germany possible. In the documentary, there is mention of statues and monuments of German soldiers, as well as a different historiography that glosses over all the atrocities of the genocide. As such, the descendants of the Herero and those of the colonizers have contrasting versions of what actually transpired. Those who committed murder and genocide are presented as heroes and have statues in their honor, while the victims of the genocide are often nameless, with no statues or monuments to commemorate them.[20]

When we consider that genocide is a foundation of empire-building, colonization of countries and theft of resources, it becomes more difficult to envision peaceful reconciliation between the colonizer and the colonized. While Namibia and the descendants of the Herero have gained political independence, the few descendants of the Herero who speak or appear in the documentary make it clear that they have not recovered their land. Instead, the children of the colonizers own most of the land that can be used for agricultural purposes. A major area of contention for the Herero includes that of buying back their land when they did not sell it in the first place. The documentary also shows the German Development Minister visiting Namibia, talking to the Herero, and asking for reconciliation and healing. However, the prospects of such reconciliation occurring appear dim, especially as most of the power (economic) lay with the colonizer and the home country of the colonizers. A redistribution of resources, including land, appears to be an idea that the colonizers seem unwilling to address.

5

The Armenian Genocide in Film: Overcoming Denial and Loss

Armen T. Marsoobian

Southern Connecticut State University

The Armenian genocide coincides with the birth of what we now know as the feature film industry in the United States. The first genocide depicted in a full-length feature film was the Armenian. Yet, just as the genocide itself faded from collective memory, save for that of the Armenian survivors themselves, the depiction of the events of 1915–1923 would have to wait over eighty years for another widely distributed cinematic treatment in the United States, while in France its treatment was only slightly earlier. The circumstances behind this lacuna are themselves worthy of filmic treatment. Geopolitical factors played a significant role in suppressing portrayals of this crime in the following decades. Unlike the Holocaust and subsequent genocides, films that place their narrative in the period of the genocide itself are rare. Ironically, one hundred years after the start of the genocide, it has taken a daring filmmaker of Turkish origin to take up the challenge of a direct depiction. Given this long period of silence, the films that have been produced in the past two decades deal not with the genocidal events themselves but with the memory and trauma of the survivors and the generations that followed.

This long period of the genocide's erasure is mirrored in the actual disappearance of the first full-length feature film about the Armenian

Genocide, *Ravished Armenia*, which was released in January 1919. *Ravished Armenia*, alternatively titled *Auction of Souls*, exists today only as a 20-minute-long fragment. The story depicts the survival struggle of one brave Armenian teenager whose story is told against the backdrop of massacres and deportations. As with the fate of many early films, the fragility of the film medium and lack of a preservation ethos contributed to its loss. The fragments themselves are discontinuous, but their places in the overall narrative are known from the fact that the script with inter-titles and scene descriptions has survived. The fragments are not outtakes and are almost exclusively dramatic action-packed scenes of violence and mayhem. The purpose behind their having been spliced together is a matter of speculation, though the most likely scenario is that they were put together in Soviet Armenia to create a documentary film on the genocide. Given the scenes depicted, it is easy to be fooled into believing that this was actual documentary footage. A videotape version of these 20 minutes appeared less than 20 years ago. Stories about the film's disappearance and rediscovery raise more questions than provide answers. There is always hope that more remnants of this classic will resurface. Just this year, a less than 2-minute segment from the beginning of the film surfaced in Paris. It had always been known that Henry Morgenthau, Sr., the American ambassador to the Ottoman Empire at the time of the genocide, had played himself, reenacting his actual confrontation with the Young Turk leadership, in particular, Talaat Bey, the interior minister. It is this rare footage that has now resurfaced.[1]

We do know that the film was loosely based on the real life story of a survivor of the genocide, Arshalouys Mardigian, whose name had been changed to Aurora Mardiganian soon after her arrival in the United States. Mardiganian had arrived in New York City on November 4, 1917, after two horrific years and a 1,400-mile journey by foot from the Anatolian interior to her eventual rescue in the Caucasus. She experienced sexual slavery and witnessed the deaths of her parents and siblings. She had come to the United States in order to bear witness to the suffering of her people and to find a surviving brother. Soon after her arrival, she was taken in by an Armenian couple who assisted her in her search. The film historian Anthony Slide has chronicled Mardiganian's saga in which her recounting of her ordeal was first converted into a best-selling book and then transformed into a major motion picture in which she would star as the lead in her own story.[2] Knowing no English and having never seen a motion picture, she signed a contract to star in a film in which she was to play herself reenacting the horrors of the genocide. Upon arriving on the film set in Southern California and seeing film extras wearing fezzes and dressed in gendarme uniforms, she thought she was being returned to Turkish captivity. Forced to continue acting even after breaking an ankle in one harrowing scene, she was required to make appearances around the country for the premieres of the film. After experiencing a nervous breakdown, she was replaced by seven lookalikes to fill in for her appearances. Slide captures this retraumatization when he writes: "Aurora Mardiganian suffered physical and emotional humiliation in her native Armenia. . . . On arrival in the United States … she was to become the victim of another form of exploitation: capitalism and a society looking for a cause worthy of its white, Christian wrath."[3]

Both the book and the film were ostensibly created to raise funds for the American Committee for Armenian and Syrian Relief, later to become Near East Relief. There were many fundraising events surrounding the premieres of the film, including one in New York City on February 16, 1919, attended by 900 well-heeled invited guests in the ballroom of the Plaza Hotel and hosted by Mrs. Oliver Harriman and Mrs. George W. Vanderbilt. The greater awareness of the Armenian genocide raised by the book and the widely screened film helped raise over 110 million dollars for relief work, an unprecedented figure that in today's dollars would be 2.5 billion. While the film was marketed in support of relief work, it was also a commercial endeavor that probably made a significant amount of money for Colonel William H. Selig, the film's producer, and Harvey Gates, the screenwriter and manager and guardian of Mardiganian. She herself had signed a contract for 15 dollars a week, but the pressure of the appearances led to her eventual escape from her managers in May of 1920. In the end she received little in the way of compensation for her work on the film or her guest appearances. Sadly, she died in obscurity at the age of 92 in 1994, after a stay in a California nursing home.

The press reviews at the time of the film's release were generally very positive, though it is sometimes hard to distinguish whether the writers were more concerned with what was being told than with the quality of how it was told. Slide, one of the world's leading experts on the silent film era, judges the film to be "Oscar Apfel's masterpiece." He writes that the 20-minute fragments "provide the viewer with more than a hint of what the finished production must have looked like. . . . But what these shots (seldom an entire scene) demonstrate is the quality of Oscar Apfel's direction. He has obviously created a film with such a documentary-like feel that it is almost *cinéma vérité*. It is actuality rather than a staged narrative. The realism is intense, and it is unimportant what the shots or scenes are meant to represent because the drama, the tragedy, the momentum is all there."[4]

Though little of the film survives, we know from the marketing and publicity stills that sex and the persecutions of the "white" Christian race were used to generate box office interest. In the pre-Production Code days of the film industry, director Oscar Apfel exercised much license in his use of visual imagery. Having a genocide victim star in a film about her own persecution added a degree of sensationalism not to be matched in the annals of filmmaking. Add to this the partial nudity on display, the Orientalist-based harem scenes of captive women, and the slave market scenes of the buying and selling of "white" female flesh, we can see the exploitative nature of the Hollywood film industry fully on display even in its infancy. Given the highly negative press portrayal of Turks and their persecution of Christians since the time of the Hamidian Massacres of the 1890s, there were no qualms in using bestial caricatures in the media marketing and stereotypical evil villain silent film gesturing in the portrayals of the perpetrators. Slide claims that the film "ran into relatively minor censorship problems in North America," having been "reviewed and passed by the National Board of Review of Motion Pictures, which described it as 'a frank straightforward exposition of sufferings of Armenia which makes a sincere and powerful appeal to every drop of red blood in America's manhood and womanhood.'" The Board concluded that the film's "entertainment value was 'impressive,' its educational value 'unusual,' and its historical value 'admirable.'[5] The cinematic rendition of the events seemed to match the "truth" of this survivor's testimony and that of hundreds of others who had witnessed the events in Turkey. Mardiganian herself in an interview years later stated that what actually happened was often worse than what could be portrayed in the film. In particular she pointed out that the iconic crucifixion scene that concludes the film was more horrific, involving the impalement of the rape victim with a sharpened wooden stick through the vagina.[6]

The film did encounter censorship problems in the United Kingdom, and this was to foreshadow the changing geopolitical reality in the Near East and South Asia in the early 1920s. Britain was in peace talks with the successor Ottoman Turkish government and was facing the early signs of a Turkish nationalist backlash and a restlessness among its Muslim colonial subjects. Securing their newly acquired oil wealth, a wealth that lay in Muslim Arab lands of the conquered Ottoman Empire, required sensitivity to Islamic sentiments. The result was the removal of all references to the word "Christian" in the intertitles and the cutting of the final crucifixion scene. This suppression was a foreshadowing of what was to become a more systematic erasure of the Armenian story in the decades to come.

Fifteen years after the publication of *Ravished Armenia*, the Czech-born German-speaking Jewish novelist Franz Werfel published what would become another worldwide best seller, *The Forty Days of Musa Dagh* (*Die Vierzig Tage des Musa Dagh*)(1933). This work of historical fiction was based upon actual events in 1915 when a group of Armenian villages resisted the deportation orders and fought off the Ottoman army for fifty-three days on the mountainside of Musa Dagh in the southern Cilician region of the empire. The Armenians were finally rescued by a French naval force that happened to be patrolling in the region. As one of the only successful resistances to the slaughter, the other being the resistance at Van, this event is celebrated by Armenians as one of the few heroic moments in an otherwise dark period in their history. Werfel had gathered his material for the novel during his travels and talks with many genocide survivors in Lebanon, Palestine and Syria. The novel garnered high praise in the German-speaking parts of Europe before pressure from the Turkish government led to the Nazi ban on the novel in February of 1934. The novel was doomed from the outset in Nazi dominated parts of Europe since many saw in it parallels to the German treatment of its Jewish citizens. The government of Turkey pressured its own Jewish and surviving Armenian citizens into denouncing the book even to the point of coercing Armenians to participate in book burnings of copies of the novel in the courtyard of their church.

Even as pressure in Germany and Turkey grew against Werfel and his novel, Hollywood saw a possible box office bonanza in this epic of resistance of good against evil. The two-volume novel was quickly translated, often in an abridged form, and eventually appeared in 34 different languages. Metro Goldwyn Mayer paid Werfel $15,000 for the screen rights in early 1934 and began development of the film even before the publication of the English translation in the fall of 1934. The potential for lucrative overseas distribution of this worldwide bestseller was an added incentive to MGM given the fact that 40 percent of Hollywood's income was derived from offshore at that time. While the over 900-page novel painted a complex and not totally faltering portrait of the Armenian resisters, the studio saw a ready-made historical epic that would have juicy roles for leading actors of the day. The role of the novel's hero, Gabriel Bagradian, a wealthy Armenian from Paris, had been tentatively assigned to the studio's rising star, Clark Gable. Other protagonists in the novel would provide good roles for the likes of William Powell and some of the leading female stars of the day. Irving Thalberg would produce it for his boss, Louis B. Mayer, and had slated Ruben Mamoulian to direct the production.

Opposition to the film by the Turkish government was swift and vehement, led by its then ambassador, Mehmet Münir. The details of the campaign against the film are too complex to trace out in detail here, but recent scholarship based upon State Department and MGM studio files chronicles this sorry business of the suppression of the truth of the genocide based upon commercial interests and realpolitik.[7] The US State Department took an active role in pressuring the studio executives to kill the project. Initially unconcerned about the loss of the Turkish film market, MGM capitulated under threats to their French market as a result of France's courtship of Turkey as a possible ally in the pending struggle against Nazi Germany. The refrain of needing Turkey as an ally – though sometimes an unreliable ally – against some greater threat to American national interests would be repeated again and again in the course of the next 80 years.

MGM held the production rights for 40 years and periodically would either announce or hint at a new effort to make the film. Given the diminishing European market with the rise of Nazism, MGM toyed with the idea of reviving their efforts in 1938, but an even stronger pushback from the State Department on the grounds of national security crushed the attempt. The same national security grounds are cited to this day by successive administrations when the question of Armenian genocide recognition is taken up by Congress. Attempts were made again in 1950 and 1969 but met a similar fate. MGM finally sold its rights to John Kurkjian, a California real estate developer with no film production experience. Unable to raise the necessary budget for a full-scale production, his director Sarky Mouradian produced a low-budget "shadow" of the originally conceived epic of the Armenian resistance to genocide. With unknown actors and an incoherent narrative due to extensive omissions from the original story line, the film failed to gain a national distributor and was eventually released on video. The critics panned it. Every few years rumors or press releases would herald a new attempt to produce a movie epic worthy of the novel's scale and reputation. Nothing would come of these efforts. Many Armenians still wait for this never-made movie epic, while others have moved on, knowing that the time has long passed for such a film. As we will see, one such filmmaker, Atom Egoyan, found a cinematic way to deal with this longing for an epic and the futility of its achievement.

Henri Verneuil, the award-winning French filmmaker, journalist, editor, film critic and radio commentator, was an artist who at first appeared to have made a successful career by "moving on" from the need to represent the genocide. Verneuil was born Ashot Malakian in 1920 in Rodosto, present-day Tekirag in the eastern Thrace region of present-day Turkey. He and his family fled the second wave of persecutions of Armenians in Turkey in the post-war period, finally settling in Marseilles in 1924. At a young age he fell in love with the movies and though trained as an engineer, he soon found himself working as a film critic and journalist. In 1952 he directed his first feature-length film and went on to direct nearly 40 feature-length films in the course of the next 40 years. He wrote many of the screenplays and worked with many of Europe and America's leading actors. He won many awards, including an Oscar, a Golden Globe and a César, the French equivalent of an Oscar. Yet for most of his voluminous output, little was produced on Armenian themes until late in his career. His last two films, *Mayrig* (1991) and its sequel, *558 rue Paradis* (1992), are autobiographical meditations on his life as an Armenian émigré in France whose family had fled the genocide.

Mayrig is the diminutive form of the Armenian word for "mother." The film was based upon his 1985 semi-autobiography with the same title that in many ways is an affectionate tribute to not only his mother but also his two aunts. Raised as he was by these three loving women and his father, his story has much in common with many such immigrant coming-of-age stories, but often lurking in the background are the ghosts of the genocide. In the book, these ghosts are subtly present, their outlines presented but their visage never detailed. The seven-year-old Azad, the boy whose life is being told, hears the stories of the horrors of 1915 when his father Hagop (played by Omar Sharif) reluctantly allows him to attend a compatriotic meeting of survivors in which such stories of suffering are shared. The stories themselves are not conveyed to the reader, only their affect: "But the time of fairies and elves had just ended its fleeting existence, face to face with reality. I was no longer a child."[8] When Verneuil transformed his book into a film, he chose to bring to the fore these horrors, first solely by the use of words and again a second time by transforming those words in moving images. The movie opens with a very evocative visual and aural reimagining of historic Armenia. Images of Mount Ararat, ancient Armenian churches, *katchkars* and beautiful landscapes at sunset precede the opening credits with a voiceover briefly chronicling the history and suffering of the Armenian people. The narration ends with a poetic cry and a haunting rendition of the Armenian song *Dle Yaman*, followed by the credits and an abrupt change of scene to a rain-soaked street in Berlin. We witness genocide survivor Soghomon Tehlirian assassinate Talaat Pasha, the former interior minister and chief architect of the Armenian genocide. Scenes of the trial follow, with a harrowing eye-witness account by a female survivor of a death march. We see the pain on the face of the witness and the reaction of the people in the courtroom. All we have are the witness's words. Later in the film, Azad overhears a family friend tell his story of the death march he endured. We are transported to visual recreation of the march, mostly of men, as it heads off into a desert land-scape. We see Apkar, the family friend, complain to a passing military officer about the conditions under which they are forced to march. The officer happens to be Jevdet Bey, the notorious governor of Van, known as "the butcher of Van." Apkar's complaint about his broken shoes results in a gruesome scene in which he has horseshoes nailed to his feet. Jevdet Bey was infamous for perfecting this form of torture, but Verneuil's scene fails by its very explicitness. The unbelievability of the reality of the torture is created by its explicit depiction. The whole sequence of the death march, which ends in a graphic massacre, may leave some viewers numb, but I, for one, find its attempt at realism too unreal. Atom Egoyan, ten years later in his film *Ararat*, depicts Jevdet Bey in the film being made within the film's narrative. Jevdet Bey orders the horseshoeing of a young boy, but this time the torture takes place off-camera. We hear the screams of this child but only see the face of his young Armenian companion, Arshile Gorky, and the perpetrator, Jevdet Bey. The scene has a greater emotional impact for me even though we are reminded at the end of the scene that this is only a film as the camera pulls back and we see the director and production crew in the background in the process of shooting this scene.

In the early 1990s, there was growing excitement in the Armenian American community when it was announced that the highly successful Academy Award–nominated director, Atom Egoyan, was making a film about the Armenian genocide. With the financial backing necessary for a first-rate production, Armenians were to get the film that they had long been waiting for, an epic rendition of the genocide. Yet for Egoyan, this was an ambition that was no longer possible. Yes, there would be an epic, but this would be a film-within-the-film, a film we witness being made in Egoyan's film. Egoyan had set himself a different, even more ambitious goal in making *Ararat*. How can one depict the aftermath of genocide, a genocide whose memory was denied and erased in the decades that followed but whose trauma still remains in the descendants of the victims? Egoyan explains his ambition:

> My film does not seek to add anything to the historical record of what happened, since the real issues for me have been why 'what happened' has been so systematically ignored, and what the effects of that ignorance have been on successive generations. *Ararat* is not so much about the past as it is about the present. It is about the responsibilities of people living now. A film that sought to depict the horrors of the Armenian Genocide would have no doubt been emotional, but it would not have dealt with the issues Armenians must live with today.[9]

In large measure, I believe, Egoyan has met his goal.

Ararat is a complicated film whose storyline, as with all Egoyan films, is not a straight linear narrative. The film is a multilayer construction with a number of interconnected story lines. The character Edward Saroyan, a famous French-Armenian film director (played by Charles Aznavour), is shooting *Ararat*, a filmed reconstruction of the massacres and the resistance that took place in Van during the early stages of the Armenian genocide. The script is based on the eye-witness account of Clarence Ussher, an American physician and missionary who was in Van. During the shooting of the film, Saroyan and his scriptwriter, Rouben (played by Eric Bogosian), ask Ani (played by Arsinée Khanjian), an art historian and specialist in the work of Arshile Gorky, to help incorporate the character of Gorky into the script. Gorky and his family were in Van during the massacres. Ani's son, Raffi, who has a job as a gofer for the movie, is involved in a love relationship with his stepsister Celia. Raffi is trying to come to terms with what happened to his father many years earlier, when he was killed trying to assassinate a Turkish diplomat. Celia, who is estranged from her stepmother Ani, is also trying to make sense of her father's supposed suicide and blames Ani for his death. Returning to Toronto from a clandestine trip to Turkey, Raffi is subjected to a long interrogation by David, a customs inspector who is on his last day of work before retiring. David suspects that Raffi is smuggling heroin inside the film canisters that Raffi claims contain exposed film that is needed for the final editing of Saroyan's film. David ultimately lets Raffi go, though he is pretty certain that the canisters do not contain film. These are not the only troubled relationships that complicate the plot.

Throughout the film, we see scenes from the film that is being shot. This film-within-the-film plays a crucial role in the overall dynamics of Egoyan's film. Saroyan's "*Ararat*" is an old-style historical costume drama that contains some highly charged and graphic scenes. Egoyan himself describes the acting in this film as "bordering on historical kitsch" and a "bit heavy-handed," but nonetheless, it depicts what those "images of the past would feel like to a culture that has never seen them before."[10] Because a major cinematic epic about the Armenian genocide had never been made, Egoyan felt compelled to depict what such a movie would be like without actually having to make it himself. By embedding fragments of this "never made film" within his film, Egoyan accomplished this goal.

Needless to say, this is a very complicated plot. When the film was commercially released, some Armenians criticized it as too hard to follow, with too many contemporary characters in troubled family relationships. I recall my aunt's remark as we left the theater at the time: "I wish there was more of the film about the actual genocide that Charles Aznavour's character was making." This was not an atypical reaction. There is a craving in the Armenian diaspora for an Armenian *Schindler's List*. But it is clear that Egoyan did not set out to make *that* film.

Egoyan's *Ararat* succeeds not on the level of a historical fiction film about the Armenian genocide but as a film about the complicated and messy psychological aftermath of the unresolved and *continuing* genocide. There are three time frames depicted in this film, roughly the years 1915, 1934, and 2000. The first marks the year in which the genocide began and in which the events depicted in Saroyan's filmic account of the siege of Van took place. The year 1934 was the year in which Arshile Gorky worked on his most famous painting, *The Artist and His Mother*, which plays a central role in the film. Its appearance may well reflect the fact that he never actually finished the painting. The never finished painting may be a symbolic gesture of not wanting to let go, to let go of his beloved mother who in real life he was not able to save. The final year, 2000, is the contemporary time in which Saroyan is making his film and in which we witness the conflicts of all the major characters in the film. Right from the opening credit sequence, Egoyan is able to seamlessly capture all three time frames, symbolically embedding the past in the present, as well as the trauma that many generations of Armenians continued to carry.

In the less than two-minute opening credit sequence, 1915 is symbolized by the photo pinned on the wall, while 1934 is depicted by Gorky's Union Square studio and his presence in it. This adult Gorky is not a character in the Saroyan film since the film depicts the child Gorky in 1915. The year 2000 is captured by both the contemporary video of Mount Ararat, which we are later to learn was shot by Raffi on his clandestine trip to Turkey, and also by Edward Saroyan's arrival at the Toronto airport, which closes this sequence of shots but opens the overall story of the film. The three time frames visually merge into each other, a technique often used in the film that follows. The traumatic past is thus constantly present.

The adult Gorky character presents an interesting and in many respects a haunting anomaly because he is not a character in the Saroyan film that is being shot. Many of the scenes from that film conclude with the camera widening out to reveal the film crew shooting the scene, thus letting the viewers know that they have been watching a film recreation. Other devices are also used to inform the viewers of the cinematic unreality of the scene, often just at the moment when suspension of disbelief is at its greatest and viewers are caught up in an emotionally horrifying event. By contrast the scenes with the adult Gorky do not employ such devices and seem to be set apart from the time sequence of the film's present narrative. This parallel story is unconnected but always present. Egoyan does breach this separation at one moment at the end of the film when he has the adult Gorky character dressed in contemporary clothing show up in the lobby of the theater at the gala opening of Saroyan's film. He interacts with no one. Standing apart, he stares at a poster depicting an image of the deportations. Is he an actor in the film or some apparition intruding into the present?

More than 10 years passed before another feature film was produced related to the Armenian genocide. Two films were released within six months of each other in the lead-up to the centennial commemorations on April 24, 2015. *The Cut* was released in November 2014, followed by the appropriately titled *1915: The Movie* in April 2015. The former was produced and directed by the award-winning director and actor Fatih Akin. Born of Turkish parents in Hamburg, Germany, he co-wrote the screenplay with the veteran Hollywood screenwriter Mardik Martin, an Iraqi Armenian born in 1936. Akin, whose reputation was made creating complex films noted for their psychological acuity and depth, took up the challenge of making a historical epic that dealt directly with the genocide and its immediate aftermath. The project was rife with symbolic significance. Here was a young diasporan Turk and a first-generation diasporan Armenian collaborating to give voice to a long-silenced crime. Akin, having been born in Germany, a nation highly complicit in this crime and carrying the moral burden of the Holocaust, challenged the nationalist narrative of Turkey. The cast included a number of well-known Armenian actors and a few of Turkish origin. No scenes were filmed in Turkey, but this is understandable both for practical and geopolitical reasons. Some have complained that the film does not do enough to contextualize the tragedy that you see unfolding. Aside from some information conveyed in opening titles placed over a map of the region, we have to draw inferences from passing remarks in the film's spare dialogue. The fact that the lead protagonist, Nazaret, is mute for a major portion of the film contributes to this lacuna. He suffered a "cut" to his throat that renders him mute. Akin claims in an interview in the Turkish-Armenian newspaper *Agos* that his film is not about genocide but is a historically based "adventure" story about one man's harrowing survival and his determination to rescue his twin daughters in the genocide's aftermath.[11] Needless to say, despite such disclaimers, both he and the newspaper soon received death threats from fascist nationalist elements in Turkey. Whether you agree with Akin or not about the classification of his film as a genocide film, he does acknowledge that his motivation in making the film was to discharge a burden and break the silence about the genocide in Turkey:

> The Armenian Genocide is a great pain that is not talked about. There are many stories. Every survivor, and every person that died have their own story. I tell the story of a single person in my film, but I have tried to weave the story of this person by combining many sources, literature, scientific books and witness accounts ... I had previously said, 'Turkey is ready to watch this film,' and tonight I see that I was right. It seems that the viewer has also relaxed. I was carrying a burden; I have now laid my burden on the shoulders of the viewer.[12]

This two-hour-and-18-minute big-budget movie shot in 35 millimeter film with Cinemascope lenses attempts to capture the feel of a historical epic in the tradition of David Lean or Elia Kazan. Filmed in five countries with a 20-million-dollar budget, the film has the sweep of such historical epics as *Doctor Zhivago* and *America, America*. Yet for some critics the time for such epics has passed.[13] Unlike Egoyan who confined his epic to a film-within-the-film in order to probe the social psychological aftermath of the genocide, Akin chose to make an epic. I leave it to audiences, whether they be Armenian or Turkish, to judge whether the time has passed for a historical epic on the Armenian genocide.

The creators of *1915: The Movie* have chosen a different path. Directed and written by relative newcomers Garin Hovannisian and

Alec Mouhibian, the film takes the approach of a play-within-a-film to tackle the traumatic memory of the genocide in the current generation of Armenians. Simon (played by Simon Abkarian, who starred in both *The Cut* and *Ararat*), a director of a Los Angeles theater company that has long stopped performing because of a tragic accident suffered by one of its actors, is determined to put on a play titled "1915." The performance is to be for one night only, April 24, 2015. The play revolves around the decision of one Armenian character, Ani, to save herself by agreeing to run off with a Turkish soldier. In doing so, she must abandon her family, her child and her nation, a scenario that evokes strong objections from the Armenian community. With a staged dramatic reenactment, the ghosts of memory, both personal and communal, will be purged that night. This is an ambitious film whose interpretation may provoke vastly different responses.

The centennial of the Armenian genocide appears to have sparked a renewed interest in the topic for cinematic treatment. I know of three film projects in their early stages of development and I suspect that there are many more yet to come.

6

The Ukrainian Famine of 1932–1933 on Screen: Making Sense of Suffering

Iuliia Kysla

University of Alberta

The cinematic representation of the Ukrainian Famine of 1932–1933, more often referred to as Holodomor,[1] although a subject of numerous documentaries, up until very recently has been limited to Oles' Ianchuk's 1991 feature film *Holod-33* (*Famine-33*), written by Serhii Diachenko and Les' Taniuk. It seemed that things may have substantially improved with the appearance of two new pictures depicting the Great Famine: *Povodyr* (*The Guide*, 2013) by Ukrainian director Oles' Sanin and the Canadian epic *The Devil's Harvest* (expected to come out in the near future), directed by a German-born George Mendeluk, which will be the first feature-length film about the Holodomor in English. However, with *The Devil's Harvest* still in its post-production phase and Sanin's film consciously avoiding direct depiction of the Great Hunger, *Famine-33* so far remains the only feature film that openly and directly addresses the complexity of the 1932–1933 tragedy. Reading Ianchuk's film in the context of other famine films like the four-part Irish television drama, *The Hanging Gale* (1995), I will begin by investigating the reasons behind the notable deficit of Holodomor films during the first two decades of Ukrainian independence. Why are directors, both Ukrainian and foreign, still avoiding the visual depiction of one of the most tragic events in Ukrainian history? Does it have something to do with the problem of expressing the inexpressible, or perhaps with the collective trauma of a post-colonial nation still unable to cope with its uneasy past? In the second part of this essay, I will take a closer look at *Famine-33* and *The Guide*, two exemplary cases of Ukrainian national narrative cinema, which are part of Ukraine's larger postcolonial project striving to distance itself from the Soviet past and create its own post-Soviet memory of the Great Famine.

"One-of-a-Kind:" Ukrainian Holodomor and Irish Gorta Mór

One of the most important challenges for artists when writing literary works or working on visual representation of the famine – whether it is the Irish "Great Famine" of the 1840s, the Ukrainian Great Hunger of the early 1930s, or the Bengali Famine of 1943 – is the limited capacity of representation: is it possible to describe all the horrors and the scale of such an historical phenomenon as famine, and are there any limitations to our ability to understand and analyze such a dreadful event? Hunger is not the only challenging topic resisting representation. Even if simple analogies between the Soviet famine of 1932–1933 and the Holocaust may to some extent trivialize and obscure the complexities of both catastrophes, as does Ukraine's lobbying the international recognition of the Famine as genocide, questions about ethics and possibility of aesthetic representation of such traumatic events often raised by Holocaust commentators are equally applicable to the famine literature. As it has been often stressed by critics, an event of such singularity as Holocaust cannot be easily explained and visualized, for there is always a risk to "transform an ontological event into a soap opera" (Elie Wiesel) or make it the "cheap consumer goods" (Imre Kertész), as it can be seen in the case of popular 1978 *Holocaust* mini-series.[2] The artistic representations of such "event at the limits" (Saul Friedländer) may thus lessen and trivialize the horror and people's suffering while making it enjoyable for the audience and exploitable for the media.

As material for the film drama, *hunger* can be "as tricky as [the] Holocaust"[3] for the very same reasons mentioned above, and it runs the risk of falling into a category of representation, which Nicholas Mirzoeff calls "exploitative," where "history and trauma are commodified for mass entertainment" and pain and suffering become normalized.[4] Similar to the experience of Holocaust, the trauma of famine, the very physical condition of an exhausted and slowly dying human body, cannot be easily comprehended and imagined by us who "living *after*" are usually well fed and sleep in warm beds.[5] One more additional thing that makes famine a challenging subject for cinematic representation, and this is exactly where it essentially departs from the Holocaust, is its dullness in visual terms. As Ian Stephens, editor of *The Statesmen,* an English-language newspaper in India, has argued in his memoirs about the 1940s Bengal, hunger has less power to engage and fascinate the spectator by the scene of violence:

> Death by famine lacks drama. Bloody death, the death of many by slaughter as in riots or bombings is in itself blood-bestirring; it excites you, prints indelible images on the mind. But death by famine, a vast slow dispirited noiseless apathy offers none of that. Horrid though it may be to say, multitudinous death from this cause looked at merely optically, regarded without emotion as a spectacle, is until the crows get at it, the rats and kites and dogs and vultures very dull.[6]

Stephens wrote this comment in regards to mass media's role in reporting the famine, but this distinction perfectly illustrates the challenge encountered by Oles' Ianchuk in 1990 when, still living in the Soviet Union, he set to recreate the terror, fear and desperation of the 1932–1933 Famine, still a taboo subject for the official Ukrainian cinematograph.[7] And this is for what Stephen Holden in his review for *The New York Times* praised Ianchuk's "grimy black-and white" movie, despite its technical "crudeness:" "The indelible images of human suffering that permeate Oles' Yanchuk's film '*Famine-33*' are memorable precisely because they are so far removed in tone from the raucous, shoot-'em-up violence and hysteria of Hollywood movies."[8]

Apart from ethical and representational problems, there is additional explanation why *Famine-33,* as well as its Irish counterpart *The Hanging Gale (1995),* has virtually remained the only fictional film produced on the subject. A number of factors may have played role here, including Ukraine's changing political atmosphere and difficult economic situation, but two obvious similarities between the Irish and Ukrainian cases are striking. One has to do with the so-called "Holocaust-mania" and lack of international interest, within the cinematographic milieu as well, in other less publicized tragedies. The centrality of the Holocaust as a "new cosmopolitan memory"[9] for the modern visual culture provided writers of other catastrophes with the universal language of suffering,[10] as we will see later when discussing Ukraine Famine films. But at the same time its privileged position tended to overshadow other forms of mass suffering. This prompted certain Ukrainian and Irish diaspora communities in North America to respond by seeking parity in recognition of their Great Famines, stressing the uniqueness of suffering incurred either by the Irish or by the Ukrainian people.[11]

The other reason for the rarity of famine films, despite the centrality of two tragedies for the development of modern Ireland and modern Ukraine, lies in the prolonged absence of public commemoration of both famines, even though reasons for this in each case varied. In the Soviet Ukraine, the memory of the Soviet manmade famine of 1932–1933, which claimed at least 3.3 million or so lives in Ukraine, the Soviet Union's richest agricultural region, had been denied and repressed for many decades. Already in the early 1990s, when Ukraine had just achieved independence, the famine turned out to be one of the most intensely debated issues of Soviet history and lately became one of the pillars in the formation of Ukrainian national identity, turning gradually into a "specific form of cultural reality that, in turn, ha[d] all features of a civil religion."[12] The hypersensitivity of the subject and its over-politicization had been further complicated by its sacral character implying that any critique of the event runs the risk of being mistaken as an attempted denial of the fact of the Famine itself.[13] More prosaically, as Olha Papash has suggested, the main reason for this might have been a "complete demise of the Soviet-Ukrainian film industry in the wake of the economic crises," for by the time the Famine had become a dominant theme in the historical narrative under President Iushchenko, Ukraine "simply lacked the facilities to engage in a cinematographic project of a similar scope."[14]

Similar to Ukraine, even though Ireland gained its independence decades earlier, the Irish Potato Famine, "as if [it] were some kind of shameful family secret, best left unmentioned,"[15] did not receive a large-scale state-sponsored public attention until the mid-1990s when the 150th anniversary of the event had been commemorated. Besides favorable economic circumstances, it was the capacity to distance itself from the past that "made possible in the 1990s a discourse that would have been unthinkable in the 1940s," the time when the Famine first entered the realm of academic discourse.[16] The only feature film to deal with the Irish Potato Famine, also a product of the 1990s memorialization project, *The Hanging Gale* by Diarmuid Lawrence, aired in Ireland and Britain in May–June 1995 and was a British–Irish co-production made by Little Bird Films for BBC Northern Ireland, with support from the Irish Film Board. Interestingly enough, this British 4-episode TV historical drama offers severe criticism of the British government for its failure to deliver help to starving Irish peasants,[17] as well as the harsh treatment of Irish tenants by landlords and their agents. Due to this self-implicating character, *The Hanging Gale* exhibits some traits of what James Young described as perpetrator's "impulse to memorialize its own victims," as was the case of Germany haunted by its Nazi past.[18]

In drastic contrast to the Ukraine Famine-*33* containing explicit anti-Russian rhetoric and the straightforward message ("Soviets are bad, Ukrainians are good"), Lawrence's characters are well balanced; the four Phelan brothers (the McGanns) demonstrating various Irish reactions to the Famine are set against the figure of a "colonizer," the English Agent "torn between his own need for survival, the blindness of his absentee master and sometimes sneaking sympathy for the peasants."[19] Framed in terms of non-violent protest and armed resistance against the foreign rule, what is exemplified by ideological choices made by the Phelan brothers, the film offers more or less a nuanced interpretation of the social causes of the Famine but, strangely enough, avoids the overt visual depiction of the hunger "spectacle," diluting the realistic gloomy landscape shots with aquamarine Goya-like romantic interludes. The only vivid famine scene, showing a priest finding a dying peasant family who are presented as half-human zombielike creatures in a tiny shelter in the wild countryside, is followed by the shot of the Agent's house to display the gap between the colonized and colonizer. The reliance on realistic photography and various sorts of testimonies drawn from historical sources (hunger is more spoken about than seen) as the main means to convey the horrors of the starvation is the director's way of resolving the problem of representation, even though his mixture of realism with romanticism may create additional problems, since film's romantic episodes, as suggested by Margaret Llwellyn-Jones, are "strong enough to outweigh the central historic injustice's traumatic power."[20] On the one hand, *The Hanging Gale*, with its balanced portrait of the enlightened English Agent, can be seen as a part of government's concern about the rising anti-English sentiment in Northern Ireland, while, on the other hand, it clearly demonstrates the ambiguity of famine memory in Irish identity politics. The Ukraine Famine sagas, by contrast, are the typical memorialization projects commemorating the martyrdom of the people where Famine occupies a central place as a symbol of foreign repression and the nation's sacrifice.

Re-Imagining the Holodomor: Collective Trauma in Feature Film

Even though today Ianchuk's *Famine-33* is the single feature film overtly portraying the Ukrainian Famine, together with Oles' Sanin's *Povodyr* (*The Guide*, 2014), it is a part of a larger spectrum which I call "national narrative" (*natsnarratyv*) cinema represented mainly by films produced in Ukraine after 1991 and often funded by the Ukrainian diaspora and, starting from 2005, by the Ukrainian government as well. Such films as Ianchuk's well-known '*Bandera series*'[21] helped to foster the collective memory of the nation and were "examples of rebuilding the national cinema" by bringing to a screen events that serve Ukrainians as a source of cultural identity, such as the Great Famine or World War II.[22] Both *Famine-33* and *The Guide* can also be treated within the category of a specific – post-Soviet – version of post-colonialism in a country that, similarly to other former Soviet republics, tries to cultivate its "new" post-Soviet national past by merging the technique of "estrangement from the past of alien [Soviet] hegemony with the romantic narrative of national history."[23]

No historical drama, as we know, reflects a true "historical reality" which, according to Evgeny Dobrenko, "lies not in the subject (representations of the past) but precisely in the time of [its] production." From feature film we can read more about its "presence" than "we can about the eras which these films (novels) were meant to 'reflect.'"[24] It is thus hardly surprising that, based on a novel *Yellow Knight* (1962) by émigré writer Vasyl' Barka and partially funded by the Ukrainian diaspora, *Famine-33* does not offer any new knowledge about the 1932–1933 Famine but rather "reflects" the existing discourse of the *Holodomor/genocide* developed by the Ukrainian diaspora in the 1980s and later appropriated by the Ukrainians in Ukraine, including Ianchuk himself.[25] It is also by no means accidental that *Holod-33* premiered on the republic-wide television channel UT-1 on the night before the all-Ukrainian referendum on independence scheduled for 1 December 1991. At the end of the film, we have an even more evident example of Ianchuks's contribution to the referendum: wandering in the woods, Andrii, the only survivor of his family, asks a skeletally thin elderly man (actually played by a former Gulag prisoner)[26] he meets by chance, where all the people have gone: "Has the plague taken them all?" "It is not the plague, son, it is the state [*hosudarstvo*]," comes the reply. His warning to a boy to "run away from here" was clearly addressed to a wider Ukrainian audience expected to vote overwhelmingly for independence from the Soviet Union. And indeed, as some critics admit, Ianchuk's film played a crucial role in determining the outcome of the 1991 referendum; no other feature film in Ukrainian history would be so influential.[27]

Shot in central Ukraine in regions that had experienced the tragedy in the 1930s, *Famine-33* chronicles Stalin's forced collectivization campaign and the hunger that followed it, focusing on a single Ukrainian peasant family slowly starving to death, one by one. In short, it is a "tale of death and unparalleled suffering in which once proud villagers were forced into cannibalism to survive in a country often referred to as the breadbasket of Europe."[28] The story of the Great Hunger is shown here through the eyes of a small boy called Andrii Katrannyk, the only survivor from his family destroyed by the repressive policy of the state. Chronologically, it covers the period from autumn 1932, when local communists confiscated the last remaining provisions from the Katrannyks, to the summer of 1933, when, under armed convoy, the surviving peasants collect the harvest from fields covered with the bodies of the dead – a comparatively short but one of the deadliest periods in Ukrainian history when at least 15 to 20 percent of Ukrainian peasants died and many more remained deeply affected by the disaster.[29] Against the backdrop of the long years of silence about the events, as well as continuing attempts of some parts of Ukraine's political spectrum to deny them, *Famine-33*, besides being a political statement, was also a project of remembrance, commemorating the memory of the victims who died, massively, in silence and total oblivion. It was also about giving them a voice which they been denied for too long.

From the very beginning, the film presents the Famine from a postcolonial perspective – as a regime-sponsored "terror" of "coercive confiscation of [Ukrainian] food and live stock," that was later exported "to finance the industrialization of the [Soviet] Union." "I wanted people to see," Ianchuk remarked in 1991, "what life was like in a colony, the inhabitants of which were mercilessly exploited in the name of a utopian ideology."[30] Depicting what he calls "humiliation by hunger"[31] exclusively as Ukrainian suffering, the director sets up Ukrainian peasants, victims of hunger and colonial brutality, against well-fed and uniformly evil Soviet party officials, "juxtaposing Ukrainian spirituality with the communist lack thereof."[32] Although the film does not conceal that there have been Ukrainian supporters of the Communist regime (the only 'good' Communist, however, has to shoot himself in order to preserve the positive image of the national community), the sociopolitical cause of the trauma passes in silence. Strangely enough, the film omits an important part of the story, the peasants' resistance to the collectivization in 1929–1930, when at least half of all peasant revolts took part inside Ukraine.[33] What could have partially explained the treatment of Ukrainian farmers in 1932–1933 and provided some positive examples for identification is absent in the film. Instead, *Famine-33* presents the Great Hunger as a spiritual torment and a "voluntary and fully conscious sacrifice" of the Ukrainian "martyrs" for the "*future* salvation of Ukraine," depicting Ukrainians as the only victims of the Soviet regime's genocidal policy. In this context, the film thus offers a more psychologically acceptable "substitute" image of the past by presenting all the horrors of life threatened by starvation as a "rationalized act of suffering for ideals and convictions."[34]

Famine-33 is very emotionally powerful film that relies more on images, than words. It is shot in gloomy black-and-white to highlight the atmosphere of the film, with occasional colorful pastoral interludes for scenes from the past – the director's debt to the Ukrainian poetic cinema of the 1960s–1970s and particularly to Iurii Illienko, with whom he worked. In terms of stylistics, Ianchuk's feature-length debut is very different from his later patriotic films made in a more traditionalist manner; overloaded with symbolism and cultural codes usually unintelligible to a foreign audience, it resembles rather a "series of tableaux of crucial moments in the lives"[35] of the film's protagonists than a conventional narrative cinema. In performing the suffering of the Ukrainian starving body, the director opts to use the close-up perspective, suitable "for the creation of distinctive symbols as well as omissions," presenting the Famine, through early-Christian rhetoric of suffering and martyrdom, as the perpetual confrontation of two absolute powers, of good (Ukrainian/Christianity) and evil (Soviet Union/Antichrist).[36]

Visually, it is not a gradual day-to-day psychological exploration of degradation and erosion of the starving body – though it would be a very interesting thing to do – but more of a monumental depiction of universal suffering of the Ukrainian people where the Famine, as demonstrated by Olha Papash, "is represented not as a tragic episode of the past, but rather as an important impulse" for the creation of an independent Ukrainian state in the future.[37] The individual spectacle of a hungry body is created predominantly through close-up images of villagers numb with despair and hunger silently waiting in the pouring rain for their bread delivery only to be brutally dispersed later by armed soldiers, or peasants staring at a pile of sacks of wheat guarded by Red Army soldiers and a dead body lying in front of them. While viewers do not see the physiological starvation in a process, they confront its visual consequences imprinted on the emaciated bodies, usually faces, of the starving people predominantly singled out as Ukrainians. As the tragedy unfolds and their suffering intensifies, we see more corpses on screen, so the ground soon becomes literally covered with bodies, particularly after the Red Army massacres unarmed peasants who are desperately trying to storm the mill where confiscated grain is being stored.

Borrowing the language from the Holocaust, Oles' Ianchuk tries to achieve a newsreel effect, apparently to "compensate for the lack of real-life images associated with the famine,"[38] and he recreates an iconic image of a dehumanized survivor as a silent, passive, weak and often unnamed living being. In one of the most poignant scenes, where Soviet soldiers unload a train, tossing down frozen bodies of the deceased and still living farmers into an unmarked mass grave, the director clearly alludes to the visual imaginary of the Holocaust and other Nazi crimes against humanity, consciously establishing a link between the murderous policies of Hitler and Stalin, and furthermore equating the Jewish tragedy with the Ukrainian one. Perhaps it was not just a mere coincidence that in 1993 Oles' Ianchuk's *Famine-33* was shown on the same day as Steven Spielberg's *Schindler's List* (1993) at the Film Forum festival in New York.[39]

As a remembrance project, Ianchuk's film offers an exclusivist model of Ukrainian identity based on sacrifice, victimhood, and martyrdom. But this representation, as Olha Papash has persuasively argued, is problematic, for by representing the famine as a conscious sacrifice of the Ukrainian people for the sake of the future Ukraine, "the film *post factum* predetermines the events of the 1930s" and thus "unwittingly" contributes to "a rehabilitation of the atrocities it was intended to condemn."[40]

Whereas after *Famine-33* Ianchuk switched to the more controversial topic of Ukrainian participation in World War II, Oles' Sanin, one of the most promising Ukrainian directors, renowned for his well-perceived epic *Mamai* (2003), spent almost 8 years writing and rewriting the script of his second feature film about the Soviet persecution of Ukrainian folk minstrels (*bandurists*) at the time of the forced collectivization, the Famine, and emerging repression of the Ukrainian nationally-minded intelligentsia in the early 1930s. His new film, *Povodyr, abo kvity maiut' ochi* (*The Guide*), released in 2013, to some extent can be seen as a sequel to *Famine-33*, even though the two films differ substantially in their stylistics and portrayal of the Hunger. Both are set in the early 1930s and aim to depict Soviet crimes against the Ukrainian nation by appealing to the most traumatic historical episodes in Ukrainian history. Both use the customary strategy of individual representation of collective suffering that leaves little room for nuance; all Soviet officials are universally evil, though the trope of a "good communist" committing suicide is present in each film. But if *Famine-33* was a political statement against "communist tyranny," *The Guide* takes one step forward towards constructing a vivid, although very blurred and fragmented, vision of the "other" non-Soviet Ukraine, that of the period of the Ukrainian national revolution of 1917–1921. In other words, the film fills the void that is left by *Famine-33*'s expressionist scenes of mass destruction and death. In contrast to Ianchuk's essentialist divide between suffering Ukrainians and Communist perpetrators, Sanin's contribution, despite all its excessive symbolism and instrumentalist approach to history, is interesting for its attempt to give a slightly more complex reading of the Soviet past, which, unfortunately, does not prevent the film from being a "set of beautiful, but discrete pictures."[41]

A patriotic blockbuster that attempts to mimic the style of filmmaking popularized by Hollywood, *The Guide* is a mixture of all possible genres, with clear allusions to the Ukrainian tradition of the "poetic cinema." Often criticized for its "schematized, devoid of semitones, lifeless" characters, stylistic dissonance and muddled plotlines,[42] the film tells the story of a young boy named Peter (Anton Sviatoslav Greene), son of an American engineer, Michael Shamrock, who came to the USSR in the 1930s to help with industrialization. Alarmed by Shamrock's intention to pass on documents about Stalin's intended famine in Ukraine to a British journalist in Moscow, a ruthless NKVD officer Vladimir (Oleksandr Kobzar) organizes the foreigner's assassination that is accidentally witnessed by his son, carrying the documents. The boy flees to the countryside where he befriends and becomes the guide for a blind folk musician, Ivan Kocherha (Stanislav Boklan), who would later become a substitute father to him. After a series of daring adventures, Peter and Ivan end up separated and are reunited only at the end of the film when the old minstrels are being conveyed to their deaths. The fate of the blind *bandurists* persecuted by Soviet authorities alludes here to the historical suffering of the Ukrainian people, which, in Sanin's own words, is the story of "unbroken human spirit. The story of people who, living in subhuman conditions, survived and remained human beings."[43]

The director's attempt to show how "in a matter of months the pride and flower of the [Ukrainian] people would disappear in the common graves"[44] is an extremely promising idea but it can be very challenging at the same time. By making his protagonists experience practically all events of the dramatic 1930s, Sanin fails to say something new about these events and instead constructs a disjointed collection of "conventional shock-scenes absolutely unintelligible for those who have the vaguest idea" about Ukrainian history.[45] Although important for Ukraine, *The Guide*, similarly to *Famine-33*, lacks that "kind of dramatic qualities that would appeal to international

97

audiences,"[46] since foreign viewers would be evidently confused by the film's incoherent narrative and symbolism decipherable only by Ukrainians. And yet, what Sanin's epic does is attempt to historicize the Great Famine, in a drastic contrast to Ianchuk' quite abstract and timeless depiction of the tragedy. At the same time, the film demonstrates the director's inability or rather reluctance to use overt depictions of the hunger, which in the film's epic structure often serves as just another test situation for his characters.

Although a central symbol, the suffering and starving Ukrainian body is not foregrounded in *The Guide*. Similarly to Lawrence's *The Hanging Gale*, in Sanin's film, the horrors of starvation are verbalized more than visualized; relying heavily on a voice over narration citing official Soviet directives about the collectivization in Ukraine, the director simply lets history explain what we cannot see for ourselves. What we see, however, is a thick milky mist, the director's metaphor for the hunger, where "all [peasants] had starved to death," as one Red Army officer, disgusted by what he had seen, tells Vladimir. In one critical episode, after which Peter lets himself be lost in a fog, he and Ivan find a young schoolteacher and her starving children in an abandoned school. Determined to save the orphans from the approaching Soviets, Kocherha promises to lead them through the fog, because, as the director admits, "in a fog, only the blind can lead, others are afraid." In the film, Sanin uses the fog to cover his heroes and disorient the enemies and at the same time to evoke a psychological effect of emptiness and loss usually associated with the famine. In his interpretation, the Ukrainian Great Famine was the

> … story of no time and no space … This is the story of a fog in which nobody knew what had been waiting for him or her; only death was there. This is the story of a dead field that remained unharvested, for there was none to harvest it. [Clear allusion to Ianchuk's final film's sequences.] This is the story of a lost boy who was searching for a man who saved him from everything and became a father to him.[47]

The famine sequences end up with an impressive shot of a lost boy wandering amidst the field of dead sunflowers, surrounded by barbed wire.

Even if not seen, the Famine runs through the film like a red thread, even though from time to time it gets lost against the background of the "half-Jedi and half-Hobbit" ragged *bandurists*[48] and their struggle with the Soviet regime, embodied in the confrontation between the saintly figure of Ivan Kocherha and Vladimir, the "villain." The film presents the catastrophic famine of 1932–1933 as a deliberate policy on the part of the Soviets to destroy the Ukrainian people, singling out two individuals, Joseph Stalin and Lazar Kaganovich, as responsible for the deaths of millions of innocent civilians. Effectively, the opening of the film shows the Ukrainian Communist, the former People's Commissar of Education of the Ukrainian SSR, Mykola Skrypnyk (in film – Sytnyk), committing suicide – a repeating image from *Famine-33* – to the sounds of jazz. Shortly before his death, Sytnyk, self-identified as "Communist and Ukrainian," asks Michael Shamrock to pass on a book (that turns out to be the 1840 edition of Taras Shevchenko's *Kobzar*) containing secret party documents about the Famine to a British journalist in Moscow, Gareth Jones, hoping that their "publication perhaps could stop the machine killing innocent people and destroying my people." Within the plotline, the party documents, enclosing the infamous resolution on "sabotage of grain procurements" (originally dated back to December 1932),[49] become an object of obsession, a fetish for Vladimir who throughout the film tries to capture Peter, who is carrying them. Interestingly enough, these documents function in a similar way as the golden chalice does in Ianchuk's drama. In *The Guide*, they become the proof of Stalin's planned genocide against the Ukrainians. And Peter Shamrock, like Jan Karski, a renowned currier for the Polish underground during World War II, takes on an important mission to deliver the message and inform the world about this dreadful tragedy. In contrast to Karski's pursuit to smuggle information from Nazi-occupied Poland to warn the rest of the world about the horrors happening to Jews in his own country, Peter's mission fails. It is hard to say from the film whether the documents ever reach their addressee, but this reference to the Holocaust suggests a clear link between the crimes conducted by Stalin and Hitler and reiterates Ukrainians' longing for the same international recognition for *Holodomor* as enjoyed by Holocaust.

As a matter of fact, *The Guide* neither conceals nor emphasizes the problem of the local executors of the terror who participated in the requisition of peasant crops during the collectivization campaign in Ukraine. In this regard, the menacing OGPU officer Vladimir, the only visible representative of Soviet authority in the film, is singled out as the main perpetrator of these "nasty things" (*merzosti*). The murder of a disobedient chairman of the collective farm committed by Vladimir's henchmen reveals to us his repressed Ukrainian identity. Preceded by the murder shot, the film's climax sequences contain one scene where Vladimir, enjoying the hospitality of the village whose grain he has to confiscate, sits down to eat something. While eating, he stains his *kosovorotka* (Russian skewed-collared shirt) and has to change it into a Ukrainian embroidered shirt, which seems like a ritual of peeling off his colonial camouflage, in Homi Bhabha's sense.[50] Downgraded to the level of the locals, he is ready to meet Ivan Kocherha, his long-forgotten archenemy, who comes to the same village for the wedding of the chairman's daughter.

The history of relations of these two men on screen is the history of trauma they both endured in 1918 in the aftermath of the legendary Battle of Kruty, when, captured by the Bolsheviks, they chose to take opposite ideological positions; one joined the Soviets by betraying his former comrades-in-arms, while the other remained faithful to his ideals.[51] Through a series of repetitive black-and-white flashbacks, Sanin is able to tell his viewers the story of Vladimir's treason, a source of his highly compromised identity and never relaxed fear. A frightening figure because of his "high percentage of [human] weakness,"[52] Vladimir exhibits some traits of what Bhabha calls "mimic" or "hybrid" colonial identity, of someone who is "almost the same [as the colonizer], but not quite."[53] The Character's marginality is demonstrated through his love of a cigarette brand named "IRA," the second-rate cigarettes produced in Moscow before the Revolution that in the 1920s were famously rebranded by Soviet Constructivists. In the film, IRA cigarettes function both as a sign of his belonging to the "Old" pre-Soviet "World" (in fact, high-ranking Soviet officials paraphrase the famous slogan, "IRA cigarettes are all [he] retains from the Old World")[54] and a material connection to the past (this is how – by the scent of cigarette smoke – Kocherha recognizes Vladimir). What is most fascinating is how the director uses these small historical artifacts, such as IRA cigarettes, or recreates, for instance, a specific noise made by a Chekists' black leather jacket in order to create a "reality effect." Language is another marker of Volodia's hybrid identity in *The Guide*. Tellingly, from time to time, he ceases to speak Russian, the language of domination and power, and switches to Ukrainian, for example, when communicating, with his wife. Overall, though an evidently negative construction, the figure of a Chekist capable of feelings alludes to Ukraine's uneasy relationship with the Soviet past, in a way, suggesting that there might be multiple readings of this past.

Conclusions

Reimagining collective trauma and extreme physical violence on the screen is a daring endeavor indeed, and the Famine, as revealed by this study, has proven to be a most challenging subject. The cinematic representation of historical suffering makes trauma endurable and, therefore, accessible to a wider audience. By "simulating victim experiences through sights, sounds, visuals," films like *Famine-33* and *The Guide* become places where "the act of remembering a distant past" provides viewers "personal access to the suffering of others where such suffering could be inconceivable in a secure society."[55] At the same time, cinema usually leaves off-screen all negativity and horrors of it. We should not forget that the Ukrainian Famine of 1932–1933, like the Holocaust, was first of all a story of survival, in which there was little room for human dignity, for to live often meant to "choose to become less human."[56] In this regard, a screen adaptation of the past runs the risk of "turning abject poverty itself, by handling it in a modish, technically perfect way, into an object of enjoyment."[57]

As the above analysis has demonstrated, the focus on performing and staging famine, be it the Irish Potato Famine or the Ukrainian Great Famine, has developed only recently, in the early to mid-1990s. Unlike the victims of the Holocaust, those of the Ukrainian Famine still await an adequate visual representation of their suffering. During and after the collapse of the Soviet Union, after many years of silence, the Ukrainian Famine of 1932–1933 appeared on the screen as the major historically based reason to support Ukrainian independence, the line of argument best illustrated by Ianchuk's 1991 film. The current visual representation of the Holodomor, even though substantially amended by Sanin's recent contribution, is still dominated by the narrative developed by the authors of *Famine-33* on the eve of Ukrainian independence, where the story of famine is told exclusively as one of passive victimization and

Christian martyrdom. As we have already noticed, such a national interpretation of famine leaves no room for nuance and obstructs the complexity of historical reality, reducing Ukrainians to the status of victims of colonial brutality and history to a number of the nation's sacrifices in the name of independence. In this context, the directors' decision to employ religious rhetoric for the depiction of the famine, to make the past more acceptable and justified, must be seen as their key strategy to counter the feared impossibility of representation.

7

The Holocaust in Feature Films: Problematic Current Trends and Themes

Jonathan C. Friedman

West Chester University

When dealing with the representation of the Holocaust in fictional media, there is no shortage of admonitions, from Elie Wiesel's famous quote that "Auschwitz defies imagination," to Theodor Adorno's misunderstood line that "to write poetry after Auschwitz is barbaric."[1] Yet for over 60 years, the performing and fine arts have helped to imbed the memory of the Holocaust in our collective consciousness. Critics may take issue with representations constructed in feature productions like *Schindler's List* or the 1978 television miniseries, *Holocaust,* but they cannot dismiss the fact that for all their shortcomings, they helped to advance both popular and academic discourse on the Holocaust. In the past few years, however, movie-going audiences have witnessed both a poor German child going to the gas chamber along with his Jewish friend (in 2008's *Boy in the Striped Pajamas*) and Jewish sadists who scalp Germans, as part of Quentin Tarantino's revenge fantasy, *Inglourious Basterds,* from a year later. As of this writing, the most recent feature films on the Holocaust and Nazi Germany with any connection to a US production company are the disappointing efforts *Esther's Diary* and *The Book Thief.* (A BBC production entitled *Woman in Gold,* about the struggle to retrieve a plundered Klimt painting from the Austrian government, premiered in April 2015).

How did we get from addressing the large scale questions and scope of the Holocaust to this? And what are the implications of this downward trend in the representation of the Holocaust in feature films? Were Wiesel and Adorno fundamentally correct in their warnings?

In order to offer commentary about the future of narrative films about the Holocaust, it is important to show their development through time. Israeli film historian, Ilan Avisar has postulated four phases of this evolution: an initial phase of propaganda and newsreels, a second phase of realism using classic Hollywood staging techniques, a third phase of what he calls modernism, which is more discordant in both content and form, and a final, post-modern phase, which appears to have absolutely no rules.[2] As has been well documented by Avisar and other scholars such as Ben Urwand and Thomas Doherty,[3] the cinematic depiction of Nazi Germany in the 1930s and 40s was minimal. The first phase of Holocaust representation included propaganda pieces like Leni Riefenstahl's *Triumph of the Will* (1935), the anti-Nazi play *We Will Never Die* (1943), and then after the war, Allied newsreels, such as the gruesome short entitled *Death Mills*. The realist phase was coterminous with the propaganda phase, but it lasted from the 1930s until the 1960s and featured classics like *The Mortal Storm* (1940), *Diary of Anne Frank* (1959), and *Judgment at Nuremberg* (1961). The French documentary, *Nuit et brouillard* (*Night and Fog*) (1955) could be considered the beginning of the so-called modernist phase, with its jarring soundtrack and jump cuts of violent imagery juxtaposed with contemporary footage of Auschwitz. The modernist use of non-traditional scenic styles and focus on suffering rather than heroism continued with films such as Sidney Lumet's *The Pawnbroker* (1964), *Sophie's Choice* (1983), and Claude Lanzmann's *Shoah* (1985).[4] Feature film productions on the Holocaust reached their numerical peak in the 1990s, the decade of Steven Spielberg's *Schindler's List* (1993) and the establishment of both the United States Holocaust Memorial Museum (in the same year) and the Survivors of the Shoah Visual History Foundation. As cultural studies scholar Deborah Staines argues: "There was a noted tendency throughout the 1980s and 1990s for cinema to articulate the Holocaust into a public discourse of memory. Indeed, one might almost say that there was a cultural demand on cinema to perform memories of Auschwitz."[5] The embrace of Holocaust memory by "baby boomers" and their concern for immortalizing the narratives of survivors, as more and more approached their final years, helped to fuel this unprecedented creative and critical output. For his part, Avisar regards *Schindler's List* as a "post-modern" Holocaust film because of its reinvention of existing iconography, and many subsequent films have fundamentally altered the form and content of Holocaust representation. Thus, in post-modern Holocaust films, ambiguity has replaced clarity vis à vis victims and perpetrators, comedy has become conflated with drama, and the trauma of the Holocaust has become a surrogate for other national traumas.[6]

A number of recent films have either blurred or inverted the traditional perpetrator/victim tropes, including Roman Polanski's *The Pianist* (2002), about the Polish-Jewish classical pianist, Władysław Szpilman, featuring a storyline about a German army officer (William Hosenfeld) who helped Szpilman in hiding. The Costa-Gavras film, *Amen,* also from 2002, centers on Kurt Gerstein, the supplier of poison gas to the camps who began leaking information about the Nazi murder program to diplomats and church officials. Even genres that one would think would be far removed from the Holocaust demonstrate role reversal, as in the superhero film, *X-Men,* whose main villain, Magneto, is a Holocaust survivor. The year 2008 was practically a banner year for films with sympathetic or at the very least relatable German characters. There was Hanna Schmitz, the illiterate concentration camp guard in *The Reader*; John Halder, the literature professor turned Nazi in *Good*; and the doomed eight-year-old Bruno in *The Boy in the Striped Pajamas.* The character of Liesel Meminger in *The Book Thief* (2013) is merely a variation of Hanna Schmitz. This time, she's a nice German who cannot read. At bottom, films like *The Reader, The Book Thief,* and *Amen* are unsettling not because they depict complex perpetrators; in this, they do a service. They are an important, popular extension of academic works like Christopher Browning's *Ordinary Men,* which demonstrates that non-Nazis could be just as murderous as the SS. Instead, these films are troubling because they almost completely elide the victims as subjects of the narrative. Their experiences seem merely utilitarian, a means to provide context for the perpetrators' stories and motivations. The most egregious case in this regard is *The Boy in the Striped Pajamas,* where the German rather than the Jewish child seems to be the target of audience concern at the end of the film.

The Grey Zone (2001) is another film that muddies the boundaries of perpetrator and victim, and although I think it is one of the most gripping and visceral fictionalized accounts of the Holocaust, I can understand its critics who find problematic the casting of recognizable stars (particularly comedian David Arquette) as well as its general premise. In terms of sheer box office numbers, the film was a flop, garnering little over $500,000 in total, compared with the approximately $320 million for *Schindler's List*. But writer/director Tim Blake Nelson clearly set out to construct an anti-*Schindler,* a film with no heroes and no redemption, basing his script on two very difficult sources: Primo Levi's 1988 essay, "The Grey Zone," and Miklos Nyiszli's memoir, *Auschwitz: A Doctor's Eyewitness Account*, which chronicles Nyiszli's experiences as a Hungarian Jewish prisoner and conscripted assistant to camp doctor, Josef Mengele.[7] The film operates on various levels. On one, befitting its title, *The Grey Zone* is a tale of moral ambiguity. On another level, the film is an unflinching look into the heart of the Nazi genocidal beast, offering some of the most graphic cinematic depictions of the gassing operation inside Auschwitz. By anchoring his story to a unit of Hungarian Jewish *Sonderkommandos*, one of a number of units of inmates forced to work in the gas chambers and crematoria until they themselves were gassed, Blake Nelson leads his audience into uncomfortable territory, to a place where spectators are forced to witness re-enactments of murder and to sit in judgment of the victims whose work, however coerced, served the Nazi murder program.

The Hungarian film, *Fateless* (2005, directed by Lajos Koltai), an adaptation of Imre Kertész' 1975 semi-autobiographical novel translated as *Fatelessness* in English, is perhaps a more effective depiction of horror and moral equivocality. The book focuses on the experiences of a 15-year-old Hungarian Jewish boy, Gyuri, during World War II, recounting his incarceration in a number of concentration camps, from Auschwitz to Buchenwald. The film and novel are unique in a number of ways. There are few cinematic representations of the Holocaust in Hungarian, and certainly few Hungarian films manage to break into the US independent market. More to theme, *Fateless* is unique in its tone. The prose of the novel is almost dreamlike, and the movie retains this. There are tableaux of the concentration camps, and they often proceed without dialogue. The audience simply sees Gyuri progressively deteriorate until the film becomes almost unwatchable. Then there is Gyuri's own assessment of the camp experience at the end of the film, which remains difficult to unpack. Kertész, through his character, Gyuri, seems to operate in a psychic no man's land, lacking any special ties to his Jewish heritage or to Israel and rejected by his country of origin, resulting in the belief that neither his Hungarian heritage nor Jewishness will guide his fate.[8]

In addition to the more abstruse messaging advanced in films like *The Grey Zone* and *Fateless*, audiences now have to contend with the use of comedic frameworks to tell the story of the Holocaust. Satires depicting the Nazi regime have a longstanding history, from Ernst Lubitsch's *To Be or Not to Be* from 1942 to Mel Brooks' *Producers* from 1968, and even Jerry Lewis' never to be released film from 1972, *The Day the Clown Cried*. In 1997, Italian filmmaker and actor Roberto Benigni waded into these problematic waters with the release of the film, *Life is Beautiful,* which featured Benigni as an Italian Jew who marries a non-Jew, winds up incarcerated in a camp with his young son, and attempts to shield him from the horror by making it seem as if the entire experience is just a game. Although the film won an Academy Award for Best Foreign Language Film, it generated strong opposition from some scholars, such as Kobi Niv, who in his book, *Life is Beautiful, but Not for Jews,* took issue with the "sham normality" of Benigni's concentration camp. Niv criticized Benigni's decision to remove the horrors of the camp for the audience, much as Benigni's character did for his son in the film.[9] He also decried the choice of character names. Benigni's character, Guido, who dies, could be seen as Judas expiating the sin of the Jews, allowing his son Joshua (Jesus?) to live happily ever after with his Christian mother. Peter Kassovitz's 1999 film, *Jakob the Liar,* a remake of a 1975 East German/Czech production but with the recognizable Robin Williams in the lead role of Jakob, fared even more poorly. A flop with both critics and movie goers, *Jakob the Liar* deals with a Jew in an unnamed ghetto who raises the morale of fellow inhabitants with lies about a Russian advance. The one part of the film that seems to operate on multiple levels is the final scene, when Jakob, who has been executed, narrates in voiceover the fate of his fellow Jews in the ghetto. He says that although they have been deported to a death camp, it is possible they have actually been rescued by the very

Russians about whom he has been lying. So while the audience sees a happy ending, it is consciously ambiguous, and the likelihood remains that this is just another ruse. With Quentin Tarantino's *Inglourious Basterds,* as well as his more recent *Django Unchained,* we have the trope of comedy stretched to its breaking point, as comedy-drama gives way to revenge fantasy – a format hailed by some critics but derided by others, like David Mendelsohn, who lamented how Tarantino managed to turn Jews into Nazis.[10]

In a 1987 review of comedic literature on the Holocaust, scholar Terrence Des Pres took issue with what he saw as the limits set on Holocaust representation, i.e., that it should be approached as a "sacred," unique event and that depictions of it should be as "accurate and faithful as possible to the facts and conditions of the event, without change or manipulation for any reason."[11] He argued in defense of humor and satire, declaring that the "value of the comic approach is that by setting things at a distance it permits us a tougher, more active response."[12] But this statement begs a host of questions, namely, does not the dramatic approach do the same thing? Is comedy more effective if we are dealing with a recreated account or something completely fictional? Are there simply some subjects which cannot achieve the kind of impact through the trope of comedy? Des Pres did not lay out criteria for the effective use of comedy in ventilating Holocaust narratives. In fact, in his conclusion, he seemed to qualify his approval, saying that the novels he was evaluating in his essay were basically serious but that they incorporated some comic elements. They recognized first and foremost the gravity of the universe into which they were venturing. Films like *Life is Beautiful* and *Jakob the Liar* both do that, while *Inglourious Basterds* does not, so why do critics generally regard the first and third as good films, while rejecting the second? In fact, of the three, *Jakob the Liar* is perhaps the most earnest and desirous to achieve verisimilitude, and it ends on a more depressing note than either *Life* or *Inglourious.* A comparison to the original East German version of *Jakob the Liar* from 1975 (*Jakob der Lügner*) is helpful here, suggesting that it is not necessarily the genre of comedy that is the problem but the way in which a particular story is constructed within the framework of that genre. Peter Stack, writing in 1999 for the *San Francisco Chronicle* in advance of a limited run of the East German film, argued that its "beauty ... is its simplicity. There's no mugging for comedic effect, no pat jokes, no elaborate fantasies ...

slowly the vise of history closes on this decent, innocent man, and the viewer is simply left speechless."[13]

Comedy can therefore work as a means of representing the Holocaust, but because of the dangers it poses to the seriousness of the subject, film-makers should proceed with caution. A semi-comedic movie with a Holocaust story that works, in my assessment, is *Everything is Illuminated*, from 2005, based on Jonathan Safran Foer's novel, which follows a fictional journey to Ukraine by Foer in search of a woman who (in this alternative universe) saved his grandfather during the German occupation. The comedy of the film, which underscores the cultural clash between an American Jew and his Ukrainian travel guides, allows the audience to acclimate itself to what is unfamiliar geography. The comedy also recedes once the complex details about Foer's grandfather and the secret identity of his elder Ukrainian guide unfold. Thus, the comedic elements serve more as commentary not only about two peoples who know next to nothing about each other, but also on the absurdity of contemporary life in the wake of World War II. The movie and novel are more about the present and remembering the past in a region of the world little known to most Americans and still insufficiently explored in Anglo-American scholarship.

An even more unexpected exploration into the Holocaust is the Chinese animated fantasy, *A Jewish Girl in Shanghai* (2010), based on the novel by Wu Lin. Well-drawn in anime style, the film has garnered praise, and it has done much to improve Sino-Israeli relations, but I would argue that, like the bulk of its comedic counterparts, it is also ineffective. In this case, it is not that the film is insensitive or degenerates into phony sentimentalism (although there is a good deal of that). Rather, my criticism has to do with the film's conflation of the Holocaust with the Chinese resistance against the Japanese occupation. At one point in the film, the heroine, Rina, a Jewish child who was able to flee with her brother from Poland to Shanghai in the early days of the war, plays her violin before her Japanese captors, but she refuses to play something pro-Japanese, so she becomes more a symbol of China's defiance, rather than a victim of Nazi genocide.

Refracting other historical narratives through the prism of the Holocaust is not a new cinematic device. In fact, there is a pattern in Israeli films of using the Holocaust as a metaphor for life in war-torn Israel. For instance, Ilan Moshenson's *The Wooden Gun* (1979) tells the tale of a gang war between young Israeli kids who ridicule their Holocaust survivor parents, in an inter-generational allegory about Israel's potentially violent future. Two more recent Israeli films from the past decade, *Walk on Water* (2004) and *Ha-Chov* or *The Debt* (2007, remade in 2011), address the dilemma posed by Israelis exacting revenge for the Holocaust. While both films have slightly different conclusions, they share a similar message; vengeance and lies corrode. *Walk on Water*, directed by Eytan Fox, is both a film on the role of Holocaust memory in constructing Israeli national consciousness, as well as a discourse on sexuality and politics. Its main character Ayal, a Mossad agent whose wife has committed suicide because of her husband's occupation, is sent undercover to kill a Nazi war criminal whose grandchildren, Pia and Axel (who is gay), are in Israel. Ultimately, Ayal rejects the course of revenge, and it is grandson Axel who takes his grandfather's life, thus expiating the sin of that generation and allowing Ayal to move past the cycle of violence.[14] *The Debt* also deals with an effort by Israeli agents to kidnap a Nazi, this time a doctor by the name of Max Rainer, a fictionalized incarnation of the infamous "Angel of Death" at Auschwitz, Josef Mengele. Similar to Mengele, who eluded Israeli captors, Rainer manages to escape after an initial capture, and the protagonists choose to fabricate a story that they killed him during this attempted flight and then disposed of his body. Decades later, news that the doctor is still alive leads the agents to a Ukrainian nursing home, where they have to carry out his execution both for restitution and to prevent their lie from being revealed. They also have to come to grips with their past failure. At neither task are they successful. One agent commits suicide, leaving the lead agent, Rachel Brener, played by Gila Almagor, to carry out her mission, which she does at the end in a gruesome scene in which both she and the doctor wind up stabbed multiple times over, and both ultimately die.

Two recent Holocaust dramas, *Sarah's Key* (2010, directed by Gilles Paquet-Brenner) and *Esther's Diary* (originally titled *Forgiveness*, from 2008, directed by Mariusz Kotowski) serve as equal parts commentary on Holocaust memory and present-day life. In this case, the settings are France and the United States, respectively. Although both productions feature multiple, intertwined storylines, the disparity between the two is vast. *Sarah's Key* relates the experiences of French Jews deported to their deaths in 1942. Sarah is a Jewish girl who tries to help her brother hide during the deportations by locking him into a secret compartment and keeping the key, not realizing that she would never be allowed to return, thus inadvertently facilitating his death. Years later, a journalist named Julia Jarmond, played by Kristen Scott Thomas, uncovers the mystery of the key and Sarah's fate while writing a piece on the July 1942 round-up of the Jews of Paris. She is also set to move into Sarah's old apartment with her fiancé, whose family took possession of the unit after the deportations. There are related subplots as well, including storylines about Julia's fiancé who wants her to have an abortion and her quest to find Sarah and her son (who wound up in Italy). While critics by and large recommended the film, I felt that the French production from around the same time entitled *La Rafle* (*The Round Up*, directed by Rose Bosch), which also deals with the fate of Parisian Jews in 1942, is better in part because of its straightforward plotting – based on the true story of survivor Joseph Weismann, who escaped from the Beaune la Rolande concentration camp. Both *Sarah's Key* and *The Round-Up* feature gripping images of the suffering which Jews endured at the hands of both German and French officials, and the portrayal of French collaboration is especially open and honest. They show the horrific conditions which Jews endured in the city's cycling arena (the Velodrom d'Hiver), where they were brought by French police in July 1942 before their deportation to Beaune la Rolande and then Auschwitz and where they had to endure for days without adequate food, water, or sanitation. Both films also have their share of problems. With *Sarah's Key* it's the convoluted plot; with *La Rafle*, it is the odd juxtaposition of scenes with Hitler and Himmler, which seem out of place and almost cartoonish. But *Round Up* is clearly a tale of the Holocaust in France, while *Sarah's Key* does not know what it wants to be. Is it about the experience of French Jews during the Nazi occupation? Is it a mystery? Is it a story about post-traumatic stress disorder? Is it a statement about relationships? In trying to be all of these, *Sarah's Key* collapses under the weight of its intricate plotting.

With *Esther's Diary*, a film that uses an eponymous diary to relay a Holocaust narrative, the problem is not intricacy, but the exact opposite. Images that feel appropriated from *Night and Fog*, and music evocative of *Schindler's List* pervade the film, which centers on two women: Maria, a psychology professor and radio-host, and Sarah, the descendant of a Holocaust survivor who was at once helped and betrayed by Maria's ancestors. The film has the feel of a low budget made-for-television melo-drama, with shoddy acting and dialogue like: "Tell them they'll never feel alone as long as they carry you in their hearts;" "I'm not afraid of dying. I faced death at an early age. When death is all around you, your soul changes;" and "I had a good day. Who am I kidding? I had a fucking rot-ten day."[15] The most ridiculous, and in my opinion, offensive moment in the movie involves the revelation that Maria's husband is having an affair, analogous to the pairing of the abortion/Holocaust storylines in *Sarah's Key*. It is this climactic event, coupled with the death of her mother, which leads Maria to set off for Poland on a quest to master her past. As the title of the famous work by historian Charles Maier aptly suggested, the history of the Holocaust might well be unmasterable.[16] And films like *Esther's Diary* do not allow audiences of any generation an effective interrogation of that past. It is unthinkable that this film would be the last word on the subject of the Holocaust from an American production company.

A more respectable Polish film from recent years is *In Darkness* (2011), based on Robert Marshall's monograph, *In the Sewers of Lvov*,[17] which chronicles the survival of a handful of Jews with the help of Lvov sewer inspector, Leopold Socha, who, along with his wife, is among the 6000 Poles recognized by Yad Vashem as Righteous among the Nations. Directed by Agnieszka Holland, who also directed the 1990 Holocaust film *Europa, Europa*, about a Jewish boy who passed as a German, *In Darkness* mirrors the turn in scholarship towards incorporating sexuality and gender into the Holocaust narrative, with its graphic depiction of sexual intercourse and pregnancy (and subsequent infanticide, which is fortunately only described rather than shown). The film is also in many ways the Polish *Schindler's List*, with its focus on a non-Jewish hero. In fact, although one of the Jewish survivors, Krystyna Chiger, wrote a memoir of her experience in the sewers, entitled *The Girl in the Green Sweater: A Life in the Holocaust's Shadow*,[18] we learn little about her in the film. She helps merely to establish the setting of the sewers – the hunger, boredom, fear, and increasing indif-ference to the vermin and filth. She suffers in the darkness with her family, but it is the drama above ground with Socha that is once again the primary focus of the audience's gaze.

By contrast, Władysław' Pasikowski's *Pokłosie* (*Aftermath*) from 2012 does not offer comfort or gratitude. Based loosely on Jan Gross' book

Neighbors, which chronicles the murder in 1941 of 1600 Jews by Poles in the small town of Jedwabne, the film forces its Polish audience to confront an unsettling history. The film's protagonist, Franciszek Kalina, returns to his hometown after living in Chicago for a number of years to reconnect with his brother Jozef. Franciszek stumbles upon remnants of a Jewish cemetery in the woods, and he begins to do research into the history of the town during the war, which sets off the natives. Meanwhile, his brother, overcome with guilt, uses the tombstones to create a makeshift memorial in his field, and his neighbors vandalize his home and eventually murder him in a shocking, and almost unbelievable way. (Franciszek finds Jozef crucified on the door of his barn). As with *In Darkness, Aftermath* has a likable Polish protagonist, but here, he has been Americanized. Meanwhile, the depiction of native Poles is uncompromisingly negative. After watching the Academy Award winning 2013 film *Ida,* by Pawel Pawlikowski, about a nun who discovers that she is Jewish and who seeks out her communist aunt to visit the village of her murdered parents, I get the sense that Polish filmmakers are having difficulty representing Jews as Jews – not as archetypes – Jews as victims, hidden Catholics, or bad communists, but rather as ordinary people. More subtlety and nuance are in order going forward as Poles grapple with the dual absence in their midst – the absence of Jews and the absence of an honest collective memory. Institutionalizing Holocaust and Jewish education in Poland is particularly pressing. In its 2014 survey of global anti-Semitism, the Anti-Defamation League found Poland to be the most antisemitic country in eastern Europe.[19]

So where does that leave us? Is there any hope of regaining some effectiveness in the cinematic representation of the Holocaust? I believe, first of all, that representation is legitimate and possible and that popular forums such as cinema, literature, music, and art are legitimate arenas in which to carry on a discourse about the Holocaust. Their reach and potential to inform are simply too vast to discount. That being said, films are just a gateway or an access point to knowledge, and they certainly should not be the final or sole sources of information. Watching a film about the Holocaust should inspire deeper and more rigorous inquiry into the subject, and because of film's potential to misinform, which deniers can seize upon, it behooves filmmakers to do their homework and create an environment that is as faithfully recreated as possible. They need to conduct research, preferably in multiple languages, into the history and historiography of the setting for their particular stories. They should shoot on actual locations and use indigenous actors or non-actors in order to present a tableau that approaches an agreed consensus and memory of the real. I am inclined to believe that the better Holocaust films are based on accounts that actually happened, and indeed, films that are more docudrama than completely fictionalized, such as *Diary of Anne Frank, Judgment at Nuremberg,* and *Schindler's List,* continue to rank highly among critics, and their attention to historical detail is as much a part of this as the overall quality of direction, writing, and acting.[20] There are groundbreaking films in the fictional realm as well, like *The Pawnbroker* and *Everything is Illuminated,* but these films have authentic settings and, more importantly, center on the lingering impact of trauma on survivors and their descendants. They allow the audience into as real an environment as possible, and they do not shy away from the "ruins of memory," to quote Lawrence Langer,[21] but in fact they foreground their stories in the psychological toll wrought by genocide. So second to historicity should be personalization and representation of trauma in all its forms on all levels.

If I were asked about what subjects I would like to see covered in Holocaust films, I would respond that there are currently 50,000 testimonies of survivors in Steven Spielberg's Shoah Foundation, now the University of Southern California Shoah Institute. Many of them touch on topics and come from regions which historians have only recently begun to explore, such as escapes from mass shootings in Belarus, Latvia, and Lithuania, and the role in which non-Nazi killers played in the executions. There is also so much more the general public needs to know about Jewish life in Europe before the Holocaust, and then during the Holocaust, how the killing centers in Poland functioned.[22] The Hungarian film, *Son of Saul* (2015), which won the the Academy Award for Best Foreign Language Film, is notable in this regard, but one could make the argument that in its fusion of *The Grey Zone's* content with *Fateless'* form, it does not so much break new cinematic ground as refine it. More representation of non-Jewish victims of the Holocaust – Roma-Sinti, people with disabilities, gay men and lesbians, Jehovah's Witnesses, and Soviet POWs – would further enrich the body of cinematic work on the subject. Films such as *And the Violins Stopped Playing* (1988) and *Korkoro* (*Alone* or *Free*, 2009) have begun the process of representing the experiences of Roma-Sinti during the Holocaust. Both films focus on groups of Roma who face deportation (Hungarian Roma in *And the Violins,* and Roma in France in *Korkoro*).[23] Both films are flawed offerings, too, with stereotypical images of Roma as soil-averse violinists and criminals. *Korkoro* also features two French protagonists, a man and a woman, who risk their lives to save the Roma troupe as part of their resistance against the German occupation. Although the film is based on a true story, it is revealing that the heroism of the French characters co-exists with, and perhaps even supersedes, Roma suffering in the film's narrative; moreover, the man survives while the woman and the Roma are deported. Whether intentional or not, the fact that this particular story was able to be told over other narratives reflects the tendency of filmmakers to play to an audience's desire for in-group male heroes.

I am hopeful that in the future more filmmakers will choose to venture into the above-mentioned sub-themes of the Holocaust and to do so in the creative, feature format, but I am aware of the forces against this prospect. The documentary form, which was outside the scope of this essay, is probably more appropriate for Holocaust representation, although, as the dispute between Claude Lanzmann and Jean-Luc Godard over Holocaust imagery attests, documentaries are not necessarily any less controversial than feature films.[24] Moreover, my critique of "post-modern" content and form and preference for a more "modernist" focus on trauma and historicity might seem outdated. The notions that "this has been done before" or "this is too difficult to watch" are powerful obstacles to new Holocaust cinema, and even films which tackle big questions and tell relatively unknown stories and which receive an initial green light might never see the light of day. Such appears to be the case for Israeli filmmaker Eytan Fox's bio-pic of gay Jewish survivor Gad Beck. Reports in 2008 circulated that Fox had signed on to the project, but as of this writing, the film is in limbo.[25] Viktor Frankl's memoir, *Man's Search for Meaning,* has also recently been optioned (as of June 2015), and it will be interesting to see, again assuming it makes its way to a premiere, how it balances its discourses of trauma and hope. In the end, it appears that the era of Holocaust representation in feature films from the Hollywood system is at best treading water, and although there is continued narrative exploration of the topic by European and Israeli

8

Slaughter in China on Film: Nanjing and "Saving Asia" through Mutilation

Mark V. DeStephano

Saint Peter's University, Jersey City, New Jersey

One of the pivotal historical events of the twentieth century, the Nanjing Massacre of 1937, also set the stage for the twenty-first century struggle between Japan and China. Nanjing (Nanking), which had intermittently been the capital of China for centuries, had been the military objective of Japanese forces since their invasion in 1931.[1] As can be imagined, the facts of what actually happened at Nanjing are confused and much contested, both for historiographical and political reasons.[2] While many historians date the massacre as occurring after the fall of the city on December 13, 1937, others, such as the Nazi John Rabe, who was arguably the most important witness to the tragedy, consider the massacre to have begun in early September, when random air raids began.[3] Especially controversial are the methods of counting victims and the actual number of those slaughtered. For example, by the reckoning of most Japanese historians, 40,000 to 200,000 were killed, whereas by Chinese accounts at least 300,000 were slaughtered, and by Nazi German testimony close to 500,000 perished.[4] There is even a dispute as to who was a "victim." Among those killed, who were the "civilians" and who were the "combatants?" Were the Japanese truly aggressors, or the saviors of an Asia that was precariously balanced over the abyss of Western domination?[5] Were the killings of the citizens of Nanjing simply a collateral effect of war, or was their killing an act of genocide?[6] When did the "Massacre of Nanjing" end, on January 30 or March 28, 1938, or on some other date?[7]

The cinematic medium is uniquely suited to offer viewers both the "truth" of historical "fact" as well as the "truth" of "fictional" representations of events, which seek to portray possible interior responses of participants in those events. This study will examine three sets of genocidal atrocities perpetrated by the Japanese in China, as they are portrayed by Chinese filmmakers: (1) the massacre at Nanking (*Black Sun: The Nanking Massacre*, 1995); (2) the mutilation of "comfort women" as part of the Nanking Massacre (*City of Life and Death*, 2009); and, (3) the rape of teenage schoolgirls by Japanese soldiers (*Flowers of War*, 2011). Through these films, Chinese filmmakers have attempted to give flesh and bones to the horrifying genocidal atrocities perpetrated in China by Japanese armed forces between 1931 and 1945. Perhaps more importantly, however, is their ability to show that these unspeakable acts also took a terrible toll on ordinary Japanese soldiers, many of whom were pawns and victims in the savage geopolitical games of their delusional leaders.

Black Sun: The Nanking Massacre (1995)

One of the earliest, and perhaps the most powerful of the Chinese films to portray the slaughter at Nanjing, Mou Dun Fei's *Black Sun: The Nanking Massacre* (1995)[8] assumes a strongly nationalistic position in its initial and final framing of the events of the tragedy. The film begins with the statement that it is, "Dedicated to all war victims, to commemorate the fiftieth anniversary of the successful conclusion of the Campaign of Resistance," which reflects a later Chinese construal of national attempts to combat occupying Japanese troops during the period of 1931 to 1945 as an organized movement. In point of fact, Chinese resistance was, at best, a piecemeal opposition, which was at times directed by forces of Chiang Kai-shek's Nationalist government and on other occasions was spearheaded by the forces of Mao Zedong's Communist insurgency. Director Mou Dun Fei immediately and starkly reveals his ideological position by next projecting what will be the theme of *Black Sun*:

On September 4, 1937, the Emperor Hirohito issued an imperial directive on the conduct of the Greater East-Asia War. It deliberately avoided reference that the Japanese military abide by the rules of warfare set by international treaties. This set the stage for the forthcoming atrocities in the Nanking Massacre.[9]

Mou unapologetically lays the blame for the slaughter at Nanjing on Emperor Hirohito for having given Japanese soldiers, in his opinion, permission to perpetrate whatever inhumane acts of savagery they wished, without any consideration for common humanity or fear of consequences. As if to defend the thesis he has just proposed, Mou then presents historical footage of Japanese troops destroying everything in their path as they sweep through China, and he establishes a strictly historical timeline that brings the audience back to July 7, 1937, which the director defines as the origin of hostilities: "Then a full-scale war with China began." Mou carefully juxtaposes text with historical footage, helping viewers to understand the chronology of Japanese aggression that led up to the terrible destruction at Nanjing: the machine-gun assault at Luguo (Marco Polo) Bridge on July 7, 1937, the attack on Shanghai on August 13, and the fall of Shanghai, Suzhou, and Songjiang in November. This series of Chinese defeats necessitated the transfer of China's capital to Chongqing on November 20, but did not stop the Japanese juggernaut that rushed towards Nanjing, the former capital.

Black Sun's reenactment of events now begins, as Mou shifts from black-and-white film to color, and brings viewers into the streets as invading Japanese wade through scores of dead bodies of men, women, and children. As they advance, the Japanese soldiers gun down unarmed citizens and break into local homes, committing untold acts of violence such as rape and murder of people of all ages. The first occupying troops are shown slaughtering Chinese citizens mercilessly, as they are ordered by their officers to, "Kill, kill, kill, kill." Mou carefully builds a case against the Japanese perpetrators as he masterfully recreates a filmic rendition of what had been the testimony of Chinese witnesses and victims of the atrocities. So as to remind spectators that he has in no way strayed from documentary evidence of the savage events, even though his film is a creative work, the director assiduously precedes each reenactment with historical footage.

In this way, Mou creates a film that is akin to a scholarly article, complete with a thesis statement, detailed proof, and even the equivalent of footnotes. He underscores the fact that *Black Sun* is not simply the product of the Chinese imagination by presenting a scene in which the Japanese officers are being filmed and interviewed regarding their successful entrance into Nanjing. Major General Sasaki Touichi voices what Mou asserts to be the Japanese command's general plan regarding its advance into China:

> History is being made. The Japanese Empire will control all Asia. This is the trend of history. I feel honored and proud to be a soldier of the Japanese Empire. If these intimidation methods work, all of China will surrender soon. Then the war will be over. It would be more fortunate for the Chinese. It will be a lot of work to establish a new Asia.[10]

Mou's reconstruction of events next leads spectators into the Japanese command center on December 2, 1937, as General Matsui Iwane (1878–1948) issues orders to subdue all of Nanjing, or, as an officer explains the operation, "The rest of the troops are cleaning up the city."

General Matsui is informed that there were over 50,000 Chinese soldiers in the city, but that Major General Sasaki's forces have killed 20,000 and captured the rest. What is to be done with them? Matsui remarks that the uncle of Emperor Hirohito, Prince Asaka Yasuhiko (1887–1981), had issued an order to kill all prisoners of war and not to leave any behind.[11] Mou clearly espouses this interpretation of historical fact and then orders Matsui to "tell the soldiers to start a killing competition; headquarters will reward the soldiers," which is also one of the most highly disputed facts of the entire Nanjing Massacre.

An interesting twist in Mou's film is his inclusion of the voice of Japanese samurai Takayama Kenshi, who engages in a discussion with his good friend Lieutenant General Nakajima Kesago (Kyogo) as to who the greatest samurai was and what the proper use of the sword should be. Takayama notes that the most famous swordsman of ancient Japan, Masamune, believed that the sword should not be used as an instrument for killing. He further asserts that the even sharper swords produced by Masamune's disciple Mura Masa, "represent the threatening power of a dictator." Nakajima disagrees, bluntly stating that, "When the enemy sees the sword, they both fear and respect it." Takayama makes the significant observation that unless the soldier has a conscience and is aware that the sword should be used for peaceful purposes, "then it becomes evil." Mou's purpose in including this scene is twofold. First, it presages the thousands of deaths of innocent Chinese perpetrated by Japanese officers with their swords. On a more conciliatory note, the director also acknowledges that the samurai tradition in and of itself is not evil. Through the voice of Takayama, Mou stresses Masamune's greatness – not simply because he was the finest swordsman in the history of Japan, but, more importantly, because he came to believe that the sword should not be used for killing. Nakajima now reiterates the Japanese army's plan for victory, this time in terms of the sword: "To deal with the Chinese, you must hold a sword …This sword is for destroying all who block Buddha's teachings. In order to have a prosperous new Asia, this must be a holy war."[12] He further explains that the war in China is not just for the purpose of creating the Greater East Asia Co-Prosperity Sphere, which had been proposed by the Japanese Foreign Ministry in 1938, but rather because, "It is also a dream to reform the world and save humanity." Takayama urges using force first, and education later. The scene is followed by Nakajima's bloody "testing" of his new sword by severing off the heads of seven bound and kneeling Chinese. The powerful and thought-provoking sequence ends with historical footage of a beheading at Nanjing, just as the head flies off the body of an innocent victim. Mou impresses his viewers with the factual nature of all of these atrocities by providing extensive historical footage of them being committed, including scenes of doctors in the International Refugee Zone showing and explaining the horrific wounds that survivors have sustained.

Black Sun continues to chronicle other Japanese acts of savagery that are documented in historical footage, but in the second half focuses the spectator's attention more on the ideological conflict within the ranks of the Japanese high command. Imperial generals bicker among themselves as to whose unit should claim the glory for the Japanese occupation of Nanjing. Lieutenant General Nakajima is informed that the Emperor has issued an edict, stating that he is "satisfied with the quick occupation of Nanking" and urging that imperial soldiers should "clean up the remains of the Chinese army." The Japanese believe that many of these soldiers are now hiding in civilian dress in the "International Safety Zone." Lieutenant General Tani Hisao urges that Japanese troops kill every Chinese person they find, stating coldly: "This will make them fear us. It will end the war and reduce casualties."[13] The ideological climax of the film comes when Mou stages a meeting of all of the officers of the Japanese high command, in which critical observations that have been made throughout the film are reiterated at once. For example, Lieutenant General Tani notes that, unlike the Russo-Japanese War and the Qing Dynasty War, the emperor's order to conduct the capture of China did not insist that international rules of war be observed; this, he argues, is not accidental. Another officer states that the soldiers have "terrible discipline," while Lieutenant General Nakajima observes that the men have just won a great victory and that, therefore, "To have more leeway with the rules is not asking much." But in a moment of tremendous tension, yet another officer pointedly asks: "You mean slaughtering, burning, and raping are mere relaxation of the rules?" Defending all of the atrocities, Tani finally remarks, "In this conflict many heroes were made." The most powerful question of the entire film is now spoken by another officer: "Killing women, children, and the disabled; how can that be called heroism?" Tani lamely responds, "Those who won are heroes … Only the winners have honor." Near the end of the film, Mou recalls the historical memory of a China enslaved by foreign domination, a threat that is now re-imagined by the conquering Japanese: "The Chinese are large in numbers and hard working. We must train them like oxen to work for men. Opium should enslave them very well."[14] As the film continues, many more savage acts are chronicled, each followed by footage of the actual event. The film's action ends with the following declaration:

> After Nanjing was occupied by the Japanese army, massive burning, killing, raping, and plundering continued for six weeks. Males, females, old, and young – none were spared. The atrocities were even worse than those shown in this film. This was not a war. It was an intentional, planned, and organized massacre.[15]

Mou completes his masterpiece with silence and then scrolls a list of victims so as to account for the Chinese estimate of 300,000 slaughtered.

Black Sun ends with the sobering verdict of the International Military Tribunal of the Far East, followed by a reporting of the sentences of each of the Japanese war criminals:

> According to the verdict of the war crimes tribunal in 1947, the Japanese army was judged to have raped over 20,000 women, and killed 300,000 Chinese during the Nanjing Massacre. One third of the city was destroyed. Property was plundered at unestimated losses. No family was spared.[16]

Mou's somber and carefully-documented study powerfully underscores the fact that, just like the innocent Chinese who were slaughtered, many ordinary Japanese soldiers – and the honor and conscience of the Japanese nation – were unalterably and forever scarred at Nanjing.

City of Life and Death (2009)

A remarkable film both because of its exploration of a hotly debated issue and because of its technical virtuosity, director Lu Chuan's *City of Life and Death* (2009)[17] chronicles the experiences of a young Japanese soldier, Kadokawa Masao, as he carries out his orders in Nanjing. Near the beginning of the film, which the director shot in black and white to create a somber and depressing atmosphere, Kadokawa's unit receives orders to pursue fleeing Chinese soldiers. Entering a nearby church, they find it filled with Chinese who are surrendering, including many Chinese soldiers. The Japanese, who appear to be terrified, call for reinforcements, but are still greatly outnumbered. At one point, a group of women push the soldiers away from a confessional box, leading the Japanese to believe that they are hiding a group of armed Chinese soldiers. Kadokawa gathers some of his comrades and fires into the confessional, only to have a number of dead women fall out onto the floor. Kadokawa, almost in shock, laments, "I didn't mean to ..." The scene ends with Kadokawa's comrades dragging him away as he tries to go to the dead women.

Later, a band of Chinese soldiers ambushes Kadokawa and his unit. All around him, Kadokawa's colleagues are gunned down, but one of their number manages to escape and sound a siren, calling for reinforcements. The Japanese come in force, destroying everything in their path with tanks and a large number of ground forces, rapidly winning the engagement. As Kadokawa staggers away, he sees Chinese soldiers, including one little boy dressed as a soldier (who, as we shall later learn, is Xiaodou), tied to posts along the street. As some Japanese soldiers shout, "Banzai!" Kadokawa sees

123

others looting. Dead bodies are strewn everywhere, and other Japanese soldiers are executing a group of civilians. A group of bound women is led off, and, as he continues along, Kadokawa passes the naked body of a dead woman. All around he sees dead bodies hanging from telephone poles, and civilians are being shot as quickly as they appear. Even more ominous is the forest of severed heads hanging from cords. Death and destruction are everywhere.

After participating in the burning of a building filled with hundreds of Chinese prisoners, Kadokawa and the other Japanese soldiers, who have been forced to kill tens of thousands of unarmed soldiers and non-combatants, find time to rest and play. Kadokawa visits the quarters of comfort women, where he meets Yuriko, a beautiful young Japanese woman. Kadokawa is inexperienced in sexual practice and recoils in fear as the woman begins to attend to him. So, kindly and sweetly, she tries to relax the young man, who folds his head into her breast and tells her his name. Yuriko cannot help but cry. For his part, Kadokawa tells another soldier that, "That is the kind of woman I want to marry." Later in the film, when he returns to her, Yuriko does not recognize him, as she almost mechanically lies down and invites him to use her. Even after he has told her his name and they begin to make love, she still does not know him. Through this, director Lu underscores the near impossibility of establishing human intimacy in this situation of suffering and uncontrolled brutality. In as much as Kadokawa wishes to step away from the events at Nanjing, even the woman he has come to love has become so dehumanized that mutual feelings of love cannot possibly develop.

After witnessing numerous acts of barbarism committed by his fellow soldiers, Kadokawa finds it increasingly difficult to perform his duties, or, at times, to stand back from the brutality. At one point, he witnesses a cart of dead, naked women being carried off from the area of the comfort women. Kadokawa is saddened to the core. In yet another shocking scene, a young Chinese woman who has been working with refugees in the international safety zone has been trying to save the lives of some men who are about to be led off to execution. The woman is eventually detected and is being led away by a group of soldiers. Suddenly, a shot rings out; Kadokawa has shot the woman in the back of the head, saving her from untold indignities that she was to suffer at the hands of her captors. His disillusionment increases deeply when he goes to visit Yuriko, only to find that she has died at the front, where she had been sent to serve the troops. Totally crestfallen, Kadokawa simply murmurs, "She was once my wife. Yuriko was once my wife."

In the penultimate scene of the film, the Japanese celebrate their great conquest of Nanjing. Kadokawa dances down the street with his fellow soldiers, and, when the troops cry out in victorious shouts, he looks to the sun, contorts his face, and lets out a heart-wrenching scream that comes from the depths of his soul. In the final scene, he and another soldier are leading two bound prisoners, the former Chinese soldier Shunzi and the "boy soldier", Xiaodou, out into the fields. Kadokawa orders the other soldier to cut the prisoners loose; solemnly, he comments that "Life is more difficult than death." Kadokawa then salutes his comrade, who bows to him, and sadly walks away. Suddenly, the soldier turns around and shouts, "Kadokawa!" and bows profoundly. The final moments of the film show Kadokawa, on his haunches, crying. He puts a gun to his head and fires, instantly killing himself. Meanwhile, Shunzi and Xiaodou continue to walk, laughing and playing. The film ends with the presentation of a series of memorial cards, the last one being that of Xiaodou, who, the caption tells us, is still alive.

Perhaps the most moving of the three films discussed, *City of Life and Death* is a masterful portrayal of the terrible sufferings endured by both the Chinese people and by many of the Japanese soldiers who perpetrated unspeakable atrocities in Nanjing in 1937. While there is no question that Japanese troops were culpable for the wholesale slaughter of hundreds of thousands of Chinese, both combatants and non-combatants, the creators of *City of Life and Death* choose to let the true tragedy of the events at Nanjing be mirrored in their effects upon those who committed them. The egregiously violent actions of the Japanese more than speak for themselves, as we have seen both in this film and in *Black Sun: The Nanking Massacre*. The writer and producers of *City of Life and Death*, who are all Chinese, have achieved the nearly impossible task of producing a profound sense of sympathy for Kadokawa in viewers, even though he must participate in some of the horrors of the Japanese conquest of Nanjing. What is more, the film attempts to perform an extremely powerful function – to enact a form of acceptance of guilt and restitution. Whereas the Japanese government has, to date, not offered an official apology for the actions of its army at Nanjing, this filmic masterpiece offers something of a culturally vicarious apology. Oddly, it is the Chinese producers and directors who give voice to what may very well have been the thoughts and feelings of many of the young Japanese soldiers who committed atrocities in Nanjing. The film does not whitewash the acts of brutality that were freely undertaken by many soldiers; however, Kadokawa represents that collective reservoir of horror and guilt that ultimately leads him to commute the sentence of the Chinese he is about to execute. He briefly tries himself in his own mind for the crime of "opposing the military leadership and embracing excessive humanity," convicts himself, and then carries out his self-imposed sentence of death. As he had stated earlier, "Life is more difficult than death." Psychologically, he is utterly incapable of living with the horrors he has witnessed, with the acts that he has committed, and with the loss of Yuriko. *City of Life and Death*, while deeply saddening, concludes with an almost resounding vote of confidence in the goodness of humanity, as represented by this personal act of recompense, which is Kadokawa's suicide and his gift of life to Shunzi and Xiaodou. As the scene concludes, Xiaodou plays with dandelions, jumps, and laughs loudly, just as children ought to do.

Flowers of War (2011)

Of the various film representations of the Massacre of Nanjing, the only one that is more of a Hollywood expansion than a truly historical representation is director Zhang Yimou's *Flowers of War* (2011), which, in a very brief written introduction, is said to be "inspired by true events." The film follows the plot of Geling Yan's novel, *Thirteen Flowers of Nanjing*, a fictionalized version of incidents recorded in the diary of Minnie Vautrin, an American missionary who saved the lives of many young women of the Ginling Girls College at the time of the Japanese invasion of Nanjing. Unlike *Black Sun: The Nanking Massacre*, the introduction to *Flowers of War* is very short and announces the deaths of over 200,000 people, but betrays no ideological leaning other than to mark the events at Nanjing as a humanitarian disaster. Film producers Zhang Weiping, Zhang Yimou, William Kong, and David Linde clearly do not wish to make any political statement that might be construed as condemning any nation or any individual, other than letting the events of the story demonstrate the reality of the Japanese slaughter:

> Marking an especially dark chapter of human history, over 200,000 people lost their lives in the relentless battle for control of the city ... Under impossible conditions, ordinary people fought for their very survival.[18]

This very sanitized prelude to the reality of what happened at Nanjing employs neutral language, such as, "over 200,000 people *lost their lives*," almost leaving the impression that these deaths were random and accidental. This introduction offers no explanation of who caused this "especially dark chapter of human history," other than to begin with the very bland statement that "In the Autumn of 1937, having conquered Shanghai, Japan turned its sights on the Chinese capital, Nanking."

At the beginning of the film, events are narrated in Chinese by Shu, one of the girls who has survived the tragedy being presented: this is the story of the last days of the Chinese army's defense of Nanjing. A group of Chinese high-school girls and one young boy, George Chen, seek to return to the Roman Catholic cathedral, where they hope to take refuge in their convent school. An American mortician, John Miller (played by Christian Bale), who has been called to the cathedral to prepare the remains of the priest there, follows the youths and enters the church, looking for money and the comforts of safety and a fine home. Shortly thereafter, a group of twelve prostitutes arrives, also fleeing the terrible wrath of the Japanese soldiers and seeking the shelter inside the church. As the story progresses, John becomes increasingly concerned with the safety of both the girls and the women, and he dons the clerical uniform of a priest in an attempt to garner respect from the increasingly hostile Japanese soldiers who come to the premises. John thwarts attempts by the soldiers to rape and carry off the women, even to the point of plotting their escape through the agency of Mr. Meng, the father of one of the girls, who is working as an aide to the Japanese.

The central episode of the film is the invitation by a cultured Japanese colonel, Hasegawa, for the girls, who have sung for him, to perform at the official celebration of the Japanese conquest of the city. One of the Japanese soldiers counts 13 girls present, and orders that there be 13 to sing at the next day's celebration. Later that night, at Shu's suggestion, the 13 girls climb the parapet of the church bell tower and prepare to commit suicide. They are only persuaded to come down when the prostitutes offer to go to the celebration in place of the girls. The 12 prostitutes convene to discuss whether all will go. Mo, the apparent leader of the group, urges all the women to go in place of the girls, as if all that the Japanese want is "pleasure," which, she quips, is "what we do." She quotes the first half of a verse of an ancient poem: "Prostitutes never care about a falling nation," while another completes it: "they sing and dance while others die." Mo rallies the others with a stirring challenge: "I think we should do something heroic and change the old way of thinking." Her appeal is so effective that even Ling, who has hesitated, agrees to sacrifice herself: "People say 'whores are heartless'; so tomorrow, let's do something honorable with our hearts."[19] Yet a problem remains: There are only 12 prostitutes.

In a remarkably sacrificial act, George, who had almost died of starvation at age six but was saved and raised by the cathedral priest, Fr. Ingleman, demands that Miller use his mortuary skills to make him up as a girl, substituting for the missing choirgirl. The following day, he and the 12 prostitutes are led off to "entertain" the Japanese, and step into history as the "Thirteen Flowers of Nanjing." The film ends with Miller, who has hidden the girls in the bottom of a truck, escaping into the countryside with them. The narrator of the film, Shu, reports that she never heard anything about the "Thirteen Flowers" again.

While popularized in many ways, *Flowers of War* still provides audiences with a stark reminder of how Japanese brutality at Nanjing also created many heroes. As it is wont to do, suffering also brought about reconciliation and a renewed optimism in the essential goodness of humanity, despite the incredible atrocities being committed by the Japanese. Miller leaves his drinking and philandering and dedicates himself to saving all of the women; he even turns back to God, praying for their deliverance and trying to embody the noble ideals of the uniform he has taken up. The prostitutes prove that they are not heartless exploiters, but rather feel love for the others and for their homeland. What is more, after their sacrifice is arranged, the prostitutes bond with the girls, with each group affectionately referring to the other as "little sister" and "big sister," respectively. The film highlights several scenes in which Miller leaves the compound in search of several prostitutes who have fled the area. Meeting foreign friends of his, the American is offered the chance to leave Nanjing safely, an offer he rejects outright because he refuses to abandon the women. Thus, reconciliation is effected at many levels of the human experience, both within the Chinese population and among the expatriates. But what of the Japanese? Director Zhang Yimou portrays only one "good" Japanese soldier: Colonel Hasegawa. As for the others, they are nothing less than emotionless machines of brutality, lust, and unrelenting slaughter. Despite the film's "Hollywood" sensationalism, *Flowers of War* does achieve its goal of presenting the struggle for survival of two groups of very ordinary Chinese women in very extraordinary circumstances of violence, death, and destruction.

Much more than simple propaganda, the films we have considered have contributed to a now highly-nuanced consideration of the many complexities of the Nanjing massacre. Based on historical facts, such as they are, the films seek to reconstruct the narrative of human lives that were either taken or forever traumatized by Japanese forces. What is more, Chinese directors, while clearly and correctly propounding a sense of national pride, also show, from many varied viewpoints, the toll that all human beings suffered – Chinese, Japanese, and other members of the international community who resided in Nanjing at the time. The Nanjing Massacre continues to be a central theme in the historical consciousness of "New China" and Japan, and, as the films show, is now more controversial and critically significant than ever.

9

Bangladesh: The Forgotten Genocide

Lynne Fallwell

Texas Tech University

For many reasons, Bangladesh's war of liberation, and the genocide that accompanied it, should not have been forgotten, even by Western media outlets and the larger international community that have been known to overlook such stories.[1] The 9 months of genocide, which started on March 25, 1971, were covered by a number of well-known journalists and became the basis of four short documentary films produced even before the conflicted had concluded.[2] One, *Stop Genocide* (1971), by Bangladeshi filmmaker Zahir Raihan, was purposely narrated in English to make it more accessible to a wider audience. References to the genocide also appeared in Western popular music; both folk singer Joan Baez and the Beatles' George Harrison released songs about Bangladesh.[3] Concomitantly, Harrison staged a huge benefit concert, which took place in front of a sold out crowd in Madison Square Gardens on August 1, 1971. The concert, along with a triple-album box set and a feature film, went on to raise millions for UNICEF and became the template for later benefits like *Live Aid*.[4] Yet, despite these efforts, and the fact that at least one feature film or documentary on the war of liberation has been released almost every year since 1971, events in Bangladesh faded from collective memory.[5]

Since the 1990s, a call to rediscover these events has coincided with a larger interest in the field of genocide studies more generally. In 1996, which marked the 25th anniversary of Bangladesh's fight for independence, the

Liberation War Museum opened in the country's capital Segunbagicha, Dhaka. The year previous, directors Tareque and Catherine Masud released *Muktir Gaan* (*The Song of Freedom*, 1995), a documentary film about a group of singing performers known as Association of Liberation Fighters/Artists of Bangladesh who traveled to refugee camps during the war to inspire resistance fighters with patriotic songs.[6] The film mixed original footage shot by American filmmaker Lear Levin with a fictional elements to "tell the story of the birth of a nation and the ideals of secularism and tolerance on which it was founded."[7] Taking almost a quarter century to produce, *Muktir Gaan* won both the 1996 *Best Film Award* from the Bangladesh Film Journalists Association, and the 1997 Special Jury Prize at the Festival of South Asian Documentaries.[8] In 2002, the Masuds released a feature film (*Matir Moina, The Clay Bird*) about the growing religious and cultural tensions in East Pakistan in the late 1960s, as seen through the eyes of a young boy. Again, the film received international recognition at both Cannes and the American Academy Awards, indicating an interest in the subject beyond the borders of Bangladesh.[9] Most recently, there has been a proliferation of internet sites providing global access to resources through online archives, discussion forums, and video sites, albeit many of the last still only in regional languages.[10] This proliferation is driven in part by the government of Bangladesh setting up an International Crimes Tribunal in 2009 to try members of the Pakistan Army as well as local collaborators for war crimes.[11] At the same time, the renewed focus has also brought great debate about how the events of 1971 are being portrayed, as controversies surrounding two films, *Meherjaan* (2011) and *Children of War* (2014) demonstrate.[12] This chapter traces how Bangladesh's War of Liberation has waxed and waned in public consciousness by looking at cinematic representations of its genocide and how they contribute to the collective memory. In order to put these filmic representations in context, I first offer a brief overview of the major events surround those 9 months of genocide in Bangladesh.

Background History: From East Pakistan to Bangladesh

As with many other genocides, the antecedents of the conflict in Bangladesh were rooted in struggles over land, religion, and cultural identity formation.[13]

They were also a byproduct of both colonialism, post-colonial rule, and Cold War geopolitics. The partitioning of the British Indian Empire in 1947 resulted in the formation of two sovereign states, India and Pakistan. While India, with its Hindu majority, occupied a contiguous land mass, Pakistan found itself divided linguistically, culturally, and geographically into two separate regions a thousand miles apart on either side of India. Although both regions were predominantly Muslim, the power between them was far from equal. Despite being demographically less dense, Punjabi-dominated West Pakistan quickly established itself as the official Pakistan, holding military power and deliberately excluding the Bengali Muslim majority of East Pakistan from the political process. Furthermore, West Pakistan quickly imposed its own colonial-type rule on its eastern counterpart, such as demanding that Urdu, spoken by less than 10 percent of the population, be the official language instead of Bengali, spoken by some 54 percent of the population, and primarily the residents in East Pakistan. Despite settling the issue in 1956 by making both languages official, West Pakistan continued to accuse the Bengali population of the east of not being "Muslim enough", and for showing too much sympathy toward their Indian Hindu neighbors.[14] Governmental regulations repeatedly attacked artistic movements and cultural endeavors of the Bengali population. Economic policies, particularly surrounding the sale of jute, left East Pakistan feeling that it was supporting West Pakistan financially without a say in how those resources were spent. In response, the Awami League, a pro-Bengali nationalist movement headed by Sheikh Mujib-ur-Rhaman, gained support in East Pakistan; at the center of its agenda was a six-point program requiring autonomy for the provinces.

Tensions mounted on both sides, growing steadily throughout the 1960s. In 1969, Muhammed Ayub Khan, who had ruled Pakistan since seizing it in a coup in 1958, resigned as president following a popular uprising. His replacement, Agha Muhammad Yahya Khan, promised to hold the first free and general elections, which extreme weather and the ensuing damages caused him to postpone.[15] When the elections were eventually held in December 1970, Sheikh Mujibur-ur-Rahman and the Awami League won a majority in East Pakistan and became the de facto president-elect for both halves of the country. However, acting-president Khan refused to cede control of the government to Rahman, and instead mounted a military action, known as Operation Searchlight, against those demanding autonomy for East Pakistan. Prepared to "kill three million (Bengalis) to stop secession," Khan launched the first attacks in the city of Dhaka on March 25, 1971.[16] Instead of suppressing nationalist sentiments, Operation Searchlight galvanized citizens of East Pakistan to join the Awami League and become freedom fighters. As with many other cases of genocide, there is no exact total of the cost of human lives during the nine months of fighting, but a commonly cited figure reports between two and three million Bengalis dead, with an additional 200,000 plus women being brutally raped, and upwards of 10 million people crossing the borders as refugees.[17]

Cinematic representations of the events that unfolded between March and December 1971 tend to fall into four categories: films depicting the horrors of genocide, films depicting the heroic efforts of freedom fighters, films using the War of Liberation as a backdrop for stories about human interaction, and films about the fate of women during the conflict. These categories are not necessarily finite, as some films fall into more than one category. In addition, many of the films are accessible only in the language of production, usually Bengali but also Hindi and sometimes Urdu, with limited subtitles in English. As a result, this chapter is not a comprehensive review of all relevant films, but rather a discussion of general trends and themes.

Reporting the Horrors of Genocide

The first films about the genocide were short documentaries that appeared while the conflict was still taking place, their aim being to get the message out about what was happening in East Pakistan. They coincided with a general change in Western media coverage of war and conflict. In the 1960s, an increase in television channels brought increased competition as stations fought to get and keep viewers. From a news standpoint, this created the "9 o'clock" phenomenon of leading with the most dramatic stories ("if it bleeds, it leads"). In his comprehensive examination of how this shift influenced coverage of the Bangladesh War of Liberation, Naeem Mohajemen indicates that as the pace of reporting accelerated, complex multifaceted issues were reduced to bilateral disagreements with clearly demarcated "good" and "evil" sides. With this, came a shortened news cycle and the idea that stories were "hot," before quickly growing "cold." This accelerated pace of reporting meant that the Bengalis became cast as simple, gentle people, "persecuted by more aggressive, militant, and more Islamic Pakistan."[18] While world attention increased, what became lost in such coverage was the agency and humanity of those involved; victims were reduced to images of heaps of bodies and wide-eyed children in refugee camps and the true protagonist of the production became the White narrator, either appearing on screen or in voiceover.[19]

Stop Genocide (1971), a 20-minute black and white production by Bangladeshi filmmaker Zahir Raihan, is among the earliest examples of this documentary style. Conceived and completed in the spring of 1971, its style is very much influenced by Cuban filmmaker Santiago Álvarez in its incorporation of found footage from newsreels, video, and photographs.[20] Raihan's work also draws attention to contemporary Cold War politics which saw support for the liberation fighters coming from India, the Soviet Union, and China, while Pakistan gained allies in the United States, Iran, and Turkey.[21] A devoted communist, Raihan opens the film with a quote from Lenin's *Right of Nations to Self-Determination*. Images of US bombings in Vietnam and pictures of the Nazi concentration camps are interwoven with those of raped women, destroyed homes, piles of dead bodies, and frightened refugees fleeing to India, setting up the connection between Western politics and the violence in East Pakistan. The contrasting image is that of a resistance fighter explaining the reasons for fighting, which links back to points raised in the opening Lenin quote. Finally, the film ends with the word STOP filling the screen.

While *Stop Genocide* was not officially endorsed by either the East Pakistan film board or the government in exile, it did receive support from Indian Prime Minister Indira Gandhi, who wanted the film circulated to a wide international audience. The fact that the film's voiceover is in English assisted this effort greatly. Based on his success with *Stop Genocide*, acting Prime Minister Tajuddin Ahmed, head of the wartime provisional government in East Pakistan, ordered Raihan to produce three more documentaries immediately. He directed *A State Is Born* and produced Babul Chowdhry's *Innocent Million* and Alamgir Kabir's *Liberation Fighters*.[22] Unfortunately, Raihan's film career was cut short when he disappeared in January 1972 while searching for his brother, noted writer Shahidullah Kaiser.[23]

Other films to use actual footage from the time period include: Chashi Nazrul Islam's *Ora Egaro Jon* (1972); the previously mentioned *Muktir Gaan* (*Songs of Freedom*, 1995) by Tareque and Catherine Masud; and Mrityunjay Devvrat's inaugural film, *The Children of War – Nine Months to Freedom* (alternative English title *The Bastard Child*, 2014). One common effect of using primary source footage in these films is to enhance the graphic nature of the 1971 genocide and to attempt to convey the scale of atrocities committed.[24] The other feature these films share is that they bookend increased public interest in events in Bangladesh, with the first examples coming out immediately following the actual events, and the second examples dating from the period of rediscovery. In both cases, inclusion of actual footage helps covey a sense of, and here I am borrowing a term used about the Nazi Holocaust, "Never Again"; never let us forget the magnitude of this event and the lives it cost.

Heroic Efforts of Freedom Fighters

Following on the heels of the initial documentary films, feature films began emerging from the newly-formed Bangladesh, many of which involved casts and crews who themselves had served as freedom fighters during the War of Liberation. Alamgir Kabir, who directed the short documentary *Liberation Fighters* (1972), is one such example. Like Raihan, Kabir was a communist, having become acquainted with politics while studying in England and subsequently taking part in the wars of liberation in both Palestine and Algeria. In East Pakistan, he became a journalist and noted movie critic. When the war broke out, he joined the radio center of independent Bangladesh, and reported the news in English using the pseudonym Ahmed Chowdhury.[25] After the war he went on to make a number of highly acclaimed feature films, including those set during the events of 1971. His first feature was *Dhire Bohe Meghna* (*Quiet Flows the Meghna*, 1973), which features the Meghna River as a backdrop for the growing tensions.

Interestingly, Kabir's film was not the first full length feature featuring the War of Liberation. That designation technically belongs to an Indian

135

production, *Joy Bangladesh* (*Hail Bangladesh*), which was released in India in 1971. However, the Bangladesh government complained that the War of Liberation was not portrayed accurately and the Indian government eventually banned the film.[26] Discounting this production, the first post-war feature to come out of Bangladesh is actually the drama *Ora Egaro Jon* (*They were a Group of Eleven*, 1972), directed by Chashi Nazrul Islam and based on a script by Al Masood.[27] The film tells the story of 11 freedom fighters (*Muktijoddha*) as they face off against the Pakistani Army. About his film, Chashi Nazrul Islam states:

> *Ora Egaro Jon* is a milestone in our film industry. If this film had not been made the masses would have missed the spirit of the freedom struggle. I got the idea of the theme from the 11-point demand of the students, which motivated our leaders to call for Independence. Moreover, the 11 heroes in the film represent the 11 sectors of our freedom struggle.[28]

Again, many members of the crew and cast, including the film's male lead, drew on personal experiences of the freedom fighters during the war.[29] The film relied on limited resources available after the war, including found footage, and using live rounds to recreate gun fire and explosions because dummy ammunition was not available. Like *Stop Genocide*, it also used actual footage of the war, the content here given to the director by a camera man from an international news agency.[30] Among the themes touched on by *Ora Egaro Jon* are the mass killings at Dhaka University, the actions of those collaborating with the Pakistani Army, and what one interview called "the sacrifices the women folk made," referring largely to the mass rapes.[31]

In total, Chashi Nazrul Islam went on to direct six films about the war, including *Shangram* (*Struggle*, 1973), about the actions of a Bangladeshi military office; *Hangor Nadi Grenade* (*The Shark, the River, and the Grenada*, 1997), the story of a mother who sacrifices her son to save the lives of two freedom fighters; and *Megher Pore Megh* (*Clouds After Clouds*, 2004), which, while set in the presentday, features events of the war as a backdrop.[32] Like *Ora Egaro Jon*, Islam's film *Shagram* (*Struggle*, 1973) features the story of men who fought to liberate Bangladesh, this time based on the diary of Major General Khaled Mosharraf, one of three brigade commanders of the Bangladesh Forces during the war. Known as politically and intellectually astute, he was noted for developing a two-pronged military strategy: the first to inspire a special guerrilla force of young urban students, intellectuals, and professionals to conduct targeted attacks within the city of Dhaka; the second to use foreign media to spread word of those attacks so that others would be inspired to commit to the struggle.[33] Creating feature films based on memoirs and stories of Bangladeshi freedom fighters is a trend that has continued from the initial period into the present, and even crosses national borders.

For example, similar narratives of grit, determination, and military prowess play out in the Indian blockbuster, *Border* (1997), directed by Bollywood producer J. P. Dutta, *Asttiety Amar Desh* (2007) directed by Khihir Hayat Khan and based on the biography of military pilot Matiur Rahman, and *Nishongo Sarati* (*Tajuddin Ahmad: An Unsung Hero,* 2007) by Tanvir Mokammel. The movie depicts the events of one night during the Battle of Longewala when 120 soldiers of the Punjab regiment of the Indian Army and their commander, Major Kuldip Singh Chandpuri, held off a tank regiment of the Pakistani Army. *Asttiety Amar Desh* (2007) tells the story of Pakistan Air Force pilot, Matiur Rahman, who, on August 20, 1971, attempted to hijack a military plane en route from Karachi, Pakistan to India in support of the liberation movement. A struggle with the captain ensured and the plane crashed, killing both men. His widow and two infant daughters were subsequently imprisoned for five weeks before being released by the Pakistan Air Force.[34] A political, rather than military, figure, Tajuddin Ahmed exemplifies the narrative of freedom fighter as General Secretary of the Awami League and later in his role as first Prime Minister of Bangladesh and head of the wartime provisional government (it was he who Raihan to produce additional documentaries following *Stop genocide*).[35]

A version of the freedom fighter narrative with a woman as the central character is *Guerrilla* (2011), directed by Nasiruddin Yousuff and adapted from the novel *Nishiddo Loban,* by Bengali writer Syed Shamsul Huq. The film opens on the night of March 25, 1971, when protagonist Bilkis Banu's husband, journalist Hasan Ahmed, vanishes. Banu, while searching for her husband, subsequently joins the liberation movement and becomes involved in the publication of the underground English-language paper, *Guerrilla*. She becomes central to the liberation movement as she smuggles out revolutionary songs by Bengali musician and activist, Atlaf Mahmud. As the film progresses, Banu suffers significant losses, including the death of her brother, a commander of the local freedom fighters. The film ends when she is captured by members of the Pakistan Army and opts to blow herself up, along with the enemy soldiers, rather than submit to their intentions of rape.[36] The commonality among all of these films is their attention to the heroic efforts of freedom fighters. Their narrative is one of good versus evil that ends with the triumph of an oppressed population, even if that triumph comes at the cost of martyrdom.

Backdrop for Human Interaction

Other films, particularly the most contemporary ones, present a more nuanced narrative of interaction that highlights the complexity of human relationships. Often, these films depict a story involving individuals representing different sides of the conflict dealing with the consequences of creating a self–other dichotomy. Two films by Tanvir Mokammel, in particular, represent this theme of "othering." *Nadir Naam Madhumati* (*A River Named Madhumati*, 1994) is set in a remote village on the banks of the Madhumati. As the events of 1971 encroach on the village, where the main character, Bacchu, decides to join the rebels. This puts him in direct conflict with his father, who opts to support Pakistan. At the same time, Bacchu's teacher and his family find their freedoms increasingly eroded as daily life become politicized.[37] In *Chitra Nadi Pare* (*Quiet Flows the River Chitra*, 1999), the story is again set in a village on the banks of a river. This time, the protagonist is a Hindu lawyer left to deal with the consequences when he and his family, unlike their Hindu neighbors, refuse to bow to increasing pressure from Muslim neighbors to leave the village.[38] Films with similar themes include *Amar Bondu Rashed* (*My Friend Rashed,* 2011), directed by Morshedul Islam, and *Matir Moina* (*The Clay Bird,* 2002), the aforementioned feature film by Tareque and Catherine Masud.

An offshoot of this theme of exclusion follows a character as he or she seeks answers for events that occurred in the past. The Bangladesh–UK co-production *Shogram* (2014), by Munsur Ali, is one example.[39] Here, the film opens with a conversation between an English reporter and an old freedom fighter. The plot tracks back to a love story between a Muslim boy, Karim, and a Hindu girl, Asha, during the war of liberation. When political events intercede into quiet village life, Karim is separated from Asha and must learn to navigate the new reality of war and revenge before they can be reunited.[40] What separates this film from earlier freedom fighter narratives is its consciousness of the passage of time. While the bulk of the film takes place in the past, it retains a link to the present and the fact that the original fighters are aging. The film is also unique due to its international collaboration. Director Munsor Ali is British-Bangladeshi, and many of the actors are noted stars from Hindi, American, and European productions. The film itself is framed by dialogue in English, with flashbacks in both Urdu and Bangla that are then subtitled.[41] As with the first documentary, *Stop Genocide* (1971), this film represents an effort to communicate with an audience beyond regional movie-goers.

Films About Women

One unique subset of the Bangladesh liberation films has to do with the experiences of women.[42] While a film like *Guerrilla* (2011), endeavors to cast its female protagonist in an almost stereotypical masculinized freedom fighter role, others take a more critical look at the objectification of women as both metaphors for the nation and victims of gendered sexual violence. Even when the focus is not on dissecting rape as a tool of genocide, contemporary films with female protagonists still tend to complicate and politicize women's roles in society. Consider the film *Hangor Nodi Grenade* (*The Shark, the River, and the Grenada*, alternative English title, *The Mother*, 1997), directed by Chashi Nazrul Islam and based on a novel with the same name by Bangladeshi writer Selina Hossian (1976). Without romanticizing the past, Hossain's writings tend to feature explorations of human interactions with the state and individuals, with a particular focus on women.[43] Set in a rural landscape in East Pakistan, *Hangor Nodi Grenade* centers on the character of Buri, the mother of a disabled son who eventually sacrifices her son's life to save two freedom fighters. Explaining Buri's choice, Hossain states:

Thus I have expanded and broadened and politicized the role of women. I have also shown how the so-called illiterate women can even exemplarily exercise their agency in terms of making the right decision at the right time. In terms of emancipation – in this instance, anticolonial liberation war – the female figure by no means remains passive, but rather active on more levels than men can afford to imagine. She not only acts in various ways, but she also offers the resources of imagination and intuition such that they all play very politically significant roles.[44]

While Hossain wrote the original story in 1976, it is significant that it took over 20 years, and a few false starts, to produce a film adaptation.[45] The cinematic retelling of Hossian's mother narrative coincided with larger scholarly debates on the relationship between women and the nation, as well as specific debates on the rhetoric of motherhood as symbol for Bangladesh.[46] Woven into these discussions is the issue of rape and representations of Bangladeshi women as weapons of war and genocide.[47] Just as recent films mirror their earlier counterparts by incorporating actual film footage into storylines, contemporary films that highlight genocidal rape are harkening back to an earlier public cinematic discourse. Between 1971 and 1973, the new Bangladesh government openly acknowledge the fate of women who had been raped by the Pakistan Army, calling them "war heroines" (*birangonas*). Rather than being shunned, as is common in other genocides, these women were recognized for their sacrifice to the nation and were often reintegrated into society by reuniting with their husbands or by arranged marriages with male freedom fighters. However, within the first few years, these initiatives quickly faded from public consciousness and the fate of rape survivors disappeared from public discourse, not to reemerge until recently.[48]

Two contemporary films show how the issue of Bangladeshi rape survivors has reentered the cinematic landscape. The first film is less controversial, and the most opaque, on the issue of rape. Masud Akando's production, *Pati (Father)*, was released Bangladesh in December 2012, and premiered at the Wiltshire Theater in Los Angeles on May 5, 2013. Set in the fictitious, predominately Hindu village of Chhoi Ana, the film capitalizes on the image of Bangladesh residents as largely simple, gentle, rural people. There are three narratives running through the production. The first features various depictions of fathers including grandfathers, single fathers, and fathers-to-be. The second shows an absence of mothers. While there are women in the film, mothers are either largely absent, replaced by an aunt or a daughter, or are yet to be, as in the case of one heavily pregnant figure. In the absence of physical mothers, the countryside stands in as the nurturing maternal which, like the children, requires protecting by the fathers. The third narrative is the growing unrest that is about to penetrate this isolated village. The climax of the film sees a father and his young sons trying to rescue their daughter/sister from the local Pakistani general. Sexual violence is implied, but never shown on screen, with the closest being a thwarted rape attempt near the very end of the film. The significance of the narrative in *Pati* is not in reintroducing the sexual victimization of women during the genocide, but rather the restitution of the paternal figure and his ability to rescue the fledgling nation symbolized through the saving of his daughter.

The other film, *Children of War: Nine Months to Freedom* (alternative title *Bastard Child,* 2014), depicts rape much more obviously and controversially.[49] It is also an Indian, rather than Bangladeshi, film, significant in that it becomes a topic taken on by a foreign government, albeit a neighboring country. The director, Mrityunjay Devvrat argues, "the film looks at human stories and personal stories of how [the civilians in East Pakistan] suffered and how they came out victorious. It is a largely fictional film made up of true stories", and that the larger intent of the film is to, "make people understand, among other things, why there are so many Bangladeshis in India."[50] In this sense, while initial depictions of rape served a purpose of reintegrating the women themselves, newer films focus on issues of educating the public at large.

On one hand, it is striking that the most recent celluloid depictions of rapes should be so controversial. In films not dealing with the war of liberation, Bangladesh has an established trope in the form of "cut pieces" or short, unrelated scenes inserted into a film sequence for the purpose of allowing the, predominantly male, audience, to engage in sexual or violence voyeurism; they usually feature actresses hired specifically for that purpose.[51] On the other hand, what makes a film like *Children of War* problematic is its extended rape scene of the film's female lead, which takes place in front of her on-screen husband, essentially victimizing her and emasculating him in his role as protector. This represents the exact opposite of the paternalistic savior figures in *Pati*.

Genocide is not an easy topic to discuss, let alone represent on a large movie screen. Yet, for Bangladesh, coming to terms with its war of liberation and subsequent national identity, have been intrinsically linked to such cinematic representations. For the first few years after 1971, graphic displays of actual genocide footage served to legitimatize the injustices bestowed upon the nation by their enemy, Pakistan. Later, depictions of liberation fighters demonstrated that the new country of Bangladesh was founded by heroes. As the immediacy of events receded and the actual participants aged, films using the war of liberation as a backdrop for human interaction allowed movie goers to contemplate the more nuanced relationships between average citizens. While the most recent spate of films depicting genocidal rapes provoke controversy, they also promote greater discussion, both inside and outside Bangladesh, about what exactly happened during those nine months in 1971. Hopefully, this increased attention will help shift the to-date inward looking Bengali-language films back onto the attention of the international stage and make the Bangladesh story part of regular conversations with the field of comparative genocide.

10

Argentina's Dirty War on Film: The Absent Presence of The Disappeared

Kristin C. Brunnemer

Pierce College

Between 1976 and 1983, Argentina's Dirty War (or "The War Against Subversion" per the military junta in power) claimed the lives of thousands of suspected anti-government dissidents. While some trace the origins of The Dirty War to political insurrections of the 1960s, most historical accounts posit the war's official beginning with Isabel Peron's 1976 removal from office. Peron, the third wife of Juan Peron and vice president until his death in 1974, succeeded to the presidency in 1974, but was removed from office through a military coup d'état that placed General Jorge Rafael Videla in the position, one he would hold for the next seven years. Securing power, Videla and his military cohorts established a reform program called The Process of National Reorganization, or El Proceso for short, whose principle objectives were "the elimination of subversion, the improvement of the economy, and the creation of a new national framework."[1] In accordance with that first objective, Videla's junta government originated task forces whose members "were divided into those who kidnapped, those who tortured, and those who collated information and kept records."[2] Conservative estimates place the number of those kidnapped, detained, tortured, and killed at 7,500, while organizations such as Amnesty International claim the number to as high as 30,000.[3] "By September 1976, "The Process" was

143

conducting an average of 30 kidnappings a day; the whereabouts of only 1 percent of these victims had been verified" and the remaining 99 percent are assumed dead.[4] Those who never returned became known as *El Desaparecido* ("The Disappeared").

Among The Disappeared were blue-collar workers, whose unions had traditionally favored Peron and Marxism (30 percent), and "liberal professionals, journalists, intellectuals, artists, university students and school teachers," who composed "more than forty percent of the disappeared."[5] Among those kidnapped were also arbitrary citizens, who had neither economic nor official ties to these unions or professions, for relatives, friends, and neighbors present or named during torture sessions "would be seized as well, on the principle of guilt by association."[6] Acquaintances named during torture sessions were also subsequently arrested, creating a political climate whereby "the possibility of publicly voicing dissent or protesting civil rights violations was out of the question, for it would not only jeopardize individual survival, but it would also place relatives and friends at risk of becoming targets of military repression."[7]

Survivors' stories about their imprisonment could be the basis for any horror film. An estimated 350 *pozos* (detention centers) were in existence during The Process's seven years in power, "each one under the supervision of a high-level military or police officer."[8] These *pozos* have often been compared with Nazi Germany's concentration camps, with ESMA (an acronym for *Escuela de Mecánica del al Armada* – Navy Mechanics School) being called "the Argentine Auschwitz."[9] Located in central Buenos Aires, ESMA housed 5,000 or more kidnapped Disappeared who were subjected to a series of psychological and physical tortures, among them the use of electric cattle prods, water and dry suffocation techniques, rectal electrocution, physical confinement in *tubos* ("spaces so tiny they were called ...tubes"), rapes, beatings, burns, food and water deprivation, and " 'death flights' in which prisoners [alive but drugged]were thrown from aircraft into the Atlantic Ocean."[10] Many *pozo* survivors later provided testimony to these abuses to commissions and in trials beginning in 1983.

Another unique membership within these *pozos* was the children brought or born there. Like their biological parents, the children of The Disappeared never returned to their biological families, but were "appropriated" ("so called because the kidnappers were generally provided with forged birth certificates that certified them as biological parents") to families with ties to the junta government.[11] By some estimates, approximately "500 newborns and infants were handed over to military families to be raised as their own."[12] These adoptions and their repercussions later formed the basis for some of Argentina's most notable films about The Dirty War.

In the midst of this humanitarian crisis, those who became the public face for civil rights and The Disappeared were *Madres/Abuelas de la Plaza de Mayo* (Mothers/Grandmothers of the Plaza de Mayo), two separate but interrelated groups that organized weekly marches around the plaza in front of Buenos Aires's Casa Rosado each Thursday, from 1977 to 2006, staging 1,500 demonstrations in all.[13] Wearing white scarves on their heads "embroidered with the names of their disappeared as a kind of uniform"[14] and carrying signs depicting pictures of their missing offspring, the Madres and Abuelas "invented a range of techniques to rescue the disappeared from obliteration in the public memory," thus "keeping the issue visible in a public space in the heart of the country's governmental and financial district"[15] Though these demonstrations were peaceful, organization members found themselves under government threat and attack, both verbally (as with the sobriquet of "*Las Locas* [The Crazy Women] *de la Plaza de Mayo*") and physically. Notably, three Madres founders – Azucena Villaflor de Vincenti, Ester Ballenstrino de Careaga, and Maria Ponce de Bianco – were themselves killed after detention in ESMA, on "death flights" where Disappeared victims were thrown, alive, from airplanes over the Atlantic Ocean.[16]

Films about Argentina's Dirty War began to emerge in the mid-1980s when The National Reorganization Process's government finally collapsed. While Videla had resigned in March, 1981, his appointed successor, Roberto Viola, was ousted just 9 months later. Thereafter, Viola's own successor, Lt. General Leopoldo Galtieri, found himself overthrown by military coup d'état in June 1982, after an unsuccessful military conflict with the U.K. over the Falkland Islands. Major St. John then held the office for 13 days before another military general, Reynaldo Bignone, assumed the presidency in July 1982. This political instability, coupled with mounting inflation, increasing public dissent, and mounting (inter) national protests regarding Argentina's human rights violations, resulted

145

in calls for elections, which brought President Raúl Alfonsín to power in December, 1983.

Five days after assuming office, Alfonsín passed legislation for a National Commission on the Disappeared (CONADEP), to investigate Dirty War crimes. Along with books and films, including CONADEP's own report and 90-minute documentary (both titled *Nunca Más[Never Again]*), other writers and filmmakers emerged to create "a narrative reconstruction, in which personal experience turned to public testimony."[17] Alfonsín also "recognized the National Film Institute ... and abolished film censorship laws that had been on the books since 1968," paving the way for the two dozen or so films focused on Argentina's Disappeared to date.[18]

While this number may not seem a substantial figure given the hundreds of films centered on genocides and atrocities worldwide, keeping in mind that Argentina's film output under the dictatorship was 15 to 20 films per year, the creation of six major motion pictures about The Dirty War by 1986, within three years after El Proceso's dissolution, is a substantial percentage.[19] Of this era, Pat Aufderheide notes, "The Argentine Public seemed primed to use the darkened movie house like a confessional."[20]

As with documentaries about The Dirty War (e.g., *The Mothers of the Plaza de Mayo* (1986), *Spoils of War*, *The Blonds* (2003), *The Disappeared* (2007), *Our Disappeared* (2008), and *Abuelas: Grandmothers on a Mission* (2013)), dramas about these years reflect the gamut of aforementioned historical topics. These include films about exile (e.g., *Angel Face* (1998), *Kamchatka* (2002), *Hermanas* (2002) and *Clandestine Childhood* (2011)) coming to terms with a loved one's disappearance - e.g., *The Girlfriend* (1988), *A Wall of Silence* (1993), *Buenos Aires Vice Versa* (1996), *A Less Bad World* (2004) and *Imagining Argentina* (2003) and portraying the horrific conditions of *pozos* - e.g., *Night of the Pencils* (1988), *Garage Olimpo* (1999), and *Chronicle of an Escape* (2006). Many films also take as their focal point the appropriation of Disappeared offspring, including *The Official Story* (1985), *Sons and Daughters* (2001), *The Lost Steps* (2011), *Cautiva* (2005), and *The Day I Was Not Born* (2010).

Perhaps what is most striking about this collective body of work is how infrequently those Disappeared occupy the films' subject positions. In most, their physical absence posits them as objects of memory rather than active subjects driving the narrative forward. The Disappeared are often relegated to supporting characters rather than principal players, their testimonies serving as the basis for the protagonists' emotional journeys. In a number of films, The Disappeared are initially absent from the main character's cognitive register, becoming only a presence through the characters' research and revelations. Quite ironically, even those films that focus on The Disappeared's kidnapping and torture experiences tend to render those characters as objectified bodies whose subjectivity is made absent by their tortured dehumanization. Collectively, these films offer a portrait of The Disappeared as still an ever-present absence in Argentina's cultural memory, a process still in negotiation 40 years later.

Such is the case for Argentina's most famous Dirty War film, *The Official Story*. Luis Puenzo's 1985 film tells its story not from the perspective of a survivor or a loved one, but from that of an upper-middle-class history teacher who increasingly becomes aware that her adopted daughter Gaby is likely the biological progeny of someone disappeared. Set in March 1983, just as the junta government is unraveling, the film establishes Alicia as a "stand-in for an internationalized middle class," someone whose bourgeois complacency has kept her from contemplating her complicity.[21] Puenzo's contends that choosing Alicia as protagonist was intentional: "there was enormous resistance to the subject of the disappeared. It had gotten to the point where people would turn off the radio if there was news about it. And I was looking for a way to break through the passive resistance."[22]

Alicia's worldview is grounded by her private school employment and her marriage to Roberto, a businessman whose success is predicated upon collusion with government officials. In her classroom, Alicia reveals her allegiance to history, telling her students, "By understanding history, we learn to understand the world. No peoples can survive without memory. History is the memory of the peoples."[23] Alicia's journey, as the title suggests, is her movement away from accepting "the official (his)story" (the film's Spanish title – *La Historia Oficial* – plays to both of these translations), toward the recognition that history belongs also to those peoples whose memories are never officially recorded.

Alicia's initial shift in perspective occurs at a high school reunion, where classmate Ana has returned from Europe for the first time in seven years. Over dinner, the gossip turns toward an absent peer who is said to have aged considerably since the exile of one son and the death of another in the Maldives (Falklands War). A smug classmate immediately contends that "all her children became subversive … If they were seized, surely there was a reason."[24] In so doing, she enacts what Nancy Hollander calls "Identification with the aggressor … a common defense, symbolized by the frequent response of those who passively observed or heard about the apprehension of a neighbor, co-worker or even family member: '*Habra hecho algo*' ('He/she must have been up to something')."[25] Ana avoids commenting until the classmate attacks Ana's return: "We can't all choose between the tough caviar of exile and home. Don't expect us to pity you."[26] Calling the classmate an "unforgettable bitch," Ana's remarks become the film's first counter-narrative to the official story.[27]

Ana also provides the film's central testimony to the horrors experienced by The Disappeared when she confides in Alicia why she left so abruptly, never writing, never telling anyone she was leaving. Crying as she remembers her 36-day imprisonment, Ana describes the blindfolds, beatings, interrogations, electric prodding, simulated drownings, and eventual rape. Alicia's questions to Ana – "But why? Why did they do that to you? Did you report it?" – reveal both Alicia's shock and her naivety about the presence of The Dirty War all around her.[28]

Ana's personal narrative soon shifts, however, to a more collective experience of those detained. After telling Alicia, "Often I didn't know if the cries were mine or someone else's," Ana shares her recollections of pregnant women whose babies were taken and sold "to families who buy them without asking questions."[29] Startled, Alicia immediately jumps to her feet, rejecting the witnessing role she has previously assumed, angrily declaring, "Why tell me that?"[30] Supposing Alicia means Ana's entire testimony, not just her mention of appropriated children, Ana confides that she's never told anyone her story before. "How unbelievable. I feel guilty," Ana declares before leaving, in what is yet another reminder of how Ana's experiences are merely the backdrop for Alicia's coming-to-consciousness narrative, a status further reinforced by Ana's brief appearance only twice more in the film.[31] Ana's story is merely a foil to trigger Alicia's own journey.

Alongside her fears that Gaby could be appropriated, Alicia also contends with students who contradict her belief in recorded history as official truth. After a heated argument with Costa, a vocal student who insists that "history's written by assassins," she arrives in her classroom to discover her blackboard covered with news clippings and photos of The Disappeared.[32] When her colleague Benitez confiscates her report to school authorities about Costa's defiance, he reveals his own encounter with a task force that shredded all of his papers, forcing him to abandon his university teaching position. Alicia questions whether it's possible that The Disappeared aren't missing, but merely relocated as he himself has been, but Benitez rejoins with a series of Socratic questions: "What do you care whether it's true? Is it your problem? It's always easier to believe it's impossible, right? Because if it were possible it would require complicity."[33] Paired with Benitez's words is Alicia's arrival in downtown Buenos Aires, where the film captures real footage of Madres, Abuelas, and supporters marching to the Plaza de Mayo. The posters, chants, pictures, and billboards slowly start to permeate Alicia's consciousness, and, physically overcome, Alicia grabs the wall for support.

Alicia's understanding of her complicity continues to grow as she searches for the truth about Gaby's heritage, a journey that leads her first to the conventional paths she has always trusted: her husband, Gaby's pediatrician, hospital and county records, even the church confessional. In none of these authoritative spaces, however, does Alicia find anyone willing to help her uncover the truth. In one ironic scene, Alicia confronts a hospital clerk who has just referred her to a neighboring clerk, who, in turn, has referred her back to the original clerk. Alicia's frustration catches the attention of a Madre/Abuela, herself searching for family members, who offers Alicia access to the organization's records. The Madres also lead Alicia to Sara Reballo, a woman convinced that Gaby's age, hip dislocation at birth, and vital statistics make for a possible match for her missing granddaughter.

Perhaps purposefully, Sara never states whether she is the mother of Gaby's (potential) biological father or mother. Instead, as she shows Alicia the four remaining photos she has of the couple, Sara narrates their love story from early childhood adoration for one another, to their wedding, pregnancy, and disappearance. Handing Alicia a photo of the couple at age five, she and Alicia both note how the girl bears a striking resemblance to

Gaby. Sara's testimonial of her missing loved ones is one of the film's most touching scenes, providing a subjectivity to The Disappeared, making their haunting absence all the more palpable.

Upon their second meeting, Alicia confides in Sara: "It's strange. I always thought that I would do anything to avoid losing what I had, that I'd be capable of anything as long as – as long as everything remained as it was. Strange, isn't it? I didn't want to lose what I love, but I couldn't ..." Alicia doesn't continue the sentence; she is still grappling with the knowledge that The Disappeared, who were once made invisible by El Proceso's official story, have been ever-present in her world all along.

However, Alicia's recent concentration on Gaby's parentage blinds her to Roberto's own struggles to maintain his standing in a world crumbling around him. With investors declining to return calls, colleagues vanishing, government officials resigning, and their replacements beginning to investigate the company's dealings, Roberto's fears rise to the surface in a seething encounters with his anarchist father (who accuses Roberto of growing rich through nefarious dealings), and with Alicia, who is now questioning, for the first time, how he acquired Gaby. As the film progresses, Roberto has increasingly come to symbolize the junta government with which he has long associated. Thus, when Alicia introduces Roberto to Sara, he mimics the government's ideological pattern of dealing with the Madres, referring to Alicia as "completely crazy" and Sara as "a nut" and a "bag lady."[34]

Roberto's symbolic link with El Proceso continues in the film's final minutes as he changes tactics, arguing that Gaby is better off with them, and that Alicia's pursuit will cause Gaby to lose the only family she knows. This, however, only confirms for Alicia that Roberto has been lying all along. When Roberto finds that Gaby is missing, he beats Alicia until she confesses that Gaby is spending the night with Roberto's parents. Bashing her head into the wall and slamming her hand in the door, Roberto enacts upon Alicia a brief yet symbolic torture session, one that is broken only by Gaby's call, her voice on the phone denoting her absent presence within their home. As Gaby sings a lullaby to mommy into the phone, Alicia wraps her bloodied hand in a cloth remarkably similar to the Madres' embroidered white head scarves, hugs Roberto goodbye, and grabs her belongings, leaving her keys in the door as she slams it shut. Alicia herself has become an absent presence, no longer present, no longer a participant in the home Roberto's wealth has created, no longer subject to the official story.

In *Confronting the 'Dirty War' in Argentine Cinema: 1983–1993,* author Constance Burcúa writes that these films posit "the family unit as the primary victim of a fascist and repressive policy of state."[35] *The Official Story* illustrates this to be the case as the war has forever altered the respective families of Sara Rebello, Anna, Alicia, Roberto, Roberto's extended family, and perhaps Gaby henceforth. As Gaby's concluding song about being lost in "the land of I don't remember" conveys, The Disappeared's absent presence is also a wound scaring them all, heretofore and hereafter.

Biraben's *Cautiva* (2003) also uses The Dirty War's adopted children to tell its story of Argentina's Disappeared. Raised in the prosperous home of former national police officer Pablo Quadri and his wife Adela, Cristina does not even know she's adopted. After all, her birth certificate and identification card state she was born to the Quadris on March 20, 1979; she even has a photo of Adela pregnant with her.

As with *The Official Story,* *Cautiva* offers several expository scenes to demonstrate Cristina's middle-class complacency, including home video images of friends and family celebrating her fifteenth birthday, the traditional *Quinceañera,* preceded by newsreel footage from the 1978 World Cup, an early revelation to Cristina's actual birth taking place on this day when Argentina both hosted and won the series. The juxtaposition of this opening footage (with images of President Videla and Former US Secretary of State Henry Kissinger in attendance) with Cristina's *Quinceañera* likewise establishes interconnectivity between these political and personal events.

Other signs of The Disappeared as both absent and present in her life begin to emerge early in the film. In her political science class, for instance, Cristina's teacher has difficulty in quelling her student Angélica's protest that "the amnesty" offered to "war criminals" is not "in reality a presidential pardon of sorts" as her teacher suggests, but, rather, "unrestricted power."[36] A battle begins between the teacher, who is trying to keep the focus on the safe recitation of facts, and Angélica, who protests that amnesty allows the president to "throw away all the evidence collected for years against these assassins.[37] The teacher's blasé suggestion that Angélica should lobby

Congress to nullify the amnesty causes Angélica to curse, thus creating an excuse to discharge Angélica for administrative reprimand. In subsequent days that follow, Angélica doesn't return to class, an absent presence noted by Cristina with resigned complacency, Angélica's empty desk a focal point for Biraben's camerawork.

Cristina also puts forth little protest to her friend Suzanne's dismissal of Angélica's parents as "leftist radicals" who "used to kill people with bombs. Even priests."[38] According to Suzanne, The Disappeared weren't detained, tortured, or killed; they simply "ran away" or "left the country," and there was no Dirty War, just a "war against Communists."[39] Suzanne dismisses Angélica's disappearance, seeing Angélica as guilty by association to subversive parents, thus modeling how "the military Junta maintained the strategic denial that complemented the physical disappearance of the victim."[40]

Abruptly, Cristina's worldview shifts when, much like Angélica, she is "summoned from her classroom, given over to the custody of a high-ranking judge and forbidden to contact her parents."[41] The judge produces blood tests taken secretly after Cristina's routine appendectomy that reveal "with 99.98% certainty" that she is really Sofia Lombardi, the daughter taken from her Disappeared biological parents during their imprisonment.[42] As the judge explains, "your case is called 'appropriation' because the transfer of your custody was executed without your natural parents' permission."[43] Cristina is just one many "who are just now learning the truth" about their biological origins.[44]

Cristina/Sofia's age and the film's 1994 setting matter; still under 18, she becomes a ward of the court, ordered to live with her maternal biological grandmother, Elisa Dominich. Biraben subtlety demonstrates the class distinctions between the two households as Elisa's home and neighborhood are shabbier and older, and Cristina/Sofia will now be enrolled in the local public school as Sofia Lombari, not the private Catholic school Cristina Quadri attended. Cristina feels captured, kidnapped from the world she has known into a completely altered reality.

In denial, Cristina runs from the judge's office and out of the court building, taking a series of public transportation options in an attempt to return to her home with the Quadris. Calling them from the train station nearby, Cristina barely opens her father's car door before unmarked police vehicles surround it. Although Pablo attempts to use his police background to extricate them from the situation, his demands fall on deaf ears. In an ironic reversal, the police vehicles once used to kidnap The Disappeared are now being employed to return Cristina/Sofia to her biological family.

Yet Cristina/Sofia feels herself to be a victim of kidnaping and captivity, and the film's early scenes of Cristina's birthday celebrations and contented family life make the Quadris seem initially more like victims than villains. Briefly reunited while she gathers her belongings, the Quadris tell Cristina that her biological parents abandoned her in infancy, on a disserted train. Per Pablo, a fellow officer knew that Adela had recently miscarried and offered Cristina to the couple. They didn't ask questions, Adela tells her, "After all we had gone through, we didn't want to know."[45]

Gradually, and through a series of vignettes and montages, Cristina/Sofia begins to soften toward her biological family; she bonds with her mother's younger sister Ana and Ana's children, and learns more about her biological parents – their careers as architects, the house they designed (in which Ana now lives) with a nursery for Sofia, their hobbies, and their tastes in music and art. These conversations and revelations, however, do more to illustrate their absence for her than to bring them to life. This absence is heightened for Cristina/Sofia when she discovers her mother's bedroom has been untouched since her disappearance, everything left exactly the same as the day she was kidnapped those 16 years past. Their ever-present absence galvanizes Cristina/Sofia to discover what happened to them, and, subsequently, what happened to her.

Cristina's search is greatly aided by Angélica, who attends Cristina's new high school and has herself been searching public records for information about her disappeared father. Angélica confesses that she remembers her early years at Orletti, a *pozo* hidden within a Buenos Aires' garage; she and her mother were released, but her father was never seen again. Angélica soon undercovers Marta, a nurse assigned to deliver Sofia, who recalls the birth for its unusual circumstances and unique date in history. Marta confirms that Cristina was born in June 1978, not March 1979, and that the birth was attended by an unknown woman who insisted that Cristina be breastfed before her appropriation. Given a photo of Cristina's birthday gathering, Marta remembers Cristina's godfather as a "main thug" called "Glow-Worm" as well.[46] As Marta provides her memories of that evening, the film uses her narrative as voiceover for accompanying imagery, featuring Sofia's mother in the agonies of both childbirth and from fresh cuts, burns and bruises from a recent torture session. Having borne witness to this and many other horrors, Marta is clearly still living with the painful presence of memory.

Naturally, these details contradict the Quadris' account of her adoption; she would have been 9 months old, not days old, calling their complicity into question yet again. This time, however, Pablo and Adela do not seek to cajole her, but, rather, argue that subversives are dangerous, and that they never wanted to know the truth of Cristina's parentage. The film's final scene focuses in on Cristina standing on the balcony of the house her biological parents designed, turning to Elisa to ask, "Nana, about their disappearance, is it forever?"[47] A crane shot to the Argentine night sky soon leads to the film's dedications, and a final note that "Those responsible, except for a few cases of house arrest, are free, protected by laws created for their benefit, by subsequent democratic governments."[48] This absence of punishment is still ever-present in collective consciousness.

As melodramatic as *Cautiva*'s plot may seem, Cristina, in many respects, is an "everyman" figure for a pertinent theme in civil law and culture: how DNA testing has altered the national dialogues about recovering lost offspring. To date, The *Abuelas de Plaza de Mayo*'s "Grandparents' Index, a human-leukocyte-antigen test that can identify a link between grandparents and their grandchildren", has been used to locate "eighty-three of the five hundred grandchildren believed to have been taken."[49] As *Cautiva* reveals, "the children of The Disappeared are potent symbols of how Argentina addresses its past."[50]

Irresolution also marks those Dirty War films based on the memoirs of those kidnapped and tortured in *pozos* who lived to tell their stories. *Chronicle of An Escape* (2006), for example, adapts its screenplay from Claudio Tamburrini's memoir of his 121-day incarceration at La Mansion Seré in Buenos Aires, while *Garage Olimpo* (1999) takes as its basis the memories of director Marco Bechis's own 10-day internment ("his Italian passport apparently saved him"), coupled with testimonies of others about their imprisonment.[51] Both are unique in their focus on The Disappeared as central protagonists in a narrative centered on their capture, torture, and escape or demise.

Yet, here, too, the subjectivity of The Disappeared is an ever-present absence. In *Garage Olimpo*, for instance, main character Maria Fabriani is "conspicuously de-politicized and deprived of a personal history."[52] Other than a short scene in which she is teaching literacy classes to poor adults, there is no other element of how or why her mother's well-connected friend claims she is "mixed up in politics;" nothing more is offered to illustrate her personality or identity before she becomes prisoner A01 at this infamous torture center.[53] The same is true for Claudio and his fellow prisoners in *Chronicle of An Escape*. An opening soccer game and shower scene with a largely silent Claudio provide viewers merely with the knowledge that he plays *fútbol* for his university. During the torture sequences, Claudio learns that a fellow prisoner and distant acquaintance named him under torture in order to give his friends time to escape, but Claudio's own ideas, preferences, and beliefs are as absent from this narrative as they are in *Garage Olimpo*.

Instead, both films concentrate their attention on realistically depicting the physical tortures experienced by detainees. For Maria, this begins with being stripped naked, blindfolded, and given 15,000 volts of electric shock before having her heart resuscitated, so that the process can continue; it ends with her slumped body falling forward on a death flight. For Claudio, this involves being blindfolded, handcuffed to a bed, beaten, and submerged in water headfirst, sometimes concurrently; it ends with his escape along with three other prisoners, all of them naked and handcuffed, perceived as outcasts on the streets thereafter. While quite graphic, these scenes also have a distancing effect, *Garage* for its use of black and white video monitor imagery for the most visceral explicit torture scenes, and *Chronicle* for its choice to cut away from these images, preferring to show the aftermath of physical torture rather than its process. Yet the camera in and of itself further participates in the characters' objectification through the use of center framing and close-ups, choices that posit these Disappeared protagonists as objects rather than subjects.

More importantly, this subject position is given to their captors, who seek mastery over their victims, and demonstrate agency in their ability to generate psychological suffering. Both characters are subjected to mock executions, games of obedience and group think. Maria particularly experiences this as one of her captors is her mother's tenant Felix, who, just coincidentally works at the *pozo* and has long tried to date her. For Maria, Felix's presence is often a source of salvation, for it is he who brings her additional food and bribes the other guards not to rape her and to give her 15 minute breaks during her electrocutions. However, it is Felix, not Maria, who has agency to protect her from her tormentors' whims and weapons.

Objectification, unquestionably, is the intent of torture, a practice meant to make absent the persecuted one's humanity. Elaine Scarry articulates this process as one by which the prisoner's "world, self, and voice are lost, or nearly lost, through the intense pain of torture," as s/he "experiences an annihilating negation."[54] Certainly, for all intents and purposes, both films' desires to portray accurately the sights and sounds experienced by The Disappeared during their imprisonment comes at the expense of providing subject positions for those characters. In these films, they are present only in body.

In "How Traumatized Societies Remember: The Aftermath of Argentina's Dirty War," author Antonious C. G. M. Robben argues that "The continual resurgence of traumatic memories from the dirty war indicates that Argentine society has not yet come to terms with its past."[55] Indeed, as films about The Dirty War continue to be made in the twenty-first century, they have mirrored and modeled this process of negotiation, creating cinematic works that continue to grapple with how best to chronicle atrocity, history, and memory.

11

Featuring Acts of Genocide in Chilean Film

Gloria J. Galindo

Roskilde University

There are a few Chilean filmmakers who have dealt with the recent historic past in feature films such as *Imagen Latente* (1987) directed by Pablo Perelman; *La Frontera* (1991) by Ricardo Larraín; *Amnesia* (1994) by Gonzalo Justiniano; *Machuca* (2004) directed by Andres Wood, Miguel Littin´s *Dawson, Isla 10* (2009) and *Allende en su laberinto* (2014). There is also the work of the documentarian Patricio Guzmán, who has made award-winning documentaries about the military coup and Pinochet´s dictatorship, including *La Batalla de Chile* (1979), *Chile, la memoria obstinada* (1997), and *Nostalgia de la luz* (2010). Although the previous films did bring the recent past to the silver screen, Larraín is the first and only filmmaker who has made three successive films dealing with this traumatic period of Chilean history, engaging in an extended analysis of the period from three different perspectives. In this essay, I explore the cinematic representation of acts of genocide perpetrated by the dictatorship in Chile through Larraín's trilogy consisting of *Tony Manero* (2008), *Post Mortem* (2010), and *NO* (2012). I include as well his first feature film *Fuga* (2006) in which the filmmaker reflects on an artist's unresolved traumatic past and its impact on the creative process. I argue that the articulation of a traumatic past and the artistic process in the film is the filmmaker's groundwork for the trilogy, which is his attempt to understand the complexity of Chile's recent past.[1]

While I will not discuss the term genocide at length here, I would like to state that I use the broader and inclusive understanding of the term coined by Raphael Lemkin. He combined the Greek word *genos* that means, "race/people" and the Latin *cīdere,* which means "to kill," in order to define genocide as "the destruction of a nation or of an ethnic group." However, he argues that genocide does not mean the destruction of an entire nation, but rather "a coordinated plan of different actions aiming at the destruction of essential foundations of the life of national groups."[2] On the contrary, the legal definition of the Convention on the Prevention and Punishment of the Crime of Genocide (CPPCG) is the result of diplomatic compromises and is therefore exclusive and discriminatory. CPPCG defines genocide as "acts committed with intent to destroy in whole or in part, a national, ethical, racial or religious group." This definition excludes politicide (the killing of a human group due to political affiliation), leaving these groups to the mercy of state-sponsored terror, although more people have been killed for political reasons than for others.

Genocide as the (partial) destruction of a nation or ethnic group must be understood as an injury to the social body since the survivors carry the indelible mark of an unthinkable event. As such, it is a traumatizing event or events with widespread cultural repercussions. Trauma is "an overwhelming experience of sudden or catastrophic events, in which the response to the event occurs in the often delayed, and uncontrolled repetitive occurrence of hallucinations and other intrusive phenomena."[3] The context of these events, often a series of events, states Turim, "becomes key to the severity of their wounding," of which one of the effects is "to distance the self not only from one's memory, but also from the experience of others, and from any collective formation." Furthermore, she claims that "individual and collective elements of trauma are often interwoven and inextricable. When one is a member of a traumatized collectivity, what has happened to others like one's self has the potential to multiply the wounds."[4] In other words, collective trauma impacts in different ways not only the victim of the injury but also the victim's family and social context by repressing or rejecting the individual or collective experience, or by transferring it to the collectivity, creating collective memories. Moreover,

Caruth understands trauma as a new possibility of history as well. If we want to write about the past, the author argues, it is imperative to register the impact of historic violence by locating it not "only in the destructive moment of the past, but in an ongoing survival that belongs to the future." Violence does not disappear with the end of the traumatic events but becomes part of the traumatized memory of those who survive and "it may be witnessed best in the future generations to whom this survival is passed on."[5]

Freund argues that genocide as subject for film, – which is also relevant, *mutatis mutandis,* to trauma – embodies a paradox due to it being "unrepresentable in the magnitude of its horror and yet its image, perhaps more than any other, represents its subject to a point of excess."[6] In this sense, film has to negotiate the impossibility of representing genocide or trauma in the intersection of aesthetics and ethics, as well as the formal and narrative aspects. As Cresswell and Karimova ask themselves, the conflict lies in whether or not "such cinematic representations 'fairly portray' [...] the experience of trauma itself? Or, to what extent they do – through stereotypical cultural representations – *reproduce* the very forms of *structural power* which may, in the first place, be trauma's generative cause?" Finally, they wonder if it is "possible to *problematize*, through the medium of cinema itself, these stereotypical representations?" In other words, the authors wonder if it is possible to reflect on trauma through cinema by questioning the characteristics of some cinematic representations that stereotype the traumatic experience, instead of thinking about the effects of trauma's causal mechanisms. In filmmakers who have experienced trauma, the authors assert, trauma affects the filmmaker's perception of subject and world in the cinematic encounter constituted by the film's form and content.[7] Kaplan reinforces the latter by arguing that the only approach to trauma is through "its figuration by either its victim, by those witnessing it, or by artists undertaking its telling." That is, the best approach to trauma is by those who have directly, or indirectly, experienced it. She argues further that cinema "may be especially appropriate to figuring the visual, aural and no-linear fragmented phenomena of trauma ... Trauma analysis aims to distinguish and understand trauma landscapes – their politics, aesthetics and impacts."[8]

Pablo Larraín's first feature film, *Fuga*,[9] is a Chilean-Argentine co-production that revolves around Eliseo, a traumatized young composer and his inability to create, not because of the difficulty of the piece but rather because he associates music with the mysterious rape and killing of his sister, which he witnessed as a child. The repeated image of the event comes to his mind as flashbacks. Flashbacks are used in film to signify "temporal occurrences anterior to those in the images that preceded it [that] concern a representation of the past that intervenes with the present flow of film narrative," and to reorganize the structure of the story.[10] On one occasion, Eliseo remembers a summer day and hearing heavy and monotone piano notes as he peers through a window and sees a bloody scene with his sister leaning back on the piano and a man leaning on her. The day of the *première* of Eliseo's masterpiece, *Danza Macabra* (*Dance of Death*), Georgina, the orchestra's pianist and his love interest, suddenly dies. He collapses, convinced that his music and violence and death are fatally intertwined, and begins a series of escapes: first from his music, and then from a mental institution where his parents have locked him up, and finally, an escape from his own life when he realizes that there is no way out, and he throws himself into the sea. I propose that the tragic death of Eliseo's sister is a signifier of the unknown and yet latent past of which the filmmaker has been deprived by his family and social environment. The rape and murder of the girl could also be an allegory for the genocide of thousands of Chilean citizens whose only crime was to be dissidents or active participants in the struggle for social change and a better and more democratic society. "Allegory in film is not a genre or a style, but a mode of representation characterized by the dialectic articulation between the tendency to construct a coherent picture of social reality and aesthetic fragmentation – as for example flashbacks or black and white images combined with color images – as the result of the failure to achieve it."[11] In this sense, rape, murder, and madness in *Fuga* are allegories used as a tool for signifying the abusive relations of power in the unrepresentable reality during the military regime that used mass genocide and rape of women in order to overpower or eliminate its dissidents. Madness, on the other hand, can suggest the impossibility of understanding traumatic events that are beyond human comprehension.

The film focuses on the impact in the present of an unresolved past, reflecting on how the protagonist deals with a traumatic memory as the aftermath of an event of which he has only partial recollection. The director attempts here to reflect on and inquire about a past as a loss – a lost past – which he, like the protagonist, has been denied. The film takes the form of a nightmarish representation of an artist's creative journey where music and childhood trauma intersect, operating as a reflection on the human condition, not as memory or reality, but as hallucination. That is why the narrative is fragmented and inconsistent with many narrative holes and a lack of a congruent backstory in order to reconstruct the truth and resolve the conflict. The intersection between the protagonist's obsession with his composition and his fragmented and unexplained recollection suggests that Eliseo does not have all the pieces of the puzzle in order to reconstruct the past. Therefore, he is unable to construe a logic system of signifiers, (i.e. a music piece) that would make sense to the latent narrative of his memory.

Although Larraín is one of the few Chilean filmmakers who confronts Chile's recent past in feature films, he does not come from a liberal or socially critical environment, but from a right wing wealthy family. Both of his parents are politicians and members of the conservative political party that supported Augusto Pinochet's military regime, and they still support his legacy. He claims that he has been ashamed of having an oblivious childhood, having been unaware of what happened during the military dictatorship, and having not been told the truth when he was younger.[12] The filmmaker does not share his parents' political beliefs, and he is a confessed anti-Pinochet. He believes that the Chilean political right as supporter of the Pinochet regime "is directly responsible for what happened to the culture during those years, not only by destroying it or restricting it, but also through the persecution of writers and artists."[13] In an interview with *The New York Times* regarding winning the Directors' Fortnight in Cannes 2012 for *NO*, he admits that when he was a child, he was completely ignorant of what was happening in Chile. He was a teenager when he became aware: "I felt that I had missed something that a lot of people had experienced, which is called fear and pain." However, he wishes to "understand it, not to experience that – not even to tell it, just to expose it." In the same interview, Larraín claims that after completing his trilogy with *No* (2012) – his last film on the dictatorship – he realizes that it has been an impossible task. He means

161

that "[t]here's a huge mystery for [him] about those days," and despite all he knows about the horrible past, there is still an "invisible truth" that he cannot grasp, and therefore he accepts that "[a]fter making three films [he] didn't get it," and therefore he is done with it.[14] Nevertheless, Larraín has made three consecutive feature films that deal with Chilean recent history, based on a fictionalized historic narrative full of tension and conflict that explore the traumatic past, unintentionally creating a trilogy on the dictatorship. However, I argue that *Fuga* is a sort of prelude to Larraín's trilogy. In *Fuga*, the filmmaker reflects on the tension that articulates art, a personal experience of loss, and the latent traumatic past that stands in the way of artistic creativity. The trilogy, however, is about fictionalized, sometimes historic, events that occurred during the military dictatorship. *Tony Manero* revolves around a serial killer under Pinochet's dictatorship. Contrary to *Fuga*, *Tony Manero* appeals to dirtiness in a mise-en-scène shaped by the blurred image of a 16mm. hand camera, by the shock of violent scenes, and by the inclusion of a sick and unpleasant protagonist. In *Post Mortem*, the history of the genocide during the military coup d'état is shown through the gaze of an apathetic morgue clerk who receives emotionlessly the bodies of the victims of the coup.[15] *NO* tells the story of the advertisement for the No-campaign during the plebiscite in 1988.

Tony Manero is not the first film to deal with the dictatorship, but it is the first to do so without being overtly political, allowing for multiple collective imaginations from that specific historical moment.[16] *Tony Manero*'s mise-en-scène is greyish, shadowy, and at times blurred, and often with jump cuts. In the film, Santiago is a curfew phantom city, where crime, military patrols, and summary executions are unpunished by the suspended rule of law of the state of exception, and fear and anxiety invade the mood.[17] The film's protagonist is a middle-aged man named Raúl Peralta, in the shadow of Pinochet's dictatorship, and who is obsessed with Tony Manero, Travolta's character in *Saturday Night Fever*. Peralta is a misogynistic, unemployed man who fashions himself a performer, a cabaret dancer in the outskirts of the city. He is a sexually impotent serial killer who works, under the cloak of state-sponsored terror, kills unrepentantly while in the background we hear the sounds of machine guns and handguns, sirens, and military vehicles along with the shouting and yelling of people during military raids in the neighborhood.

The year is 1978, Chile has been under Pinochet's dictatorship and imposed curfew since September 11, 1973, and military forces have kidnapped, disappeared, and killed thousands of Chilean citizens. Peralta is unaffected by what is happening in the country; quite the contrary, he uses the chaos to his own benefit, that is, to kill in order to acquire the necessary tools for his performance in a local bar's cabaret show, and a TV competition show for Tony Manero impersonators. On one occasion, he helps an older woman after she is assaulted by a gang of youngsters only to brutally kill her and steal her TV once inside her apartment. On another occasion, he steals the wallet and watch of a man who has been fatally beaten by paramilitary forces. Later, he kills an elderly couple who own the local theater because they replace the showing of *Saturday Night Fever* with *Grace* (1978). Finally, he kills a shop owner in order to steal the rest of the glass floor he needs for his show that he has already begun to acquire by trading the stolen TV. The figure of the serial killer is an allegory for both the society that the military regime has created, and the regime of terror people live under: As Larraín states, Raúl "acts with impunity. He is enraged. His desires reflect the enraged behavior of a government,"[18] and the arbitrariness of its crimes. In a sense, the film is an exploration of how the country in the impunity of a state of exception deals with the fact that the police force is part of the military regime and that their main goal is to persecute, disappear, and kill their opponents, instead of protecting the population against crime. The protagonist is a twofold allegory of the repressive forces' actions and the reaction to state sponsored terror. At the same time, the film attempts to construct an unresolved traumatic memory instead of an expected testimonial and final memory that could retort the past.

The second film of Larraín's trilogy, *Post Mortem*, goes back to the beginning, September 1973, days before the military coup. The opening scene is a black screen and a noise in the background that proves to be coming from a military tank that is seen from under the undercarriage driving down an empty littered street. The angle of shot is almost impossible from a human point of view, which shows, quoting Pemjean, its "unascribable status, the certainty that no one can see from this position, that no one stormed Santiago on 11 September 1973 clinging to the belly of a military truck."[19]

The next scene introduces Mario, an undaunted and lank-haired autopsy clerk, whose main spare time activity is to watch from his windows the comings and goings of his neighbor, who is a cabaret dancer named Nancy. He is a sort of voyeur who looks furtively at the dancers in the burlesque club from where Nancy has just been fired, not only for being too thin but also for getting older. The figure of the voyeur often appears "in accounts of cinema spectatorship as shorthand for gendered dynamics of power; the homology between the cinematic apparatus and the subjugation of women relies on understanding the act of unseen gazing as a form of sexual domination."[20] However, here the voyeuristic gaze could be understood as the enunciation signifier of a new power dynamic that soon will take place and symbolically will emasculate men, and frame women and other minorities as subaltern to the misogynic, masculine, and patriarchal rules reinforced by the new to be relations of power. Mario takes Nancy home after she is fired. Their journey is interrupted suddenly by a student march in the opposite direction where Nancy meets a long-haired student leader who invites her to join him, while Mario is left behind frustrated but unperturbed as they disappear into the crowd. The director envisions the crowd here more as a physical flow than a massive group of political protesters against which the protagonist and his "cadaveric" love interest are moving, suggesting a move "against the grain" of history, that is, a historic regression that will destroy a democratic tradition by the establishment of an authoritarian regime. The mass slows his car down, as if "it was a wheat field, grown grassland, or a flow of water (all figures of the mass from Canetti's *Crowds and Power* [1962])."[21] The true crowd in the film will later prove to be the mass of dead people who were either collected from the streets or supplied by the military to the Forensic Institute. After losing sight of Nancy and the student, Mario keeps moving through the mass, unaffected by the events that we will later learn were the last protests before the military coup.

A few days after, on September 11, Mario wakes up to an empty neighborhood. Nancy's house is also empty and vandalized. Santiago is in a state of siege, confining people to their homes, and reduced to ruins; cars have been destroyed by tanks, and the only sounds come from the unseen vigilant fighter planes that thunder overhead. At the morgue, dead bodies are piling up everywhere, waiting to be autopsied, obliterating the crime with

a legal death certificate, as if they were casualties of war and not mass murder against defenseless people, which becomes clear with the first autopsied body. The forensic team's first autopsy is carried out not in the institute
but in the hospital in front of a group of high-ranking military officials as
witnesses. When Mario, still unperturbed, is instructed to type directly on
an electric typewriter that he cannot even use, he is replaced by a soldier.
The special autopsy "of a brutalized body precedes the revelation that this
is [the president] Allende himself, the victim of murder or suicide."[22] After
trying to give a detailed autopsy description, the forensic doctor states that
the victim died from a short-distance gunshot wound that could have been
inflicted by himself, keeping the autopsy open for interpretation. Similar to
the fate of the crowd of dead bodies and the president, is that of Nancy and
her friend, "signaled by a lengthy close up of an egg, left frying in the pan
to a charred black."[23] The next day, Nancy is found hiding in a shed at her
home; Mario helps her until he learns that she is also hiding the longhaired
student. When Mario realizes that she is taking advantage of him, he locks
them both in the shed and blocks access to it so they disappear into the
surroundings of an occupied and deaf city. This figure of immuration operates here as a device of annunciation of the massive kidnapping and forced
disappearance of the regime's opponents that the military forces inaugurate
with the coup, using clandestine torture locations, and later mass burials
in order to hide the bodies. However, the film focuses not on the historic
event but on the protagonist's narrative as an allegory for the recent history.
Whereas the military coup is the backstory that takes place in absence, the
protagonists of recent past are a lifeless crowd piled up in the morgue. The
procedure of the autopsy can be read, as one of the scriptwriters suggests,
as the autopsy of Chile.[24] It is a reflection on the country as the death of its
democratic tradition as we knew it, or the birth of a new political order
based on torture, forced disappearances, and mass murder.

The third film of the trilogy, *NO*, which is based on *El plebiscito
(Referendum),* an unpublished play by Antonio Skármeta, is a fictionalized retelling of the advertising for the No campaign of 1988, which lob-
bied for votes against the continuation of the Pinochet regime. The film
shows the tension between the ad men and the organizers and detractors
of the campaign. Shot on U-matic cameras as a device to recreate the visual raw look and the mood of the 1980s, *No* intertwines archival footage,

blurs the line between reality and fiction, and creates an "illusion where the archival footage becomes fiction and the fiction becomes archival footage,"[25] as if past and present are flowing within each other. The film features the overlapping of footage of historic actors from 20 years ago with their present-day images. In a sense, what fascinates Larraín is a certain idea of the eternal return as memory, or the memory that keeps coming back, in terms of seeing "how a person's body says again what it once said, thinks what was once thought, returns to where it once was. It returns, and that's the work of memory."[26] In a way, he uses the advertising campaign as a metaphor to signify the common space where the "pact that Chile signed with an economic model" took place and failed, which, Larraín claims is "woven in the campaign and the referendum, because we said no to Pinochet but yes to his system. There's a piece of the Yes that won. That's why we focused on the ad man."[27] This idea coincides with the idea that in postmodernism, the market is the place of negotiation of not only commodities but also of social relations and affects. The film is a pastiche with "a strange balance between documentary and fiction," between history and narrative, which means, "the way things happen in the movie is not exactly the way they were, but the facts are the same."[28] *NO* centers around advertisement executive Rene Saavedra, son of a prominent Chilean dissident exiled in Mexico. He works at the same time with other commercial advertisements, which seek "to provide joy," in a country that is under a military regime and violates human rights.

Convinced that Chile needs to be cheered up, Eugenio García-the historic ad man who created the No campaign (in association with José Manuel Salcedo)-says that "[w]hat we need to convey, looking up at a deep blue sky, is the feeling you have when black clouds part and the sun finally breaks through. What is that word?: "La alegría!" Joy! That was the slogan: "Chile, la alegría ya viene" Chile, joy is coming."[29] The campaign strategy raised controversy among the coalition of political groups organizing the No campaign because of the brutality of the 15-year dictatorship, in which an estimated 3,000 political opponents had been killed, another 3,000 had disappeared, "and about ten times that number had been tortured, abused and raped by Pinochet's secret police. The vote was going to be a straight choice: "yes" or "no" to eight more years of the *Generalissimo*."[30] However, Larraín does not want to recount strictly the historic facts but rather to capture the cultural mood in Chile of 1988. "There was something in the air, like a sensation. It is not only about the story and about the dramatic plot. It is also about the atmosphere. I tried to capture that from the memories and feelings I grew up with. The sensation I am talking about is heavy and unsettling. It was a super grey moment in Chile's history."[31] Larraín intertwined in the film a series of black and white archival images of the military coup, the mass murder of dissidents, and the persecution of people, as the process of choosing material for the No advertisement, and doing so, he is not just telling the story of the campaign but also a story of genocide and trauma. Within this footage, the tape of the *cueca sola* (a solo dance) stands out, danced alone by women, whose husbands, sons, brothers, or fathers were among the dead or disappeared. The dance of women and its representation operates as the resignification of genocide represented by the absence of men, who disappeared and whose photos are pinned to the women's dresses or hang around their necks. The black and white footage that intertwines with fictional footage could be read here as the representation of "a certain disability of remembering or forgetting completely the traumatic experience, along with the relentless pursuit of understanding the unresolved past,"[32] which is the unifying thread along Larraín's trilogy. The trilogy is an attempt to overcome his disability of remembering and the obstinate search for understanding the unresolved past by recreating the recent traumatic history and doing so creating individual and collective memories.

The protagonist, who is a young single father divorced from his political dissident wife, seems like the other protagonists in Larraín's films, detached from the environment that surrounds him. He lives an apathetic life alone with his son and their live-in-maid. It seems as if he cannot feel any joy in his life, as if he does not believe his own discourse of joy. His commitment to the advertisement is not political but strictly professional. The apprehensions about the campaign's political and ethical issues and traumatic experiences of the campaign organizers do not concern him, because contrary to the coalition of political parties and grassroots organizations for the No campaign, he does not believe in it or he is indifferent to the arrival of a possible collective joy or democracy. Being a child of exile, his attitude of denial, detachment, or disinterest seems like a defense mechanism for avoiding the effects of a traumatic experience. In this sense, the referendum appears to be a space of resignification of the recent past by means of revisiting archives and narratives, which deepen or open the wounds of the individual and collective trauma, and affect society as a whole. All this evokes what Turim states above, that trauma is an overwhelming experience, and the reaction to it is often uncontrolled and delayed. One of the effects of trauma is the detachment from memory, from others' experiences, and from the collectivity.[33] Saavedra is a child of exile, which means that he belongs to a country that struggles with its traumatic past, meaning in turn that he is part of this national culture of trauma. The day of the referendum, half of the Chilean population is thrilled celebrating the No triumph on the street, among them all those involved in the No campaign, except for Saavedra himself, its architect. Saavedra seems not indifferent but sad and lonely because he is not able to share the joy of his colleagues, even though more than half of his fellow citizens see the No victory as a sign of hope for democracy and justice. In the final scenes, Saavedra is back to his regular job, untouched by the historic moment of the plebiscite that has just passed.

Larraín's trilogy is a singular portrayal of trauma of genocide that in each case revolves around a protagonist who can be a middle-aged or a younger single man: it can be a misogynic serial killer, a stalker forensic clerk, or an apathetic ad man, who also is sexually impotent or dysfunctional …, and whose backstories are a set of fictionalized moments around Pinochet era. In this sense, Larraín's work can be understood as a subjective trauma narrative in which he explores the tension between trauma and artistic expression, in an always-present past. However, the trilogy also operates as a narrative of a collective traumatic experience, or a post memory narrative, that attempts to recreate the unknown or the transferred past by articulating the individual and the collective experience. Trauma "is not just *reflected* by, but *constituted* in culture," and representing it "cinematically is a means to reflect it,"[34] but also to create and recreate witnesses and collective memory as legacy for the future.

Trauma narrative is not only about conflicted characters and historic backstories, or the retelling of the traumatic past, but also about a certain technology that conveys the mood of trauma or post-traumatic effects of the historic events. For Larraín, technology is a significant device in making film and a crucial tool in narrating the mood of the past. His aim is not to represent history but, as Larraín puts it, to "capture through tone and atmosphere a slice of life, a piece of humanity. And maybe then [to be] able to provide a tiny grain of understanding of what happened. Society has tried to understand what happened in [the] country through logic, and it does not work. Life is not like that."[35] Paraphrasing Bongers, Larraín is aware that since the beginning of the last century, modern history and memory are archived mainly by means of audiovisual technology. In his films, the filmmaker meticulously combines anachronistic audiovisual technologies with contemporary digital formats creating a tension between technology's history and the history of the recent past, which does not mean just rewriting the history of the recent past but also the national history of audiovisual technology.[36] Because of the scope of his project, Larraín's trilogy has created controversy among the national spectatorship questioning his entitlement to participate in (re)writing history and creating collective memory. One of the reasons for this has been that Larraín deals with fiction, or fictionalized historic events, and according to the filmmaker, the country has lost its ability to understand fiction, which is "one of the most hidden legacies of the dictatorship [...] to believe that everything works in the realm of reality, where abstraction is not possible. And abstraction is a key because with it you build imaginaries, you create poetry."[37]

12

Screening the Killing Fields: The Cambodian Genocide on Film

Cathy J. Schlund-Vials

University of Connecticut – Storrs

On April 17, 1975, during the Cambodian New Year, black-uniformed Khmer Rouge soldiers entered the capital city, Phnom Penh. Arriving on trucks, in jeeps, and on foot, the communist Khmer Rouge triumphantly declared an end to US imperialism and civil war.[1] Armed with AK-47s, Khmer Rouge troops urged, via loudspeaker announcements, Phnom Penh's denizens to welcome them as liberators and peacemakers. Notwithstanding pacifist claims, the Khmer Rouge – perhaps not surprisingly, given their bellicose dress and warlike demeanor – summarily executed those most immediately affiliated with the previous regime, namely members of the vigorously anti-communist Lon Nol administration and his army.[2] In the days and weeks that followed, the Khmer Rouge renamed the nation "Democratic Kampuchea" and systematically emptied Cambodia's cities, forcing residents – often at gunpoint – to vacate their homes and march to countryside labor camps.

Guided by the "revolutionary" desire to instantiate an agrarian utopia and turn the country back to "year zero" by eliminating all traces of Western influence, technology, and Khmer tradition, the Pol Pot-led Khmer Rouge specifically targeted and unabashedly killed those most "tainted" due to education and past affiliation: teachers, doctors, Buddhist monks, lawyers, civil servants, Royal Khmer court musicians, dancers, and artists, along with their families.[3] The Khmer Rouge likewise eradicated those deemed incapable of contributing to the regime's revolutionary agenda, particularly the weak, the sick, and the elderly. Indeed, as Cambodia's cities were emptied, hospital patients – even those anesthetized and in surgery – were abandoned, left to die.[4] In addition to banning private ownership, currency, and religion, the Khmer Rouge regime prohibited the use of "Western" medicines (such as penicillin) and proscribed formal education, insisting that one's schooling occur not in the classroom but in the fields.[5] To further ensure full allegiance to *Angka* ("The Organization"), Khmer Rouge cadres separated wives from their husbands, parents from their children. The use of familial names for "mother" and "father" was forbidden; instead, children referred to parents and other family members as "comrades."[6] In a society obsessed with purging – by any means necessary – the pre-regime, pre-Khmer Rouge past, children were considered ideal subjects because they held, by mere virtue of age, the least amount of memory.[7]

The Khmer Rouge reign of terror came to an abrupt end 3 years, 8 months, and 20 days later, when the Vietnamese army – as per the Cambodian-Vietnam War (1977–1979) – overtook Phnom Penh on January 7, 1979.[8] Despite the relatively brief time of Khmer Rouge rule, *Angka*'s impacts were dramatic, wide-ranging, and long-lasting: in the post-conflict era, 65 percent of the population was female; only nine judges remained; out of 550 doctors, 48 survived; three-quarters of Cambodia's teachers were executed or fled the country; 90 percent of Khmer court musicians and artists were dead.[9] An estimated 1.7 million Cambodians – approximately 21 to 25 percent of the nation's population – perished due to disease, execution, forced labor, and starvation. Over the next decade, faced with ongoing political instability, crushing poverty, and no infrastructure, approximately 510,000 Cambodians fled to nearby Thailand seeking asylum; another 100,000 sought refuge in Vietnam.[10] More than 150,000 Cambodian refugees eventually relocated to the United States, while others made their way to Australia and France, among other countries.[11]

Known as the period of the "Killing Fields" for those outside Cambodia and "Pol Pot time" within, this genocidal history, as Youk Chhang, director of the Documentation Center of Cambodia (DC-Cam), observes, has contributed to a sense that Cambodia is "known to the world for two things – Angkor Wat and the 'killing fields' .... Some believe one came from God and the other from hell."[12] This reading of Cambodia's past and present identity as an unreconciled genocide state is complicated by the belatedness of justice for the regime's innumerable victims. Whereas almost 40 years have passed since the regime was ousted from power, to date only three former Khmer Rouge officials have successfully been tried and convicted of crimes against humanity: Kaing Guek Eav (a.k.a. "Comrade Duch"), Nuon Chea, and Khieu Samphan.[13] These convictions – rendered in 2010 and 2014 – occurred through the context of the hybrid "Extraordinary Chambers in the Courts of Cambodia" ("ECCC," also known as the U.N./Khmer Rouge Tribunal), which is presently pursuing additional cases involving crimes of genocide.[14] Admittedly, a number of high-ranking officials have already passed away from natural causes: for instance, the regime's leader, Pol Pot, died in 1998; its general, Ta Mok (known as "The Butcher"), passed away in 2006. Most recently, Ieng Thirith, Khmer Rouge Minister of Social Affairs, was in 2012 deemed mentally unfit to stand trial due to Alzheimer's diagnosis, was released from prison, and passed away in 2015. Her husband, Ieng Sary, the regime's former foreign minister, died of heart failure in 2013 while in ECCC custody.[15]

Set against these open-ended juridical frames, wherein prosecutions have been observably slow and reparations largely non-existent, films about the Cambodian genocide are – as this chapter from the outset maintains – imbued with the prosecutorial task of identifying regime crimes, recollecting individual survivor remembrances, and delineating perpetrators from victims.[16] Incontrovertibly, this diagnostic project is made more difficult given that – with the exception of two instances involving Vietnamese Cambodians (*Khmer Khrom*) and Cambodian Muslims (the *Cham*) – the Khmer Rouge did not target a specific ethnic or racial group, leading some scholars to characterize Democratic Kampuchea as an "autogenocide" state.[17] Hence, the very claim of genocide as it is connected to the Khmer Rouge state remains legally contested. Nevertheless, as this chapter's deeper consideration of films about the Cambodian genocide makes clear, the actuality of state-authorized mass killing is not only acknowledged but operates as an incontestable first premise in such productions. To be sure, films about the Cambodian genocide, which use collective remembrance and individual memory as a means of imagining alternative reparative spaces, bear more than passing resemblance to cinematic and cultural treatments of the Holocaust.

Moreover, the extent to which films about the Cambodian genocide endeavor to recollect "life under the Khmer Rouge" as a means of reclaiming a sense of Cambodian selfhood is at the forefront of a diasporic Cambodian cinematic canon marked by refugee subjectivities. This distinct body of work – comprised of directors who have found asylum in the United States and France – is, as Cambodian-refugee-turned-Cambodia's most prominent director Rithy Panh surmises, one wherein "memory must remain a reference point."[18] As individuals forced to leave the country of origin, diasporic Cambodian directors tirelessly contemplate the conditions that brought their refugee status "into being" while concomitantly negotiating a distant and often vexed relationship with the country of origin. It is through a still-unreconciled genocidal past that refugees are able to significantly recollect their particular experiences during the Democratic Kampuchean era and reclaim a lost Cambodian selfhood. Integral to diasporic Cambodian films about the genocide, then, is a judicious investigation of the Khmer Rouge period, which remains, as Khmer American filmmaker Mike Siv notes, a "wound we [as Cambodians] carry."[19] These critical engagements with genocide remembrance, which attempt to make legible the Democratic Kampuchean period and its aftermath, cohere with what Panh notes is at the forefront contemporary "Killing Fields" filmmaking: in the absence of internationally-sanctioned justice, these productions must lead to "comprehension [about the Khmer Rouge period]" and should "not establish a cult of memory."[20]

As primary context, I return the juridical registers of Cambodian genocide film to establish the relationship between recent tribunal politics and contemporary cinematic productions which – to varying degrees and by divergent ends – restage, rehearse, and remember the Khmer Rouge period. I provide a brief overview of films which engage the period as a starting point for explorations of refugee loss and identity; I also consider works which incorporate this history as a means of calibrating and measuring the disastrous legacies of the Cambodian genocide in the present. I then situate these juridical dimensions within a now familiar "before, during, after" narrative promulgated by Roland Joffé's 1984 film, *The Killing Fields*.

As the most well-known production about the Cambodian genocide, *The Killing Fields* serves as a chief cinematic referent for audiences and template for films that use, as both backdrop and foreground, "Pol Pot Time." Notwithstanding its cinematic prominence, the specificities of the Khmer Rouge regime in *The Killing Fields* are – as initial critical assessments about it underscore – obscured within a larger story of American involvement in Southeast Asia. Whereas *The Killing Fields* occupies a central place vis-à-vis Cambodian genocide film, and while the majority of films about the Khmer Rouge era are documentaries, more recent works such as Rithy Panh's *The Missing Picture* (2013) and Arthur Dong's *The Killing Fields of Dr. Haing S. Ngor* (2015) diverge from this particular "before, during, and after" script via mixed media and combined footage.[21] I conclude with Rithy Panh's cinematic oeuvre in order to map the past, present, and future contours of Cambodian genocide film.

The majority of short- and full-length films about the Cambodian genocide are documentaries, like John Pilger's 1979 televised *Year Zero: The Silent Death of Cambodia*, or productions based on survivor autobiographies and interviews, such as Jocelyn Glatzer's *The Flute Player* (2003) and Socheata Poeuv's *New Year Baby* (2006).[22] More recently, films about the Cambodian genocide both acknowledge the almost 2 million who perished yet also recollect the time before the Khmer Rouge, particularly through narratives that focus on pre-revolutionary Cambodian artists. This mode of cultural recollection is emblematized by Greg Cahill's short film, *The Golden Voice* (2007), based on popular Cambodian singer Ros Sereysothea, and director John Pirozzi's *Sleepwalking Through the Mekong* (2007) and *Don't Think I've Forgotten: Cambodia's Lost Rock and Roll* (2015), which focuses on a vibrant, pre-Khmer Rouge imaginary. Alternatively, other works consider – as a significant narrative backdrop – Khmer Rouge legacies in diasporic Cambodian refugee communities, expressly those based in the United States. These include Spencer Nakasako's Cambodian American trilogy, *A.K.A. Don Bonus* (1995), *Kelly Loves Tony* (1998), and *Refugee* (2004); Nicole Newnham and David Grabias's *Sentenced Home* (2006); and Masahiro Sugano's *Cambodian Son* (2014).[23] Whereas these works use the Khmer Rouge era as a starting point for contemplation of the present-day Cambodian American experience, Mike Siv's forthcoming *Surviving Justice: The Trial of the*

Khmer Rouge (working title) is more directly focused on the tribunal and follows the journey of genocide survivors as they return to Cambodia to observe court proceedings.[24]

This connection between prosecutorial agendas and Cambodian genocide film is also evident in the vexed legal reception of Rob Lemkin and Thet Sambath's *Enemies of the People* (2009), which at the titular level accesses an inimical Khmer Rouge characterization of so-termed threats to the Democratic Kampuchean state. Whereas the title indirectly suggests a focus on regime victims, *Enemies of the People* concentrates its attention on perpetrators, who from the outset admit to participating in mass killings. As *Enemies of the People* progresses, however, it becomes apparent that perpetrators were also victims of a volatile regime wherein internal purges were regular and common. As background, Sambath, a Cambodian journalist who lost his mother, father, and brother during the Khmer Rouge era, began to seek out individuals willing to confess war crimes and crimes against humanity; the interviews featured in *Enemies of the People* represent a culmination of Sambath's efforts and featured aforementioned Nuon Chea ("Brother Number Two"). Prior to completing the film, Chea was in 2007 apprehended by United Nations authorities and indicted by the tribunal, which began full-scale deliberations of his case three years later, in 2010.

While the perpetrator focus of *Enemies of the People* is apparent via the subjects highlighted and the persons interviewed, the documentary's unique relationship to recent tribunal machinations render unquestionable the film's evidentiary registers. Soon after the film's European and US premiers, Marcel Lemonde (ECCC Co-Investigating Judge) requested that the directors release it as evidence in Chea's case; while Chea had been previously interviewed by a number of international news outlets, he consistently refused to answer questions about the Khmer Rouge era. In *Enemies of the People*, Chea recollected in unprecedented fashion his role in the regime, admitting to Sambath a heretofore unexpressed culpability. Facing considerable international pressure and widespread criticism, Lemkin and Sambath refused to submit the film to the ECCC on the grounds that this violated agreements made with those featured (although they did agree to allow court access once the film entered public domain).[25]

Such tribunal politics vis-à-vis *Enemies of the People* is in part indicative of the film's status as a *documentary* production, its confession focus, and its overriding perpetrator emphasis. Even more important, these juridical contestations – which converge on the film's verification of Khmer Rouge atrocity and individual culpability – underscore the relative paucity of criminal evidence. While Tuol Sleng Prison (S-21) and Choeung Ek Killing Field – particularly with regard to inmate photographs, detailed torture accounts, and inmate remains – make undeniable Khmer Rouge atrocities, there is relatively little evidence (e.g., direct correspondences and photographic evidence of criminality) linking former Khmer Rouge cadres and high-ranking officials to the genocide. In contrast to the paucity of such physical evidences, there is an abundance of survivor accounts (specifically published memoirs and biographies); these firsthand testimonials largely form the foundation of the majority of films about the Cambodian genocide, including Joffé's abovementioned, *The Killing Fields*.

Not only is *The Killing Fields* credited with introducing the Khmer Rouge period to the wide screen; the very nomenclature through which the Cambodian genocide is most commonly accessed – via "the killing fields" – was coined by Cambodian journalist Dith Pran, whose relationship with *New York Times* reporter Sydney Schanberg and his experiences of survival were the conceptual basis for the film.[26] An English-French film director who began his career in television, Joffé made his feature film debut with *The Killing Fields*, which was produced by David Puttnam, featured music by Mike Oldfield (best known for scoring the horror film, *The Exorcist*), and showcased Bruce Robinson's adapted screenplay. *The Killing Fields* also introduced Dr. Haing S. Ngor (as Pran), a first-generation Cambodian survivor, to the silver screen. The winner of three Academy Awards (including "Best Supporting Actor," "Best Cinematography, and Best Film Editing) and eight BAFTA (British Academy Film Awards), *The Killing Fields* opens in 1973, as Lon Nol's army is engaged with a civil war with the Khmer Rouge. The Vietnam War, specifically as waged on the Vietnam/Cambodian border, looms large in the first third of the film, which narrates Schanberg's (portrayed by Sam Waterston) and Pran's frenetic journeys through Phnom Penh and to various wartime fronts.

Focused on the time before, during, and after the Khmer Rouge era, *The Killing Fields* engenders by way of tripartite narrative progression what has now become the dominant temporal frame in diasporic Cambodian memoirs and films. As Teri Shaffer Yamada observes in her analyzes of Cambodian-American life writing, this schema adheres to a distinct "autobiographical chronotype."[27] Such a chronotype includes the conditions which both brought the Khmer Rouge "into being" via American foreign policy alongside the atrocities committed by the regime; it likewise encompasses the making of Cambodian refugees. Set in the United States, Cambodia, and Thailand, *The Killing Fields*'s narrative is divided between its two protagonists. Expressly, soon after the Khmer Rouge takeover of Phnom Penh, Schanberg leaves for the United States; Pran is forced to remain in Cambodia. Schanberg, riddled with guilt, endeavors to locate Pran from faraway New York City. By contrast, Pran must hide his past affiliation as a journalist and struggle with famine, disease, and Khmer Rouge brutality before he eventually makes his way to a Thai refugee camp.

Notwithstanding the film's significance as a full-feature "first," and despite its importance as a mainstream, widely circulated production about the Cambodian genocide, it is *The Killing Fields*'s initial reception – as emblematized by Roger Ebert's critical assessment – that renders visible its surprising and disremembered connection to another cinematic genre: the Vietnam War film. As Ebert surmises,

> The American experience in Southeast Asia has given us a great film epic (*Apocalypse Now*) and a great drama (*The Deer Hunter*). Here [in *The Killing Fields*] is the story told a little closer to the ground, of people who were not very important and not very powerful, who got caught up in events that were indifferent to them, but never stopped trying to do their best and their most courageous.[28]

Cinematically, the "American experience in Southeast Asia" was, by 1984, familiar to US audiences. In addition to Francis Ford Coppola's *Apocalypse Now* (1979) and Michael Cimino's *The Deer Hunter* (1978), the late 1970s and early 1980s witnessed a slew of Vietnam War-focused films, including *Go Tell the Spartans* (1978), *Good Guys Wear Black* (1978), *First Blood* (1982), *Streamers* (1983), *Uncommon Valor* (1983), *Missing in Action* (1983), and *Purple Hearts* (1984). Yet, if Southeast Asian landscapes were a familiar backdrop for films about the Vietnam War, so too was it a setting for works that privileged American bodies over Southeast Asian subjects. At stake in these productions was a meditation on the "failure of Vietnam" through the rubric of white soldier remorse and veteran trauma. Situated within this context, even though *The Killing Fields* was most certainly about the Cambodian genocide, Schanberg's negotiation of guilt occupies much of the narrative and is given equal weight as Pran's harrowing survivor story. Moreover, the film's inclusion of scenes that speak directly to US involvement in the region – namely those that feature bombings and American military personnel – further confirm a connection to the Vietnam War. Last, but certainly not least, the final scene of the film – which takes place in an aforementioned Thai refugee camp and features a reunion of Schanberg and Pran – involves the former asking for forgiveness (for abandonment) from the latter, engendering an affective connection to mainstream portrayals of the Vietnam War as regretful conflict.[29]

Notwithstanding these narratival limitations, the critical and commercial success of *The Killing Fields* significantly presages the emergence of an identifiable Cambodian genocide film canon, which indefatigably seeks to reckon with disastrous legacies of the Khmer Rouge regime. Such reckonings characterize Rithy Panh's *oevure*, which includes 16 films and spans almost 30 years.[30] As Cambodia's most prolific and celebrated director, Panh is in fact a diasporic artist: a Phnom Penh native, Panh (at the time, aged 13) and his family were – like other denizens – forced to relocate to the Cambodian countryside.[31] His father was a school teacher and primary school inspector who, like his mother, siblings, and other relatives, died under the regime. Soon after the dissolution of Democratic Kampuchea in 1979, Panh sought temporary refuge in a Thai refugee camp and eventually found permanent asylum in France.[32] While enrolled in vocational school to learn carpentry, Panh was given a video camera at an informal social gathering; this sparked a lifelong investment in filmmaking.[33] After graduating from the *Institut des hautes études cinématographiques* (Institute for Advanced Cinematographic Studies), Panh returned to Cambodia in 1990, though he maintains Paris as a key base of operations.[34]

As a total reading of Panh's work brings to light, Panh's work repeatedly references the histories, impacts, and legacies of the Khmer Rouge period. His first documentary feature, *Site 2* (1989), focused on a family of Cambodian refugees in a camp on the Thai-Cambodian border and received the "Grand Prix due Documentaire" at the Festival of Amiens. Almost 5 years later, in 1994, Panh's second film – a docudrama titled *Rice People* about a rural family struggling to subsist in Cambodia post-Khmer Rouge – received even greater attention due to its presence at the Cannes Film Festival. Its subsequent submission to the Academy Awards (as a possible nominee in the "Best Foreign Language Film" category) represented the first time a Cambodian film had been submitted for an Oscar. Panh returned to documentary filmmaking with *La terre des âmes errantes* (*The Land of the Wandering Souls*), released in 2000. As was the case with his previous two films, *La terre des âmes errantes* is set in the post-Khmer Rouge era and concentrates on a Cambodian family; members of the family dig a trench as part of a national infrastructure project. Through this excavation, the family uncovers a killing field. This discovery – which links Cambodia's present with its disastrous Democratic Kampuchean past – foreshadows Panh's subsequent cinematic return to the Killing Fields via his 2003 documentary, *S-21: The Khmer Rouge Killing Machine*.

Set in Tuol Sleng Prison, *S-21: The Khmer Rouge Killing Machine* brings together two ex-prisoners of the regime – Vann Nath and Chum Mey – and their former captors, which include guards, interrogators, torturers, a prison photographer, and an on-site doctor; while the action takes place in the present, the film revisits the Khmer Rouge period and includes on-site re-enactments by Khmer Rouge perpetrators. To contextualize, S-21 was a major Khmer Rouge torture/detention center, and the majority of those interned did not survive: out of an estimated 12,000 prisoners, a little over 200 survived their imprisonment. After forcing confessions of betrayal and wrongdoing, Khmer Rouge guards would transport prisoners to the aforementioned Choeung Ek Killing Field, a primary execution site. As the film progresses, Nath and Mey eventually confront their S-21 captors, who stress that they too were regime victims due to the fact that they were teenagers at the time. *S-21: The Khmer Rouge Killing Machine* premiered at the 2003 Cannes Film Festival where it was awarded the Prix François Chalais. It was reported that a Khieu Samphan, after seeing the film, was moved to finally admit to the existence of the prison after years of public denial.[35] And, in an instance of "life reflecting art," the ECCC actually staged in 2009 similar re-enactments as part of the first Khmer Rouge trial against the prison's head warden (known as "Case 001"). Two years later, Panh directed *The Burnt Theatre* (2005), which engages the post-Khmer Rouge era via a drama concentrated on a theatre troupe that resides in the burnt out remains of Suramet Theatre (in Phnom Penh). His next film, *Paper Cannot Wrap Up Embers* (2007), focused on prostitution, took a more presentist focus and marked a slight departure from previous work. Panh returned to S-21 and the Killing Fields era five years later with *Duch, Master of the Forges of Hell* (2012), a documentary that featured interviews with previously mentioned Kaing Guek Eav.

In the face of past acclaim and in drawing to a close, it is Panh's most recent work, *The Missing Picture* (*L'image manquante*) (2012), which is probably best known due to the fact it received Cambodia's first Academy Award nomination (in the "Best Foreign Language Film" category) and was awarded top prize in the *Un Certain Regard* section at the 2013 Cannes Film Festival. Partially based on the director's memoir, *The Elimination* (co-authored with French novelist Christophe Bataille and published in 2013), *The Missing Picture* is a blended documentary film which brings together contemporaneous news reportage, Khmer Rouge propaganda film, photographs, clips from classic Cambodian cinema, and carved, painted clay figurines (created by Sarith Mang) which, as *New York Times* critic Manohla Dargis notes, "serve as human stand-ins." These stand-ins, placed in "diorama-like sets," initially provide audiences with "an intellectual remove," which – as the film progresses and as casualties amass, shift shape and reflect the experiences of those starving, suffering, and dying under the regime. As Dargis observes, what is most "startling is the depth of emotion that Mr. Panh solicits from you as he fills in the missing picture of this lost world and ... reclaims the human individuality that the Khmer Rouge sought to obliterate."[36]

Such "reclamations of human individuality" evocatively militate against Khmer Rouge directives to conform and forget. They are also very much at the forefront of Cambodian genocide film, which labors to remember, recollect, and recall histories *of* and experiences *with* state-authorized mass violence without the benefit of reparative trial and wholesale international justice. As Panh recounts vis-à-vis *The Missing Picture*:

For many years, I have been looking for the missing picture: a photograph taken between 1975 and 1979 by the Khmer Rouge when they ruled over Cambodia.... On its own, of course, an image cannot prove mass murder, but it gives us cause for thought, to record History. I searched for it vainly in the archives, in old papers, in the country villages of Cambodia. Today I know: this image must be missing. I was not really looking for it; would it not be obscene and insignificant? So I created it.[37]

As critical archive, films about the Cambodian genocide in the end labor to record a history that continues to be overwhelming present for those in-country and in the diaspora. Such "otherwise imaginations" function as a potent mode of memory work by assiduously commemorating those who perished and unstintingly reckoning with the legacies of the Killing Fields era.

13

"This Time We're Going to Hit Them Without Mercy": Indonesian Operations and East Timor's First Feature Film

Clinton Fernandes

UNSW Canberra

Claimed by Portugal as a colonial possession in the seventeenth century, East Timor was invaded by Indonesia in 1975 and occupied for 24 years. It gained its independence in 2002. The Democratic Republic of East Timor is one of the newest members of the international community. The first feature film to be filmed and produced in East Timor, *A Guerra Da Beatriz* (*Beatriz's War*), premiered in 2013. This chapter will examine the film by exploring the cultural, historical and political terrain that underpin the plot. It will conclude with a discussion of how East Timor and Indonesia received this film and others.

The Marriage of Beatriz (Sandra Da Costa) and Tomas (Raimundo Dos Santos)

Beatriz, the eponymous character in *Beatriz's War*, at the age of 11 marries a boy of her age, Tomas. Their marriage takes place in the mountains of East Timor in 1975, the year that Indonesia invades the territory. Their families exchange gifts, as is the custom. The marriage has a political implication; the families intend to resist the Indonesian army, and this marriage fulfils the additional objective of strengthening the unity of the village.

Marriages and other social relationships played an important role in the survival of Timorese society, especially in circumstances where there was no functioning state system (in the hinterland where the Portuguese colonial presence was light) or when the state existed as a result of Indonesian rule – and was therefore resisted by the population. Under such circumstances, trust was vested in one's relatives, and marriage was more than a relationship between two people; it connected two or more families. A predominant form of marriage in East Timor is what some scholars have called the MBD marriage (mother's brother's daughter marriage) or cross-cousin marriage. In this form, a man who marries his mother's brother's daughter marries into a family that he trusts because there have been marriages between his family and her family in the past. His family thus becomes known as the Wife Taker, and her family, the Wife Giver. The wife herself is not regarded as being transferred to another family; rather, the Wife Giver family is seen as transferring fertility to the Wife Taker family. Once in the Wife Taker family, the woman gives birth and produces new life through her children, who then pass on new life to their own Wife Takers. This exchange has been called the Flow of Life.

Accompanying the Flow of Life is an exchange of goods, a cultural practice that has been noted by many scholars, known as *barlaque* (a term of Malay origin). The value of the goods to be exchanged is agreed upon by the elders of the Wife Giver and Wife Taker families, and determined by the kinship relations and the hierarchy of the respective families. After the value of *barlaque* has been agreed upon and the exchange of goods made, a ceremony occurs in which the bride joins the groom's lineage and family. The groom in turn builds a new house for them as soon as he can afford to do so.

There is, of course, no opportunity for Tomas to build a house in which Beatriz may live because Indonesian forces attack their village and the young couple must run for their lives. They connect with resistance forces in the mountains, where they live until they surrender in 1983, when Beatriz gives birth to her son. They miraculously survive one of the largest losses of life relative to a total population since the Holocaust. This episode in East Timorese history is one of the least known mass atrocities of the twentieth century, a subject to which this chapter now turns.

Beatriz and Tomas Survive the Conventional War and the Famine

When the Carnation Revolution in Portugal in 1974 saw its new, anti-fascist government formally accept the terms of the 1960 UN Resolution on Decolonisation, East Timor was officially placed on the UN's decolonization agenda. Leading Indonesian officials refused to countenance the possibility of an independent East Timor; they insisted that any decolonization process should result in East Timor being annexed to Indonesia. Inside East Timor, the two most popular political organisations were the Timorese Democratic Union (UDT – União Democratica Timorense) and the Timorese Social Democratic Association (ASDT – Associação Social Democratica Timorense), which changed its name to FRETILIN – the Revolutionary Front for an Independent East Timor (Frente Revolucionária do Timor-Leste Independente) in September 1974.

FRETILIN described itself as a front that united nationalist and anti-colonial groups for the liberation of the East Timorese from colonialism. FRETILIN's young leaders – almost all were less than 30 years old – were heavily influenced by the intellectual, cultural and political climate of the 1960s. Among other things, they criticized the Church's complicity in Portuguese colonialism, its wealth and its large land holdings. The local Bishop retaliated by describing FREITILIN as communists and forbidding Catholics to vote for them.[1] Since many UDT leaders came from conservative, land-owning families, they were threatened by a FRETILIN initiative called "alphabetização" or basic literacy. They were also worried by FRETILIN's tactic of communicating directly with the villagers rather than relying on traditional chiefs or civil servants, as they themselves did. FRETILIN's extravagant rhetoric did not help matters either. Although no elections had been held, it asserted that it was the East Timorese peoples' "sole legitimate representative." Rhetoric aside, FRETILIN's program focused on decolonization, land reform, administrative reform, popular education, and the development of small industries based on primary products like coffee.

On January 21, 1975, UDT formed a coalition with FRETILIN. Both parties agreed that East Timor should become independent and that they would form a transitional government. This government would have representatives from the Portuguese government and from UDT and FRETILIN. It would prepare a Constitution that would form the basis of an independent East Timor. However, their mutual suspicion proved to be too strong, and Indonesian intelligence exploited FRETILIN's and UDT's political inexperience, successfully playing off one side against the other. It suborned UDT's leaders, stoking the flames of suspicion and distrust. After village-level elections in Los Palos in May 1975 delivered a clear victory to village chiefs who were FRETILIN supporters, UDT formally withdrew from the coalition. Indonesian intelligence advised UDT leaders that FRETILIN was planning a coup on August 15, 1975. Indonesia, they said, would respect East Timor's right of self-determination if UDT moved against FRETILIN. Accordingly, key UDT members led a preemptive coup against FRETILIN in the early hours of August 11, 1975. FRETILIN fought back on August 20, defeating most of the UDT forces by August 30. Between 1,500 and 3,000 people are estimated to have been killed during the internal armed conflict. The Portuguese governor and his administration left the mainland for the off-shore island of Atauro, and later proceeded to Portugal. The defeated forces of UDT, now located in West Timor, signed a petition calling for the integration of East Timor into Indonesia.

Indonesia escalated its campaign of destabilisation and terror, and ultimately launched a full-scale military invasion on December 7, 1975, in order to defeat FRETILIN in battle, eliminate its leaders, and suppress any organizations associated with it, in particular its armed wing, known as the Armed Forces for the National Liberation of East Timor (FALINTIL).

These were the circumstances, it will be recalled, in which Beatriz and Tomas wed. Soon after, they fled to the ranks of the resistance in the mountains. Indonesian forces were in command of all major population centers in East Timor. FRETILIN's leaders decided to reorganize the party's national civilian and military structures in order to undertake a protracted guerrilla war. The reorganization paid dividends as many local villagers joined the armed resistance, which took advantage of Indonesian security lapses to harass outposts and ambush supply convoys. East Timor's arterial roads were severely degraded by the heavy Indonesian military traffic and by monsoonal rains that caused major landslides.

By December 1976, FRETILIN had managed to hold the Indonesian forces to a military stalemate. It was able to organize a functioning society

185

in the mountains. It struggled to provide enough food crops and basic health care to the tens of thousands of civilians who had accompanied them there. However, from August 1977, Indonesia regained the initiative through the use of air power; it deployed OV-10F Bronco aircraft that it had acquired from the USA. The significance of the Bronco was that it could be operated from the most rudimentary airfields, and its slow flying speed meant that it could identify and attack villages more effectively. It had been designed specifically for such operations. The air power offensives targeted agricultural areas and other food sources such as livestock in the liberated zones, where the population lived alongside FRETILIN, and the support bases, which surrounded the liberated zones. The Indonesian Air Force used napalm in flagrant disregard of the laws of war. According to survivors who testified before East Timor's Commission for Reception, Truth, and Reconciliation:

> The army burned the tall grass. The fire would spread quickly, and the whole area would be ablaze as if it had been doused in gasoline. Those of us who were surrounded didn't have time to escape because the flames were so big. Their strategy trapped many people ... After we got out, I could still see the old people who had been left behind by their families. They were in a sitting position. The men put on new clothes, hung belak [crescent-shaped metal chest-ornament worn around the neck] on their necks and wore caibauk [crescent-shape crown]. The women had put on gold earrings and gold necklaces, prepared their konde [traditional way of styling hair] and wore black veils as if they were going to mass. We just looked at them but couldn't do anything. The enemy was still after us.[2]

With the Indonesian army continuing its pursuit, and plagued by illness and food shortages, civilians fled to the hills and surrendered to Indonesian forces. The surrendering population was detained in camps which were often little more than huts made from palm thatch with no toilets. In many cases, the only shelter in the camps was under trees. No medical care was available. Since the detainees' food sources had been destroyed and they had walked for days in order to surrender, they were already in a weakened state when they arrived at the transit camps. A famine combined with diseases such as cholera, diarrhea, and tuberculosis resulted in mass casualties. The overall conflict-related death toll has been reliably estimated at 204,000. "Even under the most conservative assumptions," a demographic analysis concluded, "the total number of excess deaths in East Timor during the entire period of Indonesian occupation likely ranges from 150,000 to 220,000." According to a revised version of this analysis, "it is likely that 204,000 is a conservative upper-bound estimate on excess mortality. The "true" number of East Timorese who died because of the Indonesian occupation may never be known."[3] Since the population at the start of the invasion was about 648,000, this is a death toll of 31 percent.[4] The film has Beatriz and Tomas surviving the Indonesian military's genocidal operations.

Cultural Motifs

Beatriz's War (correctly) implies that a number of indigenous traditions survived the Indonesian occupation – a fact that can be observed by contemporary visitors to East Timor. Such traditions include birth ceremonies such as *fasimatan* (eye washing) and *tesifuk* (haircutting); death ceremonies such as *aifuan moruk* (bitter flowers), held one week after death; and *aifunan midar* (sweet flowers) held another week later. After the death of a relative, women family members will wear black dresses in mourning while men may wear a small piece of black cloth pinned to their shirts. One year after death, the black garments are removed in the *kore metan* ceremony.

The film also shows perhaps East Timor's best known artistic form: the traditional cloth of East Timor known as *tais*. The patterns of *tais* shown in the film are a hint of the cultural richness and diversity of East Timor. Different regions have different patterns. The *tais* of the eastern regions of Iliomar show a distinctive Portuguese influence, with traditional motifs integrated with colourful stripes and bands of small flowers of European inspiration. The *tais* of the central highlands have monochromatic designs with subtle geometric stripes whereas the *tais* of the western region have bold, Dutch-inspired floral designs. *Tais* plays an important role in birth, death and marriage ceremonies, and in other aspects of cultural and social life. The weaving of *tais* is therefore much more than an artistic form. In marriage ceremonies, a matrimonial set of male and female *tais* (*Tais Mane* and *Tais Feto*, respectively) are woven specifically for the event. The ancestral and regional affiliations of the wearer (or weaver) can be found in the various motifs and color combinations. Weaving is not an individual process but a social and intergenerational one – as many as four generations of women participate in the weaving of *tais*. It is cultural practices like these that maintained the coherence and distinctiveness of East Timorese society in the face of Indonesia's occupation, genocidal operations and attempts to make the subjugated population "good Indonesians."

Australian Complicity and *Beatriz's War*

The film then has a pregnant Beatriz – now 19 years old – surrendering to the occupying forces in 1983. The location is Kraras – a real location and the site of a crime against humanity documented by East Timor's Commission for Reception, Truth, and Reconciliation in its 2006 report. The people of Kraras were actually inhabitants of the village of Bibileo who had fled to the mountains in 1977 ahead of advancing Indonesian forces. After they surrendered, they tried to return to Bibileo but were moved to a new settlement – Kraras. They were moved because the Indonesian authorities had made dramatic changes to the East Timorese settlement pattern, forcibly closing down smaller villages that had been dispersed throughout the countryside, and imposing a settlement pattern designed to monitor the population more easily.

As it happened, Kraras was situated on a flat plain that was more fertile than the hilly Bibileo, so the people were able to feed themselves better. Here the film levels an important accusation: it explicitly points to Australian complicity. Given that Indonesia was the occupying power and Australian military forces were nowhere in the territory, the viewer may not understand the reference. The film's small budget also means that certain crucial events are assumed or are reported as having occurred off screen. The relevant background is as follows.

The leader of the armed resistance, Xanana Gusmão, met the leader of the Catholic clergy in East Timor, Apostolic Administrator Monsignor Martinho da Costa Lopes in September 1982. The meeting showed the church in East Timor that the resistance was a nationalist organization, not a communist one. The meeting led to communication between the resistance and the Indonesian-appointed governor of East Timor, Mario Carrascalão. Soon, there were talks between the resistance and the local Indonesian military commanders. The East Timorese resistance then negotiated a cease-fire with the Indonesian military in March 1983.

The newly-appointed commander of the Indonesian military, General Benny Murdani, saw Monsignor Martinho da Costa Lopes as a symbol of East Timor's resistance to Indonesian rule. He asked the Vatican's envoy to Jakarta, Monsignor Pablo Puente, to remove Monsignor Lopes from East Timor. Monsignor Lopes offered his resignation some weeks later. General Murdani also summoned Governor Carrascalão and told him that he and the Indonesian military units posted to East Timor had three months to solve the East Timor problem before military operations would resume in earnest.

The Indonesian military allowed the ceasefire to continue until an Australian parliamentary delegation led by former Australian Defense Minister Bill Morrison visited the territory. The delegation arrived in Dili on July 28, 1983, and spent a total of four days in East Timor. Four members of the resistance led by a combatant named Cancio Gama stopped the delegation near Soba (Baucău) on July 29, 1983. After a brief discussion, Gama gave the delegation a letter about conditions in East Timor.[5] Morrison's report to the Australian parliament concluded that the "administrative authority ... of the Indonesian government [was] firmly in place" and that the Indonesian government was acting in good faith in the territory.[6] While there was a dissenting statement by Senator Gordon McIntosh, the Chairman of the Senate Foreign Affairs Committee, the Official Report found no evidence of human rights abuses and no real insecurity in East Timor. The report of the delegation allowed the newly elected Hawke Labor government in Australia to reverse its policy towards East Timor's annexation. It appointed Bill Morrison as Australia's ambassador to Indonesia.

High among the Labor government's priorities was its negotiations with Indonesia on the seabed boundary. The 1972 Seabed Agreement between Australia and Indonesia resulted in a boundary much closer to Indonesia, giving Australia the lion's share of the resources. Portugal, which had then controlled East Timor, refused to conclude a similar agreement with Australia, resulting in the "Timor Gap." After the invasion, the Australian government moved to legitimize Indonesia's occupation by extending *de facto* recognition of Indonesia's sovereignty in January 1978, followed by *de jure* recognition with the opening of negotiations on the seabed boundary in the Timor Gap in February 1979. The Hawke Labor government ultimately signed the Timor Gap Treaty with Indonesia in December 1989.

"This time we're going to hit them without mercy"

The cease-fire ended shortly after the Australian parliamentary delegation left the territory. Murdani had previously warned resistance leader Xanana Gusmão not to expect help from other countries:

> There is no country on this globe that can help you. Our own army is prepared to destroy you if you are not willing to be co-operative with our republic. We are preparing an operation – Operasi Persatuan – which will come into force in August.[7]

Relations between conventional Indonesian forces and East Timorese members of Indonesian units began to break down. These East Timorese members were civilians who were selected to undergo basic military training, after which they were known as *Ratih* (*Rakyat Terlatih* or Trained Civilians). From *Ratih* some were further trained as Hansip (*Pertahanan Sipil*, or Civil Defense Force), in case of natural disaster or war. Others were further trained as *Kamra* (*Keamanan Rakyat* or People's Security Force), to assist the police. Others were trained as *Wanra* (*Perlawanan Rakyat* or People's Resistance Force), to assist the armed forces.

As such, the film adopts a narrative from East Timor's Truth Commission report, which says that members of Indonesia's Fourth Combat Engineering Battalion (*Zipur 4*) killed seven civilians in the Kraras area during the cease-fire and then molested an East Timorese woman. Beatriz's husband, a *Ratih* member, ran to the forest and complained to the armed resistance, known as the Armed Forces for the National Liberation of East Timor (FALINTIL). The armed resistance attacked *Zipur 4* along with other *Ratih* members. At least a dozen members of *Zipur 4* were killed in this attack. Word spread that the cease-fire was coming to an end. A group of Viqueque-based *Ratih* defected to the armed resistance the next day. In Lautem, hundreds of *Wanra* and *Hansip* members also defected, accompanied by other able-bodied men. An attempted defection in Iliomar (Lautem) was foiled when four East Timorese *Hansip* betrayed two resistance members who had asked them to defect. Resistance forces also fought troops from Battalion 745 in Nahareka (Viqueque). With the ceasefire successfully undermined, General Murdani declared in a speech on August 17, Indonesia's independence day, "this time we're going to hit them without mercy."[8] He launched Operation Unity (*Operasi Persatuan*, also known as Operation Clean Sweep or *Sapu Bersih*) on that day.

What has since become known as the Kraras Massacre occurred next. As tensions rose and fears mounted that the FALINTIL-Ratih attacks on Zipur 4 would be followed by an indiscriminate response, the people of Kraras fled to their original village of Bibileo and to the nearby village of Buikarin. Indonesian forces entered Bibileo and took the villagers who were sheltering there to Beloi in Viqueque. On September 7, Indonesian forces entered Kraras, which was almost completely empty. They killed all four or five people who had stayed behind, and burnt many houses. Two days later the Indonesian government declared a state of emergency. On September 16, Indonesian forces went back to Beloi, took the villagers to Caraubalu and handed them to Indonesian soldiers from a different unit. The villagers were then taken to a location called Welamo where they were told to stand in a hole and were executed. At least 55 people aged one to 61 years were killed at this time.[9] The next day, Indonesian forces went to Buikarin, collected the rest of the people from Kraras who were sheltering there, and separated the men from the women. They marched the men to the Wetuku River in the vicinity of Tahubein not far from Buikarin. At least 141 men were were executed at this location.[10] On September 22, Indonesian forces arrested and killed the father and wife of Virgilio dos Anjos (Sihik Ular), who had led the first Ratih defections to FALINTIL in Kraras.

The film continues to allude to real events, which include the resettlement of the survivors of the massacres – who were all women, very young children, or very old men – in the previously uninhabited area of Lalerek Mutin (Viqueque). This resettlement continued a policy begun after the 1978–1979 famine of making dramatic changes to the East Timorese settlement pattern. Indonesia forcibly closed down smaller villages that had been dispersed throughout the countryside and in the mountains. They imposed a settlement pattern designed to monitor the population more easily. This obviously affected indigenous forms of social organization as well as patterns of food cultivation and food consumption. Thus, the film provides a picture of Indonesia's indiscriminate killing and torture of civilians, and its attempted destruction of East Timorese society.

The CAVR Report as a Hidden Script

Tomas is missing, presumed dead. Beatriz survives Kraras along with Tomas' sister, Teresa (Augusta Soares). The film depicts Teresa becoming the mistress of the local Indonesian military commander. In this, the film follows a hidden script, albeit an impeccably well-researched one. East Timor's Commission for Reception, Truth, and Reconciliation (known by its Portuguese initials CAVR) has concluded that there was widespread evidence of sexual violence, a particularly heinous crime against humanity. Although there are cultural taboos against admitting such violations, the CAVR received hundreds of direct testimonies that showed that rape, sexual torture, and other acts of sexual violence were widespread and systematic. The CAVR found that the Indonesian authorities' "institutional practices and formal or informal policy" encouraged such behavior.[11]

Established as an independent statutory authority by the UN Transitional Authority in East Timor, the CAVR found as follows:

> Throughout the invasion and occupation there was a persistent practice of forcing East Timorese women to become, in effect, the sexual slaves of military officers. These activities were conducted openly, without fear of reprisal, inside military installations, at other official sites and inside the private homes of women who were targeted. In a significant number of similar cases, rapes and sexual assaults were repeatedly conducted inside victims' homes, despite the presence of parents, children and other family members of the victim ....
>
> The victims of this form of sexual slavery were not free to move about or travel, or to act independently in any way. It was not uncommon for the "ownership rights" over these women to be passed on from an officer who was finishing his tour of duty to his replacement or another officer. In some situations, women forced into these situations became pregnant and gave birth to children of several different officers during the years in which they were the victims of sexual slavery.[12]

Since many of the actors and extras lived the events depicted in the film, the process of filming had been a cathartic one. Village women helped the filmmakers to organize the sets correctly, and to choose the most authentic flowers and candles for a funeral scene. An Australian journalist who watched the film being shot later wrote that she was "overwhelmed by examples of art imitating life. Women extras wept unprompted during a scene in which they are forced from their homes by Indonesian soldiers, just as they were 25 years ago. A man who lived under a bridge for the final few years of the occupation, and who avoided persecution was cast as the town drunk. And former guerrillas in East Timor's Falintil resistance army have been cast, more or less, as themselves …. Some of the extras are professional mourners, or 'wailing women,' who are paid to weep at funerals. The sound is haunting, but unlike normal crying. Then Pires [a co-producer] whispers something to one of the women at the front of the truck. In the next take, the woman calls out "to save the spirits of our lost children," and the crying changes; now they are weeping for real. Soon everyone, including myself and the Australian crew, is crying."[13]

The Puzzling Absence of FRETILIN

Despite the vital role played by FRETILIN in the resistance, and the personal connections of many of the key people associated with the film, *Beatriz's War* has little to say about this political organization. The absence of FRETILIN from the movie is even more remarkable because it did not disappear from Timorese politics after independence. Quite the contrary – after the departure of the Indonesians, during the period of a United Nations-led transitional administration, the FRETILIN-dominated Constituent Assembly drafted the Constitution of the Democratic Republic of Timor-Leste. Opposition parties disliked many of its sections. According to a United Nations Special Commission of Inquiry:

> The adoption of 28 November as national independence day commemorated the 1975 unilateral declaration of independence by FRETILIN. The FRETILIN flag and anthem, *Patria Patria*, were adopted as the national flag and anthem. The recently formed FDTL [defense force] was renamed FALINTIL-FDTL (F-FDTL) in an attempt to link the future defense force with

193

FRETILIN history and overcome the 1987 withdrawal of
FALINTIL from FRETILIN[14]

FRETILIN formed the first government of an independent East Timor,
winning 55 seats out of a total of 88. In February, 2006, nearly a third of
the East Timorese military from the western areas of the country went on
strike, claiming they faced discrimination in promotion and conditions of
service relative to soldiers from the east. Soon, East Timor's security force
disintegrated as open conflict broke out between the police and the military. An Australian-led international force helped stabilize the country in
May 2006 following a request for foreign intervention from the government of East Timor. Although the country is currently at peace, the first
post-independence FRETILIN government still polarizes public opinion.
This may be one reason why the word 'FRETILIN' plays little part in the
film, and the characters are portrayed as fighting for national unity without
any hint of party membership.

Indonesia's Receptivity to the Film

Writing in the *Jakarta Post*, Indonesian commentator Windu Jusuf
remarks – correctly – that the film "depicts Indonesia under the New Order
as a colonizer." This does not sit well with many Indonesians, who regard
themselves as heirs to an anti-colonial tradition. Jusuf notes that for them,
"Timor Leste remains an unpleasant memory …. Many are still reluctant
to say that Timor Leste eventually achieved *kemerdekaan* (independence)
from Indonesia. Instead, we say *lepas* (released), since using *merdeka*
would imply that Indonesia was a colonizer or foreign occupier like the
Japanese, the Dutch or – the ultimate villain that the nation loves to hate –
the Israelis in Palestine."[15]

A different but related comparison between Indonesia/East Timor and
Israel/Palestine had been made very prominently by Karl Meyer in *The
New York Times* in 1992, when President Suharto had addressed the United
Nations in his capacity as Chairman of the Non-Aligned Movement. Among
other things, Suharto had criticized the Israeli occupation of Palestine.
Meyer, then the chief foreign affairs editorial writer for *The New York
Times*, wrote an editorial pointing out the hypocrisy of his remarks. He

accused Indonesia's invasion of East Timor as being "just as heinous as the more recent and more highly publicized territorial grabs by Iraq and Serbia. The evil continues ... there was no hint of contrition in yesterday's United Nations speech by President Suharto of Indonesia, leader of the 108-nation Non-Aligned Movement .... with respect to tiny East Timor, Jakarta behaves more like a Banana Republic. It has rejected Portugal's proposal for a referendum in the former colony, and has stonewalled efforts to permit a UN presence in East Timor. All this while General Suharto ostentatiously demands the withdrawal of foreign troops from occupied territory – along the River Jordan."[16]

The distributors *of Beatriz's War* may not have tried to distribute the film to Indonesia, given the reception received by an earlier film about East Timor – *Balibo*. *Balibo* was a major Australian feature film shown at leading international film festivals. It depicted certain events at the border town of Balibo in October 1975, when the Indonesian military was conducting a terror and destabilisation campaign in the border regions of East Timor. Five journalists employed by Australian TV stations went to East Timor to cover the conflict. The Indonesian military killed all five journalists a few days after they arrived at Balibo. That film's factual authenticity was widely acclaimed. Mukhlis Paeni, head of Indonesia's Film Censorship Agency (LSF) – which banned the movie just hours before its Jakarta premiere in December 2009 – said Balibo was "artistically extraordinary but politically dangerous."[17] Indonesia's Alliance of Independent Journalists defied the government ban and screened it around Indonesia, risking jail and/ or fines.

Beatriz's War thus adds to the contest over the recent history of Indonesia, joining films like Robert Connolly's *Balibo* (2009) and Joshua Oppenheimer's *The Look of Silence* (2014), documentaries on the killings in Indonesia and their aftermath. As a new generation of Indonesians and East Timorese artists emerges, no longer shackled by a fascist state or a military occupation, these and related debates can be expected to get an airing on film and in other forms of artistic expression.

14

The Guatemalan Genocide on Film: An Ongoing Crisis and Omission

Zachary Vincent Smith

West Chester University

In Guatemala, between 1982 and 1983, in the midst of a civil war that had been raging since 1960 and would continue until 1996, a dictatorial regime led by General Efrain Rios Montt systematically murdered several thousand Guatemalan Mayans. Unlike the Holocaust and other genocides-such as the Cambodian, Bosnian, and Rwandan, about which there are numerous scholarly and literary works-the genocide in Guatemala has only traces of an international historical memory. The cinematic representation of this genocide also pales in comparison to the many films about the Holocaust, with only a few productions, including *When Mountains Tremble* (1984),[1] *Granito* (2011),[2] *Discovering Dominga* (2003),[3] *Haunted Land: Le pays hanté, la Palabra Desenterrada* (2001)[4], and the obliquely related feature film about the 1954 coup, *The Silence of Neto* (1994).[5] Through an analysis of these films, this essay not only contributes to the discipline of cinema studies, but it also furthers the process of embedding the Guatemalan genocide into the historical record of the genocides of the twentieth century.

Guatemala has a history of oppression toward its Mayan population.[6] As a result of the revolution of 1871, a "liberal" government, led by Justo Rufino Barrios, intensified coffee production in Guatemala, which required vast land extensions and a large labor force; to find workers, Barrios created the Settler Rule Book, which forced the native, Mayan population to work for free for the landowners, the criollos[7] and later, German settlers.[8] Barrios confiscated the "vacant" native land as well as religious lands owned by the Catholic Church. This vacant land, under the protection of the previous conservative government led by Rafael Carrera, had deep roots of protection ever since the colonization of the land. Barrios distributed the land to his liberal friends, who became important landowners.[9] By enslaving the native population in this period, the colonial Guatemalan government laid the groundwork for future exploitation.

In the 1890s, successive United States governments asserted supremacy over resources and labor in Latin America. The dictators that ruled Guatemala during the late nineteenth and early twentieth century were very accommodating to US business and political aspirations. Unlike many Latin American countries (Cuba, Haiti, and Nicaragua), the United States did not use military force in Guatemala, at least initially. A Boston-based company called United Fruit (UFCO) helped to ensconce the US presence in Guatemala. The company poured vast amounts of money into the pockets of the region's politicians, which in turn led to the passing of legislation that would allow the company to purchase land at minimal prices.[10] The company became known as *el pulpo* – the octopus – to the people of the region.[11] By the 1920s, United Fruit's employment of 5,000 banana workers led them to be Guatemala's biggest employer.[12] With the help of the United States Government, in 1931, the dictator General Jorge Ubico came to power, initiating one of the most repressive militaries in Central American history. Ubico created secret police units and informants who would help torture and murder his political opponents. Ubico sided with the United Fruit Company, rich landowners, and anyone who improved his wealth. After the crash of the New York Stock Exchange in 1929, the Settlers Rule Book established by Barrios was not creating enough wealth for Ubico. Unable to keep up with production and labor, Ubico implemented debt slavery and forced labor to make sure that there was enough labor available for the coffee plantations. Ubico passed laws allowing landowners to execute workers as a "disciplinary" measure.[13] He also openly identified as a fascist; he admired Mussolini, Franco, and Hitler, saying at one point: "I am like Hitler. I execute first and ask questions later."[14] Ubico's reign lasted until 1944 when he abdicated due to economic unrest. Between 1944 and 1954, the presidencies of Juan Jose Arevalo (1945–1951) and Jacobo Arbenz Guzman (1951–1954) ushered in "Ten Years of Spring" in Guatemala. Both Arevalo and Arbenz, inspired by the policies and practices of the New Deal during the Great Depression, supported labor and challenged American businesses to adopt policies more beneficial to citizens of Guatemala. They passed laws noxious to the United Fruit Company's monopoly over the economic system of Guatemala.

From the moment Dwight D. Eisenhower took office and appointed him secretary of state, one of John Foster Dulles' top priorities was to topple the democratically elected governments of Iran and, especially, Guatemala. He set out to replace "that madman (Mohammad) Mossadegh" in Operation Apex, also desired by British Prime Minister Winston Churchill, and considered by John Foster as God's work on earth. The head of the CIA, Allen Dulles the "spymaster," John's brother, was more than happy to aid his brother in fulfilling the mission. The administration successfully installed the Shah in Mossadegh's place to reign until the coup by Ayatollah Ruhollah Khomeini in 1979.

Mossadegh in Iran and Jacobo Arbenz in Guatemala had a great deal in common: both commanded the ire of the Dulles brothers, and both were democratically elected leaders who desired to improve the living conditions of the common people in their countries by taking on the powerful neo-colonial corporate interests dominating their economies. In Guatemala, UFCO controlled vast acreages, 85 percent of which the corporation decided to leave uncultivated, seeming to mock the poor in the country. Arbenz expropriated a quarter million acres of UFCO uncultivated land and compensated the company for what it said the land was worth when it purchased it. UFCO acquired the land cheaply, with 99-year leases and no taxes, by sweetheart deals from Jorge Ubico, the corrupt military dictator of Guatemala before the reformer Juan Jose Arevalo. Arbenz then dispensed the land to peasants and workers to be cultivated for food.

As in the Iranian situation, the Eisenhower administration falsely portrayed the Arbenz reform efforts as part of a scheme to transform the country into a communist state, thus justifying a covert US intervention to stop it. The administration's incestuous relationship with UFCO rivaled the

George W. Bush administration relationship with Haliburton. John Foster Dulles and the firm of Sullivan & Cromwell had been the legal counsel for UFCO for decades. John Foster and Allen both were shareholders in UFCO. Thomas G. Cocoran was a paid consultant for UFCO while working for the CIA and helping engineer the coup. Ann Whitman, the wife of the UFCO's publicity director, was Eisenhower's personal secretary. John Moor Cabot, the Assistant Secretary of State for Inter-American Affairs, was a major shareholder in UFCO, and his brother Thomas Dudley Cabot, director of international security affairs in the state department, had been a former UFCO president.

This disturbing story of American political corruption is told in *Bitter Fruit: The Story of the American Coup in Guatemala, by Stephen Schlesinger and Stephen Kinzer.*[15] The authors reveal the administration's hidden agendas and motivations, and the lack of vigilance, oversight, and checks-and-balances to supervise their actions. Under the canard used in Iran of "anti-communism," the administration took over a democratically elected government and essentially replaced it with a dictatorship. The real reason behind the coup was the protection of the interests of a major US corporation, UFCO, which was being circumscribed by the Arbenz land reforms and labor laws.

By late June, 1954, the Arbenz government, diplomatically and economically isolated by the Eisenhower administration, concluded that resistance against the "giant of the north" was futile, and Arbenz resigned on June 27. Jose Castillo Armas marched into Guatemala City, and on July 8, 1954, Castillo Armas was elected president of the junta. The election of Castillo Armas and the overthrow of Arbenz was a great victory over "communist imperialism," according to the Dulles brothers. Many Guatemalans saw it differently. The new regime rounded up thousands of suspected communists, and executed hundreds of detainees, crushed labor unions which had flourished since 1944, and returned United Fruit's confiscated. Castillo Armas, however, did not last very long; He was assassinated in 1957. Guatemalan politics then degenerated into a series of violent coups and countercoups, coupled with brutal repression of the country's people.

The Guatemalan state, supported by US interests, then began confronting the threat of communist revolution coming from Cuba. Fidel Castro offered military training to Guatemalan insurgents and in January 1962, the insurgents accepted his help. The United States sided with the pro-business Guatemalan government and turned a blindeye to its use of terror tactics to stamp out the communist threat.[16] Over the ensuing decades, there would be four waves of terror, and each onslaught would have different tactics imposed and different levels of violence. The different waves did not target just one group, but anyone opposing the government in any form became a targeted group. The first wave of terror began with the CIA-backed coup of 1954 and lasted until 1963, when another coup was engineered. The second coup (1963–1970) used state sanctioned terror as "spectacle." Bodies of executed political opponents were left on display for the public to see. The second wave degraded the possibility of political change and targeted anyone willing to stand up against the Guatemalan government no matter what their social status. The third wave of state sanctioned terror (1970–1978) involved the near total elimination of guerilla forces in Guatemala. In 1978, the Guatemalan army began the systematic slaughter of the native Mayan population. This period of massacre, referred to as the "Silent Holocaust," led to the extermination in mass of native Mayan communities. The fourth and final wave of terror, in reaction to revolutionary victories in Latin America in the 1980s,[17] produced the largest number of fatalities in Guatemalan history.[18]

General Efrain Rios Montt seized power in a coup d'état on March 23, 1982, and immediately began targeting indigenous Mayans as communist sympathizers. Rios Montt launched a scorched-earth campaign called "rifles and beans," meaning that pacified Indians would get "beans," while all others could expect to be the target of army "rifles." His mantra was, "If you are with us, we'll feed you; if not, we'll kill you." An avowed fundamentalist Christian, he impressed the Reagan White House, and Reagan hailed Ríos Montt as "a man of great personal integrity." In October 1982, Ríos Montt secretly gave carte blanche to the feared "Archivos" intelligence unit to expand "death squad" operations, internal CIA intelligence revealed.[19]

Despite growing evidence of Guatemalan government atrocities, political operatives for the Reagan administration sought to paint a picture of a regime doing good things for its people, and it deliberately covered up atrocity stories. Reagan personally took that position in December 1982 when he met with Ríos Montt and claimed that his regime was getting a "bum rap" on human rights and atrocity claims. Reagan lifted the ban on military aid to Guatemala because political violence in the cities had "declined dramatically" and rural conditions had improved. But a different picture was coming from independent human rights investigators reporting on conditions in the countryside. On March 17, 1983, Americas Watch representatives condemned the Guatemalan army for human rights atrocities against the Indian population, including rural women suspected of guerrilla sympathies who were raped before execution. Soldiers threw children into burning homes, into the air to be speared with bayonets, and they "picked them up by the ankles and swung against poles so their heads [were] destroyed."[20]

On February 25, 1999, a Guatemalan truth commission issued a report on the staggering human rights crimes that Reagan and his administration had aided, abetted, and concealed. The Historical Clarification Commission, an independent human rights body, estimated that the Guatemalan conflict claimed the lives of some 200,000 people, with the most savage bloodletting occurring in the 1980s. Besides carrying out murder and "disappearances," the army routinely engaged in torture and rape. "The rape of women, during torture or before being murdered, was a common practice" by the military and paramilitary forces, the report found. The report added that the "government of the United States, through various agencies including the CIA, provided direct and indirect support for some [of these] state operations." The report concluded that the US government also gave money and training to a Guatemalan military that committed "acts of genocide" against the Mayans.[21]

During a visit to Central America, on March 10, 1999, President Bill Clinton apologized for the past US support of right-wing regimes in Guatemala. "For the United States, it is important that I state clearly that support for military forces and intelligence units which engaged in violence and widespread repression was wrong, and the United States must not repeat that mistake," Clinton said. Though Clinton admitted that US policy in Guatemala was "wrong" – and the new evidence of a US-backed "genocide" might have been considered startling – the US news media mostly treated the story as a one-day event. US complicity in genocide prompted no panel discussions on the cable news shows, which then were obsessed with Clinton's personal life. In 2013, a Guatemalan court convicted Rios Montt of genocide and crimes against humanity, sentencing him to 80 years in prions, but the country's Constitutional Court overturned the conviction. Montt was set to be retried in 2015, but he was found mentally unfit for trial, presumably closing the chapter on the genocide without resolution or justice.

When Mountains Tremble

The documentary *When Mountains Tremble* was an early attempt to bring the hidden history of the Guatemalan genocide to light. Directed by Pamela Yates and Thomas Sigel, the film follows Rigoberta Menchu, who testifies about her own radicalization because of the deaths of her two brothers and her father by the death squads of the Guatemalan government, using both a first-person account and documentary film footage to show was happened in the time of Montt's reign. Menchu is a Quiche Indian from the highlands of Guatemala, awarded the Nobel Peace Prize in 1992 for her autobiographical *I, Rigoberto Menchu*, an exposé of the state-sponsored genocide that swept Guatemala in the late 1970s and early 1980s and that claimed several of her family members.[22] Images from the film include day-long fights between rebel and government forces, instances of beatings of civilians by death squads, and speeches by US officials (notably President Ronald Reagan) about holding the line against communism. The use of re-enactments undercuts the film's historicity, but this is counter-balanced by the use of contemporary footage and the information obtained from Menchu's testimony. Revealing both the depth of knowledge about the genocide on the part of ordinary Guatemalans, and the culpability of the United States, the film is a raw and striking account, and it received the special jury award at the Sundance Film Festival after its re-release in 1992. Although its viewership was limited, it had a galvanizing effect on director Yates, who went on to make the 2011 film, *Granito: How to Nail a Dictator.*

Granito

Granito focuses both on the revisiting of Yates' work in *When Mountains Tremble*, as well as on the criminal investigation of Rios Montt in the late 1990s. *Granito* therefore has a dual narrative and timeframe, and the focus on the tribunal is interesting because the initial case against Montt would have proceeded in Spain, where the Constitutional Court claims universal jurisdiction for crimes. *Granito* also includes Yates' interview of Montt from June 1982. In the interview, Yates repeatedly asked Montt about all the things that she witnessed in the Highlands, where the military was attacking the civilian population, and after initial denials, Montt inadvertently admitted responsibility by saying, "If I do not control the army, then what am I doing here?"[23] Although this footage alone was insufficient to lead to an indictment, documents surfaced about army massacres in the summer of 1982 coordinated by the Guatemalan high command, leading the Spanish court to issue arrest warrants in 2006. The Guatemalan court initially blocked Montt's arrest, and he won a seat in the Guatemalan congress in 2007, making him immune from prosecution, but when his term ended, so did his immunity, and he was indicted and convicted in 2013, only to have the conviction overturned by the Guatemalan constitutional court. *Granito* is an important testimonial about justice in the wake of genocide, and the legal developments of the past two years has heightened its relevance. In 2013, with Montt's conviction, the film appeared vindicated; now, with Montt likely to avoid retrial, the film serves as a powerful indictment against both the Guatemalan and international system of justice.

Haunted Land: Le pays hanté, la Palabra Desenterrada and *Discovering Dominga*

Haunted Land: Le pays hanté, la Palabra Desenterrada, from 2001, and *Discovering Dominga*, from 2003, are two even lesser known documentaries about the Guatemalan genocide from the pre-Spanish indictment period. Both films anchor their narratives to survivor testimonies and the forensic analysis used to bring perpetrators to justice. *Haunted Land*, directed by Mary Ellen Davis, features a Mayan survivor, Mateo Pablo, and a Guatemalan photographer, Daniel Hernandez-Salazar, who travel together to the Mayan highlands to visit the site of the village of Petanac, which was destroyed by the Guatemalan government. The story of how 38 Mayans were murdered unfolds with the discovery of mass graves and interviews with survivors and eyewitnesses. The portrait is as personal as it is somber and strikingly quiet. Unlike the judicial tone of *Granito*, *Haunted*

Land has an elegiac quality, leaving historical commentary and context to other authors.

Discovering Dominga is an equally intimate and multi-layered story of a child survivor (Denese) of the Rio Negro massacres, which occurred between 1980 and 1982 and claimed the lives of approximately 4,000 to 5,000 Mayan peasants. Denese, born Dominga, was nine when she became her family's sole survivor of the massacre. Two years later, an American family adopted her. In the documentary, Denese's return home is both a fact-finding mission and a testimony to the world about the genocide. The villagers of Rio Negro (where Denese's family lived) had been marked by the government as "insurgents" for resisting their forced removal to make way for a World Bank-funded dam. Through the discovery of her childhood and of family deaths, Denese embarked on a mission to tell the truth about what happened in Guatemala in the 1980s. In the film, a United Nations Truth Commission found the Guatemalan army responsible for 93 percent of the war crimes committed in the country, and declared the killings at Rio Negro a crime of genocide. Yet as Denese discovers, the perpetrators have not been punished, and the military remains all-powerful. Outraged at the injustice, Denese decides to become a witness in a landmark human rights violation case. She joins her relatives to demand the exhumation of the Rio Negro massacre victims from an unmarked grave and their re-burial in a new gravesite called Monument to the Truth. Ultimately, the community succeeds. In a dramatic moment, Denese returns once again to Guatemala to witness a forensic team unearth the grisly remains of the victims, including the body of her beloved father.[24]

The Silence of Neto

In the past few years, there has been a proliferation of documentaries about Guatemala in general (e.g., *Living on One Dollar* (2013); *I Will be Murdered* (2013) – about a Guatemalan lawyer who predicted his own death; *B-Boy for Life* (2012), about the lives of two break-dancers in Guatemala City); and about the Maya, specifically (*Heart of Sky, Heart of Earth* (2011), and *Mayan Renaissance* (2012). Yet the realm of feature films is truly undiscovered territory when it comes to the Guatemalan genocide. One related feature is the 1994 films, *The Silence of Neto*, which does not take place in the

1980s, but rather during the coup of 1954 when US armed forces helped the Guatemalan army suppress the popular revolution. In this film, we follow a boy named Neto, whose main goal is to fly a hot air balloon. Neto watches as the arrival of the US armed forces changes his everyday life. Neto's father loses his job, his family must move from the city he loves, and one of his closet family member dies during this military operation.[25] The film's subtext is that the groundwork for the genocide perpetrated in the late 1970s throughout the early 1980s was paved by the support of right-wing dictatorships by the United States. In this we see parallels to other films critical of US foreign policy during genocides such as *Sometimes in April* (2005) about Rwanda, and *The Killing Fields* (1984), about Cambodia. Like *When Mountains Tremble*, *The Silence of Neto* received special recognition at the Sundance Film Festival, and it is one of the first of its kind as a feature film about the dark history of US involvement in regimes that committed crimes against humanity over the past five decades. Yet like *Haunted Land*, it is almost too implicit in its imagery, and the analogy too subtle to capture the true suffering of the Guatemalan people, especially for North American audiences ignorant of their own complicity in this history. It instead presents a quasi *Boy in the Striped Pajamas* view of the atrocities going on around Neto. The film undoubtedly tries to attract the attention of a wider audience, but fails to do so.

Conclusion

By looking at these films, one should take away the pressing need for more research into, and representations of, the genocide in Guatemala. The five films explored here tell stories of human rights abuses, mass murder, tyrannical regimes, and international complicity. These films may not ever catch the mainstream moviegoers' eyes, or sink into international consciousness to a degree that the Holocaust films have, but they should be incorporated into courses on the history of genocide and used as a springboards for more scholarship and cinematic attention. Although the recent legal decisions regarding Rios Montt have probably closed the door on a retrial,[26] they have heightened the importance of the films under analysis here and have provided an opportunity for human rights organizations and filmmakers to do more to chronicle

15

Cinematic Witnessing of the Genocide in Bosnia 1992–1995: Toward A Poetics of Responsibility[1]

David Pettigrew

Southern Connecticut State University

The creation of a film about the genocide in Bosnia and Herzegovina bears the weight of a great responsibility. Such a film would presumably be expected to attempt to "tell the truth" about the genocide in the sense that it would convey accurate information about what happened, and would contribute to insuring that the truth and the suffering of the victims would not be forgotten. The responsibility to truth and to memory is especially important in the current socio-cultural context, in which the leadership of Republika Srpska, the Bosnian Serb dominated entity within Bosnia and Herzegovina, denies the genocide.[2] This paper seeks to consider the extent to which films about the genocide in Bosnia have been capable of bearing authentic witness to the genocide, both in terms of truth and of memory and also in terms of bearing witness to the singularity of the suffering of the victims and survivors.

In *Sovereignties in Question*, Jacques Derrida questions the possibility of such authentic witnessing. Derrida addresses a line in Paul Celan's poem *Ashenglorie*, namely, "*Niemand zeugt für den Zeugen*" ["No one bears witness for the witness."].[3] Derrida reads this line as a prohibition that could be understood as "No one in fact bears witness for the witness, no one can, of course … because no one *should*."[4] Derrida suggests that one cannot witness for the witness because there is only *one* witness to the moment, namely the "absolute victim" who actually suffered the crime. Derrida writes of Celan's poem, "The poem says there is no witness for the witness. No one bears witness for the witness … No one can because it must not be done. The possibility of the secret must remain sealed at the very moment when bearing witness unveils it."[5] Derrida emphasizes the poem's implication that "One cannot and must not (claim to) replace the witness of his or her own death … or the witness of others' deaths, the one who was present and survived, for instance, at the hell of Auschwitz."[6] At that time, at the moment of that death, there is the deepest "secret." For Derrida, Celan's prohibition is a reminder and a command that we must hold that secret sacred, and treat it as inaccessible. Derrida's reflections open a path to thinking about the very *topos* of the impossible when he identifies an ironic capacity of Celan's poem, namely, Celan's dictum that "no one witnesses for the witness" – *witnesses*, by virtue of its own prohibition, *the impossibility of witnessing*. The poem *seals* the secret as it reveals it, bears witness to it *as* secret. The poem, he writes, "keeps its secret, all the while telling us that there is a secret, revealing the secret it is keeping *as* a secret…"[7] Derrida writes, indeed, that he wants to take us to this limit, to the *aporia* of what is "at the same time possible and impossible."[8]

The impossibility of witnessing – the inaccessibility of the secret – would seem to mean that no *one* poem or *one* translation would be able to provide a complete or final meaning.[9] "Whoever bears witness [in English in the original] does not provide proof," insofar as the experience was "singular" and "irreplaceable."[10] Derrida concludes that in the face of the impossibility of witnessing, any "responsible witnessing" would need to engage "a poetic experience of language."[11] This poetic experience of language would be able to attend to a plurality of accounts of the singularity of the suffering of the victims – an "incalculability of the word." This plurality and incalculability would not mean that there is *no* truth but rather that there would be a constellation of "truths"; a metonymic sliding of signifiers attending to the plurality of witness accounts.

How would cinema depict the plurality of accounts of the singularity of suffering at the limits of the possibility of witnessing? Given the relatively recent occurrence of the atrocities in Bosnia, cinematic accounts have been able to draw on actual events, documentary film footage, photographs, and a range of eyewitness accounts, as well as on the findings of subsequent legal proceedings. Would it be more likely for a film to tell the truth and encounter the singularity of the suffering of the other if it is based, to some extent, on actual events? Michael Winterbottom's *Welcome to Sarajevo* (1997), for example, is one such film.[12] *Welcome to Sarajevo* takes place during the siege of Sarajevo, and the plot revolves around the true story of a journalist who became personally involved in a news story about an orphanage in Sarajevo that was under attack.[13] After broadcasting the story about the orphanage, the journalist became motivated to continue to publicize the plight of the orphanage in order to protect the children. The film depicts his efforts to adopt one of the children at the orphanage into his family in England. In the course of this story, the film represents a number of other actual events during the siege, and the director interweaves archival footage into his narrative, giving the film a feeling of historical authenticity. One such archival scene involves the shelling of a bread line in which 16 civilians were killed and many wounded. The archival footage reveals the blood of the victims, and a partially severed limb that is dangling as the victim is carried to the back of a Volkswagen hatchback to be taken for medical treatment. In another use of archival footage, the film depicts a British news team's actual discovery of the Trnopolje concentration camp, including the iconic image of an emaciated Fikret Alić behind the barbed wire. Another archival clip woven into the story shows the shelling and conflagration of the National and University Library in Sarajevo, which took place from August 25 to 26, 1992. Such scenes in the film involve actual footage of the atrocities committed by the Bosnian Serbs against Bosnian Muslims (Bosniaks). Those who view the film are given an opportunity to witness the range of atrocities. The reporter in the story of *Welcome to Sarajevo*, Michael Henderson, dramatizes his own transition from detached observation (at one point he asserts confidently, "we're not here to help … we're here to report") to passionate engagement, a transition that could only result from such witnessing. After covering the story of the orphanage, Henderson is ready to take action to defend the orphanage and adopt one of the children.

Welcome to Sarajevo also dramatizes other actual events, such as the reenactment of the Miss Besieged Sarajevo contest, a contest that was immortalized in the song titled *Miss Sarajevo*.[14] In addition to actual events, the film reveals the kinds of atrocities that were suffered by the civilians in Sarajevo during the siege. For example, one of the main Bosnian characters, a driver and translator for the news team, is himself the victim of a sniper while standing in his living room. Snipers terrorized Sarajevo citizens on the streets and in their homes. As a result of the shelling and sniper attacks, more than 11,000 civilians, including more than 1,000 children, were murdered.

David Attwood's *Shot Through the Heart* (1998),[15] another film based on actual events, also depicts the horrors of life in Sarajevo under the siege.[16] The plot revolves around two lifelong friends, one Bosnian Serb (Slavko) and one Bosnian Croat (Vlado) who were professional sharpshooters. Vlado's wife is a Bosniak. Slavko is called up to serve in the Bosnian Serb Army and trains snipers to attack the city. For his part, Vlado feels compelled to assist the defenders of Sarajevo. Early in the film, his daughter's 12-year-old friend is shot to death by a sniper while sitting on the front steps of her apartment building. Later, numerous civilians are heartlessly gunned down while seeking to fill jugs with water. Eventually, Vlado assumes the responsibility of attempting to stop the snipers who are terrorizing the citizens of Sarajevo, and he moves inexorably toward a confrontation with his friend Slavko.

Baggage (2011), a film directed by Academy Award recipient Danis Tanović, offers a narrative which, although only 30 minutes in length, dramatizes *the aftermath* of the genocide for the survivors.[17] Director Tanović has said that the film is based on three stories that he has been told.[18] The main character, Amir, a refugee living in Sweden, returns to Bosnia to identify the remains of his parents who were killed during the genocide. For some reason, when he visits the morgue, he is convinced that they have not found his parents. Before returning to Sweden, Amir decides to go to his childhood village. He visits his family home, which is in ruins. Before leaving the village, he encounters his childhood friend Dušan, an ethnic Serb. Dušan tells Amir he knows someone who knows where his parents are buried, and that Amir can pay for the information. When I met with the International Commission on Missing Persons in Sarajevo in 2012, they reported that at first, the families of victims who were murdered and buried in mass graves refused, on principle, to pay for information about the whereabouts of their loved ones. However, 20 years hence, the families are willing to pay for information.[19] In the film, Amir decides to pay for the information and is shown the location of a mass grave in an area in the forest. In the gripping finale of *Baggage*, he retrieves his parents' bones, along with his father's watch, and he places them in his suitcase before driving back to Sweden.

A mass grave also anchors the plot of *Behind Enemy Lines* (2001).[20] Directed by John Moore, the film is loosely based on the downing of Scott O'Grady, a United States Air Force pilot who was shot down over Bosnia on June 2, 1995. According to the storyline of the film, the Bosnian Serbs shot down the plane because it had flown over a supposedly demilitarized zone with troops positioned near a mass grave containing the bodies of civilians who had been executed by the same Serb troops. Speaking on the telephone, the Bosnian Serb commander asserts: "I had to shoot him down. He saw everything." While fleeing to evade the Bosnian Serb troops, the pilot falls headfirst into the mud of the mass grave. At that moment of the film, his commander is following his movements via satellite surveillance and observes his heat signature, although the surveillance technology cannot discern the bodies of the victims in the grave. However, the bodies are clearly seen by viewers of the film, and at this point, there is a flashback to the execution of the civilians. The pile of bodies and the mud enable the pilot to elude his pursuers. The discovery of the mass grave in *Behind Enemy Lines* is evocative of the satellite surveillance and discovery of mass graves following the genocide at Srebrenica.[21]

Jasmila Žbanić's *Grbavica* (2006)[22] is another film based on the aftermath of the atrocities that took place. *Grbavica's* plot concerns the relationship between a mother, Esma, and her daughter Sara. Sara believes that her father died during the aggression in defense of Bosnia. Her father would therefore be considered a *shahid*, meaning a "martyr."[23] Thus, initially, we, along with Sara, are led to believe that the father of the family has been killed. Many other children in Sara's school also seem to have lost their fathers in the Serb aggression.

The complication of *Grbavica* revolves around the fact that Sara wants to go on a school field trip and that Esma needs to take on a second job as a waitress at a club in order to pay for the trip. However, Sara is expecting her mother to produce a certificate attesting to the fact that her father died

211

in the aggression. If such a certificate is produced, then Sara's participation in the field trip will be free. Eventually the film reveals that Sara's father was not a *shahid*, but rather a Bosnian Serb rapist. We learn that Esma was raped, impregnated, and subsequently brutalized repeatedly when she was pregnant. At first, Esma wanted to give up her baby, but then she responded, she says, to the child's crying, and felt a maternal longing that led her to nurse Sara to keep her alive. The moment when Esma is forced to tell Sara the truth about her conception is one of the most gut-wrenching moments in the film.

Žbanić's *Grbavica* confronts the reality that rape was wielded as a weapon during the genocide. Claudia Card has identified such "war rapes" as aimed at rending the social fabric. Card writes that "Social vitality is destroyed when the social relations – organizations, practices, institutions – of the members of a group are irreparably damaged or demolished. Such destruction is a commonly intended consequence of war rape."[24] For Card, such destruction caused by rape portends no less than a "social death," which "enables us to distinguish the peculiar evil of genocide from the evils of other mass murders."[25] In addition to the commission of rape as a form of direct violence and psychological terror, there have been allegations that Bosnian Serbs raped Bosniak women with the goal of impregnating them in order to cause an ethnic change from Muslim to Serb.[26] Further, in Foča, Bosnian Serb perpetrators were convicted, in a landmark ruling, of rape as a crime against humanity for crimes committed at the Partizan sports hall and other locations.[27] The film's storyline is located *in* Grbavica, an actual neighborhood that was under Bosnian Serb control during the siege and in which non-Serb residents were terrorized. On March 29, 2013, a certain Veselin Vlahović was convicted of crimes against humanity and sentenced to 45 years in prison. He was accused of the "crimes of deprivation of life (murder), slavery, rape, unlawful detention, physical and mental abuse (inhumane treatment), robbery and enforced disappearance of civilian non-Serb population."[28] Hence, *Grbavica* portrays the devastating social impact of the sexual violence that was part of the genocide in Bosnia.

The war crime of rape is also central to the plot of Angelina Jolie's film, *In the Land of Blood and Honey* (2011).[29] Early in the film, women from a Bosniak neighborhood are abducted and taken to a military headquarters where they are imprisoned and raped. Due to a particular plot twist, the film was strongly opposed by the Association of Women Victims of War, and the production permit was revoked. The film had to be completed at facilities in Budapest.[30] Initial reports about the plot indicated that it would involve a love story involving a Serb perpetrator and a Bosniak woman in a rape camp. On the face of it, the idea that a rape camp could provide a setting for a "love story" was completely unacceptable to those who suffered in the rape camps during the genocide. As it turns out, in the film, the main character, Ajla, is taken to the rape camp where she is recognized by her recent Serb boyfriend named Danijel. Danijel happens to be a ranking officer at the headquarters. According to the plot, Danijel seeks to protect Ajla by pretending to keep her for himself. It seems that he hopes that his action will keep her from being abused by other soldiers. When Ajla is brought to his room, Danijel tells her he is conflicted about the "war" and also that he has informed his men not to touch her, that she is his property. We also learn that his father is the ranking commander and is an ultranationalist. Danijel's integrity is perhaps confirmed when he advises Ajla on how to escape from the base, and he seems prepared to help her to do so. One could argue that Ajla sees the situation (her relation to Danijel in the camp) as the only chance to survive an impossible situation. This explanation might be granted, but at times the ensuing sexual encounters seem to be too consensual and overly romanticized, especially in relation to the brutalities to which the other women in the facility are subjected. Ajla tends to the victims who have been mercilessly raped and beaten. One of them tells her: "I want to die." Such a romanticized account of the relationship between Ajla and Danijel was, as mentioned earlier, unacceptable to many of the victims. Eventually, arrangements were made for survivors to have a private screening of the film, and then a public screening was held in Sarajevo with director Jolie in attendance. Reservations about the plot were mitigated by the fact that the film depicts the Bosnian Serbs as vile perpetrators as they are seen executing Bosniak civilians at random – at one point throwing a child to its death from a balcony, simply because it would not stop crying. When Danijel is assigned to sniper duty in the hills above Sarajevo, his assignment facilitates the film's depiction of the siege of Sarajevo as a brutal assault on civilians. In addition, the film depicts the forcible deportations of Bosniaks, the use of Bosniak women as human shields, the imprisonment of Bosniaks in a concentration camp, and the execution of a group of men standing next to a mass grave.

I attended a special screening of *In the Land of Blood and Honey* at Yale University, with the film's production designer in attendance.[31] As part of the discussion with the audience, he stated that after the "war," "the Serbs went back to Serbia." I was given the opportunity to state that the Republika Srpska had been declared as an entity in 1992 (within the sovereign state of Bosnia and Herzegovina) and that the Bosnian Serbs carried out the genocide to eliminate non-Serbs from the territory of Republika Srpska. I insisted that after the genocide, the Bosnian Serbs did not "go" anywhere. Rather, they stayed right where they were, as Republika Srpska was subsequently recognized and legitimized by the Dayton Peace Accords. In the end, prior to the credits, the film asserts that as many as 50,000 women were raped, and that there was a conviction for rape as a crime against humanity.

While films such as *Welcome to Sarajevo*, *Baggage*, *Grbavica*, and *In the Land of Blood and Honey* depict events that took place early in the genocide (the siege of Sarajevo, sniper attacks, the shelling of the breadline, incendiary attacks on the National Library, scenes from Trnopolje concentration camp, the destruction of villages, the forcible displacement of the civilian population, and rape as a weapon of war), neither the term "genocide," nor the name "Republika Srpska" are mentioned at any time in any of the films. (Only in *Shot Through the Heart* is reference made to a "Serbian Republic of Bosnia.") Further, each film offers a limited exposure to the atrocities or events that took place over the course of the three and a half years of aggression: *Welcome to Sarajevo* depicts the siege of Sarajevo and a concentration camp; *Shot Through the Heart* focuses exclusively on the siege of Sarajevo; *Baggage* depicts the phenomenon of mass graves and the destruction of civilian homes; *Grbavica* offers a portrayal of the crime of rape and its aftermath. *In the Land of Blood and Honey* also dramatizes the crime of rape while focusing primarily on the siege of Sarajevo. Without any sort of overview or explanatory context, how would the viewer know the "whole story," or at least be exposed to other dimensions of the tragedy? Where is Grbavica? Where were the concentration camps? Moreover, there is no mention, in any of these films, of Srebrenica, where the atrocities have been ruled to be genocide, nor of Višegrad, where the perpetrators were convicted of crimes against humanity for herding women and children into houses on two separate occasions, on June 14 and 27, 1992, setting the houses ablaze, and burning the victims alive.[32] Given the limited scope of each film, or given what could be termed the narrative incompletion of the witness accounts provided by such films, one wonders if a documentary film could respond to this deficiency. Perhaps with the approach of a documentary film to actual events, including interviews and the use of archival footage, a documentary could provide a better context for understanding the atrocities.

Srebrenica: A Cry from the Grave (1999), directed by Leslie Woodhead, is a documentary that contains extensive information about the Srebrenica genocide.[33] The film witnesses the thoughts and emotions of actual survivors and their struggle to cope with the disappearance in July 1995 of more than 8,000 men and boys from Srebrenica. Survivors are seen visiting the old salt mines in Tuzla where the remains of the victims who had been exhumed from the mass graves were being stored. At that point in time, the authorities did not have access to DNA technology. Indeed, when the film was made, Potočari Memorial Cemetery had not been established as a national memorial.[34]

In addition to such scenes, the viewer benefits from the narrator's background information, which is interwoven with archival footage. Further context is provided by the periodic appearance of Hasan Nuhanović, a Bosniak who served as translator for the United Nation troops assigned to the Srebrenica "safe area." Hasan recounts the arrival of thousands of refugees on July 11, to the UN base (Dutchbat), refugees who were seeking protection of the Dutch soldiers from the Serbs, only to be expelled into the hands of the Serbs by the very same Dutch troops. At one point, Hasan's father was elected to meet with Serb commander Ratko Mladić, but later, in spite of this, and in spite of Hasan's own status, six armed Dutch soldiers approached his family and ordered them to leave the UN base. At that point in the film, Hasan is unable to complete the story of his family's expulsion, as it is too painful for him. The archival footage and narration provide some background context, at least for the events of the Srebrenica genocide, as we learn about the siege of the town, about the UN intervention and creation of a "safe area," and about the introduction of a peacekeeping battalion from the Netherlands (Dutchbat). There are scenes including General Ratko Mladić, the Dutch Commander Karremans, and an execution site. *Srebrenica: A Cry from the Grave* effectively incorporates archival footage and an explanatory narrative. In addition, there are text boxes that provide dates, transitions, and facts. However, this documentary is also focused on just one aspect of the genocide (Srebrenica) and the term "genocide" is never mentioned.

Marcel Ophuls's documentary film, *The Troubles We've Seen: The History of Journalism in Wartime* (1994), addresses the role and experience of journalists in Sarajevo under siege.[35] The film reports on the Bosnian Serb encirclement of the city of Sarajevo, and the sniper attacks and shelling, as it all happens. One hears the gunfire and explosions in the background throughout the film. Ophuls visits the city of Pale, the stronghold of Radovan Karadžić, with journalists who interview Nikola Koljević (one of the founding members of Republika Srpska). When returning to Sarajevo, the journalists come upon a position from which Serbs are attacking the city with heavy machine guns and mortars.

In a later scene, Ophuls interviews a reporter from the newspaper *Oslobodjene*, whose offices are under fire, and he also meets with a Sarajevo resident who has lost his leg to a shelling. In another scene, a victim of a sniper is shown in what appears to be a morgue and *New York Times* reporter John Burns reflects on the pace of the murders. At a hospital, Dr. Mufid Lazovic speaks of operating without oxygen. In the course of the documentary, we become acquainted with journalists, their journalistic styles and concerns, along with the risks they take; through them, we witness the atrocities. Ophul's film is highly stylized and nuanced. Part of his approach is autobiographical, involving references to his father's 1940 film *De Mayerling à Sarajevo*, a film that portrays the love affair and marriage between Archduke Franz Ferdinand of Austria and Sophie, Duchess of Hohenberg, leading up to their eventual assassination in 1914 in events that triggered the First World War. Other film references are quite irreverent, such as the glance in the direction of the *Holiday Inn* (1942), including the song "Happy Holiday." At one point, Ophuls is seen prodding *New York Times* reporter John Burns to sing along to the title song, "Happy Holiday," including the lyrics:

If the traffic noise affects you
Like a squeaky violin
Kick your cares down the stairs
Come to Holiday Inn[36]

All this, of course, is a darkly satirical reference to the Sarajevo Holiday Inn, where many journalists stayed during the siege, directly under the guns of Vraca Hill.

How do we understand these historical and satirical filmic references in the context of our analysis of the cinematic witnessing of the genocide in Bosnia? I suggest that Ophuls is attempting to enact a hyper-reflectivity so as to involve us in a reflective process of witnessing that is intrinsic to the art of cinema. In other words, our awareness of such a reflective process would mean that, as we view films about the atrocities in Bosnia and Herzegovina, we would not fail to become aware that we ourselves are, to some degree, witnessing the genocide. One French journalist, Patrick Chauvel, expresses this in the following way in Ophuls' film: "We're here to show what's happening … to help people understand … look at this. Think and Judge!… – a *bon témoin* [an authentic witness]" a colleague adds. Chauvel continues, "You're a reporter first, photography is just a tool … papers and fighting men rely on us … they see us as witnesses."

The question this paper has attempted to ask is whether the films in question depict the "truth about the genocide," and whether they enact an authentic encounter with the singularity of the suffering of the victims such that we can witness the truth. The films discussed seem indeed to witness the singularity of the suffering of the victims of the genocide as they tell different stories of Sarajevo, Srebrenica, the crime of rape, the concentrations camps, and the story of the mass graves. However, as I noted earlier, each film tends to focus on one isolated aspect of Serb aggression. Further, there seems to be a lack of explanatory context that would enable someone unfamiliar with the genocide to gain a genuine understanding. In addition, I noted that the word *genocide* is not uttered in any of the films mentioned.[37] *Srebrenica: A Cry from the Grave*, which is focused on Srebrenica, is one of the few films to refer to "Republika Srpska." Would this mean that the films have fallen short of their responsibility, short of what Derrida termed a poetics of responsibility?

If we would expect films about the Holocaust to convey the truth and meaning of the Holocaust, why would we expect anything less of a film about the genocide in Bosnia from 1992–1995? One way to approach the concern about the relatively narrow focus of each film is to realize that, in their representation of specific atrocities during the genocide from 1992 to 1995, that is to say that, precisely in their isolated focus, the films have enacted an authentic witnessing. Derrida suggests that there is no one probative account that would provide a totalizing or comprehensive witnessing. In other words, there is an unspeakable or unknowable aspect of genocide that exceeds incorporation into an explanatory or probative account. Crimes against humanity may be so horrible that they cannot be interpreted, in the sense that they cannot be easily represented or comprehended. Hence, with a focus on a particular story, the films we have addressed respect the singularity of the suffering of the selected scenario, and, at the same time respect the plurality of other stories yet to be told. The films point to a need for a poetics of responsibility that would respond to the plurality of stories and to the singularity of the suffering of the victims. In the sense that they do not provide the entire context, the films perform, perhaps ironically, the witnessing of which Derrida speaks.

At the same time, the films about Sarajevo or Srebrenica bear witness to a need for other films to be made about Višegrad, Prijedor, Bihać, Kozarac, Foča, Omarska, Trnopolje, and Tomašica, all places where atrocities occurred. If we conclude that no single film can or should tell the "whole story," then there needs to be a commitment to an ongoing plurality of witnessing, a commitment to being immersed in the reflective process of witnessing that can be enacted by cinema in pursuit of truth, memory, and genocide prevention.

However, the presentation of the plurality of singular accounts, through cinema and other media, could only take place, ultimately, in a discursive culture in which citizens are able to witness, reflect, learn, and grow over time in a society free of denial and censure. At the present time, there is an utterly crucial need for films about the genocide in Bosnia to proliferate in resistance to the genocide denial that permeates the political culture of Republika Srpska. Hence, the cinematic witness accounts provided by these and other films are part of a poetics of responsibility that is no less than a struggle for truth and memory concerning the genocide in Bosnia and Herzegovina that took place from 1992 to 1995.

16

"Truth" in Films about the Rwandan Genocide

Barbara A. Moss
Georgia Highlands College

Mary Afolabi
Veritas University, Abuja, Nigeria

Beginning with *Hotel Rwanda* in 2004, followed by *Sometimes in April* and *Shooting Dogs /Beyond the Gates* in 2005, and *Shake Hands with the Devil* in 2007, audiences have been a surrogate witnesses to the 1994 genocide of over 800,000 Tutsi and moderate Hutu Rwandans by the Hutu majority, a genocide which unfolded as major world powers – numbed by indifference, political missteps in Somalia, and lack of moral will – stood by and did nothing. In this essay, we compare the different representations of the Rwandan genocide and the international responses to it in the above-mentioned films, highlighting their unique qualities and differences. The filmmakers of each production provide commentary on the state of ethnic relations before the genocide, depict the carnage perpetrated by Hutus, and bemoan the impotence of the United Nations' peacekeeping forces and the apathy of the international community. Above all, the films offer audiences a painful window into the interplay of savagery and civilization as diverse protagonists struggle to hold onto their faith in God and humanity amid the abandonment of the Rwandan people.

For those of us charged with the task of studying a past of which we were not a part, we cannot claim to recapture events as they actually happened. Although aided by primary and secondary sources, we reconstruct the past through a process of imagination, language, signs, and codes. Filmmakers operate in a realm even more disconnected from "truth" than historians, and yet when they make films about history, they aim for as "real" a depiction as possible. Nyasha Mboti argues that "the attempt to make 'truthful' films is illogical."[1] To him, "it is illogical because it is based on an elemental misunderstanding of the function of cinematic images. The function of cinematic images is to communicate specific ways – gazes – of seeing the world. Behind every film, then, is a gaze or a conscious attempt to see the world in a certain way."[2] We cannot dispute the fact that our reactions to situations differ from when we are being watched or expected to behave in a particular way; thus Mboti still emphasizes that "films, do not contain truth at all. Rather, they contain cinema."[3] Related to Mboti's claim is bell hooks's idea that "giving audiences what is real is precisely what movies do not do. They give the reimagined, reinvented version of the real. It may look like something familiar, but in actuality it is a different universe from the world of the real. That's what makes movies so compelling."[4]

Though we can agree to a certain extent with the above scholars, we cannot discard the importance of historical movies. In "Film as History/ History as Film," Patrick Vonderau asserts that "film can be regarded as being related to the history of the society in which it is produced. Film can function as history: as a source or a document not only of its own aesthetic history, but of history in general. Vice versa, history can be presented as film: 'historical movies' compete with conventional written historiographic reports for public acceptance since cinema and television have become widely available."[5] Similarly, Gary Gutting, in his article titled "Learning History at the Movies," states that "movies are the source of much of what we know – or think we know – about history."[6] Writing about Steven Spielberg's *Lincoln,* Gutting recommends historical movies as a source of knowledge not just about Lincoln and the Civil War but also about politics in general.

As analysts of films about genocide, we must acknowledge the legitimate concerns of scholars from both sides of this debate. We need to be cautious in our acceptance of such films, precisely because the dangers of reduction and distortion, but we must not make the mistake of believing that historical movies have little or nothing to offer. Questions we should be asking are: How can filmmakers responsibly compress an historical event into a two-hour movie? What characters should be considered important or unimportant for filming? Who is to blame for the genocide, and is restitution possible? Above all, how can such films convey "truth," either the reality of a fact or truth as a condition, a state of being or mind? Certainly, we cannot simply dismiss films about genocide, for to do so would be tantamount to saying that we do not wish to know or that we do not care about what happened. To do this would be to ignore the victims of the Rwandan genocide – to erase them from historical memory, yet again. The four films to which we now turn offer a useful template on which to explore these difficult questions.

Hotel Rwanda

Terry George, director of *Hotel Rwanda,* uses a blank screen and an audible news bulletin of President Clinton's concerns over the deteriorating Sarajevo situation to place Rwandan events into an international context. The Western world appears more concerned about atrocities in Bosnia while calls for violence in Rwanda, blatantly broadcast on local radio stations, go unnoticed. When the genocide begins, it is "the result of some inexplicable, uncontrollable primordial tribalism."[7] Tribalism is African, uncivilized and natural. The media, and the film, ignore the political/economic factors such as "the increasing imbalance in land, food, and people that led to malnutrition, hunger, periodic famine, and fierce competition for land to farm."[8] Although unintentional, the film threatens to dissolve into the afropessimism that critics have proclaimed is the new stereotype for Africa.[9]

The film's protagonist, Paul Rusesabagina, the African house manager of the Hôtel des Mille Collines, guides us through the maze of civilization and savagery. The hotel is the symbol of civilization, and maintaining the hotel's dignity is Rusesabagina's obsession. From his initial appointment, he follows his mandate to "never never lower the tone of the hotel."[10] It is style that matters, and immaculately dressed in a suit and tie, Rusesabagina is the purveyor of the best food, cigars, and liquor. Even as the genocide commences and Tutsi refugees stream into the hotel, he makes sure that order prevails, food is served, beds are made, decorum is followed. He convinces Sabena's president to keep the hotel open because it would hurt their reputation: "The Mille Collines is an oasis of calm for all our loyal customers."[11] Civilization is the most powerful bargaining chip that Rusesabagina has and he plays it skillfully, buying time by convincing a Hutu general that American spy satellites are watching him.

Rusesabagina is initially a devotee of Western values and culture, but the abandonment of the West amid the unspeakable brutality leads him to reject this colonial mindset, and after witnessing hundreds of bodies strewn along a river road, he strips off his shirt and tie, declaring: "I am a fool. They told me I was one of them … the wine, chocolates, cigars, style, I swallowed it … I swallowed all of it."[12] As the major Western powers send troops to rescue their foreign nationals, they leave behind the Rwandan people in their most desperate hour of need: "They are cowards. Rwanda is not worth saving for any of them – the French, British, the Americans."[13] The commander of the UN Peacekeeping Force, Colonel Oliver, explains to Rusesabagina: "The West, all the superpowers …. they think you're dirt, they think you're dung. You're worthless … you're black, you're not even a nigger. You're an African."[14] As a foreign cameraman points out, the world will see the atrocities on television and go on eating their dinners.

Active complicity by non-natives in the genocide comes through in the "bargain buy from China" as thousands of 10-cent machetes spill from a crate in a Hutu warehouse. African life is not only worthless but can be cheaply extinguished. But blame falls squarely on European shoulders as a Rwandan reporter insists that "It was the Belgians who created the division"[15] with identity cards and preferential treatment for the Tutsi under colonialism. The French add to the mayhem by supplying arms to the Hutu military. And the UN peacekeepers are as helpless as everyone else. As Colonel Oliver points out, "We're here as peace keepers, not peace makers."[16] But they can neither keep the peace nor protect anyone, including themselves.

Hotel Rwanda pulls the camera back and allows the audience to avert their eyes from horrific slaughter, showing people hacked to death from a distance or a road strewn with bodies in the haze of dawn, while a couple of bloody helmets symbolize the murder of ten UN peacekeepers.

The murderers themselves are depicted at closer range. The Hutu military are without compassion, but their officers are easily bought off with bribes and sidetracked with beer. The more numerous Hutu militias joyfully brandish machetes and bayonets (one with a teddy bear impaled on it) wearing grotesque purple wigs and hanging off trucks like circus clowns roaring into an arena. Their costumes are as incomprehensible as their language. All of it is exotic, wild, and savage. There appears to be no logic to their murderous rampage. They have been set in deadly motion.

Sometimes in April

Sometimes in April focuses as much on blaming the US for the genocide as on the genocide itself. Raoul Peck opens with rolling text describing pre-colonial Hutu-Tutsi relations, a misunderstanding of colonial occupation, and Belgian pseudoscientific tests that establish ethnic division. "It was never about civilization, never about tribe or race ... it was always about greed, arrogance and power."[17] With blame securely placed elsewhere, the film cuts to Rwandan school children watching President Clinton's 1998 apology for US inaction. The tone is set as the film dances between scenes of Rwanda's march toward genocide and US diplomats scrambling to avoid international embarrassment like they faced in Somalia as clear evidence of mass killings mount.

Our guide through this downhill slide is Augustin, a Hutu soldier with a Tutsi wife, Jeanne, who has already lost most of her family in the 1992 genocide. Yet Augustin refuses to believe the genocide rumors even though his brother Honore is a DJ who broadcasts hate messages on Radio-Television Libre des Mille Collines (RTLM). This pro-Hutu Power station was a trusted part of Rwandan's lives that connected them to the genocide.[18] The present is 2004; the genocide is told in flashbacks as Augustin travels to Tanzania to visit his brother who is on trial for war crimes.

The Hutu military is clearly in control, orchestrating and sanctioning the well-planned genocide by using community organizations. They train the militia and proudly acknowledge their debt to French support that bought "Albanian Kalashnikov rifles, Israeli Uzis, Czech grenades, M16s from the US, guns and ammo from Egypt, and machetes from China."[19]

The genocide would probably not have been possible without foreign small arms sales.[20]

The film depicts the militiamen as drunken looters, or patient vigilantes checking identity cards and awaiting orders to kill at roadblocks, or as zombie-like murderers, waving machetes and clubs, marching silently toward their helpless prey at schools and churches. Both in urban and rural areas, they obey the directives to kill – "to go to work" – without question. Farmers reach for machetes and clubs and head off to murder instead of tending to their farms. It is their calm that is unnerving. It is the ordinariness of these people that begs for an explanation of their deeds.

The camera is not shy; it wants the victims to be seen as human beings, individuals whose lives are brutally snuffed out. Huddled in churches, some are led out for execution, seemingly resigned to their fate, kneeling quietly, staring straight into the camera as it slowly pans past their faces. Students at a Catholic girls' school refuse to be separated by ethnicity and are shot and hacked to death, falling upon each other in a bloody heap. Truckloads of bloody bodies, collected like so much garbage, are jostled through the streets.

The tale is more complex than brother against brother. The larger issue of how Rwanda will heal itself is played out in the personal struggles of Augustin and Honore. Augustin finally listens to his brother's testimony at the International Tribunal in Arusha Tanzania, where Honore admits complicity with his radio broadcasts. But Augustin finds it difficult to remove his wedding ring after losing his wife and children. And local Rwandan communities hold *gacacas*, to present testimony against accused perpetrators while trying to find peace in a country split by internationally abetted fratricide.

As the genocide churns on, US officials try to cajole Rwandan military officials with threats of intervention. These have no teeth as a Hutu commander sarcastically reminds them: "We have no oil here, we have no diamonds, we have nothing you need in Rwanda, why would you come?"[21] There is no "political will" to intervene; the cost is considered too high and there are no clear strategic advantages to do so. Only with the RPF takeover of Kigali is the US off the hook and able to send humanitarian aid. US bureaucrats intone, "In terms of national interest, we did everything right … As far as moral imperative we did not do the right thing."[22]

225

Beyond the Gates

Michael Caton-Jones brings the issue of faith to the discussion in *Beyond the Gates*. Civilization is articulated through an elderly Catholic priest, Father Christopher, and a young English schoolteacher, Joe, who is stationed at the *École Technique Officielle*. Father Christopher questions whether his work has made any difference among Rwandans after discovering the bodies of murdered nuns sprawled across the furniture and floor of their convent. "People have been coming to mass here for God know how long, they get up, they go to church, they sing, they genuflect, and they leave … because they're told to. They just go through the motions without the slightest understanding of what it is they're engaged in – whether they're being told to eat a wafer or hack their own flesh and blood."[23] Joe's privileged life and idealism blinds him to the evil that is pervasive until he witnesses a man hacked to death and sees their groundsman among the killers with a bloody machete. Joe then begins to question God's part in all of this.

UN troops are stationed at the school that becomes a sanctuary for terrified Tutsi when the genocide begins. Yet they cannot shoot unless fired upon. Their commander, Capitaine Delon, comes from a family that hid Jews from the Nazis. So his heart is in the right place, but his hands are tied. The UN's primary concern is the Europeans who have fled to the school for safety. Delon makes sure that they have the proper facilities and gives them updates on their situation. The Africans, meanwhile, are ignored. Rachel, a BBC reporter, reiterates this racial divide. She finds it difficult to identify with Rwandan victims although she had spent the previous year in Bosnia where she cried everyday. "Strangely enough over here, not a tear … Any time I saw a dead Bosnian woman, white woman, I thought that could be my Mum. Over here, they're just dead Africans … We're all just selfish pieces of work."[24]

The film shows Hutu soldiers before the genocide begins, strolling down the streets and manning the roadblocks harassing Tutsi. But once the genocide starts, it is the Hutu militia who are the real killers, singing, dancing, chanting, blowing whistles, swinging spiked clubs, hatchets, and machetes. There is perverse joy in their actions; this is not work for them. And yet they are the common people – François, the school's groundsman and Julius, the local shopkeeper. They are somehow transformed into smiling vicious, blood-splattered murderers.

The camera's focus here is close and detailed, recording buzzing flies around the dead and glistening blood on the corpses, and capturing the palpable fear of trembling victims. The bloody bodies of children and nuns who have been raped intensify the cruelty. However, the intended victims – Rwandan refugees flooding into the school – are far from sacrificial sheep awaiting slaughter. They organize themselves into work details to prepare food, get fuel, and provide security. They are actively involved in their own survival. As the UN prepares to abandon them, they try one last time to determine their fate by asking that UN soldiers shoot them and spare them the pain of being hacked to death by machetes. As the UN leaves, Father Christopher reaffirms his faith that God is with the Rwandan people in their suffering and so he cannot leave them. In his ultimate sacrifice he smuggles some children out and buys them enough time at a roadblock so that they can escape their killers. The epigraph by Elie Wiesel reads, "The opposite of faith is not heresy but indifference."[25]

Shake Hands with the Devil

Roger Spottiswoode shows the genocide and its impact on the commander of the UN peacekeepers, Lieutenant General Romeo Dallaire, in *Shake Hands with the Devil*. In an extremely personal exposé, we see his struggles with the UN bureaucracy, foreign ambassadors, and politicians, while he valiantly tries to stop the genocide. His mission is doomed from the start; he has too few men, insufficient ammunition, and no authority to take the offensive, "not even to protect the slaughter of the innocent."[26]

Early on Dallaire realizes that there is another game being played, one to which he is not invited or made privy to its rules. When a credible Hutu extremist defects with clear proof of a planned genocide, Dallaire decides to raid three arms caches. Inexplicably the UN not only forbids the raids, but also requires that he inform the Rwandan government of the allegations. And after President Habyarimana's plane is shot down, UNAMIR (the United Nations Assistance Mission for Rwanda) is prevented from firing unless fired upon, leaving them helpless prey to the Hutu military. When they attempt to protect Prime Minister Agathe, a Hutu moderate, they are disarmed, taken to a military base and murdered.

Their bodies are left in a bloody heap behind the morgue of the military hospital. The Prime Minister is assassinated as Dallaire listens to the gunfire on the telephone. With no real opposition, the Rwandan military take control, barely masking their disdain for Dallaire and his UN troops. They know that there will be no international intervention, as General Bagosora boasts, "Rwanda is a small African country little noticed by the world. Haven't you found that so?"[27] As Rwandans flee to UN headquarters and protected sites, Dallaire battles his superiors while their supplies of food, water, and fuel dwindle. When UN Secretary Boutros-Ghali orders them to leave, Dallaire disobeys the order. With his force reduced to 260 volunteers, Dallaire decides to remain "to bear witness to what the rest of the world does not want to see."[28] Meanwhile reporters are being sent to Bosnia and Sarajevo; Rwanda is "just one more African mess."[29]

In the film, the French share blame with the Hutu killers. Dallaire explodes when the French want to intervene after the RPF have taken Kigali:

> The reason France wants to come in now is to save their old clients because they're losing the war .... The first people France saved here were the people who planned this genocide. I saw them get on the plane to Paris. France sold them the weapons, France trained the presidential guards, France stood back for 72 days and let their Rwandan protégée try to exterminate the Tutsi and the Hutu moderates.[30]

It is the ethical compromises that begin to tear Dallaire apart. When he meets with militia leaders to arrange a civilian exchange with the RPF, he is forced to shake hands with them, one of whom has blood on his sleeve. The episode sickens him. He is shown calmly cutting his thighs with a razor blade to "feel good. It took away the pain."[31] As the genocide continues, Dallaire becomes reckless, courting death.

Through his eyes we see ugly carnage: streets so littered with bodies that the UN vehicles are unable to drive around them. Dallaire and his men gingerly pick up the dead and lay them on the sides of the road. After an RPF bombing of a hospital, dismembered limbs are strewn all over the grounds. He sees decomposing bodies choking streams, and notices dead women – rape victims – in the streets, mouths open in a silent scream, thighs bloody. "The evidence was there, looking at a skeleton you could see the pain, humiliation."[32] He imagines the dead alive and laughing in the beauty of the countryside. Holding onto his sanity by a thread, he asks to be relieved of his command. Back home, he tries to commit suicide with pills and alcohol, but fails. While the dead continue to haunt him, he admits his failure to his therapist, "My body wants to forget Rwanda now. I can't let that happen. I have to finish my mission."[33]

Comparisons

While all four movies succeeded in raising awareness of what happened during the fateful summer months of 1994 and they share similar narrative elements, they offer their own perspectives as well – on pre-genocide ethnic relations, the actual carnage, and finally, the complicity of the international community.

With respect to pre-genocide ethnic relations, all four films feature some kind of description of the relationship that existed between the two contending ethnic groups in Rwanda – the Hutus and the Tutsis. Each film offers background information into the reasons for ethnic divisions in the country, whether through narration or by on screen text, and regardless of the beginning point in each film, there are undertones of looming danger. *Shake Hands with the Devil* presents a cross section of the Rwandan people living normal lives and going about their daily activities, and Brigadier General Dallaire thinks the country is simply a beautiful place. But when Dallaire questions a female trader on the identity of street singers he notices that the woman is afraid to talk, out of fear that they are in the Hutu militia. In *Hotel Rwanda*, we feel the ethnic tension and fear just as quickly; there are rumors in town about the elimination of the Tutsis, and there are roadblocks to check the ethnic identities of the people. One such rumor comes to the attention of Paul when his brother-in-law and wife visit him at the hotel, telling him in confidence of a warning by a Hutu militia friend that there is a plot to eliminate the Tutsis, but Paul refuses to acknowledge the statement. In *Beyond the Gates*, we see varying degrees of interethnic conflict; the first time we are introduced to this is when François, the *École Technique Officielle* groundsman is driving with Joe, the school teacher, and they encounter

a roadblock where soldiers ask for François's identity. The verifying officer is quite harsh until he sees that François is a fellow Hutu, which leads
to an immediate change in his demeanor; meanwhile, while François's
identity is being checked, Joe witnesses the abuse of another man and
woman. When Joe asks François who they are, François answers cynic-
ally, "Tutsis." Later, Marie, a student in the *École Technique Officielle,* having just concluded a race and while tying her shoes, comes under attack
from teenage boys who scream "*Inyenzi*" and throw stones at her. Joe,
Marie's teacher, comes to her rescue and chases away the boys. He asks
what *Inyenzi* means, and she tells him – cockroaches. There is also a scene
in which Tutsis seek refuge at the school, and a couple tries to communicate with Joe, but because he does not understand the local language, he
calls Francois to assist him to interpret, but knowing and seeing that he
is Hutu, the couple refrains from speaking. Francois is also harsh to them
as he talks in the native language, and the couple leaves in fear. When
Joe asks Francois what transpired, Joe starts to spew anti-Tutsi venom,
declaring that it was the Tutsis who shot down the Hutu President of
Rwanda's plane and that it was the Tutsis who have a plan to enslave the
Hutus. In *Sometimes in April,* ethnic relations begin at a low point as
Hutu government soldiers give an intensive training to new recruits, and
Xavier shares with his friend Augustin that he has heard rumors of killings. The training looks more like an incitement to mass murder as train-
ees use machetes to behead effigies of ethnic Tutsis. In the end, the films
share a similar sense of both despair and inevitability as the breakdown
in interethnic relations unfolds in pre-genocide Rwanda.

Although more subtly in agreement in their negative assessment of ethnic interaction prior to the genocide, each film differs more noticeably in
their "spectacle of carnage." In *Hotel Rwanda,* director George shows the
audience mostly the *impact* of the murders. However, he does include the
shocking scene when Paul and Gregoire go for supplies to provide for the
many refugees at the hotel. On their way back, they drive on what they
perceive to be a bumpy road, which leads Paul to tell Gregoire to stop. Paul
goes out and falls on human corpses, an incident that leaves him shaken.
Beyond the Gates gives us more vivid and unrestrained images of atrocities.
These were murders committed at close range and by hand; the murder
weapon of choice was the machete. From the murder of a Tutsi man at a

roadblock to the hacking to death of Tutsi escapees from the *École*, *Beyond the Gates* does not shy away from forcing the audience into the traumatic role of murder witness. There is also the verbal carnage which the audience cannot ignore – the hate messages towards the Tutsis which filled the increasingly toxic airwaves. At one point, Marie and two other children listen to the radio at the *École*, and she interprets what they said to Joe: "Who will fill the empty graves? The cockroaches who are hiding in the churches and the schools." While *Sometimes in April* dwells more in the realm of the aftereffects of genocide, anchoring its story on the quest for justice and healing, the carnage of the past frequently ruptures the film's narrative of the present, whether it is the murder of Augustin's family or the horrific mass shooting of the girls at the Catholic Convent. *Shake Hands with the Devil* also presents the audience with upsetting images like scattered limbs and decomposing bodies half-eaten by wild dogs and rats; we also see desolation in a once beautiful country and hear the cries of the dead. The depiction of the carnage in this movie drives home the point of Dallaire's book *Shaking Hands with the Devil: The Failure of Humanity in Rwanda*, that witnessing the most insidious form of evil and not doing enough to vanquish it can inflict a trauma all its own.

For all the themes thus far examined, the role of the United Nations Peacekeeping Force remains one of the most misconstrued by Rwandans who did not fully comprehend the U.N.'s mandate. It is Dallaire who sheds light on this when he declares that his mandate is only to *keep* the peace and not *make* it. The peace keepers are to serve as impartial participants – referees – and not coaches. They are not to fire at machete-wielding Hutu extremists even when the murders occur in their presence, so long as the peacekeepers are not fired upon. Their possession of weapons is only for self-defense. Initially, Dallaire upholds this mandate, and that leads him to tell his soldiers that "peacekeeping is the highest military job on earth which he believed could be done, because where there's a will, there's a way." Dallaire's optimism gives way to pessimism as the murders increase and Dallaire's requests for help go unanswered and his forces are ordered to evacuate. The scene in *Hotel Rwanda* in which Colonel Oliver tells Rusesabagina that the UN is going to abandon the country is yet another cinematic expression of the outcry against Western inaction. In *Beyond the Gates*, the audience sees more indifference – in this case the indifference of the Belgian Captain Delon to the killings outside the gates of the *École*. He insists that he and his men can only maintain the school as a "military base," and not step outside the gates or even protect the 2,500 Rwandan refugees inside. So when at a later time, the captain tells Father Christopher that he wants an order for the shooting of the dogs that were scavenging the bodies littering the floor outside the gates, Father Christopher asks him sarcastically "if the dogs fired the first shot." *Sometimes in April* does not go into detail about the activities of the UN Peacekeepers; however, the film includes a scene in which Augustin tries to find his way to the Hôtel des Mille Collines when he hears the UN has sent in more troops for the possible evacuation of refugees, but he is surprised and disappointed they are evacuating only Europeans.

It still remains quite incomprehensible to the world how such killings of close to a million people was carried out in the modern era without the intervention of the international community, either by the Organization of African Unity (OAU), the immediate and nearest neighbor to the Rwandans of which the country were a member, or the United Nations, which not only served as an international watchdog in such cases, but had, prior to the genocide, sent peacekeepers to the country, despite reports from the commander on the ground. This directs us to the involvement of many Western powers before the genocide started. In the beginnings of the above films, we see how arms of various types made their way into the country. From Paul's accidental sighting of a container of machetes in *Hotel Rwanda*, to Augustin's witness of an influx of arms in the military base in *Sometimes in April* to information derived by Dallaire from a Hutu informant about hidden weapons all over town in *Shake Hands with the Devil*, the films point to the fact that these arms made their way into Rwanda from different Western powers – France (the chief supplier), China, and the UK-owned company, Mil-Tec Corporation. Why were these countries involved in providing the weapons that annihilated so many a people? There is a pressing need for more historical inquiry and cinematic representation into this question.

Films of the genocide also grapple with the neglect of the United States. *Hotel Rwanda* shows Rwandans listening to this classic exchange on the radio:

Does the State Department have a view as to whether or not what is happening could be genocide?

We have every reason to believe that acts of genocide have occurred.

How many acts of genocide does it take to make genocide?

Allen, that's just not a question that I am in a position to answer.

Is it true that you have specific guidance not to use the word genocide in isolation but to preface it with acts of?

I have guidance to which I … which I try to use as best as I can. There are formulations that we are using that we are trying to be consistent in our use of…[34]

Sometimes in April provides a longer version of the same segment, showing Christine Shelley, State Department spokeswoman, reading a long definition of genocide from the 1948 UN convention. Peck allows the audience to see the US stumble over its own feeble logic. In Beyond the Gates, the same segment is audible as Marie is running down body-strewn roads at night and then the scene shifts to a close up of Shelley's face as she gives her explanation. Just as she says "clearly not all of the killings that have taken place in Rwanda are killings to which you might apply that label,"[35] the scene shifts to hundreds of bodies, clothes awry, blood seeping from them, surrounded by whatever they were carrying, laying as they fell at the school. Dogs nose among the bodies. It is a damning indictment of US hypocrisy. Shake Hands With the Devil omits Shelley's explanation; instead Dallaire blatantly states the obvious: "The Americans are working like beavers to make sure as little as possible gets done in the long run. They have been fighting using the word genocide from day one … because under international law it requires them to act."[36] The enormity of the genocide provides plenty of blame to go around. As the filmmakers produce images, we get glimpses of the truth. Perhaps we do not want the whole truth anyway. As one Rwandan genocide survivor reflected, "It is impossible to show what really happened … nobody could watch what really happened. Their eyes would be closed."[37]

It was in fact the Rwandan Patriotic Front (RPF) in early July 1994 which brought an end to the genocide when the rebels took control of Kigali. The role played by the Rwandan Patriotic Front, the Tutsi led political party in exile, has been depicted uniquely by each of the movies. In *Hotel Rwanda*, we see how after witnessing and experiencing some travail, Paul, his family, and the hotel refugees are finally able to leave the besieged hotel in a UN convoy. They travel through retreating masses of refugees and militia to reach safety behind Tutsi rebel lines. We do not see the RPF's role being pictured in *Beyond the Gates*; perhaps the idea was not to focus on how the genocide ended, but that undermines the understanding of viewers who might wonder how Marie got out of the country and is re-united with Joe. *Sometimes in April* gives us a limited portrayal of the role of the RPF; we see that in Martine and Victorie's attempt to survive amidst corpses in a swamp, until they are finally rescued by the rebels. In *Shake Hands with the Devil*, we see General Dallaire in constant negotiation with both sides, but it is only in this movie that the RPF under the leadership of Paul Kagame is given a face. Although the climate in Rwanda is currently more about reconciliation and healing, future films about the genocide would benefit from a focus on efforts by the RPF to end the Hutu reign of terror.

To conclude, the Rwandan genocide as depicted in movies shows multiple truths; the films show the scale of the horror and the personal loss. They show trauma inflicted on victims and the inaction of onlookers. They ask – are justice and healing possible? We have argued that motion pictures are different from history, and that no matter how close a movie approximates reality, it is not reality and cannot be considered as such. The reality of the event cannot ever be replicated as it truly was. To find a possible way out of this, Gutting affirms that

> any truth the film presents needs to be grounded in the meticulous work of historians. But good historians do not merely accumulate data. They need sympathetic perception and imaginative interpretation to turn their data into a plausible historical story. The sympathy and imagination of creative artists can also operate on the materials historians supply. This is why a good historical film (or novel or play) can make its own contribution to our historical understanding. Actors, writers and directors who have immersed themselves in the history can provide their own distinctive insights into its meaning. But to benefit from these insights, we need to make our own connection with the historians' work. It's not nearly enough just to go see the movie.[38]

234

17

Stop a Genocide or Act in the National Interest?: A Comparative Examination of *Hotel Rwanda* and *Attack on Darfur*

Glen M.E. Duerr

Cedarville University

Hotel Rwanda[1] remains one of the more popular films to document the human tragedy of genocide. Featuring A-list Hollywood actors Don Cheadle, Nick Nolte, and Joaquin Phoenix, the film depicts the dramatic surge of radical ethnic Hutu extremism in the early part of 1994, which culminated in the 100-day genocide of the Tutsi population. Cheadle, who plays Paul Rusesabagina, the manager of Hôtel de Mille Collines in Kigali, is central to the film's characterization of how average Rwandans bore witness to the slaughter of an estimated 800,000 fellow citizens while the international community shirked its responsibility to stop the atrocities; indeed, an estimated 200,000 Hutus actually participated in the killings.[2]

Nolte's character, Colonel Oliver – who is loosely based on Canadian, Lt. Gen. Romeo Dallaire, leader of the United Nations Assistance Mission for Rwanda (UNAMIR),[3] abandons the imperiled Tutsis, and the United States government fails to intervene, citing the failed battle of Mogadishu in 1993, which resulted in the deaths of 18 US soldiers.[4] Rusesabagina, a moderate Hutu married to a Tutsi woman, Tatiana (Sophie Okonedo), is then confronted with the choice to do nothing, or to use his Western-style hotel as the only means to stop more killing in the midst of the genocide. He eventually accepts 1,268 refugees into the hotel and saves them from being killed.[5]

In a similar vein, *Attack on Darfur*[6] highlights the atrocities committed in the western part of Sudan during the mid-2000s. The movie depicts a visit by six Western journalists accompanying the small African Union forces unit to a small village in the midst of the brutal civil war. The civil war in Darfur, depending on the figures, has led to the deaths of up to almost half a million people either through execution, or genocide by starvation and disease.[7] In the film, the Westerners are confronted by the Janjaweed[8] militia – an armed group aligned with, and guided by, the Sudanese government. While some of the journalists leave when they have the opportunity, others stay to fight and are killed in the backdrop of the conflict. The film highlights the brutal nature of genocide, and in particular, exposes the use of rape as a weapon of war.

This essay starts with an overview of both movies, and then presents a wider, in-depth investigation of key political issues alluded to in the films, revolving around the debate between acting to stop a genocide versus acting in the national interest. These issues include: the reluctance of Western governments to intervene in Rwanda or Sudan, the role of prominent international organizations like the United Nations and the African Union, international media reporting genocides since the Holocaust, and the creation of new international norms to stop crimes against humanity which include the "Responsibility to Protect" and the establishment of the International Criminal Court.

Each movie serves as a warning of what can happen if foreign governments and intergovernmental organizations are not willing to intervene to make – or keep – the peace. Countries like the Central African Republic and South Sudan, as of April 2015, remain vulnerable to episodes of violence that could draw comparisons with Rwanda and Darfur. Furthermore, there are risks of genocide in other parts of the world. For example, the Rohingyas (a predominantly Muslim Bengali/Bangladeshi group) in Myanmar are in a very vulnerable position at the present, and evidence is mounting that majority of Rohingya villages have been vanquished. Genocide remains a threat in the world in the twenty-first century, but movies like *Hotel Rwanda* and *Attack on Darfur* raise the level of awareness about the horrors of ethnic cleansing around the world.

Overview of *Hotel Rwanda*

A full overview of the causes, events, and outcomes of the Rwandan genocide is outside the scope of this chapter, but some of major background
information is necessary to provide context for the movie.[9] Rwanda
is a small country in the Great Lakes region of sub-Saharan Africa. It
borders some much larger countries like the Democratic Republic of
Congo, Tanzania, and Uganda. Rwanda also borders a much smaller
neighbor, Burundi, with whom it has similar demographic features.
Notably, Rwanda's neighbors, with the exception of Tanzania, have been
embroiled in their own internal conflicts; tragically for Rwanda, a major
variable correlated with the onset of civil war in a country is a war-prone
and undemocratic neighboring country.[10] Within the country, there are
three (major) distinct ethnic groups: the Hutu (84 percent), the Tutsi
(15 percent), and the Twa (1 percent).[11] The vast majority of Rwandans
are Christian, broadly defined. However, the major schism in society has
occurred, historically, around the issue of ethnicity. During the Belgian
colonial period, the Tutsi were given favor, and an opportunity to govern the country; this changed upon independence in 1962 when the
majority Hutu took power. Periodically, the two ethnic groups clashed
over access to power, for example, in 1959, when thousands of Tutsis
were forced to flee the country.[12] The pretext for the genocide was the
Rwandan Civil War (1990–1994), during which the Hutu-led government battled against the Tutsi-led rebel group, the Rwandan Patriotic
Front (RPF). In the midst of this conflict, Hutu extremism grew to the
point where the Tutsis were dehumanized in media outlets, and ethnic Hutus faced a dilemma: participate in the killing, or be killed by
extremist Hutus.

Hotel Rwanda is a movie that was made in early 2004, premiered in late
2004, and then was shown to all audiences in early 2005, approximately 10
years after the Rwandan genocide. Shot in Kigali, Rwanda, and Johannesburg,
South Africa as a joint production of Lions Gate Films and United Artists,
Hotel Rwanda was nominated for numerous awards in a range of different categories, and it won several, including the American Film Institute
Award, as well as awards from both the Toronto and Berlin international
film festivals.

Hotel Rwanda essentially tracks the events leading up to the genocide in 1994, including the most horrendous events from April to June wherein Hutu killers murdered *approximately* 800,000 ethnic Tutsis and moderate Hutus. On numerous occasions throughout the movie, there are references to the wider context of the genocide and the reactions of the international community. There are numerous comments assuming that the Americans – or the international community – would intervene to stop the killing. As killing in the movie progresses, the likelihood of intervention decreases as it becomes apparent that no outside force will get involved. World leaders preferred to hide behind the safe wall of their "national interests," rather than attempt to stop the genocide.

The movie starts with Paul Rusesabagina managing his hotel. It is relatively peaceful, but, as the movie progresses, the scenes become progressively more violent. Hutu nationalism begins to rise and Hutu marches are depicted in the film. There is a quick and clear spiral towards anarchy as some of Rusesabagina's employees become more radical in their views, and begin to assert themselves against their employers in favor of being part the "Hutu power" campaign. One employee, Gregoire (Tony Kgoroge), in particular, starts to become more of assertive, and he begins to take advantage of the situation to provide himself with more luxuries. In a later scene, he in essence extorts Rusesabagina in order to occupy one of the best guestrooms in the hotel, in exchange for not telling the Hutu nationalist leadership what he is doing. This scene shows how some Hutus simply wanted to gain from the background situation, but did not have overt desires to join the killing.

In another early scene, two Western journalists ask a Rwandan, Benedict, about the differences between Hutus and Tutsis. He gives a robust answer, noting the Belgians picked certain characteristics so as to differentiate between the two groups – and to divide and conquer the population. Joaquin Phoenix, who plays one of the journalists named Jack Daglish, then turns to two young women beside him in the hotel, and asks them their ethnicity. One replies, "Tutsi," the other "Hutu." Phoenix responds, "they could be twins," revealing that there is no noticeable physical difference between the two peoples. For many outsiders, the distinction between Hutus and Tutsis is very difficult to observe; moreover, even for Rwandans at that time, ethnic distinctions were not always obvious except for what was listed on a person's identification card.

The use of political propaganda was a major political theme in the movie. When Rwandan (Hutu) president Juvénal Habyarimana was killed in a plane crash, both sides initially sought to blame the other. For the extremist Hutus, in particular, this act was then used as political propaganda to initiate the genocide. One of the most important components of the movie is delving into the issues of propaganda, and how certain groups are stigmatized. The phrase, "Cut the tall trees" serves as code by broadcasters in an extremist radio station to start the conflict – meaning that Tutsis (the taller ethnic group) are to be killed. On other occasions, the same broadcasters refer to Tutsis as "cockroaches." When considering genocide, one group engages in a campaign to dehumanize the other, thus legitimating violence against them (at least in their own self-perception). The language used in *Hotel Rwanda* clearly demonstrates how words shape minds and in this case create the psychological conditioning needed for genocide.

As a result of this radio propaganda campaign, very quickly the genocide becomes evident. The ethnic lines in the society become more overt as the movie progresses as well. One of Rusesabagina's workers – his van driver, Dube (Desmond Dube) – is identified as a Tutsi. Additionally, Rusesabagina's wife – as well as her family members – is also identified as a Tutsi meaning that Rusesabagina himself would probably be viewed as a traitor by extremist Hutus. The movie builds in intensity as incidents begin occurring in Rusesabagina's neighborhood. As the film continues, one of his Tutsi neighbors, Victor, is assaulted and taken away by the Hutu militia. Rusesabagina shrugs off the situation and reasons that Victor was a spy for the rebels and was captured by the armed forces for a reason.

Despite the initial horrors, the warring parties negotiate an update to earlier peace accords, giving many of the characters in the movie hope that a wider conflict will be averted. Soon after the peace agreement, however, Rusesabagina returns home to find dozens of Tutsis seeking protection after Hutus burned down their homes. His son, Roger, in the next scene is found in the neighbor's yard covered in blood with the unspoken implication that he witnessed a violent act. Extremist Hutu militiamen begin to set up roadblocks throughout Kigali to find Tutsis, and Hutus murder many of Rusesabagina's neighbors. Rusesabagina is thus given a choice – shoot Tutsis or be killed himself. Instead of having to go through with the decision, he bribes the militia general. Noting that the situation is quickly spiraling out of control, he manages to take his family – and some of his neighbors – to his hotel to try to save them.

As one might expect, many Tutsis, knowing that they might find refuge at the hotel, arrive to seek sanctuary. Supplies quickly dwindle. At this point, Rusesabagina then faces the challenge of trying to find new supplies for the people seeking shelter at the hotel. He and one of his workers venture out of the hotel compound to find supplies, only to find none. The horrors of the genocide become fully known at this point. As Rusesabagina drives down a road at night in a dense fog, his car starts hitting bumps. When he stops the car, opens the door, and the fog clears, he notices that all the bumps are actually people who have been killed in the genocide; the street is literally covered with dead bodies. In a later scene, a videotape is shown of civilians being bludgeoned to death. The characters come to realize that even this shocking footage might not be enough to get the outside world to act. Phoenix's character, Jack Daglish, says "(people will think) …. this is horrible, and then go on eating their dinners." At this point, there is another escalation in the violence. The Interhamwe – a group of notoriously violent Hutu extremists – surround the hotel compound and kill 10 members of the UN force, all of them from Belgium. Despite this, some UN presence remains as a few soldiers are left to guard the gate of the hotel. The situation seems increasingly precarious, but security is maintained at the hotel. In the midst of this, it becomes known that the Interhamwe have been murdering children. As an official with the Red Cross notes, "they are targeting the children to wipe out the next generation."

Slowly, as the violence increases, foreigners begin to leave. The Red Cross, meanwhile, remains – and brings 20 orphaned children to the hotel for safety. Nolte is livid that all of the foreigners have left and that the UN is unwilling to intervene more; all of the white foreigners, as well as the French, Italian, and UN Belgian soldiers then leave. In total, only 300 UN peacekeepers are left for the entire country, and their mandate is to not shoot at the Interhamwe. Nolte has a feeling of helplessness as chaos ensues, and he simply does not have the resources to stop the killing.

Many Westerners depicted in the movie leave Rwanda ashamed. They are unable to do anything to stop the violence. White people are separated from Black people in the movie, with the known expectation that the Black people will probably be killed in the ensuing days. Issues of race and colonialism are key components of the backdrop of the movie. The Hôtel des Mille Collines had Belgian ownership, and the Belgians were responsible for instituting the marking of Hutu and Tutsi ethnicity on identification cards beginning in the 1930s.[13] With the legal distinction between the groups cemented, tensions grew, and in the late 1950s, the so-called Hutu Manifesto called for the creation of a democratic and independent Rwanda, within which, the Tutsis were to leave because they were "foreign invaders."[14] Smaller scale skirmishes erupted, but only in 1990 did a full scale civil war start.

At the end of the movie, the Tutsi RPF begins to make gains, while refugees flee from Rwanda to neighboring countries, especially the more stable Tanzania. Eventually, a UN truck – with Rusesabagina's family rescued from the hotel – crosses the front line of the conflict. Although deposited in a refugee camp with an uncertain future, Rusesabagina and his immediate family survive and even reunite with two nieces. It is a happy ending to a very tragic story, and it stands in marked contrast to the film, *Attack on Darfur*.

Overview of *Attack on Darfur*

As with Rwanda, a full overview of the genocide in Darfur is outside the scope of this chapter.[15] However, some points are important in order to discuss the movie in context. Darfur is a region of Sudan in the western part of the country. The Darfur region borders Libya, Chad, and Central African Republic to its west and, since 2011, South Sudan to its south. Like Rwanda, some of Darfur's neighbors are war-prone and undemocratic, which increases the likelihood for the onset of civil war.[16] Formally, Sudan is divided into 18 states, five of which are within the Darfur region including: Gharb Darfur (West Darfur), Janub Darfur (South Darfur), Sharq Darfur (East Darfur), Shimal Darfur (North Darfur), Wasat Darfur (Central Darfur).[17] The major point of distinction between Darfur and the rest of Sudan is ethnicity. Unlike the divisions between Sudan and South Sudan, which largely hinged upon religious identification and ethnicity, the conflict over Darfur is largely ethnic in nature (although many other variables such as income disparity, autonomy, and culture among others are also integral to understanding the nature of the conflict). In essence, both Darfurians and Khartoum-Sudanese are Muslim, but the Darfurians are Black Africans, whereas the Khartoum-Sudanese are majority Arab. After the British colonial period ended in 1956 (the British and Egyptians co-governed Sudan from 1899 to 1956), Sudan was embroiled in conflict with its aforementioned southern region from 1956–1972, and then again from 1983–2005. A new front in Darfur opened in 2003 when similar secessionist claims were made by the Darfurians, specifically the Sudan Liberation Movement/Army (SLM/A) and Justice and Equality Movement (JEM) rebel groups.

Attack on Darfur was not as popular as *Hotel Rwanda*, but its depiction of the horrific violence in warfare is certainly comparable. The movie was released in 2009, chronicling a genocide that began 6 years earlier and continues to the present day. Although the conflict has also merged at times with other conflicts in the region, the central component of the war has been the struggle to stop the secession of the western Darfur region of Sudan. Although this conflict, like many other conflicts, has significant complexities, the baseline conclusion is that genocide is being committed against the Black African population of Darfur by the predominantly Arab government and its supporters. The Sudanese government has employed a militia, known as the Janjaweed, to carry out atrocities on its behalf and to halt what it perceives as secessionism in the region. A major issue which *Attack on Darfur* addresses is the pervasive rape perpetrated by members of the Janjaweed, one of the most horrific – and often underreported – aspects of the genocide in Darfur.

The central characters of the movie, four Western journalists – played by Billy Zane, Edward Furlong, Kristanna Loken, and David O'Hara – become central to the major event in the story, an attack on a Darfurian village carried out by the Janjaweed militia. Although in the movie the African Union (AU) has a presence in the region, it has limited formal power to stop the Janjaweed. A central character in the movie is Nigerian AU Captain Jack Tobamke, who tries to do everything he can to counsel, shame, cajole, and hinder the Janjaweed militia from committing atrocities in the village, all to no avail. In knowing of mass slaughter in the village, the

Western journalists are faced with a dilemma: stay and attempt to chronicle the violence against the villagers, or flee and allow the killers to work in the dark.[18] In the end, two of the journalists opt to leave, while the others remain behind hoping to expose the killers to outside condemnation. Much of the latter part of the movie centers on the two journalists who join the fight to try to stop the killing in the village.

At the end of the movie, the rest of the journalists return to the village only to find everyone dead, including their colleagues. The ending is particularly devastating because it depicts one village that was razed completely to the ground and all of its inhabitants murdered for the mere fact of their ethnic background. Moreover, and perhaps more chillingly, despite knowledge of the atrocities, from documentaries to films such as *Attack on Darfur*, there has been an utterly inadequate response from the international community. In 2014 alone, over 3,000 villages in Darfur came under attack by Sudanese and militia forces, resulting in the deaths or displacement of tens of thousands of Darfurians.[19]

Changes to International Law

Movies such as *Hotel Rwanda* and *Attack on Darfur* have done a service to the world not only by raising awareness of the two genocides, but also by reinforcing the international community's legal response to human rights abuses. The two significant changes to international law which the Rwandan genocide brought were the creation of the concept of the "Responsibility to Protect" and the International Criminal Court (ICC), which the United States and six other countries (including China, Iraq, Israel, Libya, Qatar, and Yemen) actually voted against. The concept of "Responsibility to Protect" was initiated under the UN system in 2005 as a means of stopping genocide and undercutting a long established international norm – state sovereignty – as an argument. By nullifying the idea that a government can do whatever it wants on its own territory, the international community may be better positioned to stop future genocides from occurring. In the words of the UN position statement:

> Sovereignty no longer exclusively protects States from foreign interference; it is a charge of responsibility that holds States accountable for the welfare of their people…[20]

> Prevention requires apportioning responsibility to and promoting collaboration between concerned States and the international community. The duty to prevent and halt genocide and mass atrocities lies first and foremost with the State, but the international community has a role that cannot be blocked by the invocation of sovereignty. Sovereignty no longer exclusively protects States from foreign interference; it is a charge of responsibility where States are accountable for the welfare of their people. This principle is enshrined in article 1 of the Genocide Convention and embodied in the principle of "sovereignty as responsibility" and in the concept of the Responsibility to Protect.[21]

When the "Responsibility to Protect" fails, as it has in the case of Darfur, the International Criminal Court becomes the next level of enforcement. In the aftermath of the Holocaust, there was no formal procedure to try people who committed ethnic cleansing or crimes against humanity. Both the Nuremburg and Tokyo trials in the late 1940s attempted to bring the perpetrators to justice, but one of the major criticisms was that the laws and rules had been created after the fact. With the creation of the United Nations system, the International Court of Justice (ICJ) was also created, which gave the UN the ability to mediate disputes between countries in order to avoid war. The problem here, however, was that the ICJ was not given a mandate over people – only to resolve disputes between states. In 1994, the UN created the International Criminal Tribunal for Rwanda (ICTR), which has held over 60 trials and convicted over two dozen individuals (a number some might find to be shockingly low).

Years later, with the signing of the Rome Statute, the International Criminal Court[22] assigned the court a similar mandate of bringing *individuals* to justice for war crimes and crimes against humanity. When the Rome Statute came into force in 2002, it then allowed the world community to prosecute those charged with committing acts of genocide in any area under any circumstances. While the ICTR is set to close at the end of 2015, the ICC remains actively involved in pursuing cases against individuals who have committed atrocities in Darfur, indicting seven individuals including Sudanese president Omar al-Bashir. Problems remain, however; only two of the seven suspects are actually standing trial. The others, including President al-Bashir, are fugitives. Even officials from countries that have signed on to the ICC, like Kenya, Chad, and Djibouti, have refused to take al-Bashir into custody when he has visited on official state business. If the ICC continues to be undermined in this way, and if major powers (especially the United States) remain uncommitted or weak in their responses, the tragedy in Darfur will worsen, and the deterrence principle of the entire system will collapse.

Conclusions

Both *Hotel Rwanda* and *Attack on Darfur* examine the concept of genocide in detailed and nuanced ways. *Hotel Rwanda* depicts both individual heroism and collective inaction in the wake of genocide, ultimately ending with optimism (even though in reality Rusesabagina lost so many people from his immediate family, including four of his siblings, his brother-in-law and his family, his wife's mother, and her sister and six children). *Attack on Darfur*, by contrast, focuses on violence against women and rape as genocidal actions and is the darker of the two films, perhaps appropriately so, as the Darfurian genocide continues to this day without any hope for an end. The central question posed by the title of this chapter: stop a genocide, or act in the national interest, provokes a binary choice for the viewer. Either the international community acts to stop the violence or it does not. The response of the world leaders has been quite different across these two cases, but in one, the violence has stopped. In Rwanda, there is almost universal international recognition of the reality of the genocide, and there have been prosecutions of war criminals. In Darfur, however, there has been a much more limited response from the international community, much more like the response of the world while the Rwandan genocide was unfolding. Most governments acknowledge that atrocities have been committed against the people of Darfur, but the international community has still failed to act in a manner that reinforces the system the it has put in place to prevent and prosecute these atrocities. The end result in both countries from world inaction has been the same – the continuation of genocide. And while films like *Hotel Rwanda* and *Attack on Darfur* have contributed to the popular awareness of the two genocides, it remains to be seen if the legal process will either tarnish or burnish their legacy.

18

Adults in Children's Bodies: *Disabling* Children in Bahman Ghobadi's Films

Eda Dedebas Dundar

Bogazici University, Turkey

First off, Number one … My name is Birahima and I'm a little nigger. Not 'cos I'm black and I'm a kid. I'm a little nigger
because I can't talk French for shit …. Number two … I didn't
get very far at school; I gave up in my third year in primary
school …. Number three … I'm disrespectful … and I swear
like a bastard …. Number four … *I suppose I should apologize
for talking right at you like this, on account of how I'm only a kid.
I'm maybe ten, maybe twelve … and I talk too much ….* Number
five … To make sure I tell you the life story of my fucked-up life
in proper French, I've got four different dictionaries …. *Number
six … Don't go thinking that I'm some cute kid, cos I'm not.*[1]

(author's emphasis)

In his introduction to his life story as a child soldier, Birahima in Ahmadou
Kourouma's novel *Allah is not Obliged* relinquishes his stance as an
endearing kid and instead disorients the Western reader with the image
of an unruly child.[2] His deliberate attempt to defamiliarize and infanti-
lize his readers is notorious as his voice appears as a full-fledged adult
in a child's body. Similarly, Iranian director of Kurdish descent Bahman
Ghobadi takes on a parallel approach in his treatment of Kurdish children
in his movies and names them "adults in children's bodies."[3] Endeavoring

246

to depict the plight of Kurdish children in Iran, Ghobadi challenges the strict division between adults and children; usually the former become dependent on the latter's guidance and destabilizes traditional roles of an adult and a child. Moreover, his persistent attention to the suffering of Kurds under Saddam Hussein's regime further situates him in a unique place as being one of the very few Middle Eastern directors to publicize the Kurdish genocide of 1988.[4]

Kristi Wilson and Tomas Crowder-Taraborrelli's book *Film and Genocide* and Leshu Torchin's *Creating the Witness: Documenting Genocide on Film, Video, and the Internet* have been the two influential books in their discussions of representing genocide in film.[5] Both books are groundbreaking not only in establishing public awareness on the atrocities but also in questioning the politics of witnessing and representation. Despite their extensive scope of the genocides worldwide, they fail to give adequate attention to the Kurdish genocide perpetrated by Hussein's Ba'ath Party in 1988 as part of the so-called Al-Anfal Campaign. Torchin underscores the lack of sources that address the Al-Anfal Campaign, and the Kurdish genocide is, unfortunately, not mentioned in Wilson and Crowder-Taraborrelli's study.[6]

In an attempt to build on the existing criticism and fill the gap on the portrayal of Kurdish genocide in film, this chapter argues that Ghobadi's movies, particularly *Turtles Can Fly* (2004), not only create public awareness of the massacres but also challenge the Western perspective on the US invasion of Iraq as being reconciliatory for the Kurds. Moreover, they provide an alternative narrative, which not only presents victims whose plight seem to be permanent even after the coming of the US soldiers, but also criticizes the rendering of an optimistic humanitarian discourse that emphasizes an "enabling fiction" – to quote Joseph Slaughter.[7] Ghobadi's movies have a two-fold purpose: first, they bear witness to the suffering of the Kurds and also depict disadvantaged children – refugees, orphans, children with disabilities, abused children – who, despite their dire circumstances, take on adult roles, negating the Western perception of a vulnerable and victimized child. In this chapter, first I am going to provide a review of the Al-Anfal Campaign and the movies that delineate it. The second section foregrounds Ghobadi's treatment of children and his attempt to give voice to the Kurds who have been victimized and abused under Saddam Hussein's regime.

Finally, I am going to do a close reading of *Turtles Can Fly* and argue that the movie stands out as a "disabling" and disturbing narrative in the affirmative sense and contests the validity of Western humanitarian efforts.

Grievability and the Al-Anfal Campaign

In *Frames of War: When is Life Grievable?*, Judith Butler raises provocative questions about how grief and grievability are categorized and how losses are deemed to be recognizable.[8] Wars, she argues, have come to establish certain frames, making a clear-cut distinction between grievable and ungrievable lives. Moreover, she argues that we are "constituted politically in part by virtue of the social vulnerability of our bodies" and that the socially constructed nature of our bodies determines whose life is deemed to be grievable.[9] In a similar vein, Saddam Hussein's Al-Anfal Campaign and his military operation based on chemical weapons and the notorious Halabja massacre of the Kurds have not found their due place in literary and cultural history. Despite the abundant movies about other massacres of the world, Kurdish lives and deaths have not been acknowledged as being precarious and grievable by film directors.

The Ba'ath Party's Al-Anfal Campaign, a brutal counterinsurgency campaign against the Kurds in Northern Iraq and other non-Arab minorities was waged mainly in the final stages of the Iran–Iraq War, between February 1988 and September 1988. Human Rights Watch estimates a total of 100,000 people massacred and about 4,000 destroyed Kurdish villages.[10] The word "Al-Anfal" derives its name from the eighth *sura* (or chapter) of the Koran in which the prophet Muhammed wages a war against non-believers, thus endowing the massacre with religious justification. Under the leadership of Saddam Hussein's cousin Ali Hassan al-Majid, notoriously known as "Chemical Ali," the genocide included mass killings, use of chemical weapons such as mustard gas and sarin and had a gendered dimension as well since it included gang raping of Kurdish women and massacres of battle-aged men. Out of the eight stages of the genocide, the Halabja massacre of March 16, 1988, is the deadliest one annihilating around 5,000 noncombatant civilians in a town near the Iranian border.

The Al-Anfal Campaign has been of little interest to Western and Middle Eastern directors. Among the few existing examples are Samira

Makhmalbaf's *Blackboards* (2000) and Hiner Saleem's *Kilometre Zero* (2005).[11] Makhmalbaf's *Blackboards* narrates the story of two Kurdish teachers who have recently survived the genocide and live on the edges of starvation. They wander through the mountains with their black-boards attached to their bodies, searching for students. Though subtle, Makhmalbaf alludes to the genocide at the beginning of the movie as the teachers are shot running away from the bombings. Saleem's *Kilometre Zero*, on the other hand, thoroughly depicts the atrocities committed during the genocide with its scenes of violence committed against the Kurds in Iraq, who are forced to enlist in the military during the war. The dichotomy between the Arabs and the Kurds is made discernible in par-ticular scenes. For instance, when the Arab soldier accompanies Ako, the Kurdish protagonist, on his mission, the enmity between the two soldiers is palpable. Despite its gruesome scenes and barren backdrops, Saleem presents a happy ending in the flash-forwarded final scene when Ako and his wife Selma rejoice upon learning of the overthrow of Hussein, and they anticipate being rescued by US forces. Ghobadi's movies, on the other hand, are far more pessimistic. His skepticism about the US inva-sion and his shooting of the damages committed by the US contradict Saleem's optimism.

Taha Karimi's recent documentary *1001 Apples* (2013) tells the story of Faraj, one of the 10 survivors of the 350 mass graves.[12] Having taken refuge in the US, Faraj together with four other survivors initiate an "Iraqi Mass Graves Survivors" group. The documentary opens with a blank computer page as an anonymous person writes, "This email is for you. Maybe it is the last chance," exhorting viewers to bear witness to atrocities.[13] Returning to Iraqi Kurdistan, Faraj and his friends bring 1001 apples with them, each one of which symbolizes a victim of the genocide. The movie is about remembering and forgiving. Realizing that people are unaware of what happened to the Kurds, Faraj and his friends begin a journey of remem-bering and commemorating the victims. However, Karimi's *1001 Apples* pinpoints forgiveness as a form of healing as well. In the climactic scene in which the relatives of the victims release their apples to the river ending in Baghdad, the survivors and the mourners bridge a gap between their vil-lage and Baghdad where "the Ba'ath Party thought about the crime of 'Anfal Campaign'...; Saddam Hussein decided to commit the crime of Anfal...;

[and from where] Ali Hassan al-Majid came."[14] Through this effective and visually striking scene, Karimi portrays a reconciliatory perspective of the genocide and its aftermath.

In his article "Enabling Fictions and Novel Subjects: The *Bildungsroman* and International Human Rights Law," Joseph Slaughter defines human rights and the *Bildungsroman* as "mutually enabling fictions" in which "each projects an image of the human personality that ratifies the other's vision of the ideal relations between individual and society."[15] Laying out the similarities between human rights and *Bildungsroman* in that they both envision an artificial sense of citizen in the nation-state, Slaughter is critical of the Third World *Bildungsromans* as well since they "make legible the inequalities of this egalitarian imaginary. [...] Consequentially, some of the not-yet-hegemonic norms of universal human rights begin to become internationally legible in the appropriations and transformations of the *Bildungsroman*'s normative generic conventions."[16] Likewise, Bahman Ghobadi, a film director famous for casting non-professional actors and children in his movies, refutes the idea of a narrative of development that mimics the hegemonic discourse and valorizes an appropriate story of maturation and fulfillment. Instead, his movies render a reversal of development, or an *Unbildung*, in which *adults in children's bodies*, as Ghobadi identifies them, learn to become children again.

Portrayal of Kurdish Children and Vulnerability in Ghobadi's films

In an interview with Boris Trbic, Ghobadi explains how he grew up in harsh financial circumstances and quit school for a few years at 15 to support his family.[17] Moreover, in the rest of the interview, he narrates a funny story of his first endeavor to shoot a film, in which he created an imaginary setting with a bench and cigarette butts with the help of his mother. His first film "won an award for best animation at a film festival in Tehran."[18] Moreover, he ventures into the film industry with his short films, as an actor in Samira Makhmalbaf's *Blackboards* (2000), and as an assistant director to Abbas Kiarostami's *The Wind Will Carry Us* (1999).[19]

The popularity of rendering children in Iranian cinema can be observed in Samira Makhmalbaf's *The Apple*, Majid Majidi's *Children of Heaven*,

Abbas Kiarostami's *The Wind Will Carry Us* (1995), Jafar Panahi's *The White Balloon* – to name a few examples.[20] Ghobadi's movies have displayed Kurdish children in calamitous circumstances, and he has manifested his interest in filming children several times. In the same interview with Trbic, Ghobadi reveals his infatuation with children and his choice of using them as such: "I'm in love with children. I consider myself a child and believe I'm spending part of my childhood now. All Kurdish children are from birth thrown into the adult lives of 20 and 30-year-olds. They are deprived of their childhood."[21] Working with non-professional children and spending time with his "actors" has been an integral part of his directing.[22]

Ghobadi's first full-length movie *A Time for Drunken Horses* (2000) delineates the survival story of five orphaned siblings who live on the border of Iraq, which "takes on a double meaning in the story connoting both livelihood and death. While border trade is the basic means of employment, hence survival, for Kurdish villages, it also means putting one's life in danger every day because of military zones, territorial conflicts, and landmines."[23] Despite the fact that the storyline does not mention the Al-Anfal Campaign and the Kurdish genocide, it delineates the suffering of the Kurds in a vivid way, particularly in the scenes where the siblings learn of the death of their father and where Ayoub, a 12-year-old boy and the new breadwinner of the family, crosses the border with his crippled elder brother Madi.[24] After the father's death, Ayoub and Rojine, the eldest healthy son and daughter, take the roles of surrogate parents to their three siblings, namely Madi, the eldest son who was born with a disability and needs to be operated soon; Amaneh, the narrator; and Kolsoum, the youngest one, whose birth caused their mother's death. Ghobadi takes a similar approach in depicting the children as "adults in children's bodies." In their self-sacrificing endeavors, both Ayoub and Rojine take on larger-than-life responsibilities. In an attempt to find the money for Madi's operation, Ayoub finally convinces his uncle to take his father's place, not only in his role as a breadwinner but also in his occupation as a smuggler. However, when he is unable to collect the money, Rojine intervenes and accepts a pre-arranged marriage with an older man, who agrees to pay the money as a dowry. However, when this attempt also fails, Ayoub takes their mule to Iraq to sell it. The reversal of adult and child roles reaches a peak when Ayoub, at the end of the movie, persuades the smugglers to take his mule with him by fervently stating "I am not a child."[25] A similar sense of disruption of maturity and chronological time exists when the viewer finds out that Madi's biological age is 15, which clashes with his small and disfigured body combined with his inability to utter meaningful words. Although he is three years older than Ayoub, Ayoub is the one who takes the responsibility of his elder, similar to the way Satellite acts towards the elders of the village in *Turtles Can Fly*. That Madi is older than Ayoub establishes a paradigmatic shift in the world of normality and the Western perception of hierarchy. Moreover, by casting a small disfigured child and a non-professional actor as the eldest male member of a family Ghobadi plays with the conventions of maturity.

Ghobadi's second film *Marooned in Iraq* (2002) centralizes the Al-Anfal Campaign and the chemical weapons used during the genocide through the story of Mirza, a renowned Kurdish musician whose wife Hanareh eloped to Iraq 23 years ago. Upon receiving her call for help, Mirza sets out on a journey across the Iraq–Iran border with his two sons. Narrated in Kurdish, the film portrays the tragic story of the Kurdish people, whose suffering is partly alleviated through music and storytelling. In Ghobadi's tragicomedy, these three adult Kurdish men, the heads of their families, need to leave their village so as to witness what their fellow people are enduring. Different from *A Time for Drunken Horses* and *Turtles Can Fly*, children play a less significant role in *Marooned in Iraq*. Two remarkable scenes, however, highlight the vulnerability of children surviving in war zones. On their way to Iraq, Mirza and his sons, Audeh and Barat, meet a teacher who is instructing a group of kids amidst bombings. In this symbolic scene, the teacher describes a plane as "something that flies. Like a bird. Humans have invented something that flies like a bird in the sky. A plane has two purposes. First, it transports goods between cities. But there is also a negative side. And what is it? It's the bombing;" the teacher draws attention to the sound of bombings and continues "at this moment, somebody's house is being destroyed."[26] Advising his students to work hard and fly on planes in the future, he instructs them to fly the paper planes that they had prepared at home, which are set as backdrops against the constant roaring of the jet planes overheard throughout the movie. Moreover, the paper planes flown over the hill present a tongue-in-cheek reply and contrast to the military aircraft simultaneously appearing in the sky.

Ghobadi's depiction of the genocide occurs in a mind-blowing scene when Mirza and sons come across a mass grave towards the end of their journey. Amidst wailing women shoveling the snow to find the corpses of the male members of their families, they are delineated as helpless and vulnerable men as opposed to the mourning women who are taking a more active role in identifying and burying their male relatives. Furthermore, upon meeting the two strong women who reprimand Audeh for searching for an eighth wife in order to have a son, he is convinced to adopt two sons who have been orphaned after the massacres. It is through Audeh's encounter with these two women that he discovers the vast number of orphaned children after the genocide. These three boastful and proud Kurdish men of the earlier scenes suddenly become incapable of having to digest such great horror and the paradigmatic gender roles in a patriarchal society are turned upside down. Ghobadi intentionally renders this reversal of gender roles and power relations so as to create an emphatic effect on the viewer. Just like Mirza and his sons, viewers are forced to bear witness to atrocities and re-think the conventional definitions of children and women. A similar role-reversal exists in the final scene when Mirza arrives at the Iraqi village to find Hanareh and is shocked at the mourning Kurdish women. Unbeknownst to him, he finally finds – but does not recognize – Hanareh, whose face is disfigured due to the chemical weapons, and agrees to adopt her daughter. By picturing Hanareh as having lost her voice, Ghobadi, once again, plays with the idea of subjectivity in an ironic way. A disabled and voiceless woman appears to possess more power and endurance than her ex-husband, who is a well-known and respected musician of the region.

Similar to *Marooned in Iraq*, *Half Moon* (2006) concentrates on a famous Kurdish musician, Mamo, and his journey to Iraq for "a cry of freedom" concert to celebrate the fall of Saddam and thus the end of the prohibition of Kurdish music and folk dances.[27] Serving as a double to Mirza, Mamo undertakes this voyage across the border with his sons and is appalled by the atrocities done by the Ba'ath regime and US soldiers. The title *Half Moon* symbolically refers to the half-lived joy of the Kurdish people, who are rescued from Saddam's dictatorial regime and failed to have their expectations fulfilled afterwards. With the coming of US troops, their predicaments have not been altered in a substantial way. Following *Turtles Can Fly*, *Half Moon* critiques US humanitarian intervention as well. *Turtles Can Fly* remains the epitome of Ghobadi's movies in which he not only manifests his reservations about the humanitarian intervention but also publicizes the Al-Anfal Campaign through his rendering of children in destabilizing roles.

Disabling and Disturbing Children in *Turtles Can Fly*

In "Savages, Victims, Saviors: The Metaphor of Human Rights," Makau Mutua argues that current Eurocentric discourse of human rights is based upon the triangle of a barbaric savage, a vulnerable victim, and a White Christian savior. Stating that the construction of the three-dimensional prism "falls within the historical continuum of the Eurocentric colonial project, in which actors are cast into superior and subordinate positions," Mutua calls for a change in the human rights discourse, which perpetuates the savage-victim-savior triangle.[28] In a similar vein, Ghobadi challenges this paradigm as a response to the Western-based human rights discourse that is oriented towards vulnerability and sees humanitarianism as a civilizing mission. For instance, in *Half Moon*, Mutua's triangle is invalidated as the travelers witness the destruction in the aftermath of the US invasion of Iraq. Among Ghobadi's films centering on the Kurdish population in the region, *Turtles Can Fly* critiques the Eurocentric colonial project with its plot based on the anticipation for the coming of US soldiers.

Turtles Can Fly opens with a sharp contrast between the barren land and the striking burgundy dress that Agrin – the female protagonist, who was raped during the genocide – is wearing when walking towards the edge of a cliff before committing suicide. As the movie progresses, death hovers above the Kurdish refugees and the orphaned children in the camp on the border between Iran and Turkey. The movie centralizes the lives of orphaned Kurdish children, who make a living by defusing landmines and selling them to the UN under the leadership of a self-sustained child, Satellite, played by Soran Ebrahim. The power dynamics and the hierarchical relations are disrupted upon the arrival of the two siblings, Agrin and Hengov, with a blind toddler named Riga, whom the kids presume to be their young brother. Hengov's competency in defusing the landmines with his mouth and his premonitions diminish Satellite's influence on the villagers. Moreover, falling in love with Agrin, Satellite further loses his control over the refugee children and becomes vulnerable.

Ghobadi, once again, uses capable and mighty children and overturns the limits of normalcy by incorporating a whole cast of non-professional children, most of whom have a physical disability due to war, and by making adults dependent on them.[29] Among the Kurdish children of the camp, Satellite, the leader, takes on many adult roles. From organizing the kids to work in the fields, to negotiating their salaries, from setting up a satellite for the elders so that they could learn about the US attacks, to selling the mines to the UN, Satellite becomes a surrogate father to the Kurdish orphans in the camp.[30] However, he meanders between adulthood and childhood, solemnity and merriment when he realizes his English is not good enough to translate the official news from CNN and George Bush's speech aired on TV. In his indisputable belief in and optimism about the US arrival, he relies on the hope of a free Kurdistan and dreams of his possible union with Agrin.

Hengov, on the other hand, is located as an antagonist to Satellite and what he stands for: outspokenness, optimism, and fabrication. Having arrived at the camp from Halabja, he is capable of a number of tasks: demining the fields despite his lack of arms, leading the kids and directing them to the fields despite his continuous silence, and taking better care of Riga despite his disability. He is contrasted with Satellite's enthusiasm and buoyancy and stands out as a threat to his dominance. His visions present a marked contrast to the official news of the war and ironically turn out to be truer than CNN. When Satellite begs to learn the upcoming news from him as a last attempt to save his reputation among the villagers, he refuses to do so since "he made predictions twice, it brought [them] bad luck twice," foreshadowing some unrevealed gruesome details about their past.[31] The brutal truth is revealed in the middle of the movie when Riga turns out to be Agrin's son, who was conceived as a result of a gang rape when Arab soldiers ransacked their village.

In *Turtles Can Fly*, Agrin has an outstanding place among the other children of the camp. In her liminal and ironic position as a mother who takes care of Hengov and Riga and as a child who continuously refuses to act as a mother, Agrin resists settling into strict binary oppositions.[32] In her constant disagreement with Hengov, Agrin is determined to leave Riga in the village so that he will be "an abandoned child, not a permanent trauma."[33] The disagreement becomes ironic when Hengov, as the head of the family, utters the final word "We'll all go together" by refusing to leave Riga behind in the scene where Agrin literally feeds Hengov like a baby due to his disability.[34] Hence, his role as the head of the family diminishes when it is revealed that he is incapable of taking care of Agrin and Riga.

In *Turtles Can Fly*, Bahman Ghobadi resists Western conceptions of humanitarianism, progress, and optimism by creating a powerful scene of US helicopters flying over the refugee camp. In an attempt to dismantle Mutua's triangle and to challenge the Western humanitarianism discourse as suggested by Mutua, he pictures the refugees in a euphoric mood as the helicopters approach. Ironically, the leaflets distributed from the helicopters read: "It's the end of injustice, misfortune and hardship. We are your best friends and brothers. Those against us are our enemies. We will make this country a paradise. We are here to take away your sorrows. We are the best in the world."[35] However, Ghobadi hints at the impossibility of ending injustice and hardship given the dilemma of Kurdish children. This influential scene is symbolic in that the events unfolding after their arrival – Satellite's losing his leg upon stepping on a landmine, his visions, and finally Agrin's murder of Riga and her suicide – herald further catastrophes to be revealed.

By delineating adult-children, who not only direct the adults but also survive under the dire circumstances, Ghobadi pushes the boundaries of normalcy and defies the Western concept of a child as being vulnerable.[36] In *Iranian Cinema and Philosophy*, Farhang Erfani underlines some unusual instances for the Western viewer, such as kids playing with gas masks and having a toothache numbed by kerosene are Ghobadi's deliberate attempts to alienate his audience: "Even an issue we could identify with, such as a toothache, is healed in the most unusual way. These orphaned refuges live in a norm that has no semblance of normalcy for most viewers."[37]

At the end of the movie, Satellite's optimism is replaced by his deep silence and ability to have visions similar to Hengov's. He almost experiences an Oedipal transformation when he loses his voice, love, power, and leg and sees things clearly. In that, he is similar to the blind toddler Riga, who, despite his loss of vision, is capable of grasping the gravity of war and their predicament and his position as "a bastard," a word repeatedly used by Agrin. Despite its optimistic title and use of metaphor likening Kurds to turtles – wanderers who carry their homes literally and metaphorically on their backs, the movie culminates with a final shot of Satellite who is numbly staring at US tanks when his right-hand man Pashow, still maintaining his enthusiasm, asks "Didn't you want to meet the Americans?"[38]

Conclusion

Highlighting his reservations about Western narratives of development, Joseph Slaughter states: "This projection is the formal gambit of both contemporary human rights and a still largely NATO-centric 'world literature' that eagerly consumes and canonizes […] narratives of the historically marginalized […], narratives that intensify the dominant enabling fictions that human rights and *Bildungsroman* are intrinsically universal and fundamentally egalitarian."[39] Ghobadi's *Turtles Can Fly* problematizes the prevalence of enabling fictions that foreground a fake sense of fulfilling narrative by casting mature and self-supporting children, who are physically disabled. The children in *Turtles Can Fly* are not disabled in the traditional sense, but rather they are *disabling* – to adopt and re-appropriate the term from Slaughter – and *disturbing* to the Western viewer as they not only have power over the elders but also overcome their victimized and vulnerable status nullifying the need for a Western savior. The predominance of *adults in children's bodies* disavows the existence of a coming-of-age story and annuls the romanticized vision of a victimized non-Western child rehabilitated by the US.[40] With his portrayal of adults in children's bodies surviving after the Al-Anfal Campaign, Bahman Ghobadi makes an ethical call to his viewers to bear witness to the Kurdish Genocide and invites them to reverse their expectations of an image of a victimized child.

Epilogue

Jonathan C. Friedman

West Chester University

In his speech at the opening of the new Holocaust museum in Yad Vashem in 2005, Elie Wiesel spoke of the need for the post-Holocaust generation to be the messengers for the survivors.[1] At the same time, Wiesel has spoken, and continues to speak, of the fundamentally unknowable nature of the Holocaust. Criminologists Michelle Brown and Nicole Rafter offer a similar sentiment in their recent article on genocide in film. In their words, "One cannot understand or remember the genocides of the past in any direct manner. Their inaccessibility impedes us from working toward complex understandings of these events and appropriate ways of responding to them."[2] Is it possible to reconcile this contradiction?

Both notions are correct. Scholars across disciplines study genocide, educators teach the subject in classrooms, and artists represent it in different visual and performing media. There is an assumption that the Holocaust and genocides *are* knowable events whose content must be conveyed from messenger to messenger. Yet no one except those who experienced it, suffered it, and died as a result of it can literally know their truths. We, the second tier messengers, own abstractions and borrowed memory, and when we try to convey the message through a medium such as fiction, we add another layer of constructed truth – or untruth. Some purists would rather have vetted elites construct this memory, which they could then bless as authentic and tightly control, but the task should be to transmit historical memory as widely as possible, and the academy cannot do this on its own. That is the power of popular media, not just because, in the words of human rights scholar Sonia Tascon, "visual images are imbued with a particular type of power due to their visual textuality,"[3] but because of the very fact that they *can be* popular and not elitist. The pop culture industry can generate huge audiences and bring massive organizational prowess to bear, reaching potentially billions of people. Although popularization often brings simplification and fabrication, it is clearly the consensus of the authors of this monograph that it is better to have the cultural access point to begin the conversation than to not have it at all.

That is not to say that quality of format and content do not matter or that educators should not be a part of the process of creating or studying or advocating on behalf of a film about genocide. On the contrary, they should be centrally involved. They should direct students towards effective films, much like they would do for any primary or secondary source; and in this book, the authors have laid out first and foremost historicity and attention to trauma as key criteria for effective representation. Educators should also assist film industries across the globe, Western and non-Western, to seek out effective narratives and formats though which to explore these narratives. My point is that the endeavor is a shared one – with necessary participation from above and below.

When I was teaching one of my courses on race, gender, and class in feature film, a student posed the question: who is the audience for a genocide film? Francesco Casetti's *Inside the Gaze* is a good place to begin to help answer this question. In Casetti's theoretical framework, films not only have an inherent expectation of the existence of a spectator, there is a constant interface and exchange which allows for the spectator a to both reinvent and reinterpret the meanings of a film's narrative and to transform their own perspectives, which means that a film can alter a state of consciousness. In Cassetti's words, "film constructs a spectator, assigns the spectator place, sets him upon a certain course … the spectator designated by the film is thus all this at once: someone presented as a possible counter-proposition, someone who reconstructs the original version of the story, and someone who guarantees something said."[4] Films enunciate a vision and require that spectators "accomplish a true journey,"[5] and the audience engages this vision, mediates the space, and filters the myriad symbols and signifiers to reach a destination. In the case of films about genocide, filmmakers have instructional and moral aims. They seek to impart both morality and history. The latter is something that has happened in reality (an "event" so to speak), as well as a construction of language (a collection of imaginary signifiers). History is also a contradiction in a number of ways. History can be boring and violent, often at the same time. Most people, one presumes or at least hopes, do not have a personal experience with murder in their lives, but undoubtedly, they have experienced the loss of family members to illness and old age. Natural death is ubiquitous; wrongful death is outside the realm of "reality" for most people. A filmmaker making films about genocide wants to insert this latter reality into the consciousness of the spectators. Genocide films may have a built-in audience of committed activists, but the filmmaker's desire is to articulate an idea with global reach and impact. The audience for a film about genocide, therefore, is the audience which the filmmaker seeks out and has the ability to construct, ideally a global spectator.

A few films about genocide have been able to accomplish this global reach. An even fewer number have been transformational (films like *Schindler's List*), that is to say that they have not only effected a global interface and conversation between the "I" of the filmmaker and the "you" of the audience, but they have taken the additional step that so many filmmakers do not once production wraps. They create an infrastructure to continue to educate and change minds. A film like *Schindler's List* was only the beginning, not the end of the relationship between filmmaker and audience. This goes to the heart of the questions as to what genocide films are supposed to accomplish. According to Brown and Rafter, such films raise "questions about witnessing, remembering and the possibility of closure," and they must "critique state power, exploring its ideal limits and constraints."[6] They should "challenge, change and even radically disorient their viewers. In keeping with public criminology, this complex treatment calls for an active response akin to witnessing, not just passive, 'feel good' spectatorship."[7] Creating institutions like the Survivors of the Shoah Visual History Foundation, which Steven Spielberg did after *Schindler*, or the organization Witness, established by singer/songwriter Peter Gabriel, are therefore central to the task of achieving and maintaining the effectiveness of works in the performing arts about genocide. Numerous perils await filmmakers venturing into this difficult terrain – from audience rejection and denial to historical inaccuracies to the potential fetishization of, and desensitization towards, violence, but the potential of their actions for good far outweighs all the disadvantages.

Epilogue: Genocide Art or "Kitsch"?

William L. Hewitt

West Chester University

An astronaut crew crash lands on a planet in the distant future where intelligent talking primates are the dominant species. Human beings are an oppressed and enslaved species on the planet and the lone surviving astronaut, George Taylor, played by Charlton Heston, finds himself captive, and he is threatened with castration and a lobotomy from the head simian scientist who fears that Taylor, poses a threat to his world. Dr. Zaius (Maurice Evans) says to Taylor during one of their confrontations: "Why, man is a nuisance. He eats up his food supply in the forest, then migrates to our green belts and ravages our crops. The sooner he is exterminated the better. It's a question of simian survival."[1]

Consider the moral dilemmas raised in these fictional situations. Your society is threatened by outsiders. Your government makes a very convincing argument for keeping those outsiders from entering your society. Would you support the decision to keep the outsiders from entering your society?[2] Philosopher Bruce Wilshire describes this fear: "The X Factor in genocide is any home group's dread pollution by the other group: the infectious smearing and disintegration of its world-experience, and the consequent annihilation of themselves." If the argument were made that the outside society could be eliminated, and the threat to your society would be eliminated for all time, would you support such a decision?[3] Consider this dilemma from an episode of *Doctor Who*:

The Doctor: Do I have the right? Simply touch one wire against the other, and that's it. The Daleks cease to exist. Hundreds of millions of people, thousands of generations can live without fear … in peace, and never know the word 'Dalek.'

Sarah Jane: Then why wait? *If it* was a disease or some sort of bacteria you were destroying, you wouldn't hesitate![4]

The Holocaust in discourse and art arguably remains the touchstone in genocide comparisons, rightly or wrongly. Imre Kertesz, in his insightful essay, "Who Owns Auschwitz" observes: "The artist hopes that, through a precise description, leading him once more along the pathways of death, he will finally break through to the noblest kind of liberation, to a catharsis in which he can perhaps allow his reader to partake as well." He then goes on to say there are very few such artists. What especially rankles Kertesz is the reduction of suffering to meaningless entertainment and commodification.[5]

An example of what concerns Kertesz is thoughtfully discussed in *The History Boys* (Nicholas Hyter, 2006).[6] The setting is a 1980s English grammar school where Alan Bennett's play (the basis for the film) focuses on eight boys preparing for entrance exams to Oxford and Cambridge. Hector is a literature teacher whose lessons have the students mostly memorizing poetry and performing scenes from plays and movies. Hector's goal is to produce "rounded" human beings, but the headmaster thinks his methods are inadequate and inefficient and unquantifiable. The headmaster, consequently, hires Irwin who employs a special technique using fact and quotations, teaching the students to challenge the established interpretations of history.

Their contrast in methodologies and philosophies comes into full view when Irwin suggests the Holocaust as a topic.

Hector reacts:

Good Gracious! How can you teach the Holocaust?
That would do as a question, Can you, should you, teach the Holocaust?
Anybody? Come on.
It has origins, it has consequences.

The students, using Irwin's approach, make it relative.

It's a subject like any other.

Not like any other, surely, not like any other at all.

No, but it's a topic. They go on school trips there nowadays, don't they? Auschwitz? Dachau.

What's always concerned me is where do they have their sandwiches?

The visitor's center. It's like anywhere else.

Yeah, but do they take pictures of each other there?

Are they smiling?

Hector objects to having the established historical view of the Holocaust challenged and relative for the sake of the entrance exam.

Why can you not simply condemn the camps outright as an unprecedented horror?

The boys apply what they have learned from Irwin:

No point sir. Everybody will do that. That's the stock answer sir … the camps an event unlike any other.

The evil unprecedented.

Et cetera. Et cetera.

No! Can't you see that even to say et cetera is … monstrous?

Et cetera is what the Nazis would have said.

The dead reduced to mere verbal aberration.

Alright, not et cetera. But given that the death camps are thought of as unique, wouldn't another approach be to show precedents?

Put them, well, in proportion.

Proportion?

Not proportion, then, putting them in context.

And if it can be explained then it can be explained away.

But to put them into context is a step towards saying it can be understood and explained.

Kertesz applied the word "kitsch" to what Hector fears might happen with popularization of the Holocaust. He is quite aware of many people's surprise to his application of the word to Steven Spielberg's *Schindler's List*[7]. He acknowledged that the film lured millions into movie theaters, and provoked interest and study of the Holocaust.[8] Kertesz sees the problem in failing to get to the wide-ranging ethical consequences of Auschwitz. He sees a vast pool of "kitsch" produced out of the:

> representation of the Holocaust that is incapable of understanding or unwilling to understand the organic connection between our own deformed mode of life (whether in the private sphere or on the level of 'civilization' as such) and the very possibility of the Holocaust. Here I have in mind those representations that seek to establish the Holocaust once and for all as something foreign to human nature; that seek to drive the Holocaust out of the realm of human experience.[9]

Then Kertesz praises Roberto Benigni's *Life is Beautiful*[10] as: "Authentic, and it moves us with the power of the oldest kind of magic, the magic of fairy tales." He says of the end of the film, and the main character's death:

> We don't see Guido's death when it comes says much about the film's unerring taste, its faultless style ... At the end, the boy sees his 'prize' rolling toward him – the 'real tank;' But here sadness over the ruined 'game' overwhelms the story. We now understand that, somewhere else, the 'game' would be called civilization, humanity, freedom – everything that humans ever regarded as valuable.[11]

For Lawrence L. Langer, to the contrary, *Life Is Beautiful*'s

> allure is based on a willing suspension of disbelief: that in Benigni's version of a death camp milieu it really was possible for a victim to preserve enough physical and spiritual mastery to 'outwit' singlehandedly the murderous intensions of the Germans. Benigni seems unconcerned that by infusing the gloom of his Holocaust scenario with the comic ingenuity of his character he allows Guido's antics to profane the solemn impact of the surroundings.[12]

Three exterminationist films, just to name a few examples, illustrate the moral quagmires, obvious and obscure, in film. At the start of World War II, the Nazis produced two notorious propaganda films. Producer Franz Hippler's *Der Ewige Jude*,[13] *The Eternal Jew* (1940), included not so subtle scenes of Jews depicted as rats scurrying from a sewer grating and infesting the surroundings. The other German propaganda film, also produced in

1940, Viet Harlan's *Jud Süss*,[14] revolves around Joseph Süss Oppenheimer (Ferdinand Marian) who is the treasurer to a Duke (Heinrich George). The Jew Oppenheimer almost brings the Duke's realm to ruin through his scheming, and he commits the outrage of raping a wholesome German girl, Dorothea Sturm (Kristina Soderbaum), and imprisoning her father and fiancée. The Duke Succumbs to a heart attack, and the community elders bring the Jew to justice. Rather than live with the stigma of her defilement by Oppenheimer, Dorothea drowns herself in the river.

Another opprobrious example of the X factor occurred in Rwanda in 1994, when exterminationist propaganda became commonplace. Radio station RTLM (Radio-Television Libre des Mille Collines) began broadcasting with funding from Christian Democratic International in 1993. RTLM, run by the Hutu majority, designated the Tutsi minority as *inyenzi*, or "cockroaches." The airwaves carried messages of hate, such as, "The cruelty of the inyenzi is incurable, the[ir] cruelty ... can only be cured by their total extermination."[15] A scene in *Hotel Rwanda*[16] reinforces the role of Radio in motivating the *genocidaires*, as well.

This is the challenge for all chroniclers of genocide to make sure that the event is not removed from the realm of human experience by the artists, showing victims, bystanders, and even perpetrators as Kertesz says, from "universal experience."[17] A genocide survivor turned filmmaker who attempts to meet this call is Rithy Panh, a survivor of the Cambodian genocide under the Khmer Rouge from 1975 to 1979. Born in 1964, Panh labored in a "rehabilitation" camp during the Khmer years. His most famous film, representing the years of the genocide, is *S-21, la machine de mort Khmere rouge* (2003) focusing on Toul Sleng, the former school converted into a detention and torture center under the notorious commandant Duch.

In *L'Image Manquante* (*The Missing Picture*, 2013),[18] Panh adopts a very unique "documentary" technique using a combination of claymation, propaganda footage, and less-than-linear-structure to tell his story. Reviewing the film for *Genocide Studies and Prevention*, Lior Zylberman speculates: "If the images Panh is seeking to capture had been recorded through technical means, such as film or photography, reproducing them would have become unbearable for the viewer (and also for Panh). In this way, Panh's film entails a challenge towards horror representation, noteworthy for its search for new expressions to represent genocidal violence."[19]

Praise for *The Missing Picture* abounded, including the *Chicago Tribune's* Michael Phillips, who offered this comparison:

> As brilliantly as Art Spiegelman examined his parents' experiences of the Holocaust in the graphic novel *Maus*, the Cambodian-born filmmaker and author Rithy Panh relives his own survival of the Khmer Rouge Regime in *The Missing Picture*. It's a fantastic film …[20]

Reviewer Jake Wilson has a much different assessment reflecting Kertesz's concerns:

> When Panh shows a clay family soaring in an imagined heaven, what exactly is the intended balance between deliberate phoniness and feeling? More generally, how do we respond to a film that could be described both as solemn act of mourning and as a study in different types of kitsch?

He says that on one level the film is "childlike whimsy" juxtaposed with implicit horror, risking "bad taste", in Wilson' opinion, Wilson concedes, "Given his background, Panh escapes any such suspicion." Nevertheless, Wilson continues,

> The poetic flourishes of the narration grow tiresome, and it's difficult to say if this strange method brings us any closer to Cambodia's past. Perhaps the point is that any effort to represent suffering of this order necessarily betrays and falsifies the truth.[21]

Would this "truth" be closer to what Irwin was trying to teach his students in *The History Boys*? Or as Andrew O'Hehir, reviewer for *Salon* said of *The Missing Picture*, "I'd personally be interested in a more encyclopedic treatment of the Khmer Rouge years…" Panh's "testimony", in its unique form, would strike many viewers as strange, and possibly less than "true" than the testimonies of "authority", a talking head such as the subjects in formal taped interviews available at the United States Holocaust Memorial Museum Oral History Project.

The American popular culture has undermined the survivor testimony as bearers of unique and terrible memories, nevertheless. Why face the uncompromising horror and fatalism of testimonies, or the realities of Auschwitz or S-21, when one can turn instead to the pathos and ultimate uplift of films like *Schindler's List* and *The Killing Fields*?[22]

Notes

Introduction

1 http://www.chicagotribune.com, accessed December 7, 2014; "Cinema Therapy" or "Popcorn Therapy" is the somewhat derisive term used to describe mental health practitioners who use film as a tool in therapy. A few examples are: Birgit Wolz, *E-Motion Picture Magic* {Kindle Edition} Glenbridge Publishing, Ltd. (August 22, 2010); Gary Solomon, *The Motion Picture Proscription: Watch The Movie and Call Me in the Morning: 200 Movies to Help You Heal Life's Problems* (Fairfield, Connecticut: Asian Publishing, 1998); and his *Reel Therapy: How Movies Inspire You to Overcome Life's Problems* (Fairfield, Connecticut: Asian Publishing, 2001).

2 Yet Lemkin lived in poverty and died in obscurity in 1959 with only seven people attending his funeral.

3 https://treaties.un.org/doc/Publication/UNTS/Volume%2078/volume-78-I-1021-English.pdf, accessed January 7, 2015.

4 Adding the suffix "cide" as synonym for genocide, for many scholars, denudes Lemkin's original neologism and meaning. Examples include: classicide; demo-cide; ecocide; femicide; fratricide; gendercide; linguicide; omnicide; politicide; pooricide; and, urbicide.

5 http://www.preventgenocide.org/law/icc/statute/part-a.htm, accessed January 7, 2015.

6 http://www.theatlantic.com/international/archive/2013/03/whats-the-difference-between-crimes-against-humanity-and-genocide/274167/?single_page=true, accessed January 7, 2015.

7 Vahakn Dadrian, "A Typology of Genocide," *International Review of Sociology*, Vol. 5, No. 2 (1975): 201–12; Leo Kuper, *Genocide: Its Political Use in the Twentieth Century* (New Haven, Connecticut: Yale University Press, 1981); *The Prevention of Genocide* (New Haven, Connecticut: Yale University Press, 1992); Helen Fein, *Genocide: A Sociological Perspective* (London: Sage, 1993); R. J. Rummel, *Death By Government: Genocide and Mass Murder in the Twentieth Century* (New Brunswick, New Jersey: Transaction Publishers, 1994); Frank Chalk and Kurt Jonassohn, *The History and Sociology of Genocide* (New Haven: Yale University Press, 1990); and, Robert Melson, *Revolution and Genocide: On the Origins of the Armenian Genocide and the Holocaust* (Chicago: University of Chicago Press, 1992).

8 Richard Corliss, "The Pleasures and Perils of Biopics: True-life dramas: must be Oscar time," *Time*, January 26, 2015, 60–1.

9 Alison Landsberg, *Prosthetic Memory: The Transformation of American Remembrance in the Age of Mass Culture* (New York: Columbia University Press, 2004), 125.

10 Suzanne Keen, *Empathy and the Novel* (New York: Oxford University Press, 2007), 16–17; 68–75.

11 Landsberg, *Prosthetic Memory,* 14, 30.

12 Isaac Butler, "The Realism Canard, Or: Why Fact-Checking Fiction is Poisoning Criticism," *Parabasis,* October 9, 2013, http://parabasis.typepad.com/blog/2013/10/the-realism-canard.html, accessed January 15, 2015.

13 Noah Berlatsky, "How *Twelve Years a Slave* Gets it Right by Getting it Wrong," *The Atlantic,* October 28, 2013, http://www.theatlantic.com/entertainment/archive/2013/10/how-em-12-years-a-slave-em-gets-history-right-by-getting-it-wrong/280911/, accessed January 15, 2015,

14 Yosef Hayim Yerushalmi, *Zakhor: Jewish History and Jewish Memory* (New York: Shocken Books, 1989), 94.

15 Paul R. Bartrop and Steven Leonard Jacobs, *Fifty Key Thinkers on the Holocaust and Genocide* (London and New York: Routledge, 2011), 25–31.

16 Wayne S. Booth, *The Company We Keep: An Ethics of Fiction* (Berkeley, Los Angeles, and London: University of California Press, 1988), 70–1.

17 Ibid., 72.

18 Irwin Rosen, "The Effects of 'Gentleman's Agreement' on Attitudes Towards Jews," *Journal of Psychology*, Vol. 26 (October 1948): 532–6.

19 Russell Middleton, "Ethnic Prejudice and Susceptibility to Persuasion," *American Sociological Review* (October 1960): 686. Middleton used Theodor Adorno's ten item list of anti-Semitism, developed in *The Authoritarian Personality,* as part of his questionnaire, positing the following scenarios and asking for agreement or disagreement.

1. Anyone who employs many people should be careful not to hire a large percentage of Jews.

2. One trouble with Jewish businessmen is that they stick together and connive so that a Gentile doesn't have a fair chance in competition.

3. The Jewish districts in most cities are the results of the clannishness and stick-togetherness of Jews.

4. Persecution of Jews would be largely eliminated if the Jews would make really sincere efforts to rid themselves of their harmful and offensive faults.

5. Jewish leaders should encourage Jews to be more inconspicuous, to keep out of professions and activities already overcrowded with Jews and to keep out of the public notice.

6. I can hardly imagine myself marrying a Jew.

7. The trouble with letting Jews into a nice neighborhood is that they gradually give it a typical Jewish atmosphere.

8. No matter how Americanized a Jew may seem to be, there is always something different and strange, something basically Jewish underneath.

9. There may be a few exceptions, but, in general, Jews are pretty much alike.

10. There are too many Jews in the various federal agencies and bureaus in Washington, and they have too much control over our national policies.

20 Elizabeth Levy Paluck, "Reducing Intergroup Prejudice and Conflict Using the Media: A Field Experiment in Rwanda," *Journal of Personality and Social Psychology*, Vol. 96, No. 3 (2009): 574–87.

21 http://www.genocidetext.net/gaci_filmography.htm, accessed January 7, 2015.

1. Settler Colonialism and Genocide in Australia

1 Henry Reynolds, *Forgotten War* (Sydney: New South Publishing, 2013), 49.

2 Edward Cavanagh, "History, Time, and the Indigenist critique," *Arena Journal*, Vols. 37/38 (2012): 24. See also Lorenzo Veracini, *Settler Colonialism: A Theoretical Overview* (Basingstoke: Palgrave Lorenzo, 2010) and Lorenzo Veracini "Settler Colonialism: A Global and Contemporary Phenomenon," *Arena Journal*, Vols. 37/38 (2012): 322–36.

3 Elizabeth Strakosch and Alissa Macoun, "The Vanishing Endpoint of Settler Colonialism," *Arena Journal*, Vols. 37/38 (2012): 41.

4 Patrick Wolfe, *Settler Colonialism and the Transformation of Anthropology: The Politics and Poetics of an Ethnographic Event* (London: Cassell, 1999), 2.

5 See Sarah Maddison, *Black Politics: Inside the complexity of Aboriginal political culture* (Sydney: Allen & Unwin, 2009).

6 The first feature film by an Aboriginal director was William Syron's *Jindalee Lady* (1992). Fifteen features films were directed by Indigenous filmmakers between 1992 and 2015. For a complete list see http://www.creativespirits.info/resources/movies/, accessed April 15, 2015.

7 The Aboriginal and Torres Strait Islander peoples of Australia belong to more than 200 distinct language groups or nations and cannot be treated as a single homogenous group or nation.

8 Peter Krausz, "Screening Indigenous Australia – An Overview of Indigenous Australia on Film," *Australian Screen Education Online*, no. 32 (Spring 2003): 90–95 – online at: http://search.informit.com.au/documentSummary;dn=8205 26615263733;res=IELHSS, accessed 13 April 2009.

9 Chris Healy, *Forgetting Aboriginies* (Sydney: UNSW Press, 2008), 10.

10 Maddison, *Black Politics*, 36–42.

11 Quoted in Dominik J. Schaller and Jürgen Zimmerer, "Raphael Lemkin: The 'Founder of the United Nation's Genocide Convention' as a Historian of Mass Violence," *Journal of Genocide Research*, Vol.7, No.4 (2005): 447.

12 The United Nations convention on genocide (ratified in Australia in 1951) developed Lemkin's original conception of the term to encompass 'any of the following acts committed with intent to destroy, in whole or in part, a national, ethnical, racial or religious group, as such:

(a) Killing members of the group;
(b) Causing serious bodily or mental harm to members of the group;
(c) Deliberately inflicting on the group conditions of life calculated to bring about its physical destruction in whole or in part;
(d) Imposing measures intended to prevent births within the group;
(e) Forcibly transferring children of the group to another group (see Human Rights Web 1997 for full text).

13 Christopher Powell, "The Morality of Genocide," in *New Directions in Genocide Research*, ed. Adam Jones (New York: Routledge, 2011).

14 Peter Read, *The Stolen Generations: The Removal of Aboriginal Children in New South Wales 1883 to 1969*, NSW Ministry of Aboriginal Affairs, Occasional Paper (1983), 21.

15 Tony Barta, "After the Holocaust: Consciousness of Genocide in Australia," *Australian Journal of Politics & History*, Vol. 31, No. 1 (April 1985): 154–61.

16 See A. Dirk Moses, "An Antipodean Genocide? The Origins of the Genocidal Moment in the Colonization of Australia," *Journal of Genocide Research*, Vol. 2, No.1 (2000): 89–106; Colin Tatz, "Genocide in Australia," *AIATSIS Research Discussion Paper*, No. 8 (Canberra: AIATSIS 1999); Maddison, *Black Politics*.

17 Colin Tatz, "Genocide in Australia."
18 Human Rights and Economic Opportunity Commission, *Bringing Them Home: Report of the National Inquiry into the Separation of Aboriginal and Torres Strait Islander Children from Their Families* (1997): 218.
19 Doris Pilkington (Nugi Garimara), *Follow the Rabbit-Proof Fence* (Brisbane: University of Queensland Press, 1996).
20 See Geoffrey Robertson, 'Well-Intentioned Genocide' at http://www.geoffrey-robertson.com/pdf/rabbit_proof_fence.pdf (n.d.)
21 Roger Ebert, "Rabbit-Proof Fence," *Chicago Sun Herald,* http://www.rogerebert.com/reviews/rabbit-proof-fence-2002, accessed May 7, 2016.
22 Kristy M. Wilson & Tomas F. Crowder-Taraborelli, *Film & Genocide* (Madison, Wisconsin: University of Wisconsin Press, 2012): 129. For a scrupulously fair discussion of this debate, see Peter Cochrane, "Rabbit-Proof Fence: the Question of 'Intent' in History," at http://www.guerreroalcazar.es/guias/rabpdf.pdf, accessed April 12, 2015.
23 Beth Roberts, *Manganinnie: A Story of Old Tasmania* (Melbourne: Sun, 1980).
24 Cited in Richard Kuipers, "Curator's Notes" at http://aso.gov.au/titles/features/manganinnie/notes/ (n.d.), accessed May 7, 2016.
25 Karen Jennings, *Sites of Difference: Cinematic Representations of Aboriginality & Gender* (Melbourne: AFI, 1993), 29.
26 Ibid.
27 Rob Gowland, *The Guardian,* 22 September 1999, http://www.southaustralian-history.com.au/elseystation.htm, accessed May 7, 2016.
28 For a detailed critical analysis of these two films see: Louis Nowra, *Walkabout* (Sydney: Currency Press & NFSA, 2003); Henry Reynolds, *The Chant of Jimmie Blacksmith* (Sydney: Currency Press & NFSA, 2008).
29 Keneally has said he would not now presume to write in the voice of an Aboriginal person, but would have written the story as seen by a White character. Ten years later Keneally wrote the novel *Schindler's Ark*, also based on a real life story, which was the source of Steven Spielberg's *Schindler's List*.
30 Films do not, in fact, have a language. They possess not grammatical laws but codes and conventions developed by individual filmmakers and cinemas. US film scholar James Monaco points out that because "film is very much like a language … it is useful to use the metaphor of language to describe the phenomenon of film." Cited in Jane Mills, *Love and Hating Hollywood: Reframing Global and Local Cinemas* (Sydney: Allen & Unwin, 2009), 56.
31 Colin Thomas Johnson (born August 21, 1938), better known by his *nom de plume* Mudrooroo, is a novelist, poet, essayist and playwright. For a full discussion of this film and critical readings, see Jane Mills, *Jedda* (Sydney: Currency Press & NFSA, 2012).
32 For Paul Byrne's curator notes, see http://aso.gov.au/titles/features/tracker/notes/ accessed 7 May 2016.

33 Various alternative spellings exist for Gamilaroi, such as Gomeroi, Gamilaroi, Gamilaraay, Gumillaroy, Kamilaroi and Comelroy, all of which are attempts at transliteration to the Latin alphabet.

34 For more detail, see Peter Robb, "A journey through north-western NSW with filmmaker Ivan Sen," *The Monthly* (November 2011), http://www.themonthly. com.au/issue/2011/november/1326604262/peter-robb/journey-through-no rth-western-nsw-filmmaker-ivan-sen, accessed 7 May 2016.

35 *Samson and Delilah* won the Camera d'Or for best first feature film at the Cannes Film Festival, 2009.

36 Therese Davis, "Love and Social Marginality in Samson and Delilah," *Sense of Cinema*, Issue 51 (July 2009), at http://sensesofcinema.com/2009/ feature-articles/samson-and-delilah/, accessed 7 May 2016.

37 Kaytetye is the name of the Indigenous Australians who live around Barrow Creek and Tennant Creek in the Northern Territory. Alternative spellings for Kaytetye include Kartetye, Kartiji, Kaytej, Keytej and Katish.

38 Terese Davis, "Love and Social Marginality."

39 See Jane Mills, "Cosmopolitanism and Bordering Practice in Ivan Sen's *Toomelah*," *Screening the Past*, No. 39 (August 2015).

2. No Good Samaritans: Explaining African Colonialism and Underdevelopment in Popular African Films

1 Robert Porter, "European Activity on the Gold Coast, 1620–1667," (PhD diss., University of University of South Africa, 1975), 1.

2 Porter, "European Activity."

3 Porter, "European Activity" and Latoya M. Burns, "The Rwandan Genocide and How Belgian Colonization Ignited the Flame of Hatred," (PhD diss., Texas Woman's University, 2014), 27.

4 Amy M. Fowler, "The Visual Rhetoric of Colonization: A Historiography of Representations of the Congo Free State," (PhD diss., University of Kansas, 2005), 15–16.

5 Jennifer Kopf, "Spaces of Hegemony and Resistance in German East Africa," (PhD diss., University of Kentucky, 2005), 4.

6 "The White Man's Burden," Kipling Society, accessed 3 May 2015, http://www. kiplingsociety.co.uk/poems_burden.htm

7 Clara Henderson, "When Hearts Beat Like Native Drums:" Music and the Sexual Dimensions of the Notions of 'Savage' and 'Civilized' in Tarzan and His Mate, 1934," *Africa Today*, Vol. 48 (2001): 93.

8 Henderson, "When Hearts Beat," 106.

9   Henderson, "When Hearts Beat," 99.

10 Walter Rodney, A. M. Babu, and Vincent Harding, *How Europe Underdeveloped Africa*. (Washington, D.C.: Howard University Press, 1981), 105.

11 Ibid.

12 Ibid.

13 "Synopsis for *Zulu*," IMDb, accessed May 2, 2015, http://www.imdb.com /title/ tt0058777/synopsis

14 Ibid.

15 Ibid.

16 Rachael Gilmour, "Missionaries, Colonialism and Language in Nineteenth-Century South Africa," *History Compass*, Vol. 5 (2007): 1764.

17 Russell Scott Houser, "American and English Missionary Perceptions of the Zulus in an Era of Leveling the Mountains, Bridging the Oceans, Civilizing and Christianizing the "Heathen" (PhD diss., Baylor University, 2004), 97.

18 Ibid., p. 43.

19 "Heart of Darkness," Spark Notes. May 5, 2015, http://www.sparknotes. com/lit/ heart/summary.html

20 Vincent Viaene, "King Leopold's Imperialism and the Origins of the Belgian Colonial Party, 1860–1905," *The Journal of Modern History*, Vol. 80 (2008): 758.

21 "Joseph Conrad, Heart of Darkness," The Iron Maiden Commentary, accessed May 2, 2015, http://www.ironmaidencommentary.com/?url=album10_xfactor/ heartofdarkness&lang=eng&link=albums

22 Viaene, "King Leopold's Imperialism," 758.

23 Ibid., 752.

24 Teresa A. Booker, "The Last King of Scotland," *Teaching Sociology*, Vol. 36 (2008): 186.

25 Kirk Arden Hoppe, "Lords of the Fly: Colonial Visions and Revisions of African Sleeping-Sickness Environments on Ugandan Lake Victoria, 1906–61," *Africa: Journal of the International African Institute*, Vol. 67 (1997): 87

26 Paul Marion, "The Uganda Railway: A Study in Late Nineteenth Century British Imperialism" (PhD diss., Sir George Williams University, 1974), 10.

27 Agnes Asiimwe, "Why Idi Amin expelled the Asians. (Cover story)," *New African*, No. 521 (2012): 32

28 Booker, "The Last King," 186.

29 Kwame Anthony Appiah, Henry Louis Gates Jr, and John Thornton, "Africana: The Encyclopedia of the African and African American Experience," *The New York Times Book Review*, Vol. 24 (2000): 188.

30 Teresa A. Booker, "*Blood Diamond*, directed by Edward Zwick, produced by Paula Weinstein, Edward Zwick, Marshall Herskovitz, Graham King, and Gillian Gorfil," *Political Communication*, Vol. 24 (2007): 353.

31 Joseph Jusuf Bangura, "The Temne in Freetown History: Rethinking the History of the Sierra Leone Colony, 1890–1961," (PhD diss., University of Dalhousie, 2006), 1.

275

3. "White Saviors" Unable to *Save* the "Other" in Hollywood's Genocidal West

1 Thomas R. Eddlem, "*Avatar*: A Visually Stunning and Perfect Historical Allegory," http://www.thenewamerican.com/reviews/movies/items/6496-avatar-a-visual-ly-stunning-and-perfect-historical-allegory; *New York Times*, http://www.ny-times.com/2010/01/08/opion/08brooks.html?_r=0.

2 A prime examples of the critique that makes capitalism the enemy: Reihan Salam, "The Case Against "*Avatar*"" *Forbes* (December 21, 2009), http://www.forbes.com/2009/12/20/avatar-media-james-cameron-opinions-columnists-reihan-salem-html.; and. 'Avatar<, torture for conservatives, *Los Angeles Times*, January 19, 2010, http://articles.latimes.com/2010/jan/26/opinion/la-oe-boaz26-2010jan26.

3 *Avatar*, DVD, directed by James Cameron (2009; Century City, CA: Twentieth Century Fox Film Corporation, Dune Entertainment, Ingenious Film Partners); http://www.imdb.com/title/tt0499549/?ref_=fn_al_tt_1.

4 *Dances with Wolves*, DVD, directed by Kevin Costner (1990; Burbank, CA: Tig Productions, Majestic Films International), http://www.imdb.com/title/tt0099348/?ref_=fn_al_tt_1.

5 Nicholasn, "*Avatar*: an Allegory of the West, "*High Country News*, https://www.hcn.org/blogs/goat/avatar-an-allegory-of-the-west-1.

6 *The New York Times*, http://www.nytimes.com/2010/01/08/opnion?/08brooks.html?_r=0.

7 Mathew Hughey, *The White Savior Film: Content, Critics, and Consumption* (Philadelphia: Temple University Press, 2014); Herman Vera and Andrew M. Gordon, *Screen Saviors: Hollywood Fictions of Whiteness* (Lanham, Maryland: Rowman and Littlefield Publishers, Inc., 2003).

8 Vera and Gordon, *Screen Saviors,* 40.

9 *Last of the Mohicans*, DVD, directed by Michael Mann (2009; Los Angeles: Morgan Creek Productions), http://www.imdb.com/title/tt0104691/?ref_=fn_al_tt_4.

10 *Last of the Mohicans*, DVD, directed by George B. Seitz (1936; Los Angeles: Edward Small Productions), http://www.imdb.com/title/tt0023119/?ref_=fn_al_tt_8.

11 *Last of the Mohicans*, DVD, directed by Ford Beebe, B. Reeves Eason (1932; Los Angeles: Mascot Pictures),http://www.imdb.com/title/tt0027869/?ref_=fn_al_tt_5.

12 The Motion Picture Production Code was a set of industry moral guidelines applied to most United States motion pictures released by major studios from 1930 to 1968. Popularly known as the Hays Code, after Will H. Hays, who was the president of the Motion Picture Producers and Distributors of America (MPPDA) from 1922–1945, the Code spelled out what was acceptable and what was unacceptable content for motion pictures produced for a public audience in the United States.

13 *A Man Called Horse*, DVD, directed by Elliot Silverstein (1970; Los Angeles: Cinema Center Films), http://www.imdb.com/title/tt0066049/?ref_=fn_al_tt_1.

14 Dan Georgakas, "They Have Not Spoken: American Indians in Film," in *The Pretend Indians: Images of Native Americans In The Movies*, ed. Gretchen M. Bataille and Charles L. P. Silet (Ames, Iowa: Iowa State University Press, 1980), 136.

15 Philip J. Deloria, *Playing Indian* (New Haven, Connecticut: Yale University Press, 1998), 183.

16 *Lawrence of Arabia*, DVD, directed by David Lean (1962; Los Angeles: Horizon Pictures [II]), http://www.imdb.com/title/tt0056172/?ref_=fn_al_tt_1.

17 Raymond William Stedman, *Shadows of the Indian: Stereotypes in American Culture* (Norman, Oklahoma: University of Oklahoma Press, 1982), 222, 260. The film is pronounced to be "the most accurate and authentic ever made," and "history as it really was." Ward Churchill, "American Indians in Film: Thematic Contours of Cinematic Colonization," in *Reversing The Lens: Ethnicity, Race, Gender, and Sexuality Through Film*, ed. Jun Xing and Lane Ryo Hirabayashi (Boulder, Colorado: University Press of Colorado, 2003), 52.

18 Robert Bird, "Going Indian: Discovery, Adoption, and Renaming Toward a 'True American,' from *Deerslayer* to *Dances with Wolves*," in *Dressing in Feathers: The Construction of the Indian in American Popular Culture*, ed. S. Elizabeth Bird (Boulder, Colorado: Westview Press, 1996), 201.

19 Michael Medved, *Hollywood vs. America: The Explosive Bestseller that Shows How-and Why-the Entertainment Industry Has Broken Faith With Its Audience* (New York: Harper Perennial, 1993).

20 Vera and Gordon, *Screen Saviors,* 134–5.

21 *Dances With Wolves*, DVD, directed by Kevin Costner (1990; Burbank, CA: Tig Productions, Majestic Films International), http://www.imdb.com/title/tt0099348/?ref_=fn_al_tt_1.

22 Huhndorf, 19. J. W. Shultz, *My Life As An Indian* (New York: Fawcett Columbine, 1981), 9–10.

23 Huhndorf, 21.

24 Huhndorf, 31.

25 Ward Churchill, *Fantasies of the Master Race: Literature, Cinema and the Colonization of American Indians* (Monroe, Maine: Common Cause Press, 1992), 243–7, "Lawrence of South Dakota: Dances with Wolves and the Maintenance of American Empire;" Stephen Powers, David J. Rothman, and Stanley Rothman, *Hollywood's America: Social and Political Themes in Motion Pictures* (Boulder: Westview Press, 1996), 186.

26 Michael Coyne, *The Crowded Prairie: American National Identity in the Hollywood Western* (New York: I.B.Tauris Publishers, 1997), 188.

27 Shari M. Huhndorf, *Going Native: Indians in the American Cultural Imagination* (Ithaca, New York: Cornell University Press, 2001), 4.

28 Bird, 196.

29 Bird, 197. R. W. B. Lewis, *The American Adam Innocence, Tragedy, and Tradition in the Nineteenth Century* (Chicago: University of Chicago Press, 1955), 5.

30 Medved, 225–226; Richard Grenier, "Hollywood's Foreign Policy: Utopian Tempered by Greed," *The National Interest*, Summer 1991, 76–7.

31 Bird, 204.

32 Ibid., 201.

33 Medved, 225–6; Richard Grenier, "Hollywood's Foreign Policy: Utopianism Tempered By Greed," *The National Interest*, Summer 1991, 76–7.

34 James A. Axtell, *Beyond 1492: Encounter in Colonial North America* (New York: Oxford University Press, 1992), 260–663; James A. Clifton, "Alternate Identities and Cultural Frontiers," in *Being and Becoming Indian: Biographical Studies of North American Frontiers*, ed. James A. Clifton (Chicago: Dorsey Press, 1989), 6.

35 Huhndorf, 5.

36 Ibid., 3.

37 Ibid., 5.

38 Bird, 202.

39 Tom Engelhardt, *The End of Victory Culture: Cold War America and the Disillusioning of a Generation* (New York: Basic Books 1995), 279.

40 Ibid., 279.

41 Annette Hamilton, "Fear and Desire: Aborigines, Asians, and the National Imaginary," *Australian Cultural History* 9 (1990): 13–35.

42 Huhndorf, 4.

43 Ibid.

44 *Hidalgo*, DVD, directed by Joe Johnston (2004; Burbank, CA: Touchstone Pictures, Casey Silver Productions, Dune Films), http://www.imdb.com/title/tt0317648/?ref_=nv_sr_1.

45 *The Last Samurai*, directed by Edward Zwick (2003, Warner Bros., Bedford Falls Company, The, Cruise/Wagner Productions), http://www.imdb.com/title/tt0325710/.

46 *Thunderheart*, directed by Michael Apted (1992: Culver City, CA: TriStar Pictures, Tribeca Productions, Waterhorse Productions), http://www.imdb.com/title/tt0105585/?ref_=fn_al_tt_1.

47 Jack G. Shaheen, *Reel Bad Arabs: How Hollywood Vilifies a People* (New York: Olive Branch Books, 2001), 19, "Sheikh" means, literally, wise elderly person.

48 Shaheen, 22, stereotypical Arab women are portrayed as "bosomy belly dancers."

49 Shaheen, 20, a prevalent stereotype has Arab men kidnap and seduce women.

50 Matthew Bernstein and Gaylyn Studlar, eds., *Visions of the East: Orientalism in Film* (New Brunswick, Jersey: Rutgers University Press, 1997), 57.

51 Churchill, 70.

52 Bernstein and Studlar, 56.

53 Stephen J. Ducat, *The Wimp Factor: Gender Gaps, Holy Wars, & the Politics of Anxious Masculinity* (Boston: Beacon Press, 2004), 210–11.

54 Berstein and Studlar, *Visions* of the East, 54.

55 Larry McMurtey, *Oh What A Slaughter: Massacres in the American West: 1846–1890* (New York: Simon & Schuster, 2005), 160.

56 Linda Williams, "Melodrama Revised," in *Refiguring Film Genres*, ed. Nick Brown (Berkeley, California: University of California Press, 1998), 61.

4. Genocide as European Empire Building: The Slaughter of the Herero of Namibia

1 T. E. Sole, "The *Sudwestafrica Denkmünze* and the South West African Campaigns of 1905–1908," *Military Journal*, Vol. 1, No. 3 (1968): 19–23

2 George Steer, *Judgment on German Africa* (London: Hoddler and Stoughton, 1939).

3 J. Swan, "The Final Solution in South West Africa," *Military History Quarterly*, Vol. 3, No. 4 (1991): 36–55.

4 M. R. Louis, "Great Britain and German Expansion in Africa 1884–1919," in *Britain and Germany in Africa: Imperial Rivalry and Colonial Rule*, ed. P. Gifford and M. R. Louis (New Haven, CT: Yale University Press, 1967), 3–34.

5 Richard Morrock, *The Psychology of Genocide and Violent Oppression: A Study of Mass Cruelty from Nazi Germany to Rwanda* (New York: McFarland, 2010).

6 Jürgen Zimmerer, *War, Concentration Camps, and Genocide in South-West Africa: The First German Genocide* (Berlin: Merlin Press, 2008).

7 Jeremy Sarkin-Hughes, *Germany's Genocide of the Herero: Kaiser Wilhelm II, His General, His Settlers, His Soldiers* (Cape Town: University of Cape Town Press. 2011).

8 *Namibia: Genocide and the Second Reich*, DVD, directed by David Olusoga (Bristol City, United Kingdom, 2005).

9 Hannah Arendt, *The Origins of Totalitarianism* (New York: Harcourt Brace, 1975).

10 *The Canary Effect*, DVD, directed by Robin Davey and *Yellow Thunder Woman* (2006, CA: Tribeka Films).

11 For Hegel, Europe remains "the center and end of universal history …. [Europeans] are the carriers of the world spirit, and against that absolute right, the spirit of other peoples has no right to exist," (Hegel, as quoted in David Smith. *Trying to Teach in a Season of Great Untruths: Globalization, Empire and the Crises of Pedagogy* [Rotterdam: Sense Publishers, 2006], 59).

12 *Namibia: Genocide and the Second Reich*.

13 Sarkin-Hughes, 57.

14 "Against non-humans, one cannot conduct war humanely." Von Trotha, as quoted in as quoted in Jeremy Sarkin-Hughes, 2009, 121.

15 H. Stoecker, *German Imperialism in Africa: From the Beginnings to the Second World War* (London: C. Hurst & Company, 1986).

16 Enrique Dussel, "Eurocentrism and Modernity," in *On Cosmopolitanism and Forgiveness*, ed. Jacques Derrida (London: Routledge, 1993).

17 Martin Louis, "Great Britain and German Expansion in Africa 1884–1919," in *Britain and Germany in Africa: Imperial rivalry and colonial rule*, ed. P. Gifford, M. R. Louis (New Haven, CT: Yale University Press, 1967)

18 "At this point we leave Africa, not to mention it again. For it is no historical part of the World; it has no movement or development to exhibit. Historical movements-that is in its northern part-belong to the Asiatic or European world …. Egypt will be considered in reference to the passage of the human mind from its Eastern to its Western phase, but it does not belong to the African Spirit. What we properly understand by Africa, is the Unhistorical, Undeveloped Spirit, still involved in the conditions of mere nature, and which had to be presented here only as on the threshold of the World's History," (as quoted in Peter Armstrong, ed., *Heart of Darkness* [New York and London: W.W. Norton & Company, 2006], 212).

19 As quoted in Armstrong, 2006, 211.

20 Bruce Wilshire, "Get 'Em All! Kill 'Em!" *Genocide, Terrorism, Righteous Communities* (Lanham, Maryland: Lexington Books: 2005), xxii.

5. The Armenian Genocide in Film: Overcoming Denial and Loss

1 This footage had its first public showing in the Armenian Genocide Museum in Yerevan on 26 April 2015 during a ceremony to honor Henry Morgenthau, Sr., attended by three generations of members of his family.

2 Anthony Slide, ed., *Ravished Armenia and the Story of Aurora Mardiganian* (Jackson, Mississippi: University Press of Mississippi, 2014). This book contains the full text of Mardiganian's memoir.

3 Ibid., 11.

4 Ibid., 29.

5 Ibid., 17–18.

6 Ibid., 10.

7 Two important scholarly articles expose the Turkish government's campaign against the film. David Welky, "Global Hollywood Versus National Pride: The Battle to Film *The Forty Days of Musa Dagh*," *Film Quarterly*, Vol. 59, No. 3 (Spring 2006), and Edward Minasian, "The Forty Years of Musa Dagh: The Film That Was Denied," *Journal of Armenian Studies*, Vol. III, Nos. 1–2 (1986–1987).

8 Henri Verneuil, *Mayrig*, trans. Elsie Antreassian Bayizian (New York: St. Vartan Press, 2006), 48.

9 Atom Egoyan, "In Other Words: Poetic Licence and the Incarnation of History," *University of Toronto Quarterly*, Vol. 73, No. 3 (Summer 2004): 892–3.

10 Ibid., 894.

11 "I don't see my film as a film about genocide. What would a film about genocide be like? What are the rhetorical tools of such a genre? Or, for that matter, is there a genre we could call 'genocide films'? The genre I chose was the Western. This is a film in the genre appropriated by Sergio Leone and of course, Eastwood, it is an adventure film. It is an epic, in the tradition of John Huston and David Lean. . . . It does not belong to the tradition of 'Schindler's List' or 'The Killing Fields'. . . . The greatest inspiration for this film was Elia Kazan's 'America, America'. I have read here and there that this film, too, has been described as a genocide film in the past, but I would disagree. In my opinion, 'America, America' is both an epic and an adventure film at the same time." Interview with Fatih Akin, *Agos*, July 30, 2014.

12 Interview with Maral Dink, *Agos*, December 4, 2014.

13 Hamid Dabashi writes in *Al Jazeera*: "The key issue in telling any epic story of dispossession, exodus, catastrophe or Holocaust is precisely the manner in which the story is to be told in the literary and cinematic context when all such grand narratives have become suspect. By virtue of a sustained course of more than one hundred years of poignant and powerful remembrance, the Armenian tragedy has advanced far too deeply into our political consciousness for a tired old cliché kind of cinematic narrative to do justice to it. If a director is not aware of that fact, he walks perilously between tragedy and kitsch." September 18, 2014.

6. The Ukrainian Famine of 1932–1933 on Screen: Making Sense of Suffering

I wish to thank John-Paul Himka for sharing his ideas and valuable comments on the earlier draft of this article.

1 The term was developed in the 1980s by the Ukrainian diaspora in North America to explain the intentional extermination of the Ukrainian people on a mass scale through hunger and later appropriated as a ready-made model by politicians and historians in independent Ukraine.

2 Elie Weisel, "Art and the Holocaust: Trivializing Memory," *New York Times*, 1989. See also, Claude Lanzmann, Seminar at Yale 1990, and Imre Kertész, "Who Owns Auschwitz," *The Yale Journal of Criticism*, Vol. 14, No 1 (Spring 2001): 267–72.

3 John Naughton, *The Manchester Guardian*, June 11, 1995.

4 Yasmin Ibrahim, "Holocaust as the Visual Subject: The Problematics of Memory Making through Visual Culture," *Nebula: A Journal of Multidisciplinary Scholarship*, Vol. 6, No. 4 (December 2009): 103.

5 George Steiner, *Language and Silence. Essays on Language, Literature and the Inhuman* (New York: Antheneum, 1967), 168.

6 Ian Stephens, *Monsoon Morning* (London, 1966), 1984.

7 With the first official reference to the 1932–3 Famine in 1987, the documentary directors were the first to address this topic on a screen: *'33 ... Eyewitnesses' testimonies (33-y ... spohady ochevydtsiv, 1989)* by Mykola Laktionov-Stezenko and *Oy, hore, tse zh hosti do mene* (1989) by Pavlo Fareniuk. See, Vira Syvachuk, "Vidobrazhennia trahedii Holodomoru v suchasnomu ukrains'komu kinematohrafi," *Naukovyi visnyk Kyivs'koho natsional'noho universytetu teatru, kino i telebachennia im. I. K.Karpenka-Karoho, Vyp. 15* (2014): 99–105; and Mykola Loktionov-Stezenko, "Smak travy," *Dnipro*, Nos. 1–2 (2003): 117–40. The received wisdom is that the Ukrainian 1932–1933 Famine was not represented on Soviet screens. The only known cinematic allusion to it is to be found in 1957 film by Mykola Makarenko and Oleksandr Kozyr *Distant and near* (Daleke i blyz'ke) that, showing the night panorama of the Ukrainian village, starts with a short phrase framed as voice-over: "It was a hard [suvoryi] 1933." (Vadym Skurativs'kyi, "Z pryvodu odniei zaekrannoi frazy," *Kino-Teatr*, Vol. 2 (2002).

8 Stephen Holden, "A Family's Struggle in Stalin's Man-Made Famine," *The New York Times,* December 15, 1993.

9 Daniel Levy, Natan Sznaider, "Memory Unbound. The Holocaust and the Formation of Cosmopolitan Memory," *European Journal of Social Theory*, Vol. 5, No. 1 (2002): 87–106.

10 Steven Marcuse, "Hunger and Ideology," in *Representations: Essays on Literature and Society* (New York: Columbia University Press, 1991), 3–16.

11 Christian Noack, Lindsay Janseen, and Vincent Comerford, ed., *Holodomor and Gorta Mór. Histories, Memories and Representations of Famine in Ukraine and Ireland* (London-New York-Delhi: Anthem Press. 2012), 1. In Ukraine, the general public gradually adopted the term Holodomor introduced by the diaspora activists, while in Ireland there developed a practice to call the Great Famine of by its Irish language name, *An Gorta Mór*.

12 Heorhii Kas'ianov, *Danse macabre. Holod 1932–1933 rokiv u politytsi, masoviy svidomosti ta istoriohrafii (1980-ti-pochatok 2000-kh)* (Kyiv: Nash chas, 2010), 206–214.

13 Kas'ianov, *Danse macabre*, 208–10, 12.

14 Olga Papash, "Collective Trauma in a Feature Film: Golod-33 As One-Of-A-Kind," in *Holodomor and Gorta Mór,* 198.

15 John Naughton, *The Manchester Guardian*, 11 June 1995.

16 Vincent Comerford, "Grievance, Scourge or Shame? The Complexity of Attitudes to Ireland's Great Famine," *Holodomor and Gorta Mór*, 67.

17 For a detailed discussion of how ideology impacted the government's contemporary treatment of the Great Famine, see Steven Marcuse's provocative essay, "Hunger and Ideology," 3–16.

18 James Young, *The Texture of Memory: Holocaust Memorials and Meaning* (New Haven, CT: Yale University Press, 1993), 25.

19 Margaret Llwellyn-Jones, *Contemporary Irish Drama and Cultural Identity* (Bristol: Intellect Books, 2002), 33.

20 Llwellyn-Jones, 33–4.

21 The series include films directed by Oles' Ianchuk – *Atentat: Osinnie ubyvstvo v Miunkheni* [*Assassination: the Autumn Murder in Munich*, 1995], *Neskorenyi* [*The Undefeated*, 2000], and *Zalizna Sotnia* [*Company of Heroes*, 2005]." Even though only *Atentat* directly touches the life of the OUN leader Stepan Bandera, all three films romanticize the figures of the Ukrainian nationalists, such as Roman Shukhevych and Mykhailo Duda.

22 Bohdan Y. Nebesio, "The First Five Years with No Plan: Building National Cinema in Ukraine, 1992–1997," *Canadian Review of Comparative Literature* (September, 2007), 291. In fact, many historical dramas of the 1990s and early 2000s happened to be nothing more than mere political statements, with idealized "flat-bed as if carved out of cardboard" protagonists and naïve quite banal plots, which in their portrayal of the Ukrainian nationalists, for instance, tend to rely heavily on the Soviet films about partisans. See, Aleksandr Fedorov, "Ukrainskie povstantsy 1940-kh-1950-kh godov v ekrannoi versii Olesia Ianchuka: mediakriticheskiy analiz," http://www.kino-teatr.ru/kino/art/kino/3596/print/.

23 Serguei Alex. Oushakine, "V poiskakh mesta mezhdu Stalinym i Gitlerom: o postcolonial'nykh istoriiakh sotsializma," *Ab Imperio*, Vol. 1 (2011), 232.

24 Evgeny Dobrenko, *Stalinist Cinema and the Production of History. Museum of The Revolution* (New Haven and London: Yale University Press, 2008), 4.

25 In one of his interviews, Ianchuk admits that, "knowing almost nothing" about the Famine before 1990; he learned about the tragedy from the books he read in the USA, where he was invited by the Harvard Ukrainian Research Institute to work on his film. http://www.spilka.pt/index.php?option=com_content&view=article&id=798:2010-02-24-00-36-08&Itemid=50&lang=uk.

26 See director's detailed interview in a documentary film about *Famine-33*, https://www.youtube.com/watch?v=fzIRyRq44n8

27 Vadym Skurativs'kyi about Ianchuk's films, https://www.youtube.com/watch?v=fzIRyRq44n8; ibid., "Z pryvodu odniei zaekrannoi frazy," *Kino-Teatr*, Vol. 2 (2002); Liubomyr Hoseiko, *Istoriia ukraiins'koho kinematohrafa. 1896–1995* (Kyiv: Kino-Kolo, 2005), 386–387. Interestingly enough, this was not only Ukraine's strategy; for instance, the Bengali famine of 1943 likewise became an argument for Indian independence. [Margaret Kelleher, *The Feminization of Famine. Expression of the Inexpressible* (Durham: Duke University Press, 1997), 162–231].

28 Nebesio, 291.

29 Andrea Graziosi, Lubomyr A. Hajda, and Halyna Hryn, ed., *After The Holodomor. The Enduring Impact of the Great Famine on Ukraine.* (Cambridge, Massachusetts: Harvard University Press, 2013), xxxvi.

30 "Film Shows Ukraine Famine," *The New York Times*, December 1, 1991.

31 Ianchuk's interview in a documentary film about *Famine-33*, https://www.youtube.com/watch?v=fzIRyRq44n8.

32 Papash, "Collective Trauma In A Feature Film," 201.

33 For an in-depth analysis of the so-called "national interpretation" of the Ukraine Famine, see the ground-breaking book by Terry Martin, *Affirmative Action Empire: Nations And Nationalism in the Union, 1923–1939* (Ithaca, NY: 2001), Chapter 7; for recent research on the famine impact on Ukraine, see *After The Holodomor*).

34 Papash, "Collective Trauma in a Feature Film," 208.

35 Holden, "A Family's Struggle."

36 Papash, "Collective Trauma In A Feature Film," 204.

37 Papash, Ibid., 210.

38 Andrei Rogatchevski, "Oles' Ianchuk: Famine '33 (Holod-33, 1991)," *KinoKultura* Special Issue 9: Ukrainian Conema (December 2009), http://www.kinokultura.com/specials/9/famine33.shtml.

39 Liubomyr Hoseiko, *Istoriia ukraiins'koho kinematohrafa. 1896–1995*, 410.

40 Papash, "Collective Trauma In A Feature Film," 210.

41 Maryna Ponomarenko, "Povodyr. Retsenziia," http://cineast.com.ua/review/2014-11-17-503-Povodir_-Retsenz__ya.html

42 Daria Badior, "Mif o ukrainskom zritel'skom kino," November 12, 2015, http://culture.lb.ua/news/2014/11/12/285768_povodir.html; Maryna Ponomarenko, "Povodyr. Retsenziia", http://cineast.com.ua/review/2014-11-17-503-Povodir_-Retsenz__ya.html; Aleksandr Guzeev, "Premiera nedeli: muzei voskovykh figur," http://life.pravda.com.ua/culture/2014/11/14/183915/; Alli Kinsella, "Review of the 'The Guide', 2014, director Oles Sanin," http://www.columbia. edu/cu/ufc//news/2014_10_16.html; Neil Young, " 'The Guide' ('Povodyr'): Odessa Review," http://www.hollywoodreporter.com/review/guide-povodyr-odessa-review-724141.

43 Jeremy Kay, Interview with Oles Sanin, http://www.screendaily.com/features/oles-sanin-the-guide/5080654.article

44 Aleksandr Guzeev, "Premiera nedeli: muzei voskovykh figur," http://life.pravda.com.ua/culture/2014/11/14/183915/

45 Ibid.

46 Nebesio, "The First Five Years with No Plan," 291.

47 Anna Cherevko "Oles' Sanin: 'Kinoteatry Skhodu vidmovliaiut'sia demonstruvaty "Povodyria." Boiat'sia, shcho iikh spaliat'," http://glavcom.ua/articles/24380.html.

48 Neil Young, "'The Guide' ('Povodyr'): Odessa Review," http://www.hollywoo-dreporter.com/review/guide-povodyr-odessa-review-724141.

49 See 'Resolution of the Ukrainian SSR RNK and CC CP(b)U on Blacklisting Villages that Maliciously Sabotage Grain Procurements' signed by V. Chubar and S. Kosior, in *Holodomor of 1932–1933 in Ukraine. Documents and Materials* (Kyiv: Kyiv Mohyla Academy Publishing House, 2008), 62–3. The original document, by the way, does not contain the last phrase cited in a film (the order to "remove all food stocks"), which was apparently added by the scriptwriters to signal the murderous policy of the state. The film also distorts the historical reality by making viewers think that this party 1932 resolution was the main stimulus for Skrypnyk to shoot himself in July 1933.

50 Homi Bhabha, "Of Mimicry and Man. The Ambivalence of Colonial Discourse," in *Location of Culture* (London: Routledge, 2004), 85–92.

51 Battle of Kruty was an attempt of the student battalions of the Ukrainian People's Republic to hold the Red Army's offensive towards Kyiv in January 1918. In Ukrainian collective memory, the Kruty as a very powerful symbol of victimhood and Ukrainian struggle for the independence is heavily mytholo-gized, and it has become common to compare the fighters of Kruty with the 300 Spartans of Thermopylae.

52 From the interview with Oleksandr Kobzar who played Vladimir in *The Guide*, https://www.youtube.com/watch?v=W--XGAa0JbI

53 Homi Bhabha, "Of Mimicry and Man," 85–92.

54 Advertising poster for IRA cigarettes (text V. Mayakovsky / design A. Rodchenko, 1924), "IRA cigarettes are all we retain from the Old World" ("Nami ostavliaiut-sia ot starogo mira tol'ko papirosy IVRA"), in *Soviet Commercial Design of the Twenties*, ed. Mikhail Anikst and Elena Chernevich (New York: Abbeville Press, 1987), 31.

55 Ibrahim, "Holocaust as the Visual Subject," 111.

56 Steiner, *Language and Silence*, 167.

57 W. Benjamin, 1973, cited in Llwellyn-Jones, *Contemporary Irish Drama,* 33.

7. The Holocaust in Feature Films: Problematic Current Trends and Themes

1 Elie Weisel, "Does the Holocaust Lie Beyond the Reach of Art?" *New York Times,* April 17, 1983, Michael Marrus, *The Holocaust in History* (New York: Meridian, 1987), 3, and Theodor Adorno, "Cultural Criticism and Society," *Prisms,* trans. Samuel and Shierry Weber (Cambridge, MA: MIT Press, 1967), 34. See also: http://www.marcuse.org/herbert/people/adorno/AdornoPoetryAuschwitzQuote.htm. According to Harold Marcuse, "It's a misquote, in as much as it's a phrase inside of a sentence which is usually left out: 'The critique of culture

is confronted with the last stage in the dialectic of culture and barbarism: to write a poem after Auschwitz is barbaric, and that corrodes also the knowledge which expresses why it has become impossible to write poetry today.'"

2 Ilan Avisar, *Screening the Holocaust: Cinema's Images of the Unimaginable* (Bloomington, IN: Indiana University Press, 1988) and Avisar, "Historicizing the Holocaust in Film," in *Performing Difference*, ed. Jonathan Friedman (Lanham, MD: University Press of America, 2008).

3 Urwand, *Collaboration: Hollywood's Pact with Hitler* (Cambridge, MA: Belknap, 2013) and Doherty, *Hollywood and Hitler, 1933–1939* (New York: Columbia University Press, 2013). These books follow the recent publication by Lawrence Baron, *Projecting the Holocaust into the Present: The Changing Focus of Contemporary Holocaust Cinema* (Lanham, MD: Rowman and Littlefield, 2005), Terri Ginsberg, *Holocaust Film: The Political Aesthetics of Ideology* (Newcastle, UK: Cambridge Scholars, 2007), Toby Haggith, and Joanna Newman, eds., *The Holocaust and the Moving Image: Representations in Film and Television Since 1933* (London: Wallflower, 2005), and Joshua Hirsch, *Afterimage: Film, Trauma, and the Holocaust* (Philadelphia, PA: Temple University Press, 2003). See also Miriam Borenstein, "Heroes, Victims, and Villains: Character Inversion in Holocaust Cinema," (MA Thesis, West Chester University, 2009). Each of these books owes much to the works by Judith Doneson, *The Holocaust in American Film* (Philadelphia, PA: Jewish Publication Society, 1987) and Annette Insdorf, *Indelible Shadows: Film and the Holocaust* (New York, NY: Random House, 1983).

4 See especially Margaret Olin, "Lanzmann's *Shoah* and the Topography of the Holocaust Film," *Representations*, No. 57 (Winter 1997): 1–23.

5 Deborah Staines, "Knowledge, Memory, and Justice: Some Grey Areas in Contemporary Holocaust Research," *Journal of Contemporary History*, Vol. 42, No. 4 (October 2007): 657, 658.

6 See Janet Ward, "Holocaust Film in the Post 9/11 Era: New Directions in Staging and Emplotment," *Pacific Coast Philology*, Vol. 39 (2004): 29–41.

7 Levi, "The Grey Zone," in *The Drowned and the Saved* (London: Summit Books, 1988), and Nyiszli, *Auschwitz: A Doctor's Eyewitness Account* (reprint, New York: Arcade, 2011),

8 See Imre Kertész, *Fateless* (Evanston, IL: Northwestern University Press, 1992).

9 Kobi Niv, *Life is Beautiful, But Not for Jews: Another View of the Film by Benigni* (Lanham, MD: Scarecrow Press, 2003). A more positive assessment of the film comes from Maurizio Viano, "*Life is Beautiful*: Reception, Allegory, and Holocaust Laughter," *Film Quarterly*, Vol. 53, No. 1 (Autumn 1999): 26–34.

10 Daniel Mendelsohn, "Review: Inglourious Basterds: When Jews Attack," *Newsweek*, August 14, 2009.

11 DesPres, "Holocaust Laughter," *Writing and the Holocaust*, ed. Berel Lang (New York, NY: Holmes and Meier, 1987), 217.

12 Ibid., 232.

13 Peter Stack, "East German 'Liar' is Truly Devastating," *San Francisco Chronicle,* November 5, 1999.

14 *Walk on Water,* DVD, directed by Eytan Fox (2004; Culver City, CA: Sony Pictures, 2005).

15 *Esther's Diary,* Amazon Instant Video directed by Mariusz Kotowski (2011; Austin, Texas: Bright Shining City Productions, 2008).

16 Charles Maier, *The Unmasterable Past: History, Holocaust, and German National Identity* (Cambridge, MA: Harvard University Press, 1988).

17 Robert Marshall, *In the Sewers of Lvov: A Heroic Story of Survival from the Holocaust* (New York, NY: Scribner, 1991).

18 Krystyna Chiger, *The Girl in the Green Sweater: A Life in the Holocaust's Shadow* (New York: St. Martin's Press, Media Tie-In Edition, 2010).

19 http://global100.adl.org/#country/poland, accessed March 30, 2015.

20 A caveat here, especially on *Schindler,* as the film has a number of historical inaccuracies, including, as David Crowe alleges, the origins of the actual list itself. See Crowe, *Oskar Schindler: The Untold Account of His Life, Wartime Activities, and the True Story Behind the List* (New York, NY: Basic Books, 2007). A very negative review of the film comes from Liel Leibovitz, who called it a "moral and aesthetic disaster, an embodiment of much that is wrong with American-Jewish life." See "Listless," *Tablet,* December 13, 2011, http://tabletmag.com/jewish-arts-and-culture/85945/listless, accessed 5 May 2015.

21 Lawrence Langer, *Holocaust Testimonies: The Ruins of Memory* (New Haven, CT: Yale University Press, 1991).

22 A documentary on Belzec appeared in 2010, written and directed by Guillaume Moscovitz. *Belzec,* DVD, directed by Guillaume Moscovitz (2010; Santa Monica, CA: Meneshma Films, 2010).

23 For a consideration of the few films on the experience of the Roma during the Holocaust, see Susan Tebbutt, "Between Distance and Proximity: Film Images and After-images of the Genocide of the Romanies," *Framework: The Journal of Cinema and Media,* Vol. 44, No. 2, (Fall 2003): 72–80.

24 Lanzmann objected to using archival images of corpses, while Godard favored their usage; indeed, Lanzmann once declared that if he discovered footage of murder in the gas chambers, he would destroy it. See, Richard Brody, "Claude Lanzmann: Movie Time," *The New Yorker,* March 13, 2012, http://www.newyorker.com/culture/richard-brody/claude-lanzmann-movie-time, accessed May 1, 2015.

25 https://variety.com/2008/film/news/eytan-fox-filme-pair-for-war-project-1117980613/, accessed May 1, 2015.

8. Slaughter in China on Film: Nanjing and "Saving Asia" through Mutilation

1 Nanjing had been the capital of China on various occasions over the centuries: 229–581 A.D., 937–976 A.D., 1368–1403 A.D., 1853–64 A.D., 1928–38 A.D., and 1940–9 A.D.

2 A thorough and objective study of the historiographical issues that are raised by the events of the Nanjing Massacre may be found in "The Challenges of the Nanjing Massacre" by Daqing Yang, Chapter 4 of *The Nanjing Massacre in History and Historiography*, ed. Joshua A. Fogel. (Berkeley, CA: University of California Press, 2000), 133–79. Several other comprehensive studies of the political dimensions of the massacre have been published over the last 30 years, such as: Iris Chang, *The Rape of Nanking: The Forgotten Holocaust of World War II* (New York, NY: Basic Books, 1997); Kitamura Minoru, *The Politics of Nanjing: An Impartial Investigation*; trans. Hal Gold (Lanham, MD: University Press of America, Inc., 2007); Xu Zhigeng, *Lest We Forget: Nanjing Massacre, 1937*, trans. Zhang Tingquan and Lin Wusun (Beijing: Chinese Literature Press, 1995); Yoshida Takashi, *The Making of the "Rape of Nanking"*: *History and Memory in Japan, China, and the United States* (Oxford and New York: Oxford University Press, 2006); and Honda, Katsuichi (1999) *The Nanjing Massacre: A Japanese Journalist Confronts Japan's National Shame*; ed. Frank B. Gibney; trans. Karen Sandness. Armonk, NY: M.E. Sharpe. (All citations of Japanese and Chinese names are listed surname first, followed by the given name)

3 See John Rabe, *The Good Man of Nanking: The Diaries of John Rabe*, trans. John E. Woods. (New York, NY: Knopf, 1998), 4.

4 Yoshida Takahasi, *The Making of the "Rape of Nanking"* (Oxford, UK: Oxford University Press, 2006), 181–2; Iris Chang, *The Rape of Nanking: The Forgotten Holocaust of World War II*, (New York, NY: BasicBooks, 1997), 139.

5 A sixth-grade Japanese textbook used in 1941 described the events in China thus: "After the Manchurian Incident was settled, our country concluded a cease-fire agreement with China. Moreover, our country pursued the establishment of eternal peace in the East based on the cooperation of Japan, Manchukuo, and China. However, the Chinese government, assisted both by European countries and the United States, did not understand our sincerity and persistently tried to exclude our country … Therefore in the interest of justice, our country decided to send the military to rectify China's mistaken ideas and to establish eternal peace in the East. Since then our military, both navy and army, has accomplished significant achievements. The people on the home front have sincerely been giving solid support to this campaign and are rushing forward in order to carry out this great mission. The foundation for eternal peace in Asia is gradually being laid." Yoshida, *The Making of the "Rape of Nanking"*, 14.

6 Joshua Fogel observes that in China the tragedy at Nanjing is referred to as the "Nanjing Massacre," whereas many in Japan call it the "Nanjing Incident," 144.

7 Compare the reasoning for various dates as described by Kitamura, 72–3, and Fogel, 104.

8 *Black Sun: The Nanking Massacre* (*Hei Tai Yang: Nan Jing Da Tu Sha*; International title: *Black Sun: The Nanking Massacre* and *Men Behind the Sun 4.*), DVD, directed by Mou Dun Fei (1995; Hong Kong: Unearthed Films, 2004).

9 Director's commentary, *Black Sun,* DVD.

10 *Black Sun.*

11 According to Iris Chang, this order was not issued by Prince Asaka but by Taisa Isamo (40), a fact which is questioned by Honda Katsuichi and Frank B. Gibney (xxi).

12 *Black Sun.*

13 Ibid.

14 Ibid.

15 Ibid.

16 Ibid.

17 *City of Life and Death* (*Nan Jing! Nan Jing!*; International title: *City of Life and Death*), DVD, directed by Lu Chuan (2009; Hong Kong: Kino Lorber Films, 2011.

18 *Flowers of War,* DVD, directed by Zhang Yimour (2011; Beijing: Beijing New Picture Film Company).

19 Ibid.

9. Bangladesh: The Forgotten Genocide

1 A tragedy forgotten by Americans, a new study exposes the roles Nixon and Kissinger played in the moral collapse of American foreign policy and U.S, leadership during these events; Gary J. Bass, *The Blood Telegram: Nixon, Kissinger and a Forgotten Genocide* (New York, NY: Alfred A. Knopf, 2013); see also Rounaq Jahan, "Genocide in Bangladesh", in Samuel Totten and William S. Parsons, eds., *Century of Genocide: Critical Essays and Eyewitness Accounts* (New York, NY: Routledge Taylor and Francis Group, 1997), 296–321; Francis Kofi Abiew, "The East Pakistan (Bangladesh) Intervention of 1971", in Samuel Totten and Paul R. Bartrop, eds., *the genocide studies reader* (New York: Routledge Taylor and Francis Group, 2009), 390–5.

2 Mark Dummet, "Bangladesh War: The Article That Changed History" *BBC News,* December 16, 2011, http://www.bbc.com/news/world-asia-16207201; "Video: Village Massacre," *ABC News,* November 30, 1971, http://www.genocidebangladesh.org/video-village-massacre/; "Bangladesh Genocide: Dhaka Massacre," *NBC News,* January 7, 1972, https://www.youtube.com/watch?v=sMg9Ly9nK0g

3 Joan Baez, "Song of Bangladesh," http://www.joanbaez.com/Lyrics/bangladesh. html; George Harrison, "Bangladesh," https://www.youtube.com/watch?v=VPR wzB_1YEk

4 http://theconcertforbangladesh.com/theconcert/

5 Examples include: http://www.londoni.co/index.php/history-of-bangladesh? id=169; http://freedomfightofbangladesh.blogspot.com/; http://www.geno-cidebangladesh.org/wp-content/uploads/2012/03/FILM-ON-LIBERATION-WAR.pdf

6 *Muktir Gaan* (original title) *Song of Freedom*, directed by Manik Ratan (1995), http://www.imdb.com/title/tt0325853/

7 *Muktir Gaan* (original title) *Song of Freedom* (1995), http://tarequemasud. org/films/muktirgaan/

8 *Muktir Gaan* (original title) *Song of Freedom,* (1995), https://corkolkata.word-press.com/welcome/calendar/day-2/muktir-gaan/

9 *Matir Moina* (original title) *The Clay Bird*, directed by Tareque Masud (2002; Audiovisio, MK2 Productions), won, among others, the FIPRESCI Prize in the Director's Fortnight at Cannes in 2002 and became the first film from Bangladesh to compete for the Academy Award for Best Foreign Language Film in 2002, http://www.imdb.com/title/tt0319836/awards?ref_=tt_awd

10 Bangladesh Genocide Archive, http://www.genocidebangladesh.org/; Geno-cide Watch http://www.genocidewatch.org/bangladesh.html; Liberation War Museum http://www.liberationwarmuseum.org/

11 International Crimes Tribunal Bangladesh, http://www.crimesofwar.org/ commentary/international-council-of-jurists-expunges-critique/attachment/ ictbd4_thumb/

12 "Review: Director Slapped the Glory of Bangladesh," http://goodcomedymov-ies.mymovielive.com/meherjaan/; "Rape Scenes Not for Selling Film: 'Children of War' director (Interview), *Business Standard,* February 27, 2014, http:// www.business-standard.com/article/news-ians/rape-scenes-not-for-selling-f ilm-children-of-war-director-interview-114022700251_1.html

13 Ben Kiernan, *Blood and Soil: A World History of Genocide and Extermination from Sparta to Darfur* (New Haven, CT: Yale University Press, 2009).

14 Genocide Watch, "The 1971 Bangladesh Genocide," http://www.genocidewatch. org/bangladesh.html

15 Craig Baxter, "Pakistan Votes – 1970," *Asian Survey*, Vol. 11, No. 3 (March 1971): 197–218.

16 Genocide Watch, "Bangladesh".

17 Ibid.

18 Naeem Mohaiemen, "Accelerated Media and the 1971 Civil War in Bangladesh," *Economic and Political Weekly*, Vol. 43, No. 4 (Jan. 26–Feb. 1, 2008): 36–40. Here, pp. 36, 38, 39.

19 Mohaiemen, "Accelerated Media," 40.

20 James Leahy, "Films that Make a Difference ... Santiago Álvarez and the Politics of Bengal: *Ciclon*," *Cinémathèque Annotations on Film*, Vol. 23 (December, 2002), http://sensesofcinema.com/2002/cteq/alvarez_ciclon/

21 Roger Vogler, "The Birth of Bangladesh: Nefarious Plots and Cold War Sideshows," *Pakistaniaat: A Journal of Pakistan Studies*, Vol 2., No. 3 (2010): 24–46, here p. 31; Richard Sisson and Leo E. Rose, *War and Secession: Pakistan, India, and the Creation of Bangladesh* (Berkeley, CA: University of California Press): 46–9, 237–65. http://www.scholarlyexchange.org/ojs/index.php/PKN/article/viewFile/5458/5047

22 Leahy, "Make a Difference".

23 "The Making of *Stop Genocide* and the Disappearance of Zahir Raihan," *The Daily Star*, December 19, 2008. http://archive.thedailystar.net/newDesign/news-details.php?nid=67680

24 For the same effect through eyewitness testimony, see Kawsar Chowdhury, *Sei Rater Kotha Bolte echechhi* (*Tale of the Darkest Night*, 2001), which recounts the killing of students, faculty, and staff at Dhaka University on the night of 26 March, 1971. *Daily Star News* (Bangladesh) 6 Sept 2002, *Bangladesh Genocide Archive*, http://www.genocidebangladesh.org/reviews-tale-of-the-darkest-nights/; http://www.filmsouthasia.org/film/shei-rater-kotha-bolte-eshechi-tale-of-the-darkest-night/

25 "Almgir Kabir," *Bangladesh Film Day*. http://bangladeshfilmday.weebly.com/alamgir-kabir.html

26 "Films on the Liberation War," *The Daily Star*, March 1, 2013, http://archive.thedailystar.net/newDesign/news-details.php?nid=270855

27 Raihan's, *Jibon Thekey Neya* (1970), technically predates the War of Liberation, but could be considered the first feature film of the movement in its coverage of the Bengali Language Movement. Fahmida Akhter, "Jibon Thekey Neya (Glimpses of Life, 1970): The First Political Film in Pre-Liberation Bangladesh and a Cinematic Metaphor for Nationalist Concerns," *Journal of the Asiatic Society of Bangladesh*, Vol. 59, No. 2 (December 2014): 291–303.

28 Ershad Kamol, "Chashi Nazrul and His Inspiring Creations," *The Daily Star*. Vol 5, No. 201, December 16, 2004. http://archive.thedailystar.net/2004/12/16/d41216140289.htm

29 Mainul Hassan, "Ora Egaro Jon and Chashi NAzrul Islam," *Daily Sun,* December 16, 2011, http://www.daily-sun.com/old_version/details_yes_16-12-2011_Ora-Egaro-Jon-and-Chashi-Nazrul-Islam_435_1_7_1_0.html#sthash.oyIn4tri.dpuf

30 Ibid.

31 Ibid.

32 Kamol, "Chashi Nazrul"

33 "Remembering Khaled Mosharraf," *WordPress*, November 7, 2010, https://jrahman.wordpress.com/2010/11/07/remembering-khaled-mosharraf/

34 "Matiru Rahman (military pilot)", *Revolvy,* http://www.revolvy.com/main/index.php?s=Matiur%20Rahman%20(military%20pilot)&item_type=topic

35 "Tajuddin, a Biopic and our History," *The Daily Star,* 1 April, 2013. http://archive.thedailystar.net/beta2/news/tajuddin-a-biopic-and-our-history/

36 "Guerrilla (2011 film), *Revolvy,* http://www.revolvy.com/main/index.php?s=Guerrilla%20(2011%20film)&item_type=topic; Gendercide is gender-selective mass killing. The term was first used by Mary Anne Warren in her 1985 book, *Gendercide: The Implications of Sex Selection.* Warren drew "an analogy between the concept of *genocide*" and what she called "*gendercide.*" Citing the Oxford English Dictionary definition of genocide as "the deliberate extermination of a race of people," Warren wrote:

> By analogy, gendercide would be the deliberate extermination of persons of a particular sex (or gender). Other terms, such as "gynocide" and "femicide," have been used to refer to the wrongful killing of girls and women. But "gendercide" is a sex-neutral term, in that the victims may be either male or female. There is a need for such a sex-neutral term, since sexually discriminatory killing is just as wrong when the victims happen to be male. The term also calls attention to the fact that gender roles have often had lethal consequences, and that these are in important respects analogous to the lethal consequences of racial, religious, and class prejudice.

37 "Alternative Movies", October 6, 2005, http://parallelcinema.blogspot.com/2005/10/nadir-naam-madhumati-1994-river-named.html.

38 Ibid.

39 Another is *Meherjaan* (2011), directed by Rubaiyat Hossain, itself a controversial film because of its "feminine re-visiting of the war," as well as its blatant depictions of rape.

40 *Shongram,* directed by Munsur Ali (2014; Shongram Motion Pictures)," "Shongram", http://letterboxd.com/film/shongram/

41 "Shogram – a Munsur Ali film – Official Movie Trailer," January 25, 2014, https://www.youtube.com/watch?v=48pT54mRONA

42 Lisa Sharlach, "Rape as Genocide: Bangladesh, the Former Yugoslavia, and Rwanda", *New Political Science,* Vol. 22, No. 1 (2000): 89–102. Targeted gender by perpetrators is an increasingly important focus of genocide research.

43 Selina Hossain, "By Writing about the Past, I Renew History," May 9, 2013, http://www.generallyaboutbooks.com/2013/05/by-writing-about-past-i-renew-history.html

44 Melissa Lee Hussain, *Women, (Under)Development, Empire: The Other(ed) Margins in American Studies*. Dissertation, Washington State University, May 2010, http://www.dissertations.wsu.edu/Dissertations/Spring2010/M_Hussain_041910.pdf

45 "The Film that Satyajit Ray Never Made," *The Hindu*, January 12, 2015, http://www.thehindu.com/todays-paper/tp-in-school/the-film-that-satyajit-ray-never-made/article6778447.ece.

46 Nayanika Mookherjee, "Gendered Embodiments: Mapping the Body-politic of the Raped Woman and the Nation in Bangladesh," *Feminist Review* 88 (2008): 36–53.

47 Lisa Sharlach, "Rape as Genocide"; For examples of heated debates surrounding the issue of rape see: Akhtaruzzaman Mandal and Nayanika Mookherjee, "'Research' on Bangladesh War," *Economic and Political Weekly*, Vol. 42, No. 50 (December 15–21, 2007): 118–21; Nayanika Mookherjee, "A Prescription for Reconciliation?" *Economic and Political Weekly*, Vol. 14, No. 36 (September 9–15, 2006): 3901–3903; Sarmila Bose, *Dead Reckoning: Memories of the 1971 Bangladesh War*, (New York, NY: Columbia University Press, 2011).

48 Angela Debnath, "The Bangladesh Genocide: The Plight of Women," *Plight and Fate of Women During and Following Genocide*, ed. Samuel Totten, (London: Transaction Publishers, 2009), 47–66.

49 See also the controversy surrounding *Meherjaan: A Story of War and Love* (2011), "Bangladesh Liberation Film Opens Old Wounds," *Agency France-Press*, February 20, 2011.

50 "Bollywood Film on Bangladesh War Horrors Opens in India," *DAWN*, May 16, 2014, http://www.dawn.com/news/1106727.

51 Lotte Hoek, *Cut Pieces: Celluloid Obscenity and Popular Cinema in Bangladesh*, (New York, NY: Columbia University Press, 2014).

10. Argentina's Dirty War on Film: The Absent Presence of The Disappeared

1 "Argentina Dirty War – 1976–1983," *Global Security.Org.*" Accessed April 30, 2015. http://www.globalsecurity.org/military/world/war/argentina.htm

2 Paul H. Lewis, *Guerrillas & Generals: The 'Dirty War' in Argentina* (Westport, CT: Greenwood Press, 2001), 150

3 Lewis, *Guerrillas & Generals*, 147, and Amnesty International, "Argentina Convicts Former Military Officials for 'Dirty War' Crimes, last modified October 21, 2001, https://www.amnesty.org/en/articles/news/2011/10/argentina-convicts-former-military-officials-edirty-ware-crimes/.

4 Marguerite Feitlowitz, *Lexicon of Terror: Argentina and The Legacies of Torture* (New York, NY: Oxford University Press, 2011): 28.

5 Mark J. Osiel, "Constructing Subversion in Argentina's Dirty War," *Representations*, Vol. 75, No. 1 (Summer, 2001): 122.

6 Lewis, *Guerrillas & Generals,* 150.

7 Carolina Rocha, "Bearing Witness Through Fiction," *CLC Web: Comparative Literature and Culture*, Vol. 9, No. 1 (March 2007): 3. http://docs.lib.purdue.edu/clcweb/vol9/iss1/17.

8 Lewis, *Guerrillas & Generals,* 151.

9 Thomas C. Wright, *State Terrorism in Latin America: Chile, Argentina, and International Human Rights* (Lanham, MD: Rowman and Littlefield, 2007), 110.

10 Ibid., 111, 112.

11 Ari Gandsman, "'A Prick of a Needle Can Do No Harm:' Compulsory Extraction of Blood in the Search for the Children of Argentina's Disappeared," *The Journal of Latin American and Caribbean Anthropology*, Vol 14. No. 1 (April 2009): 162.

12 Ibid.

13 Sonia Cardenas, *Human Rights in Latin America: A Politics of Terror and Hope* (Philadelphia, PA: University of Pennsylvania Press, 2010, 105.

14 John Charles Chasteen, *Born in Blood and Fire: A Concise History of Latin America* (New York, NY: W. W. Norton, 2001), 286.

15 Nora Amalia Femenía and Colos Ariel Gil, "Argentina's Mothers of the Plaza: The Mourning Process from Junta to Democracy," *Feminist Studies*, Vol. 13, No. 1 (1987): 15, 14.

16 Garciela di Marco, "Madres de Plaza de Mayo," *Encyclopedia of Activism and Social Justice*, eds. Gary L. Anderson and Kathryn G. Herr (Thousand Oaks, CA: Sage Publications, 2007), 887.

17 Antonius C. G. M. Robben, "How Traumatized Societies Remember: The Aftermath of Argentina's Dirty War," *Cultural Critique*, Vol. 59, No. 1 (Winter 2005): 134. See also: http://www.jstor.org/stable/4489199.

18 Tamara L. Falicov, "Film Production in Argentina under Democracy, 1983–1989: The Official Story (La Historia Oficial) as an International Film," Vol. 39, No. 4 (Summer 2001): 123.

19 Ibid.

20 Pat Aufderheide, "Awake, Argentina" *Film Comment,* Vol 22, No. 2 (1986): 54.

21 Falicov, "Film Production in Argentina," 129.

22 Aufderheide, "Awake, Argentina," 54.

23 *The Official Story,* DVD, Directed by Luis Puezo (1985; London: Arrow Films, 2005).

24 Ibid.

25 Nancy Caro, Hollander. "Psycho-political Dynamics of the Bystander in Luis Puenzo's 'The Official Story'. *International Journal of Applied Psychoanalytic Studies*, Vol. 8, no. 2 (2011): 151, accessed April 1, 2015. Doi: 10.1002/aps.

26 Ibid.

27 Ibid.
28 Ibid.
29 Ibid.
30 Ibid.
31 Ibid.
32 Ibid.
33 Ibid.
34 Ibid.
35 Constance Burcúa, *Confronting the 'Dirty War' in Argentine Cinema* (Suffolk: Tamesis: 2009): 165.
36 *Cautiva*, DVD, directed by Gastón Biraben (2003; Los Gatos, CA: Red Envelope Entertainment, 2005).
37 Ibid.
38 Ibid.
39 Ibid.
40 Frank Graziano. *Divine Violence: Spectacle, Psychosexuality & Racial Christianity in the Argentine "Dirty War"* (Boulder, CO: Westview Press, 1992), 17.
41 A. O. Scott, "Observe with Caution: She's Not The Girl She Appears to Be (Not Even to Herself)," *New York Times,* November 10, 2006, E12.
42 *Cautiva*, DVD.
43 Ibid.
44 Ibid.
45 Ibid.
46 Ibid.
47 Ibid.
48 Ibid.
49 Francisco Goldman, "Children of the Dirty War: Argentina's Stolen Orphans," *The New Yorker,* March 19, 2012, accessed on March 15, 2015, http://www.newyorker.com/magazine/2012/03/19/children-of-the-dirty-war and Michelle D. Bonner, *Sustaining Human Rights: Women and Argentin Human Rights Organizations* (University Park, PA: Penn State University Press, 2007).
50 Bonner, *Sustaining Human Rights,* 184.
51 Amy Kaminksy, "Garage Olimpo: Cinema of Witness," *Jumpcut* No. 48 (Winter 2006). http://www.ejumpcut.org/archive/jc48.2006/GarageOlimpo/text.html
52 Oscar Hemer, *Fiction and Truth in Transition: Writing the Present Past in South Africa and Argentina* (Zurich: Lit Verlag Münster, 2012), 399.
53 *Garage Olimpo,* Amazon Instant Video, Directed by Marco Bechis (1999; New York, NY: Under the Milky Way Studios, 2014).
54 Elaine Scarry, *The Body in Pain* (New York, NY: Oxford University Press, 1985), 35, 36.
55 Antonius C. G. M. Robben, "How Traumatized Societies Remember," 152.

11. Featuring Acts of Genocide in Chilean Film

I would like to thank Marcus Welsh for his close readings and insightful comments during the preparation of this article.

1 *Fuga*, directed by Pablo Larraín, (2006; Santiago: Fábula); *Tony Manero*, directed by Pablo Larraín, (2008; Santiago: Fábula, Prodigital (Brasil)); *Post Mortem*, directed by Pablo Larraín, (2010; Fábula, Canana (México), Autentika (Alemania)); *NO*, directed by Pablo Larraín, (2012; Santiago: Fábula, Participant Media).

2 Raphael Lemkin, *Axis Rule in Occupied Europe: Laws of Occupation, Analysis of Government, Proposals for Redress* (Washington D.C.: Carnegie Endowment for International Peace, Division of International Law, 1944), 79.

3 Cathy Caruth, "Unclaimed Experience: Trauma and the Possibility of History," *Yale French Studies*, Vol. 79 (1991): 181.

4 Maureen Turim, "The Trauma of History: Flashbacks upon Flashbacks," *Screen*, Vol. 42, No. 2 (2001): 210.

5 Cathy Caruth, "Violence and Time: Traumatic Survivals," *Assemblage*, Vol. 20 (1993): 25.

6 Peter Freund, "Film and the Problem of Witnessing," *Latin American Perspectives*, Vol. 39, No. 6 (2012): 234.

7 Mark Cresswell and Zulfia Karimova, "'Misfortune's Image': the Cinematic Representation of Trauma in Robert Bresson's *Mouchette* (1967)," *Film-Philosophy* Vol. 17, No.1 (2013): 154–5, accessed April 9, 2015, http://www.film-philosophy.com/index.php/f-p/article/view/358.

8 E. Ann Kaplan, "Melodrama Cinema and Trauma," *Screen*, Vol. 42, No. 2 (2001): 201–5.

9 The Spanish word *fuga* has different meaning in English depending of the context: fugue, escape, flight, leak, elopement, drain.

10 Maureen Turim, *Flashbacks in Film: Memory & History* (New York, London: Routledge, 1989), 19.

11 Tzvi Tal, "Alegorías de memoria y olvido en películas de iniciación: Machuca y Kamchatka," *Aisthesis*, No. 38 (2005): 139.

12 Andrew Chernin, "Entendiendo a Pablo Larraín," *La Tercera*, accessed 12 March 2014, http://www.latercera.com/noticia/cultura/2013/01/1453-504671-9-entendiendo-a--pablo-larrain.shtml

13 Pablo Larraín, interview by *La Tercera*, "Cineasta Pablo Larraín dice que la derecha es "responsable directa" del apagón cultural sufrido por el país." *La Tercera*. July 31, 2008, accessed February 21, 2014, http://www.latercera.com/contenido/29_35492_9.shtml

14 Pablo Larraín, interview by Manohla Dargis, *The New York Times* (22 May 2012) accessed May 23, 2012.

15 "De *Fuga* a *No*: La historia del cineasta Pablo Larraín, *La Tercera*, August 7, 2012, Cultura, accessed October 12, 2014, http://www.latercera.com/noticia/cultura/2012/08/1453-476737-9-de-fuga-a-no-la-historia-del-cineasta-pablo-larrain.shtml.

16 Iván Pinto Veas, "*Tony Manero*, acechos," *la Fuga*, accessed March 25, 2015, http://www.lafuga.cl/tony-manero/100.

17 Matt Losada, "Review," *Chasqui*, Vol. 39, No. 1 (May 2010): 219–220.

18 Pablo Larraín, interview by Michael Guillen, "*TONY MANERO – The Evening Class* Interview with Pablo Larraín," *The Evening Class* (blog) (2008), accessed May 23, 2012, http://theeveningclass.blogspot.dk/2008/12/tony-manero-evening-class-interview.html.

19 Pablo Corro Pemjean, "Post mortem: La muerte de Pinochet y Violeta se fue a los cielos," *la Fuga*, accessed March 23, 2014, http://www.lafuga.cl/post-mortem-la-muerte-de-pinochet-y-violeta-se-fue-a-los-cielos/491.

20 Kevin Ohi, "Voyeurism and Annunciation in Almódovar's *Talk to Her*" *Criticism*, Vol. 51, No 4, (2010): 521–57

21 Pablo Corro Pemjean, 'Post mortem"(see endnote 20).

22 Paul Julian Smith, "At the Edge of History," *Film Quarterly*, Vol. 64, No. 2 (Winter 2010): 12–13.

23 Julian Smith, "At the Edge of History."

24 R. González and D. Espinoza, "El 11 de septiembre según el director de *Tony Manero*," *Latercera.com*, accessed 12 April 2009, http://www.latercera.com/contenido/661_118336_9.shtml.

25 Pablo Larraín, interview by José Miguel Palacios, "The Problems of Fiction," *The Brooklyn Rail*, accessed June 11, 2014, http://www.brooklynrail.org/2012/11/film/the-problems-of-fictionpablo-larran-with-jos-miguel-palacios.

26 Larraín, interview by José Miguel Palacios.

27 Ibid.

28 Larry Rohter, "One Prism on the Undoing of Pinochet," *The New York Times* (8 February 2013), accessed February 10, 2013, http://nyti.ms/18WNb2y.

29 Paul Kendall, "How Chile's Ad Men Ousted Pinochet: The Real Life Story Behind New Film 'No,'" *The Telegraph*, February 7, 2013, accessed November 9, 2014, http://www.telegraph.co.uk/culture/film/9842723/How-Chiles-ad-men-ousted-Pinochet-the-real-life-story-behind-new-film-No.html.

30 Ibid.

31 Pablo Larraín, interview by Kiko Martinez, "Q&A: Oscar-nominated Director Pablo Larraín Revisits 1988 Chile in *NO*," *AXS Entertainment*, accessed May 24, 2013, http://www.examiner.com/article/q-a-oscar-nominate-director-pablo-larra-n-revisits-1988-chile-no.

32 Antonius Robben, "How Traumatized Societies Remember: The Aftermath of Argentina's Dirty War," *Cultural Critique*, Vol. 59 (2005): 122.

33 Cathy Caruth, "Unclaimed Experience" (see footnote 3), 181.

34 Mark Cresswell and Zulfia Karimova, " 'Misfortune's Image' " (see endnote 7).

35 Pablo Larraín, interview by Demetrios Matheou, "The Body Politic: Pablo Larraín on Post Mortem," *Sight & Sound Magazine*, accessed January 28, 2015, http://www.bfi.org.uk/news-opinion/sight-sound-magazine/interviews/body-politic-pablo-larra-on-post-mortem.

36 Wolfgang Bongers, "La estética del (an)archivo en el cine de Pablo Larraín," *A contracorriente*, Vol. 12, No. 1 (2014), 194.

37 Pablo Larraín, interview by José Miguel Palacios, "The Problems of Fiction" (see endnote 25).

12. Screening the Killing Fields: The Cambodian Genocide on Film

1 This particular allusion to "US imperialism" was linked to the second Indochina War, known more familiarly as "the Vietnam War." Notwithstanding "contained" nomenclature, the war involved multiple Southeast Asian fronts and, as the subsequent discussion of Roland Joffe's *The Killing Fields* makes clear, the illegal bombing of the Cambodian countryside.

2 Following a *coup* which deposed Prince Norodom Sihanouk, General Lon Nol served as Cambodia's head of state between 1970–1975. Unlike his predecessor Sihanouk, who declared neutrality vis-à-vis the Vietnam War, Lon Nol was vehemently anti-communist and enjoyed considerable support from the US government. During his administration, the nation was embroiled in a civil war involving his forces and Khmer Rouge troops. Lon Nol fled to Indonesia and then to the United States during the Khmer Rouge takeover of Phnom Penh.

3 "Pol Pot" was the nom de guerre for Saloth Sar, "Brother Number One." See Cathy J. Schlund-Vials *War, Genocide, and Justice: Cambodian American Memory Work* (Minneapolis, MN: University of Minnesota Press, 2012).

4 This is recounted in Dr. Haing S. Ngor's posthumously published memoir, *Survival in the Killing Fields* (2003), co-authored with Roger Warner. Ngor was an obstetrician prior to the Khmer Rouge takeover and hid this identity during the regime's reign. In *Survival in the Killing Fields*, Ngor recollects Khmer Rouge troops interrupting doctors as they were in the midst of performing operations.

5 This Khmer Rouge proverb is mentioned in Rithy Panh's *The Missing Picture* (2013).

6 See Ben Kiernan, "Introduction: A World Turned Upside Down" in *Children of Cambodia's Killing Fields*, ed., Kim Depaul and Dith Pran (New Haven, CT: Yale University Press, 1999): xi–xvii.

7 During the Khmer Rouge period, children were encouraged to report particular "violations" committed by their adult counterparts (e.g., stealing food,

connections to the previous regime, and other pre-revolutionary affiliations). Children were also forced to fight as soldiers during the Cambodian-Vietnamese War. Within Cambodian American literature, the majority of memoirs are written by individuals who "grew up" under the Khmer Rouge; these works, as I have previously argued, militate against the Khmer Rouge directive to forget. See *War, Genocide, and Justice: Cambodian American Memory Work* (2012).

8 During the Vietnam War, the North Vietnamese communists and the Khmer Rouge had formed an alliance; however, by 1975, relations between the two entities had broken down considerably. The Chinese-backed Democratic Kampuchea and the Soviet-supported Socialist Republic of Vietnam were engaged in clashes over land and maritime territories in 1975–7. In 1978, the Socialist Republic of Vietnam launched a full-scale invasion of Cambodia which ended with the Vietnamese takeover of Phnom Penh in early 1979, ushering in a period of Vietnamese occupation (and the formation of the People's Republic of Kampuchea). The Khmer Rouge, while ousted, was still actively engaged in anti-Vietnam campaigns in country, which came to an end in 1991 via United Nations intervention.

9 See Ben Kiernan, "Recovering History and Justice in Cambodia," *Comparativ*, Vol. 14 (2004): 76–85.

10 See Leitner Center for International Law and Justice, "Removing Refugees: US Deportation Policy and the Cambodian-American Community," Southeast Asian Resource Center, Spring 2010. <http://www.searac.org/sites/default/files/2010%20Cambodia%20Report_FINAL.pdf.>

11 Leitner Center for International Law and Justice, "Removing Refugees."

12 The Documentation Center of Cambodia (DC-CAM) has played a key role vis-à-vis the UN/Khmer Rouge Tribunal and is a leader in genocide remembrance and education in Cambodia. In particular, DC-CAM has provided much of the evidence for the prosecution. See "Genocide Site in Cambodia Draws Tourists" in *USA Today*, August 14, 2006. <http://usatoday30.usatoday.com/travel/destinations/2006-08-14-cambodia-genocide-tourism_x.htm>

13 Duch's verdict was delivered on July 26, 2010 as per "Case 001" of the Extraordinary Chambers in the Courts of Cambodia. Of the almost 20,000 inmates interned at S-21, approximately 200 survived. On August 7, 2014, under the auspices of "Case 002/01," Chea and Samphan (former Khmer Rouge Prime Minister) were convicted and received life sentences for crimes against humanity during the Khmer Rouge era. Chea and Samphan are currently facing crimes of genocide under the rubric of Case 002/02; Case 002 was divided to delineate between crimes against humanity and crimes of genocide.

14 There has been some heated debate with regard to further prosecutions; Prime Minister Hun Sen, a former Khmer Rouge foot soldier, has repeatedly stated that he would not seek more prosecutions; two other possible defendants have

been identified. Nonetheless, the tribunal has faced severe criticism with regard to claims of corruption and juridical inconsistency.

15 Ieng Thirith was the second woman in international tribunal history to be charged with crimes of genocide. Pauline Nyiramasuhuko was the first woman to be charged and convicted of genocide (for the 1994 Rwandan genocide).

16 The ECCC as a juridical body has tried criminal cases along with cases involving what has been termed "symbolic reparation," which includes museums, memorials, and education centers. However, with the exception of a planned genocide education complex (through the Documentation Center of Cambodia), very little has been done to provide reparations for victims.

17 This notion of "autogenocide" is predicated on the fact that the Khmer Rouge directive was concentrated around a class-based revolution; those most targeted by the regime tended to be from the upper or middle classes. The current charges of genocide against former Khmer Rouge leaders necessitate proving that the regime specifically targeted Vietnamese Cambodians (as an ethnic group) and Cambodian Muslims (as an identifiable religious community).

18 Quoted in Manohla Dargis's *New York Times* review of Rithy Pan's *The Missing Picture*. See "Returning, in His Own Way, to the Killing Fields," March 18, 2014. <http://www.nytimes.com/2014/03/19/movies/the-missing-picture-rithy-pa nhs-look-at-1970s-cambodia.html?_r=0>

19 This was the original title of Siv's film. Email correspondence with author (May 4, 2015).

20 Quoted in Manohla Dargis's *New York Times* review of Rithy Pan's *The Missing Picture*. See "Returning, in His Own Way, to the Killing Fields," March 18, 2014. http://www.nytimes.com/2014/03/19/movies/the-missing-picture-rithy-panhs-look-at-1970s-cambodia.html?_r=0

21 As is discussed later in this chapter, Panh uses clay figurines and dioramas over the course of *The Missing Picture*, along with film clips from classic Cambodian cinema. Dong's *The Killing Fields of Dr. Haing S. Ngor* uses animation in addition to photographs and excerpts from televised interviews.

22 *The Flute Player* is based on Cambodian survivor Arn-Chorn Pond, who would become the founding director of Cambodia Living Arts, an organization intent on resurrecting and preserving traditional Khmer arts. *New Year Baby* follows Poeuv's journey, with her parents, to Cambodia; as the film progresses, it is revealed that Poeuv's parents were forced to marry one another during the Khmer Rouge era.

23 *Refugee*, like *New Year Baby*, is a "return narrative" insofar as the film follows three Cambodian-American protagonists as they return to Southeast Asia

(Cambodia) for the first time since the Killing Fields era. *Sentenced Home* and *Cambodian Son* are focused on a different type of Cambodian-American return: both films consider the criminalized and involuntary deportation of Cambodian Americans in the post-9/11 era.

24 Siv's *Surviving Justice* focuses its attention on a group of Cambodian-Americans (specifically refugees) who have, through the Applied Research Institute of Cambodia (ASRIC), filed testimonials and are potential witnesses for the court. This return journey is led by justice activist Leakhena Nou, a professor at California State University, Long Beach and ASRIC founder. Inadvertently, Nou and Siv encounter Hong Siu Pheng, Kaing Eak Guev's son, who was largely unaware of his father's crimes.

25 Lemkin and Sambath are presently working on a sequel to *Enemies of the People*, tentatively titled, *Suspicious Minds*, which will feature more perpetrator testimonials.

26 This story was featured in Schanberg's 1980 *New York Times Magazine* exposé titled, "The Death and Life of Dith Pran: A Story of Cambodia."

27 See Teri Shaffer Yamada, "Cambodian American Autobiography" in *Form and Transformation in Asian American Literature*, ed., Zhou Xiaojing and Samina Najmi (Seattle, WA: University of Washington Press, 2005).

28 See Roger Ebert, *Roger Ebert's Four Star Reviews: 1967–2007* (Kansas City, MO: Andrew Walker & Company, 2007).

29 See "Screening Apology: Cinematic Culpability in *The Killing Fields* and *New Year Baby*," in *War, Genocide, and Justice: Cambodian American Memory Work*, Cathy J. Schlund-Vials (Minneapolis, MN: University of Minnesota Press, 2012).

30 Ibid.

31 See Rosa Ellen, "Rithy Panh: The Director on Cannes Glory and Haunted Life," *The Phnom Penh Post*, May 31, 2013. http://www.phnompenhpost.com/7days/rithy-panh-director-cannes-glory-and-haunted-life

32 See Lekha Shangkar, "Cambodian Director Talks about his Work and the 'Nuclear Bomb' That Struck His Homeland," February 3, 2006, *Thai Day*. http://www.manager.co.th/IHT/ViewNews.aspx?NewsID=9490000015095

33 Ibid.

34 Ibid.

35 See Robert Turnbull, "Staring Down Horrors of the Khmer Rouge," *New York Times*, April 5, 2007, http://www.nytimes.com/2007/04/05/arts/05iht-fmlede6.1.5159770.html

36 Manohla Dargis, "Returning, in His Own Way, to the Killing Fields," *New York Times*, March 18, 2014, http://www.nytimes.com/2014/03/19/movies/the-missing-picture-rithy-panhs-look-at-1970s-cambodia.html?_r=0

37 From 2014 English-language trailer, *The Missing Picture* (2013).

13. "This Time We're Going to Hit Them Without Mercy": Indonesian Operations and East Timor's First Feature Film

1 P. Smythe, *The Heaviest Blow: The Catholic Church and the East Timor Issue* (Munster: Lit Verlag, 2004: 36).

2 Commission for Reception, Truth and Reconciliation (CAVR), Chega, Executive Summary, 118.

3 S. Staveteig, *How Many Persons in East Timor Went 'Missing' During the Indonesian Occupation Results from Indirect Estimates* (Austria: International Institute for Applied Systems Analysis, 2007), 14.

4 C. Fernandes, *The Independence of East Timor: Multi-Dimensional Perspectives* (Eastbourne: Sussex Academic Press, 2011).

5 Commonwealth of Australia, *Official Report of the Australian Parliamentary Delegation to Indonesia, Led by The Honourable W. L. Morrison, M.P., July–August 1983* (Canberra: Australian Parliament House, 1983).

6 J. Taylor, *East Timor: The Price of Freedom* (London: Zed Books, 1999), 140–2.

7 C. Budiardjo and L.S. Liong, *The War against East Timor* (London: Zed Books, 1984), 47, 139.

8 John Taylor, *Indonesia's Forgotten War* (London: Zed Books, 1991), 143.

9 Commission for Reception, Truth and Reconciliation (CAVR), *Chega*, Vol 7.2, 169–71.

10 *Chega*, Vol 7.5, 13.

11 *Chega*, Executive Summary, 118.

12 *Chega*, Chapter 7.7.

13 Natalie Craig, "Of Love and War," *Sunday Age*, January 1, 2012.

14 Report of the United Nations Independent Special Commission of Inquiry for Timor-Leste.Geneva, October 2, 2006.

15 Windu Jusuf, "*Beatriz's War* and Us," *Jakarta Post*, December 21, 2014.

16 Editorial, "The Cemetery Called East Timor," *New York Times*, September 25, 1992, 32.

17 "*Balibo* Great But Dangerous, Says Indonesian Film Censor," *The Australian*, December 3, 2009.

14. The Guatemalan Genocide on Film: An Ongoing Crisis and Omission

1 *When Mountains Tremble*, directed by Newton Thomas Sigel and Pamela Yates (1983; Brooklyn, NY: Skylight Pictures).

2 *Granito*, directed by Pamela Yates (2011; Brooklyn, NY: Skylight Pictures).

3 *Discovering Dominga*, directed by Patricia Flynn (2003; Jaguar House Films).

4 *Haunted Land: Le pays hanté, la Palabra Desenterrada*, directed by Mary Eleen Davis (2001; New York: Cinema Guild).

5 *The Silence of Neto*, directed by Luis Argueta (1994; Buenos Dias).

6 Frank M. Afflitto and Paul Jesilow, *The Quiet Revolutionaries* (Austin, TX: University of Texas Press, 2007), 3.

7 Those of Spanish descent born in the New World.

8 Regina Wagner, Cristóbal von Rothkirch and Eric Stull, *The History of Coffee in Guatemala* (Bogotá, Colombia: Villegas Editores, 2001), 85.

9 Wagner, *The History of Coffee*, 88.

10 Afflitto, *The Quiet Revolutionaries*, 16; Matthew Redinger, "Managing the Counterrevolution: The United States and Guatemala, 1951–1961 (review)," *Hispanic American Historical Review*, Vol. 82, No. 4 (November 2002): 840–1.

11 Gore Vidal, "In the Lair of the Octopus," *Nation*, June 5, 1995, 792–4.

12 Afflitto, *The Quiet Revolutionaries*, 17.

13 Stephen M. Streeter, *Managing the Counterrevolution: The United States and Guatemala, 1954–1961* (Columbus, OH: Ohio University Press, 2000), 11

14 Max Paul Friedman, *Nazis and Good Neighbors: The United States Campaign against the Germans of Latin America in World War II* (Cambridge: Cambridge University Press, 2003), 82–3.

15 Paul J. Dosal, "Bitter Fruit: The Story of the American Coup in Guatemala, and: Secret History: The CIA's Classified Account of its Operations in Guatemala, 1952–1954" (review) *Hispanic American Historical Review*, Vol. 80, No. 3 (August 2000): 633–637; Michelle Denise Getchell, "Revisiting the 1954 Coup in Guatemala: The Soviet Union, the United Nations, and "Hemispheric Solidarity," *Journal of Cold War Studies*, Volume 17, No. 2 (Spring 2015): 73–102; Deborah Levenson-Estrada, "The Life That Makes Us Die/The Death That Makes Us Live: Facing Terrorism in Guatemala City," *Radical History Review*, Issue 85 (Winter 2003): 94–104.

16 Afflitto, *The Quiet Revolutionaries*, 23.

17 Ibid., 24.

18 Ibid., 25.

19 Ibid.

20 Victoria Sanford, "Command Responsibility and the Guatemalan Genocide: Genocide as a Military Plan of the Guatemalan Army under the Dictatorships of Generals Lucas Garcia, Rios Montt, and Mejia Victores," *Genocide Studies International*, Volume 8, Number 1 (Spring 2014):. 86–101; Cindy Forster, "Violent and Violated Women: Justice and Gender in Rural Guatemala, 1936–1956," *Journal of Women's History*, Volume 11, Number 3 (Autumn 1999): 55–77.

21 The full report can be read at: http://www.aaas.org/sites/default/files/migrate/uploads/mos_en.pdf

22 Victoria Sanford, "From I, Rigoberta to the Commissioning of Truth: Maya Women and the Reshaping of Guatemalan History," *Cultural Critique*, Volume 47 (Winter 2001): 16–53.

23 *Granito*.

24 *Discovering Dominga*.

25 *The Silence of Neto*.

26 On July 8, 2015, Rios Montt was diagnosed as mentally unfit to be tried in court. Kelly McEvers, "Guatemalan Ex-Dictator Rios Montt Found Mentally Unfit For Genocide Retrial," (NPR, July 8, 2015), http://www.npr.org/2015/07/08/421225062/guatemalan-ex-dictator-rios-montt-found-mentally-unfit-for-genocide-retrial, accessed, July 15, 2015.

15. Cinematic Witnessing of the Genocide in Bosnia 1992–1995: Toward A Poetics of Responsibility

1 My thanks to Hikmet Karčić, Elmina Kulašić, Rijad Gvodzen, Hari Šešić, and Bruce Shapiro for our many discussions about films bearing on the genocide in Bosnia. I regret that it was not possible to consider in this essay all of the films that we discussed. With additional space I would have liked to address others, including Srdan Golubović's *Circles* [Krugovi] (2013), Dino Mustafić's *Remake* (2003), and Jasmila Žbanić's *For Those Who Can Tell No Tales (2013)*. Thanks also to Ken Gatzke, Sheila Magnotti, and Eric Cavallero in the Philosophy Department at SCSU, for their help with the final preparation of the text.

2 Republika Srpska [Serb Republic] was officially founded on January 9, 1992 within the territory of Bosnia and Herzegovina. In early April of the same year, the Bosnian Serb leadership, including Radovan Karadžić and Ratko Mladić, began the process of attempting to remove all non-Serbs from the so-called Serb Republic. Their tactics included forcible deportation, concentration camps, the siege of civilian centers such as Sarajevo, the destruction of villages, mosques, and schools, murder, and the hasty burials of the victims in mass graves. Republika Srpska was recognized by the Dayton Peace Accords as part of an effort to end the violence. Most members of the founding leadership of Republika Srpska have been charged with or convicted of crimes against humanity or genocide. The massacre of 8,100 men and boys at Srebrenica has been ruled to be genocide by international courts. However, to this day the President of Republika Srpska denies the genocide.

3 Paul Celan, *Selected Poems and Prose of Paul Celan*, trans. John Felstiner (New York, NY: W.W. Norton & Co., 2001), 260.

4 Jacques Derrida, *Sovereignties in Question: The Poetics of Paul Celan*, eds. Thomas Dutoit and Outi Pasanen (New York, NY: Fordham University Press, 2005), 87.

5 Ibid.

6 Ibid., 91.

7 Ibid., 96, my emphasis.

8 Ibid., 70.

9 Jacques Derrida, "On Cosmopolitanism," in *On Cosmpolitanism and Forgiveness*, trans., Mark Dooley (New York: Routledge, 2001), 30.

10 *Sovereignties in Question*, 77.

11 Ibid., 66.

12 Michael Nicholson, DVD, *Welcome to Sarajevo* (1997; Miramax, UK/USA).

13 The film *Welcome to Sarajevo* is based on Michael Nicholson's *Welcome to Sarajevo: Natasha's Story* (New York, NY: Miramax Books, 1997).

14 Passengers, "Miss Sarajevo," in *Original Soundtracks 1,* Island Records, 1995.

15 *Shot Through the Heart*, DVD, directed by David Attwood (1998; HBO Films, Canada/USA).

16 Nancy Jalasca Randle, "The Human Cost of War," October 4, 1998, accessed May 2015, http://articles.chicagotribune.com/1998-10-04/entertainment/9810050019_1_vlado-snipers-serbs

17 *Baggage* [Prtljag], DVD, directed by Danis Tanović (2011; Bosnia and Herzegovina).

18 "Oscar-winner Danis Tanovic's 'Baggage' Revisits Aftermath of the Bosnian War," July 30, 2011, accessed May 1, 2015, http://www.dailystar.com.lb/Culture/Film/2011/Jul-30/144955-oscar-winner-danis-tanovics-baggage-revisits-aftermath-of-the-bosnian-war.ashx

19 Personal Conversation with Lejla Čengić, International Commission on Missing Persons, Sarajevo, Bosnia and Herzegovina, July 12, 2012.

20 *Behind Enemy Lines*, DVD, directed by John Moore (2001; Twentieth Century Fox Film, USA).

21 Samantha Power, *"Problem From Hell": America and the Age of Genocide* (New York, NY: HarperPerennial Edition, 2007), 419.

22 *Grbavica*, DVD, directed by Jasmila Žbanić (2006; Bosnia and Herzegovina).

23 The Oxford English Dictionary defines *"shahid"* as "martyr." The etymological origin of the term is traced to the Arabic *"šahīd,"* meaning "witness." See the *Oxford English Dictionary*, accessed May 1, 2015, http://www.oed.com.

24 Claudia Card, "Genocide and Social Death," *Hypatia*, Vol. 18, No. 1 (2003): 69.

25 Ibid., 63.

26 See Beverly Allen, *Rape Warfare: The Hidden Genocide in Bosnia-Herzegovina and Croatia* (Minneapolis, MN: University of Minnesota Press, 1996), John Hagan, *Justice in the Balkans: Prosecuting War Crimes in the Hague Tribunal* (Chicago, IL: University of Chicago Press, 2003), and Alexandra Stiglmayer, ed., *Mass Rape: The War Against Women in Bosnia-Herzegovina* (Lincoln, ME: University of Nebraska Press, 1994).

27 *International Criminal Tribunal for the former Yugoslavia, Appeals Chamber Judgment*, Dragoljub Kunarac, Radomir Kovac, and Zoran Vukovic (IT-96-23 & IT-96-23/1-A), June 12, 2002, accessed May 1, 2015, http://www.icty.org/x/cases/kunarac/acjug/en/kun-aj020612e.pdf

28 Court of Bosnia & Herzegovina, Vlahović Veselin (S1 1 K 005540 11 KRI) Case Information: Factual Allegations in the indictment, http://www.sudbih.gov.ba/?opcija=predmeti&id=411&zavrsen=1&jezik=e. Also see: "Bosnia's 'Monster of Grbavica' Gets 45 years," March 29, 2013, accessed May 1, 2015, http://www.aljazeera.com/news/europe/2013/03/2013329102645826837.html

29 *In the Land of Blood and Honey*, DVD, directed by Angelina Jolie (2011; GK Films).

30 "Angelina Jolie Denied Film Permit in Bosnia," October 14, 2010, accessed May 1, 2015, http://variety.com/2010/film/news/angelina-jolie-denied-film-permit-by-bosnia-7318/

31 The screening was held Wednesday, December 7, 2011, in the Whitney Humanities Center at Yale.

32 *International Criminal Tribunal for the former Yugoslavia, Judgement, Milan Lukić-Sredoje Lukić* (IT-98-32/1-T), *Judgement, §740, Trial Chamber III, July 20, 2009*, http://www.icty.org/x/cases/milan_lukic_sredoje_lukic/tjug/en/090720_j.pdf

33 *Srebrenica: A Cry from the Grave*, DVD, documentary, directed by Leslie Woodhead (1999; PBS/WNET, UK/US).

34 Office of the High Representative, Sarajevo, "Decision Establishing and Registering the Foundation of the Srebrenica-Potocari Memorial and Cemetery," 10 May 2001, accessed May 1, 2015, http://www.ohr.int/decisions/plipdec/default.asp?content_id=125; and "Decision Enacting the Law on the Center for the Srebrenica-Potocari Memorial and Cemetery for the Victims of the 1995 Genocide," June 25, 2007, accessed May 1, 2015, http://www.ohr.int/decisions/plipdec/default.asp?content_id=40028

35 *The Troubles We've Seen: The History of Journalism in Wartime* [*Veillées d'armes*], documentary, DVD, directed by Marcel Ophuls, (1994; Milestone Films).

36 *Holiday Inn*, DVD, directed by Mark Sandrich (1942; Paramount Pictures, USA).

37 The word "genocide" only appears in a text at the end of *Behind Enemy Lines*, when we read that the photographic evidence of the mass grave led to a conviction for genocide.

16. "Truth" in Films about the Rwandan Genocide

1 Nyasha Mboti, "To Show the World as It is, or as It is not: The Gaze of Hollywood Films about Africa," *African Identities*, Vol. 8, No. 4 (2010): 317–32, http://dx.doi.org/10.1080/14725843.2010.513240, accessed March 18, 2015.

2 Ibid.

3 Ibid.

4 Bell Hooks, *Reel to Real: Race, Sex and Class at the Movies* (New York, NY: Routledge, 1996).

5 Patrick Vonderau, "Film as History/History as Film, Working papers: Gemenskaper Gemeinschaften," Volume 21, https://www2.hu-berlin.de/skan/gemenskap/inhalt/publikationen/arbeitspapiere/ahe_21.html

6 Gary Gutting, "Learning History at the Movies," November 29, 2012 http://opinionator.blogs.nytimes.com/2012/11/29/learning-history-at-the-movies/?_r=0, accessed 3 February 2015.

7 Jo Ellen Fair and Lisa Parks, "Africa on Camera: Television News Coverage and Aerial Imaging of Rwandan Refugees," *Africa Today*, Vol. 48, No. 2 (Summer, 2001): 36.

8 Paul Magnarella, "Explaining Rwanda's 1994 Genocide," *Human Rights & Human Welfare*, Vol. 2, No. 1 (2002): 34.

9 Martha Evans and Ian Glenn, ""TIA – This is Africa": Afropessimism in Twenty-First Century Narrative Film," *Black Camera, An International Film Journal*, Vol. 2 No. 1 (Winter 2010): 14–35.

10 *Hotel Rwanda*, DVD, directed by Terry George (2004; Kigali, Rwanda and Johannesburg, South Africa: Kigali Releasing Ltd, 2004), DVD.

11 Ibid.

12 Ibid.

13 Ibid.

14 Ibid.

15 Ibid.

16 Ibid.

17 *Sometimes in April*, DVD, directed by Raoul Peck (2005; Rwanda, Paris, and Washington: Home Box Office Inc., 2004).

18 Darryl Li, "Echoes of Violence: Considerations on Radio and Genocide in Rwanda," *Journal of Genocide Research*, Vol. 6, No. 1 (2004): 9–27.

19 *Sometimes in April*.

20 Stephen D. Goose and Frank Smyth, "Arming Genocide in Rwanda," *Foreign Affairs*, Vol. 73, No. 5 (1994): 86–96.

21 *Sometimes in April*.

22 Ibid.

23 *Beyond the Gates*, DVD, directed by Michael Caton-Jones (2005; Rwanda and UK: Twentieth Century Fox Home Entertainment LLC, 2007).

24 Ibid.

25 Ibid.

26 *Shake Hands with the Devil*, DVD, directed by Roger Spottiswoode (2007; Rwanda: Dallaire Productions Inc./Seville Productions Inc., 2007).

27 Ibid.

28 Ibid.
29 Ibid.
30 Ibid.
31 Ibid.
32 Ibid.
33 Ibid.
34 *Hotel Rwanda.*
35 *Beyond the Gates.*
36 *Shake Hands with the Devil.*
37 Marc Lacey, "Rwandan Hotel Is Still Haunted by Horror," NYTimes.com, February 28, 2005.
38 Gary Gutting, "Learning History at the Movies."

17. Stop a Genocide or Act in the National Interest? A Comparative Examination of *Hotel Rwanda* and *Attack on Darfur*

1 *Hotel Rwanda*, DVD, directed by Terry George (2004; Los Angeles, CA: United Artists).
2 Lars Waldorf, "Revisiting Hotel Rwanda: Genocide Ideology, Reconciliation, and Rescuers" *Journal of Genocide Research*, Vol. 11, No. 1 (2009): 102
3 See Roméo A. Dallaire (with Brent Beardsley). *Shake Hands with the Devil: The Failure of Humanity in Rwanda* (Toronto: Random House Canada, 2004). In the book, Lt. Gen. Dallaire notes the correct term for UNAMIR, the United Nations Assistance Mission *for* Rwanda, not *in* Rwanda
4 Dallaire, *Shake Hands with the Devil.*
5 Waldorf, "Revisiting *Hotel Rwanda*," 102
6 *Attack on Darfur*, DVD, directed by Uwe Bolle (2009; Toronto: Phase 4 Films).
7 Alexander De Waal, *Famine that Kills: Darfur, Sudan* (Oxford: Oxford University Press, 2005).
8 Rex O'Fahey, "Conflict in Darfur Historical and Contemporary Perspectives," *DARFUR* (2006), 24.
9 For more information, please see John Hagan and Wenona Rymond-Richmond, *Darfur and the Crime of Genocide* (Cambridge: Cambridge University Press, 2009); Dallaire, "Shake Hands with the Devil;" Christian Jennings, *Across the Red River: Rwanda, Burundi and the Heart of Darkness* (London: Phoenix, 2001); Mahmood Mamdani. *When Victims become Killers: Colonialism, Nativism, and the Genocide in Rwanda* (Princeton, NJ: Princeton University Press, 2001); Carol Off, *The Lion, the Fox and the Eagle* (Toronto: Vintage Canada, 2000); Prunier, Gérard, *The Rwanda Crisis: History of a Genocide* (New York, NY: Columbia University Press, 1995).

10 Hegre, Håvard, and Nicholas Sambanis, "Sensitivity Analysis of Empirical Results on Civil War Onset," *Journal of Conflict Resolution*, Vol. 50, No. 4 (2006): 508–535.

11 CIA Factbook, "The World Factbook." See also: https://www.cia.gov/library/ publications/the-world-factbook (2015), Rwanda.

12 Jennings, *Across the Red River*.

13 Amy Chua, *World on Fire: How Exporting Free Market Democracy Breeds Ethnic Hatred and Global Instability* (New York, NY: Anchor, 2004), 166.

14 Ibid., 167

15 For more information, please see, Alexander De Waal, "*Famine that Kills;*" Gerard Prunier, *Darfur: The Ambiguous Genocide* (Ithaca, NY: Cornell University Press, 2005); Scott Straus. "Darfur and the Genocide Debate," *Foreign Affairs* (2005): 123–33; O'Fahey, "Conflict in Darfur."

16 Hegre and Sambanis, "Sensitivity analysis of empirical results..."

17 CIA Factbook- Sudan.

18 *Attack on Darfur.*

19 http://www.dailymail.co.uk/wires/ap/article-2923794/UN-3-300-villa ges-destroyed-Sudan-fighting-early-2014.html, accessed May 1, 2015.

20 United Nations. "The Responsibility to Protect." http://www.un.org/en/pre ventgenocide/adviser/responsibility.shtml, accessed on April 22, 2015.

21 United Nations, "The Responsibility to Protect."

22 International Criminal Court, http://www.icc-cpi.int/EN_Menus/icc/Pages/ default.aspx, accessed on April 30, 2015.

18. Adults in Children's Bodies: *Disabling* Children in Bahman Ghobadi's Films

1 Ahmadou Kourouma, *Allah is Not Obliged*, trans. Frank Wynne (New York, NY: Anchor Books, 2007), 1–4.

2 For a detailed analysis of Birahima's language and his "disabling" narrative, see Eda Dedebas, "*A Long Way Gone* and *Allah is Not Obliged*: The 'Disabling' Child Soldier Narrative and Representation of Vulnerability," *Journal of Commonwealth and Postcolonial Studies* Vol. 16, No:2 (2010): 56–74.

3 Boris Trbic, "Turtles Can Fly and Tales of Lost Youth: An Interview with Bahman Ghobadi," *Metro Magazine*, June 2005, 73.

4 For other films that depict the Al-Anfal Campaign of 1988, see Samira Makhmalbaf's *Blackboards* (2000), Hiner Saleem's *Kilometre Zero* (2005) and for a recent documentary, see Taha Karimi's *1001 Apples* (2013).

5 Kristi Wilson and Tomas Crowder-Taraborrelli, *Film and Genocide* (Madison, WI: University of Wisconsin Press, 2012), and Leshu Torchin, *Creating the Witness: Documenting Genocide on Film, Video, and the Internet* (Minneapolis, MN: University of Minnesota Press, 2012).

6 Torchin, *Creating the Witness: Documenting Genocide on Film, Video, and the Internet*, 19.

7 Joseph Slaughter, "Enabling Fictions and Novel Subjects: The *Bildungsroman* and International Human Rights Law," *PMLA*, Vol. 121, No. 5 (2006): 1405–23.

8 Judith Butler, *Frames of War: When is Life Grievable?* (New York, NY: Verso, 2009), 24.

9 Judith Butler, *Precarious Lives* (New York, NY: Verso, 2004), 20.

10 Human Rights Watch, 1993, *Genocide in Iraq: The Anfal Campaign Against the Kurds*. New York: HRW. Available at: http://www.hrw.org/reports/1993/iraqanfal/

11 *Kilometre Zero*, DVD, directed by Hiner Saleem (2005; Paris: Memento Films, 2007). *Blackboards,* DVD, directed by Samira Makhmalbaf (2000; New York, NY: Wellspring, 2004).

12 *1001 Apples,* DVD, directed by Taha Karimi (2013; Manchester: Ava Media, 2013).

13 Ibid.

14 Ibid.

15 Joseph Slaughter, "Enabling Fictions and Novel Subjects: The *Bildungsroman* and International Human Rights Law," 1407.

16 Ibid., 1418–9.

17 Farhang Erfani, *Iranian Cinema and Philosophy* (New York: Palgrave Macmillan, 2012), 159.

18 Boris Trbic, "Turtles Can Fly and Tales of Lost Youth: An Interview with Bahman Ghobadi," 72.

19 Farhang Erfani, *Iranian Cinema*, 158.

20 For a detailed description, see Hamid Reza Sadr, "Children in Contemporary Iranian Cinema: When We Were Children," in *The New Iranian Cinema: Politics, Representation and Identity*, ed. Richard Tapper (London: I.B. Tauris, 2002), 227–37.

21 Boris Trbic, "Turtles Can Fly," 72.

22 Furthermore, Fran Hassencahl argues that the children in *Turtles Can Fly* are very autobiographical. See Fran Hassencahl, "Experiencing Huzun through the Loss of Life, Limb, and Love in Bahman Ghobadi's *Turtles Can Fly*," in *Never There: Lost and Othered Children in Contemporary Cinema*, ed. Debbie Olson (New York, NY: Lexington Books, 2012), 318.

23 Asuman Suner, "Outside In: 'Accented Cinema' at Large," *Inter-Asia Cultural Studies*, Vol. 7, No. 3 (2006): 369.

24 *A Time for Drunken Horses*, DVD, directed by Bahman Ghobadi (2000; Laguna Niguel, CA: Iranian Movies, 2002).

25 Ibid.

26 *Marooned in Iraq*, DVD, directed by Bahman Ghobadi (2002; New York: Wellspring Media, 2003).

27 *Half Moon,* DVD, directed by Bahman Ghobadi (2006; Culver City, CA: Strand Releasing, 2008).

28 Makau Mutua, "Savages, Victims, and Saviors: The Metaphor of Human Rights," *Harvard International Law Journal*, Vol. 42, No:1 (2001): 204.

29 A similar scene exists in *Blackboards* when Rebedoir, played by Bahman Ghobadi, finds himself at the mercy of mule kids, who finally agree to provide him some bread in exchange of his teaching skills. Makhmalbaf plays with the conventional dichotomy between an expert teacher, who is ready to relay knowledge to his pupils, and novice students, who remain in an inferior status in this power dynamics.

30 Rahul Hamid, "The Cinema of a Stateless Nation: An Interview with Bahman Ghobadi," *Cineaste*, Vol. 30, No:3 (2005): 42.

31 *Turtles Can Fly*, DVD, directed by Bahman Ghobadi (2004; Culver City, CA: MIJ Film, 2005).

32 Lan Dong, "Childhood in War and Violence: *Turtles Can Fly* and *The Kite Runner*," in *Portrayals of Children in Popular Culture: Fleeting Images*, eds. Vibiana Bowman Cvetkovic and Debbie Olson, (New York: Lexington Books, 2014), 198.

33 Farhang Erfani, *Iranian Cinema*, 165.

34 *Turtles Can Fly*, directed by Bahman Ghobadi.

35 Ibid.

36 Reminiscent of the teacher in *Blackboards*, the teacher in *Turtles Can Fly* is ignored by Satellite and other children.

37 Farhang Erfani, *Iranian Cinema*, 165–6.

38 *Turtles Can Fly*, directed by Bahman Ghobadi.

39 Joseph Slaughter, "Enabling Fictions and Novel Subjects: The *Bildungsroman* and International Human Rights Law," 1419.

40 In "Innocents Abroad: Western Fantasies of Childhood and the Iconography of Disaster," Erica Burman claims that the child images depicted in stories from Third World emergencies perpetuate the adulthood of Western world or the North over the South. On page 239, she further argues that the concept of dependency that is associated with childhood in the North is bolstered through the dependency of the South on the North.

Epilogue

1 http://www.yadvashem.org/yv/en/about/events/pdf/museum_opening/wiesel.pdf, accessed 9 May 2015.

2 Michelle Brown and Nicole Rafter, "Genocide Films, Public Criminology, and Collective Memory," *British Journal of Criminology*, Vol. 53 (2013): 1017.

3 Sonia Tascon, "Considering Human Rights Films, Representation, and Ethics: Whose Face?" *Human Rights Quarterly*, Vol. 34, No. 3 (August 2012): 865.

4 Francesco Casetti, *Inside the Gaze: The Fiction Film and its Spectator* (Blooming-ton, Indiana: Indiana University Press, 1998), 14, 120

5 Casetti, *Inside the Gaze,* 126.

6 Brown and Rafter, "Genocide Films," 1020.

7 Ibid.

Epilogue: Genocide Art or "Kitsch"?

1 *Planet of the Apes,* DVD, directed by Franklin J. Shaffner (1968; Los Angeles, CA: Twentieth-Century Fox Studios).

2 "Common Ideologies Foment and Justify Genocide", http://clg.portalxm.com/library/keytext.cfm?keytext_id=183; Alex Alvarez, "Justifying Genocide: The Role of Professionals in Legitimizing Mass Killing," *Idea*, Vol. 6. No. 1 (December 2, 2001). www.ideajournal.com/articles.php?sup=10.

3 Carol Tavis and Elliot Aronson, *Mistakes Were Made (But Not By Me): Why We Justify Foolish Beliefs, Bad Decisions, and Hurtful Acts* (New York, NY: Houghton-Mifflin, Harcourt, Inc., 2008).

4 Doctor Who, "Genesis of the Daleks", www.tvtropes.org/pmwiki/pmwiki.php/Main/GenocideDilemma.

5 Imre Kertesz [Translated by John MacKay], "Who Owns Auschwitz?" *The Yale Journal of Criticism*, Vol. 14, No. 1 (Spring 2001), 268. Two works supporting Kertesz are: Tim Cole, *Selling the Holocaust: From Auschwitz to Schindler: How History's Bought, Packaged, and Sold* (New York: Routledge, 2000), Chapter 3, "Oskar Schindler;" Norman G. Finkelstein, *The Holocaust Industry: Reflections on the Exploitation of Jewish Suffering* (New York: Verso, 2000).

6 *The History Boys,* DVD, directed by Nicholas Hyter (2006; Los Angeles: Fox Searchlight Pictures).

7 *Schindler's List,* DVD, directed by Steven Spielberg (1993: Universal City, CA: Universal Pictures, Amblin Entertainment).

8 Defenses of *Schindler's List* are numerous, a good example being: Alison Landsberg, *Prosthetic Memory: The Transformation of American Remembrance in the Age of Mass Culture* (New York: Columbia University Press, 2004),

9 Kertesz,"Who Owns Auschwitz?" 270.

10 *La Vita e bella* (original title), *Life Is Beautiful*, DVD, directed by Roberto Benigni (1997; Cecchi Gori Group Toger Cinematografica, Melampo Cinematografica).

11 Kertesz,"Who Owns Auschwitz?" 272.

12 Lawrence L. Langer, *Using and Abusing the Holocaust* (Bloomington, IN: Indiana University Press, 2006), 30–1.

13 *Der ewige Jude* (original title), *The Eternal Jew*, DVD, directed by Fritz Hippler (1940; Berlin: Deutsche Filmherstellungs-und-Verwertungs-Gmbh, Berlin (DFG).

14 *Jud Süss*, DVD, directed by Veit Harlan (1940; Berlin: Terra-Filmfunst).

15 Linda Melvern, *A People Betrayed: The Role of the West In Rwanda's Genocide* [2nd Edition] (London: Zed Books, 2000), 155.

16 *Hotel Rwanda*, DVD directed by Terry George (2004; United Artists, Lions Gate Films, Industrial Development Corporation of South Africa).

17 Kertesz,"Who Owns Auschwitz?" 270.

18 *The Missing Picture*, DVD, directed by Rithy Panh (2013; Catherine Dussart Productions (CDP), Arte France, Bophana Production).

19 Lior Zylberman, "Film Review. *The Missing Picture*. Directed by Rithy Panh, 2013". *Genocide Studies and Prevention*, Vol. 8, No. 3 (Fall 2014), 104.

20 Michael Phillips, Review: "The Missing Picture," *Chicago Tribune*, March 13, 2014. articles.chicagotribune.com/2014-03-13/entertainment/ct-missing-picture-review-20140313_1_the-missing-picture-rithy-panh-marc-marder.

21 Jake Wilson, "The *Missing Picture* Review: False Idols Bear Testament to Brutal Truth. http//www.smh.comau/entertainment/movies/the-missing-picture-false-idols-bear-testament-to-brutal-truth-20140319-352rf.html.

22 Sophia Marsman, "From the Margins to the Mainstream? Representations of the Holocaust in Popular Culture," *eSharp*, 6:1. www.gla.acuk/media/media_441177_en.pdf; *The Killing Fields*, DVD, directed by Roland Joffe (1984; Goldcrest Films International, International Film Investors, Enigma Productions).

Index